T0302256

Institutional Change after the Great Recession

This book combines demand-led growth models and the institutionalist approach, in order to explain the macroeconomic performance of the main European countries in recent years, offering a coherent explanation of the institutional change since the Great Recession, including the economic policy response to the economic and financial crisis (2008) and to the debt crisis (2010).

A comparative political economy analytical framework provides an institutional base to the different European growth models, in general terms, over the period 1995–2018. The results link diverse growth dynamics to the changes in the institutional framework as a consequence of the economic and financial crises. Each chapter of the country case studies (France, Germany, Italy, Spain, Greece, Sweden, the UK, and Poland) presents an introduction with a general characterization of the country and the most relevant changes that have occurred subsequently (the main legislative milestones or changes in the behavior of social agents), especially the process of dualization or deregulation of the European economies. In addition, an analysis of the macroeconomic evolution and the situation of the labor market before and after the crisis from a demand-side perspective is included, concluding with the links between both issues and the characterization of the growth model.

Institutional Change after the Great Recession will be of special interest to all students and postgraduates in such subjects as Applied Economy and International Economic Structure but it can also be useful to researchers, doctoral students and teaching staff who want to expand their knowledge of comparative political economy, institutions and the European Union. In general, this book is of relevance to all those who are interested in the evolution of Europe today.

Luis Cárdenas is an Associate Researcher at the Complutense Institute for International Studies (ICEI) and Associate Professor of Macroeconomics at the Complutense University of Madrid. He has also been a visiting researcher at the National Autonomous University of Mexico (UNAM). His research has focused on macroeconomic analysis and labor economics, and has been published in Structural Change and Economic Dynamics, the Cambridge Journal of Economics, the British Journal of Industrial Relations, International Labour Review, the Review of Keynesian Economics, the Spanish Journal of Economics and

Finance, among others. He has a PhD in Economics from the Complutense University of Madrid.

Javier Arribas is an Associate Lecturer at the Complutense University of Madrid and at the Rey Juan Carlos University. He holds a PhD in Economics from the Complutense University of Madrid. His PhD was funded by a doctoral research fellowship granted by the Madrid City Hall. He has been a Visiting Lecturer and visiting researcher in Quito in Ecuador and Mar del Plata, Argentina. His research has focused on public services, institutional economy and the history of economic thought. His research has been published in the Journal of Economic Issues and Ola Financiera.

Routledge Frontiers of Political Economy

Preventing the Next Financial Crisis
Victor A. Beker

Capital Theory and Political Economy
Prices, Income Distribution and Stability
Lefteris Tsoulfidis

Value and Unequal Exchange in International Trade
The Geography of Global Capitalist Exploitation
Andrea Ricci

Inflation, Unemployment and Capital Malformations
Bernard Schmitt
Edited and Translated in English by Alvaro Cencini and Xavier Bradley

Democratic Economic Planning
Robin Hahnel

A History of Monetary Diplomacy, 1867 to the Present
The Rise of the Guardian State and Economic Sovereignty in a Globalizing World
Giulio M. Gallarotti

Markets in their Place
Context, Culture, Finance
Edited by Russell Prince, Matthew Henry, Carolyn Morris, Aisling Gallagher and Stephen FitzHerbert

China's Belt and Road Initiative
The Impact on Sub-regional Southeast Asia
Edited by Christian Ploberger, Soavapa Ngampamuan and Tao Song

For more information about this series, please visit: https://www.routledge.com/Routledge-Frontiers-of-Political-Economy/book-series/SE0345

Institutional Change after the Great Recession

European Growth Models at the Crossroads

Edited by
Luis Cárdenas and Javier Arribas

LONDON AND NEW YORK

First published 2021
by Routledge
2 Park Square, Milton Park, Abingdon, Oxon OX14 4RN

and by Routledge
52 Vanderbilt Avenue, New York, NY 10017

Routledge is an imprint of the Taylor & Francis Group, an informa business

British Library Cataloguing-in-Publication Data
A catalogue record for this book is available from the British Library

Library of Congress Cataloging-in-Publication Data
A catalog record has been requested for this book

ISBN: 978-0-367-89698-0 (hbk)
ISBN: 978-1-032-00724-3 (pbk)
ISBN: 978-1-003-02058-5 (ebk)

Typeset in Times New Roman
by Taylor & Francis Books

We see that everything changes, but feel that something remains.
To our families, to those who made us possible.
To (Olm)otto, to the future.

Contents

Figures

Tables

Contributors

Ignacio Álvarez is an Associate Professor in the Department of Economic Structure, at the Autonomous University of Madrid, Spain, and Research Associate at the Complutense Institute of International Studies (ICEI). He is currently on leave of absence, since he has recently been appointed Secretary of State for Social Rights. He is the co-author of the following books: *Fracturas y crisis en Europa* (Clave Intelectual), *¿Qué hacemos con el paro?* (Akal), *Economía política de la crisis* (Ed. Complutense), *La financiarización de las relaciones salariales. Una perspectiva internacional* (La Catarata), *¿Qué hacemos con la deuda?* (Akal), *Wage Bargaining under the New European Economic Governance: Alternative Strategies for Inclusive Growth* (ETUI), *Ajuste y salario. Las consecuencias del neoliberalismo en América Latina y Estados Unidos* (FCE). He has published, among others, the following research works: Villanueva, P., Cárdenas, L., Uxo. J. and Alvarez, I. (2020) "The role of internal devaluation in correcting external deficits: the case of Spain." And Febrero, E., Álvarez, I. and Uxó, J. (2019) "Current account imbalances or too much bank debt as the main driver of gross capital inflows? Spain during the Great Financial Crisis." He has a PhD in Economics from the Complutense University of Madrid. http://orcid.org/0000-0003-2801-3447

Javier Arribas is an Associate Lecturer at the Complutense University of Madrid and at the Rey Juan Carlos University. He has a PhD in Economics from the Complutense University, Madrid. His PhD was funded by a doctoral research fellowship granted by the Madrid City Hall. He has been a Visiting Lecturer and visiting researcher in Quito in Ecuador and Mar del Plata, Argentina. His research has focused on public services, institutional economy and the history of economic thought. His research has been published in the *Journal of Economic Issues* and *Ola Financiera*.

Luis Buendía is Associate Professor of Applied Economics at the University of León, Spain. Previously he taught and performed research at the Isabel I University, University of A Coruña, Syracuse University in Madrid, University of Santiago de Compostela and the Complutense University of Madrid. He has been also a visiting researcher at the *Institutet för* *framtidsstudier* and Stockholm University (both in Sweden). He has recently co-edited the book, *The Political Economy of Contemporary Spain: From Miracle to Mirage* (Routledge, 2018). He has also published articles in *Socio-Economic Review*, the *Cambridge Journal of Economics, Social Indicators Research* and *International Journal of Health Services*, among others. He has a PhD in Economics. https://orcid.org/0000-0002-8507-7538

Luis Cárdenas is an Associate Researcher at the Complutense Institute for International Studies (ICEI) and Associate Professor of Macroeconomics at the Complutense University. He has also been a visiting researcher at the National Autonomous University of Mexico (UNAM). His research has focused on macroeconomic analysis and labor economics, and has been published in *Structural Change and Economic Dynamics*, the *Cambridge Journal of Economics*, the *British Journal of Industrial Relations*, the *International Labour Review*, the *Review of Keynesian Economics*, the *Spanish Journal of Economics and Finance*, among others. He has a PhD in Economics from the Complutense University of Madrid.

Andrea Carrera is a Lecturer in Economics at Nebrija University, Madrid, Spain. He has academic and business experience in both Europe and North America. Andrea holds a PhD (Switzerland) and an MPhil (Spain) in economics. His publications include *A Macroeconomic Analysis of Profit* (Routledge, 2019).

Oana Cristian is currently working as a consultant for the OECD. She has a PhD in Economics from the Complutense University of Madrid and specializes in the study of financial crises, banking regulations and financial markets. She has worked for the European Central Bank and as an economic advisor in the European Parliament. She has relevant experience in banking and financial regulation with several important financial institutions She contributed to the report published by the Advisory Group on Market Infrastructures and Payments for Securities and Collateral, AMI-SeCo (2017) "The potential impact of DLTs on securities post-trading harmonisation and on the wider EU financial market integration"; and to Muro, C. (2020). *An Institutionalist Approach to Finance and an Illustrative Application to Investment Banking in the United States (1981–2008)*; and to Ruiz, J.R., and Cristian O. A. (2019) "The Spanish crisis from a Minskyan perspective: A new episode of financial fragility," *Journal of Post-Keynesian Economics.*

Daniel Herrero is a post-doctoral Research Fellow in Economics at the Complutense University of Madrid (UCM) and an Associate Researcher at the Complutense Institute for International Studies (ICEI). His research interests are comparative political economy, institutional economics, and labor market and industrial relations systems. He has investigated the effects of labor market and industrial relations institutions on the economic performance in both Germany and Spain. The results of his research have been published in journals like the *International Labour Review*. https://orcid.org/0000-0001-5950-8747

Julián López is a PhD research scholar in Economics at the Complutense University of Madrid (UCM). He is also an Associate Researcher at the Complutense Institute for International Studies (ICEI). His research has focused on comparative political economy, economic sociology and institutional economics. In particular, he has investigated the effects of labor market dualism and industrial relations institutions on unemployment in Spain and other advanced economies. He is currently working on a PhD on the liberalization process in advanced economies, focusing on labor market dualism, industrial relations segmentation and employment policies. The project is being funded by a pre-doctoral research fellowship granted by the Complutense University of Madrid and Santander Bank.

Marcin Roman Czubala Ostapiuk is an Assistant Professor at National Distance Education University (UNED), Spain. He has a BA in European Studies from Warsaw University and also an MA in International Politics: Sector and Area Studies from the Complutense University of Madrid. He has a PhD in Political Science with "Summa Cum Laude," European Doctor Mention and Extraordinary Doctorate Award. His latest publication is Puente Regidor, M. & Czubala, M. R. (2016) "Central banking and the crisis: A comparison of the Federal Reserve and the European Central Bank measures, and the ECB's changing role in the EU economic governance system."

Mónica Puente Regidor is a Lecturer in Applied Economics in the Faculty of Political Science and Sociology of Complutense University of Madrid. She has a degree in Political Science and Administration from the Complutense University of Madrid, a degree in Law from the Universidad de Educación a Distancia (UNED), a PhD in Political Science and Administration from the Complutense University of Madrid, and a Master's degree in European Political Economy from the London School of Economics and Political Science. Some of her latest publications are Puente Regidor, M., Czubala, M. and Mitxelena Camiruaga C. (2015) "Los cambios en el modelo de gobernanza económica de la Unión Europea a partir de 2011: el efecto en su legitimidad democrática," and Puente Regidor, M. and Sánchez Jiménez, V. (2018) "El papel de los trabajadores en las actuaciones de responsabilidad civil empresarial. El caso español." https://orcid.org/0000-0003-0089-5898

Pedro M. Rey-Araújo has a PhD in Economics from the University of Santiago de Compostela, Spain. His main research interests include the various strands of critical political economy, discourse theory, and the sociology of time. His ongoing research has appeared in journals such as *Science & Society, Rethinking Marxism* and the *Review of Radical Political*

Economics, and he is also the author of *Capitalism, Institutions and Social Orders: The Case of Contemporary Spain* (Routledge, 2021). https://orcid.org/0000-0002-0008-4633

Adrián Rial is a PhD research scholar at the Complutense University of Madrid. As part of his research, he is studying the relationship between the tertiarization process and the US productivity slowdown. He also incorporates into his analysis the role of global value chains in order to assess the impact of offshoring on the expansion of the service economy and labor productivity growth. https://orcid.org/0000-0002-1185-033X

Juan Rafael Ruiz is currently an Associate Professor in the Faculty of Economics and Business Sciences of the Complutense University of Madrid and works as an adviser to regional governments in Spain and Latin America. He has a PhD in Economics from the Complutense University of Madrid and specializes in the study of financial crises. His latest publications are Ruiz, J. R., and Cristian O. A. (2019) "The Spanish crisis from a Minskyan perspective: A new episode of financial fragility," and Stupariu, P., Ruiz, J. R. and Vilariño, Á. (2019) "The disparity in PD and LGD estimates within the IRB framework and prospects for future improvement."

Vicente Sánchez Jiménez is a Lecturer in Applied Economics in the Faculty of Political Science and Sociology at the Complutense University of Madrid. He has a PhD in Political Economy from the Complutense University of Madrid. His research interests include public policy, social responsibility, Europeanization, global governance and the labor market. He also earned an MBA and a Master's Degree in Integrated Management of Resources, Intellectual Capital and Human Resources from the Polytechnic University of Madrid. His work has appeared in several scholarly journals and anthologies, including: Sánchez Jiménez, V. Serrano-Pascual, A. and Jepsen, M. (Eds.). *The Deconstruction of Employment as a Political Question: 'Employment' as a Floating Signifier* (Springer, 2018) and Sánchez Iglesias, E., and Sánchez Jiménez, V. *Towards a Global Analysis of the Functioning of World Capitalism. Christian Palloix and the Theory of the Internationalization of Capital.*

Jorge Uxó is an Associate Professor in the Department of Economic Analysis, University of Castilla-La Mancha. He has also been the Vice-Dean of the Faculty of Social Sciences (University of Castilla – La Mancha), and the Dean of the Faculty of Economics and Business Administration, and the Head of the Department of Economics, at the University CEU San Pablo (Madrid, Spain). He has a PhD in Economics from the Complutense University of Madrid. His main research interests are macroeconomics and economic policy in the EMU, and post-Keynesian economics. His research is currently focused on the recovery of the Spanish economy, particularly in the interaction between income distribution, demand and economic growth. His recent publications are Álvarez, I., Uxó, J. and Febrero, E. (2019) "Internal devaluation in a wage-led economy: The case of Spain," and Uxó, J., Álvarez, I. and Febrero, E. (2018) "Fiscal space on the Eurozone periphery: The case of Spain." https://orcid.org/0000-0002-2218-1004

Paloma Villanueva is a PhD student in Economics at the Autonomous University of Madrid and an Associate Researcher at the Complutense Institute for International Studies (ICEI). She completed a five-month internship at the Tax and Fiscal Policies unit of the Macroeconomic Policy Institute (IMK) in Düsseldorf and worked as a Research Assistant at the External Sector and Competitiveness unit of the Bank of Spain. Her current main line of research is the relationship between redistribution of income and the current account imbalances. Her work has been published in *Structural Change and Economic Dynamics*, the *British Journal of Industrial Relations*, the *Cambridge Journal of Economics* and the *Journal of Monetary Economics.* https://orcid.org/0000-0001-5409-1049

Acknowledgments

We would like to thank all the authors who have participated with their knowledge and effort in the realization of this book. Without them it would not have been possible. For helpful comments and suggestions, we are grateful to participants of several seminars held at the Complutense Institute for International Studies. We would also like to thank the economic collaboration of the Department of Applied, Public and Political Economy of the Complutense University of Madrid for the linguistic revision of this work.

Abbreviations

AAA	*Allocation d'aide au Retour à l'Emploi (ARE) and the Allocation Spécifique de Solidarité*
ACTES	*Accords sur les Conditions et Temps du Travail, l'Emploi et les Salaires*
AENC	Agreement on Employment and Collective Bargaining
AIFM	Alternative Investment Fund Managers
AMLP	active market labor policies
ANC	Inter-Confederal Agreement for Collective Bargaining
ANI	Accord National Interprofessionnel
B&P	Baccaro and Pontusson
BE	Baumol effect
BGK	Bank Gospodarstwa Krajowego
BoP	Balance of Payments
CA	current account
CAC	collective action clauses
CBC	Collective Bargaining Coverage
CC	comparative capitalisms
CCOO	Workers' Commission
CDD	*Contrat à Durée Déterminée*
CDU	*Contrat à Durée Indéterminée*
CEEC	Central and Eastern European
CEOE	Spanish Confederation of Employers' Organizations
CFDT	French Democratic Confederation of Labor
CFE-CGC	French Confederation of Management-General Confederation of Executives
CFTC	French Confederation of Christian Workers
CGPME	General Confederation of Small and Medium Enterprises
CME	coordinated market economy
COFER	Currency Composition of Official Foreign Exchange Reserves
CPE	Comparative Political Economy
CPI	consumer price index
CRD IV	Capital Requirement Directive IV
DE	Denison effect

DME	dependent economy
DQP	diversify quality production
DR	demand regime
EBA	European Banking Authority
ECB	European Central Bank
EEMU	European Economic and Monetary Union
EFSF	European Financial Stability Facility
EIOPA	European Insurance and Occupational Pensions Authority
EMU	Economic and Monetary Union
EPL	Employment Protection Legislation
EPLRC	EPL on Regular Contracts index
EPLTC	EPL index for temporary contracts
ESM	European Stability Mechanism
ESMA	European Securities and Markets Authority
ESRB	European Systemic Risk Board
FCA	Financial Conduct Authority
FCMA	Financial Services and Markets Act 2000
FDI	foreign direct investment
FERs	foreign exchange reserves
FIRE	finance, insurance and real estate
FPC	Financial Policy Committee
FSB	Financial Stability Board
FSS	Financial Stability Strategy
GDP	gross domestic product
GFC	global financial crisis
GFCF	gross fixed capital formation
GM	growth model
GPE	Global (International) Political Economy
GSSS	General Social Security Scheme
GVA	gross value added
GVC	global value chain
HICP	harmonized indices of consumer prices
HPGI	high productivity growth industries
HPRCE	High Protection on Regular Contracts Economies
IC	international currency
ICU	International Clearing Union
IFS	International Financial Statistics
IIRR	industrial relations
IMF	International Monetary Fund
IPO	initial public offering
ISPSC	international system of payments settlement and clearing
KIBS	knowledge-intensive business services
LME	liberal market economy
LO	Swedish trade union
LOLR	lender of last resort

LORCE	Low Protection on Regular Contracts Economies
LPG	low productivity growth industries
LSE	London Stock Exchange
LTROs	long-term refinancing operations
MEDEF	Mouvement des entreprises de France
MME	mixed market economy
MW	minimum wage
NATO	North Atlantic Treaty Organization
NBP	National Bank of Poland
NCAs	National Competent Authorities
NFC	non-financial corporations
NYSE	New York Stock Exchange
OCA	Optimum Currency Area
OECD	Organisation for Economic Co-operation and Development
OMT	Outright Monetary Transactions
PASOK	Panhellenic Socialist Movement
PLMP	passive labor market policies
PP	Popular Party
PPAE	*Projet Personnalisé d'Accès à l'Emploi*
PPE	pure productivity effect
PPS	purchasing power standards
PRA	Prudential Regulation Authority
PSE	*Plan de Sauvegarde de l'Emploi*
QE	quantitative easing
R&D	research & development
REER	real effective exchange rate
RMI	*Revenu Minimum d'insertion*
RSA	*Revenu de Solidarité Active*
RT	Regulation Theory
RW	rest of the world
SAE	selected advanced economies
SAF	Swedish employers association
SDRs	special drawing rights
SEC	Securities and Exchange Commission
SGP	Stability and Growth Pact
SME	small and medium-sized enterprise
SMP	Securities Markets Programme
SOEP	Socio-Economic Panel
SREP	Supervisory Review and Evaluation Process
SRM	Single Resolution Mechanism
SS	social-structural
SSM	Single Supervisory Mechanism
TARGET2	Trans-European Automated Real-time Gross-settlement Express Transfer system
TEU	Treaty on European Union

TFEU	Treaty on the Functioning of the European Union
TLTRO	targeted longer-term refinancing operation
UGT	General Workers' Union
ULC	unit labor cost
UPA	Union of Local Businesses
VA	value added
VIS	vertical integrated sector
VoC	Varieties of Capitalism
WPIs	Workers' Protection Institutions
YoY	year-on-year

1 Introduction

Javier Arribas and Luis Cárdenas

COMPLUTENSE UNIVERSITY OF MADRID AND REY JUAN CARLOS UNIVERSITY

1 Introduction

This book combines demand-led growth models and the institutionalist approach, in order to explain the macroeconomic performance of the main European countries in recent years. It then sets out a coherent explanation of institutional change since the Great Recession, including the economic policy response to the economic and financial crisis (2008) and the debt crisis (2010).

Our analysis includes the reaction of the European institutions and case studies covering eight countries. Chapters 2 and 3 devoted to the analysis of supranational European institutions will provide an explanation of the fiscal and monetary policies implemented since 2008, respectively. Additionally, in each chapter covering a country case study, there will be an introduction with a general description of the country and the most relevant changes that have occurred subsequently (main legislative milestones or changes in the behavior of social agents). Every chapter also includes an analysis of the macroeconomic evolution and the position of the labor market before and after the Great Recession from a demand-side perspective before concluding with the links between both issues and the characterization of the growth model.

We build a "comparative political economy" (CPE) analytical framework and provide an institutional foundation for the different European growth models, in general terms and for the period 1995–2018. In the last few decades, the CPE field has been focused on the comparison of the different types of capitalism, in what is known as the comparative capitalisms (CC) approach. This field of research (Nölke, 2019) goes back to the early works by Polanyi (1944), Shonfield (1965), Olson (1982) and Albert (1993). Unlike other approaches, such as global (international) political economy (GPE), which analyzes the role of states on the global stage, CPE, and in particular CC, are based on the differences between different types of capitalism.

Institutions are understood as the legitimate rules of behavior of social agents in different countries (especially in the West), focusing on the way in which social and political variables influence the functioning of various economic areas and, therefore, influence the economic results of different countries (Block, 2007; Jackson & Deeg, 2008; 2012). Thus, this literature has studied the diversity of institutions and the change in their comparative forms (Aoki, 2001; Beramendi, Häusermann, Kitschelt, & Kriesi, 2015; Berger & Dore, 1996; Coates, 2000; Crouch, 2005; Mjøset & Clausen, 2007) while essentially focusing on how social and political variables influence the functioning of various economic spheres and thus influence the economic performance of different countries (Block, 2007; Hay, 2019; Jackson & Deeg, 2008). Complementarily, the liberalization processes of advanced societies have been widely studied within CPE from a historical institutionalism perspective. This branch of the literature will be used in order to analyze the causes of institutional change.

Within CC, the most common approach is the Varieties of Capitalism (VoC) paradigm, introduced in the early 2000s by Hall and Soskice (2001). VoC is characterized by offering an institutional supply side theory, i.e. focused on how institutions affect the inputs for the production of goods and services, such as the characteristics of the supply of labor, capital, innovation, etc. Together, these socially integrated institutions produce a specific logic of action at the national level to the extent that there is complementarity between them, and they thus configure the different taxonomies of capitalism. In turn, VoC proposes a taxonomy with three types, namely, coordinated market economies (CME), liberal market economies (LME) and mixed market economies (MME), which can be associated with the productive features of national economies and their different comparative institutional advantages (Molina & Rhodes, 2007; Reale, 2019; Schneider & Paunescu, 2012; Witt & Jackson, 2016).

As various authors have pointed out (Becker, 2009), VoC fails to take into account disruptive institutional change or systems. It also omits the elements of class and the characteristics of capitalist economies (Becker & Jäger, 2012; Bruff, 2011) and, therefore, there is a need to move toward broader approaches (Bruff & Horn, 2012). An example of this is the analysis of the Great Recession (Ryner, 2015) carried out from the VoC perspective, which is based mainly on exogenous shocks. This is probably its main analytical weakness when used to analyze the responses to the economic crisis and the weakening of the position of workers that this implied (Heyes, Lewis & Clark, 2012). All these shortcomings underlie the functionalism that characterizes most jobs in the VoC tradition and that ignores the power relationships between social agents.

Likewise, CC scholars emphasize the study of institutional change and how it varies with different types, in a literature that can be grouped under the term "varieties of liberalization." This literature is framed within "historical and sociological institutionalism," which is characterized by the analysis of broad contexts and processes that interact and shape public policy design. It places a special emphasis on long-term processes, such as path dependence or "critical junctures," which are characterized by sequences of transformations in macro contexts and with the combined effects of institutions and processes. Thus, institutional change processes are analyzed from a dynamic perspective that emphasizes conflict and negotiation among social agents.

Recently, and especially after the financial crisis of 2008 that led to the Great Recession (Tooze, 2018), there has been increased interest in the macroeconomic aspects that led to the crisis and in the outcome of the economic policies implemented (Lallement, 2011), along with the institutional architecture of the European Union (Iversen, Soskice & Hope, 2016; Jessop, 2014; Johnston & Regan, 2015). There is also work that incorporates other elements of CPE, such as "labor process theory" (Hauptmeier & Vidal, 2014).

Traditionally, CPE has focused on an exclusively supply-side approach. However, there is a growing branch of literature within CPE, arguing that the socio-institutional analysis can be improved by the incorporation of a Kaleckian (demand-led) perspective (Baccaro & Pontusson, 2016). We believe that expanding that theoretical framework offers better research prospects. For example, by including wages as a relevant variable in determining the volume of consumption and investment, the usual recommendations for wage restraint do not necessarily have a positive effect on economic growth. On the contrary, since the main European economies are wage-led, wage restraint has negative effects on economic growth. Therefore, by including demand-side issues, we will be able to have a better understanding of the consequences of institutional change in Europe.

In fact, Regulation Theory (RT), in its French (Boyer, 1990), English (Jessop, 1990) and American (Bowles, Gordon & Weisskopf, 1986; Gordon, Edwards & Reich, 1982) versions, has previously addressed the relationship between economic growth and institutional characteristics. RT is strongly influenced by the Marxian, Kaleckian, and Keynesian traditions, giving great weight to the institutions, economic policy and the structural instability of capitalism. This approach considers that the stability of each country's macroeconomic structure can create a crisis endogenously. Thus, the breakdown of one accumulation regime forms the basis for the start of the next one. RT has mainly been used to study the transition from Fordism to post-Fordism, but has also been used to reflect on a new regulatory paradigm after the Great Recession (Bieling, Jäger & Ryner, 2015; Block, 2011; Rey-Araújo, 2017). In addition, RT has been used to propose a taxonomy of countries. Amable (2003) identifies four types of European economy and a specific type of Asian economy (Market-based economics; Social-democratic economic; Asian capitalism; Continental European capitalism; and South European capitalism). This classification is based on five aspects: (1) product-market competition; (2) the wage-labor nexus and labor-market institutions; (3) the financial-intermediation sector and corporate governance; (4) social protection and (5) the education sector.

We consider that this combination of theoretical frameworks provides a set of analytical tools offering many possibilities and is better equipped to explain the macroeconomic and institutional evolution of European countries. In this work we offer a study that combines both research lines, the starting idea being that the socio-institutional aspects, specifically those of employment and industrial labor relations, are linked to certain macroeconomic patterns that constitute the growth model.

The aims of this book are as follows:

1 To identify and characterize the key aspects of the institutional frameworks of the main European economies within the CPE framework, especially the process of dualization or deregulation in the European economies.
2 To analyze the institutional changes that have taken place in these areas because of the Great Recession's economic and financial crisis. To what extent are these changes transforming the existing institutional frameworks?
3 To analyze the macroeconomic structure of these countries and their outcomes in terms of macroeconomic performance: unemployment, price stability, nominal wage restraint, exchange rate stability and trade balances.
4 To link the macroeconomic performance of these countries to the different institutional changes seen, especially in terms of economic growth, external balance, employment performance and inequality. To identify the different "growth models" by linking the institutional structure to the evolution of aggregate demand.

Sections 2 and 3 provide an introduction to the foundations of institutional change and the macroeconomic structures of the different countries included in the book. On the basis of these two areas, Section 4 is dedicated to answering the research questions posed in the book.

2 Institutional change and liberalization

Institutions are the result of the previous exercising of power but also condition the decision making of social agents by creating opportunities and imposing limits. Consequently, institutional change can be the result of either exogenous shocks, which function as a new critical point and trigger unforeseen change, or endogenous processes derived from the very evolution of institutions, in the case of contradictions (Mahoney & Thelen, 2010, Streeck, 2010).

In this regard, Streeck and Thelen (2005) point to five paths for institutional change: (1) *displacement*: when there is a slow increase in the importance of previously subordinate institutions; (2) *stratification (layering)*: new elements attach to existing institutions and gradually change their status and structure; (3) *drift*: changes in practice due to institutional abandonment, even if there is no formal change; (4) *conversion*: old institutions adopt a new role; and (5) *exhaustion*: gradual disappearance of institutions over time.

These institutional changes must be understood within historical processes that combine path-dependent situations, where institutional change is relatively slow (Armingeon, 2004), but where there are also "critical junctures" (Capoccia, 2015), at which point institutions can transform rapidly and generate a new path for institutional evolution. After these critical junctures, the institutional framework continues its path-dependence due to the existence of the veto capacity of the different agents (Palier, 2010).

However, it must be understood that these relationships are not determined *a priori*. Wright, (2000) distinguishes between "associational power," the forms of power that result from the formation of collective organizations of workers, and "structural power," power from the location of workers within the economic system. Power relationships occur in three spheres: (1) the sphere of exchange; (2) labor markets and various other kinds of commodity markets; the sphere of production, the labor process and technology; and (3) the sphere of politics. The institutional framework therefore depends on the specific configurations of power and interests that characterize the relationship between the capitalist and the working classes. In this way, the new trends in CC tend to consider that socio-economic institutions are the product of conflicts and agreements (Streeck & Thelen, 2005).

According to Baccaro and Howell (2018), the liberalization process includes any political or institutional change aimed at expanding the discretionary power of companies and employers, mainly (although not exclusively) in the form of labor legislation and collective regulation. According to these authors, institutional deregulation implies changes to the structural and associational power of workers in all three spheres (exchange, production and politics), the commonest of which are the following:

1 A decentralization of collective bargaining from higher levels (sectoral or national) to lower levels (company or workplace).
2 A greater recourse to individual negotiation between the employee and the employer or to unilateral decision-making by the employer.
3 A reduction in the capacity of class actors to organize collectively.
4 A reduction in the level and duration of unemployment benefits, making the payment of benefits conditional on active search and willingness to accept available jobs (conditionality).
5 A reduction in employment protection and, in general, the elimination of all mechanisms that interfere with the free satisfaction of the demand for labor.

A common feature of liberalization as institutional deregulation and liberalization as institutional conversion is that they both allow for greater employer discretion in wage determination, personnel management strategies, work processes and hiring and firing. However, liberalization in advanced economies takes place within the existing institutional frameworks. This is why although there is a common trend toward liberalization (Baccaro & Howell, 2018; Etchemendy, 2011), it takes different forms in each national institutional setting (Thelen, 2014), depending on its previous tradition and social embeddedness.

In dynamic terms, from a "historical and sociological institutionalism" approach within CPE, so-called "varieties of liberalization" have been proposed (Palier & Thelen, 2010) for the liberalization processes in advanced societies (post-industrial or post-Fordist). Thelen (2014) highlights the existence of three types of liberalization path:

1 *Deregulation*: involves the displacement of collective regulatory mechanisms in favor of "free market" agreements and is a typical liberalization path for Anglo-Saxon liberal economies.
2 *Dualization*: this involves the commercialization of some activities that particularly affect groups located on the periphery and is characteristic of the coordinated economies of continental Europe.
3 *Embedded flexibilization*: this includes the deregulation of activities and the effects are compensated for through social action programs.

In conclusion, CPE has been able to develop explanations for institutional change that offer greater analytical depth than previously seen.

3 Macroeconomic structures at a glance

This section introduces the main features of the behavior of aggregate demand in order to give an initial overview of the macroeconomic structures detailed in each chapter of the book. There is no single way to approach the phenomenon of the composition of aggregate demand. For example, when analyzing growth models, Baccaro and Pontusson (2016) chose to analyze the growth rates of the components of aggregate demand and focus on the trade-off between consumption and net exports.

In contrast, Hein, Paternesi Meloni and Tridico (2020) preferred to analyze contributions to economic growth, considering that these are more representative than growth rates since weighting gives a better approximation of the growth paths of aggregate demand. Behringer and van Treeck (2019) analyzed the sector balances of the economy, distinguishing between households, companies, the public sector and the foreign sector.

In addition, Stockhammer (2016) analyzed the evolution of household indebtedness as a key variable in the growth of consumption in the post-Fordist stage. As Barredo (2019) points out, the deterioration of the foreign balance is associated with the external and total indebtedness of the economy, which makes it a much more fragile model that depends on international financial flows. This explains the drastic adjustment that took place as a result of the Great Recession. This also points to complementarities between real and financial flows between countries.

Gräbner, Heimberger, Kapeller and Schütz (2020) also used a supply-side approach and argued that the fundamental divergence between export-led and debt-led models is due to "structural polarization" in technological capabilities and business efficiency.

The two main post-Fordist growth models usually mentioned are the debt-financed consumption-led demand regime (debt-led) and the export-driven demand regime (export-led). In the first, domestic demand plays a leading role, accompanied by a deterioration in net exports, generating significant debt. In the second, it is positive net exports that generate the growth in the economy, implying a creditor position for these economies. There is an intermediate case in which the growth of domestic demand does not imply a significant deterioration in net exports, so it is a domestic demand-led model.

Following these authors, Table 1.1 illustrates the macroeconomic evolution of the countries studied (Germany, Spain, France, Greece, Italy, Poland, the United Kingdom, and Sweden), showing both the contributions to growth (since the rates of variation may not correctly reflect the expansion paths of aggregate demand) with the shares of each component in aggregate demand as a whole. The figures are given for three phases, the entire period of study of the book (1995–2018) and the two stages within this period defined by the economic crisis of the Great Recession: the pre-crisis period (1995–2008), and the post-crisis period (2009–2018).

Analyzing the macroeconomic imbalance from a Keynesian point of view implies considering that investment is the variable that determines savings (domestic and foreign) and, therefore, the national accounting equation on the aggregate demand side can be reorganized as follows.Therefore, from a theoretical approach it is necessary to consider the relative importance of consumption and net exports in aggregate demand and whether there is a trade-off between consumption and export growth, as proposed by Baccaro and Pontusson (2016). However, it is also necessary to examine whether there is a trade-off between investment and/or consumption with the external sector (defined as net exports), in order to analyze the composition of aggregate demand as a whole.

An analysis of the data in Table 1.1 shows that in terms of aggregate demand growth, there are two clearly distinct patterns. First, Poland, Germany, and Sweden show either continuity in their growth rates in both the period before the Great Recession and the period after it, or high growth in the post-crisis stage as well. Second, Spain, France, Italy, Greece, and the United Kingdom show a greater discontinuity, having average growth rates below 1 percent during the second expansionary phase (the United Kingdom grew slightly faster but also showed a reduction in its growth rates).

Therefore, the analysis of the average growth over the period may lead to a mistake since in countries such as Greece, Italy and Spain, most of the economic growth took place during the years 1995–2008, with economic stagnation after that period. In contrast, although Germany has lower growth rates (1.5 percent), these are stable throughout the phases of the business cycle. In contrast, in countries such as Sweden and Poland, the fall in gross domestic product (GDP) was much less intense and entirely linked to external factors, such as the fall in exports due to the slowdown in the world economy, and after a short period of time they returned to growth rates similar to those of the pre-Great Recession phase.

An analysis of the contributions to aggregate demand growth shows that, as might be expected, consumption was the main source of growth (as a result of its high weight in aggregate demand). Investment, despite being the most volatile variable and the one that determines the business cycle in the short term and capital accumulation in the long term, made a smaller contribution

Table 1.1 Composition and contributions to aggregate demand growth

		Germany	*Spain*	*France*	*UK*	*Greece*	*Italy*	*Poland*	*Sweden*
Variables		*1995–2018*							
Consumption share	C/Y	55.0	58.8	54.4	65.0	67.5	59.9	61.5	46.5
Investment share	I/Y	21.4	23.7	22.1	17.5	20.0	19.8	21.5	23.2
Public consumption share	G/Y	19.2	18.3	23.3	18.9	19.7	18.9	18.3	25.5
Net exports share	Xn/Y	4.3	-0.7	0.3	-1.4	-7.3	1.4	-1.3	4.9
Consumption contribution	ΔC/C*C/Y	0.6	1.2	0.9	1.6	0.7	0.5	2.4	1.1
Investment contribution	ΔI/I*I/Y	0.2	0.5	0.4	0.4	0.0	0.1	1.1	0.8
Public consumption contribution	ΔG/G*G/Y	0.3	0.5	0.3	0.4	0.2	0.1	0.6	0.3
Net exports contribution	ΔXn/Xn*Xn/Y	0.3	0.1	-0.1	-0.1	0.0	0.0	0.0	0.2
Aggregate demand growth	ΔY/Y	1.5	2.2	1.6	2.2	0.9	0.7	4.1	2.5
		1995–2008							
Consumption share	C/Y	55.8	59.0	54.2	65.3	66.2	59.4	62.6	46.7
Investment share	I/Y	22.2	26.5	21.8	18.2	24.7	20.8	22.1	22.6
Public consumption share	G/Y	19.0	17.2	22.8	18.1	18.9	18.5	18.4	25.2
Net exports share	Xn/Y	3.0	-2.7	1.2	-1.5	-9.8	1.3	-3.1	5.5
Consumption contribution	ΔC/C*C/Y	0.5	2.0	1.2	1.9	2.4	0.8	2.9	1.2
Investment contribution	ΔI/I*I/Y	0.2	1.2	0.7	0.5	1.2	0.5	1.5	1.0
Public consumption contribution	ΔG/G*G/Y	0.3	0.7	0.3	0.5	0.7	0.2	0.8	0.2
Net exports contribution	ΔXn/Xn*Xn/Y	0.5	-0.5	-0.1	-0.1	-0.9	-0.1	-0.6	0.5
Aggregate demand growth	ΔY/Y	1.5	3.4	2.1	2.8	3.5	1.4	4.6	2.9

		2009–2018							
Consumption share	C/Y	53.9	58.5	54.6	64.7	69.4	60.7	60.0	46.2
Investment share	I/Y	20.3	19.7	22.6	16.5	13.4	18.3	20.5	24.0
Public consumption share	G/Y	19.6	19.7	23.9	20.1	20.9	19.6	18.2	25.9
Net exports share	Xn/Y	6.2	2.1	-1.1	-1.4	-3.7	1.4	1.3	4.0
Consumption contribution	ΔC/C*C/Y	0.7	0.0	0.5	1.0	-1.8	0.0	1.7	1.0
Investment contribution	ΔI/I*I/Y	0.3	-0.5	0.1	0.2	-1.6	-0.4	0.5	0.6
Public consumption contribution	ΔG/G*G/Y	0.4	0.1	0.3	0.2	-0.6	-0.1	0.4	0.4
Net exports contribution	ΔXn/Xn*Xn/Y	0.0	0.9	-0.1	-0.1	1.3	0.2	0.7	-0.1
Aggregate demand growth	ΔY/Y	1.4	0.5	0.9	1.2	-2.6	-0.3	3.3	1.9

Source: Adapted from the OECD database.

since its weight in GDP is low (with some notable exceptions such as Spain, which it reached an average of 26 percent in the stage prior to the Great Recession).

Likewise, public consumption tends to be counter-cyclical as a result of the automatic stabilizers, being an autonomous component of aggregate demand, so its weight is generally greater in the post-crisis stage. However, in terms of its contribution to growth, this declined in all countries (except France and Germany, where it remained constant), probably as a result of the austerity policies introduced in response to the sovereign debt crisis in Europe (2010–2012).

Finally, net exports tend to make a low contribution, due to the simultaneous effect of imports and exports. This, however, does not mean that net exports are not important for economic growth; on the contrary, this is reflected in the shares of GDP, since it is the adjustment variable between investment and domestic savings. Thus, there are economies that see their net exports over GDP increase from one phase to the next, such as Germany, Spain, Greece and Poland, others where this does not vary, such as the United Kingdom and Italy, and others where it decreases, such as France and Sweden.

This descriptive analysis is not sufficient to look at possible trade-offs between the components of aggregate demand. Figure 1.1 shows the correlation between private consumption (the most important component) and net exports (the most dynamic component), leaving aside public consumption which, as noted above, has some peculiarities since it is autonomous consumption and has a weaker relationship with the foreign sector.

The first conclusion to be drawn from the analysis in Figure 1.1 is that in all the economies analyzed (with the notable exception of the UK), there is a negative relationship between the weight of investment and the weight of net exports, although there are some interesting differences between them that need to be studied further.

In contrast, there is only a trade-off between consumption and net exports in two countries: Germany and Poland. In these two countries, if the weight of consumption and investment is reduced, the trade balance expands. This phenomenon is also observed in France, but its importance is significantly lower than in the other cases. Similarly, in Greece the opposite is true, the trade balance contracts if the weight of consumption is greater. This is undoubtedly due to the drastic adjustment in the Greek economy, which is unprecedented and meant that autonomous consumption gained weight as a result of the fall in all other components, especially investment.

Second, it is also possible to observe the patterns of adjustment of the external balance that have been previously pointed out: Germany, Spain, Greece, Italy, and Poland significantly reduce their investment share, which translates into an improvement in their trade balance. This suggests that the linear and negative relationship between investment effort and net exports is maintained. Thus, the collapse of investment as a result of the Great Recession and its financial and economic crisis, with the consequent financial restriction, is the main cause of the adjustment to the foreign sector. For their

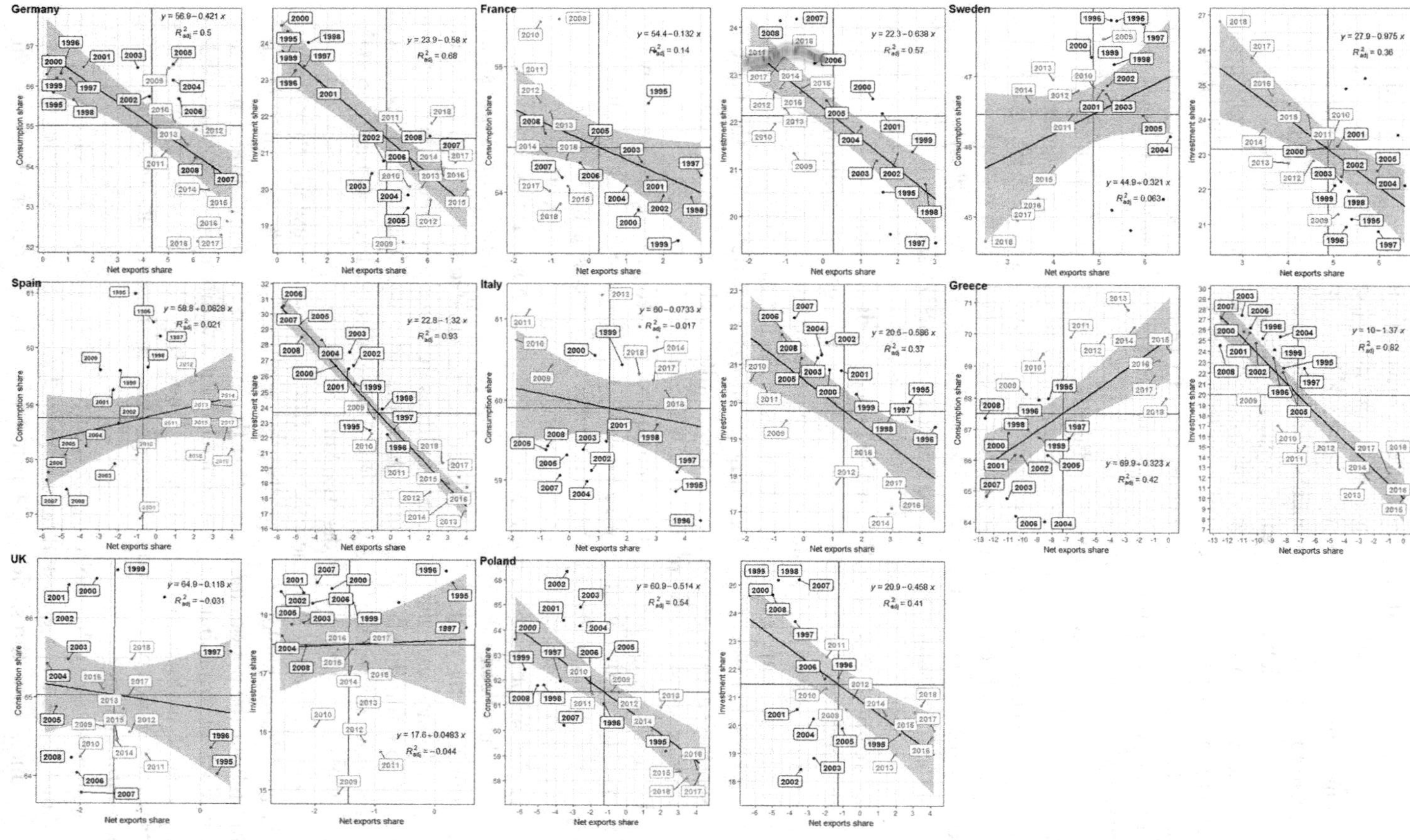

Figure 1.1 Consumption share vs. net exports share
Source: Adapted from OECD database.

part, France and Sweden increased their investment share and thus deteriorated their trade balance, as this effect was not offset by the fall in the share of consumption. The case of the United Kingdom is striking, as it has no correlation between the components of aggregate demand, possibly because it has an external deficit in all cases, regardless of the business cycle.

In short, the investment share (measured as the weight of Gross Capital Formation over GDP in real terms), is revealed as the main explanatory element of the evolution of net exports. In other words, the fundamental trade-off is between I/Y and Xn/Y, and the trade-off with consumption is only relevant for some countries.

A third aspect to consider is that while the sign of the I/Y and Xn/Y correlation is always negative, it does not have the same intensity or characteristics in all countries. Specifically, the constant is the maximum value that I/Y can reach, with Xn/Y equal to zero, which reflects the economy's capacity to save domestically, which allows savings to be issued abroad (foreign surplus), and above which the increase in I/Y has to be financed by foreign savings (foreign deficit). In other words, the constant is the I/Y "threshold," above which the economy needs foreign savings and will therefore have a foreign deficit.

The economic interpretation of these statistical relationships from a Keynesian perspective is that if, in response to an increase in investment, the productive capacity does not generate an increase in domestic production, I/Y increases rapidly, resulting in an external deficit. As the patterns are similar to those of other countries, ultimately a very low investment threshold suggests a severe problem with productive capacity.

The clearest case among the countries considered is that of Greece, which has an external deficit of only 10 percent of I/Y, while in most countries the constant is around 20 percent. This reflects Greece's productive weakness, based on low productivity sectors, and dependence on imports. As discussed in Chapter 6, the main problem with the Greek economy is that its productive structure has been weakening since its entry into the euro and the adjustment resulting from the troika's intervention has exacerbated this. The other country with the highest external deficit, Spain, does not have the same issue of a particularly low threshold, but instead these figures reflect that it had investment shares above the threshold very often and these were particularly high due to the pre-2008 housing bubble (as discussed in Chapter 8).

At the opposite end of the spectrum from the Greek case is Sweden, which has an I/Y threshold of 28 percent, a remarkably high value not reached throughout the period, indicating that the Swedish economy always maintains a positive external balance. As Table 1.1 shows, this is not the result of low investment in Sweden, but rather the fact that the productive capacity is strong enough to respond to the growth in investment, thus generating domestic savings.

This investment threshold is observed for all economies, but Germany and Poland also have a consumption threshold as well. For example, Germany has a maximum threshold of 24 percent I/Y and 57 percent C/Y for Xn/Y equal to zero. Poland is also a striking case since the correlation of net exports is greater with consumption than with investment, clearly showing that the rapid growth of the external surplus is due to the containment, in terms of the weight in GDP, of both elements, private consumption and investment.

In summary, it can be seen that all countries (except the UK) have a trade-off between investment share and net exports share. However, the key to determining whether the model is export-led or debt-led is the threshold at which a deficit is incurred. Thus, economies such as Sweden can simultaneously keep both variables high while countries such as Greece rapidly deteriorate their trade balance with increasing investment. It is in this sense that growth models become particularly important for understanding the comparative evolution of European countries.

4 Research questions

From the introduction to the main institutional and macroeconomics characteristics, the following questions arise:

- Can the country be considered as falling into a proper categorization of types of comparative political economy?
- Has the institutional structure that existed before the Great Recession been transformed, for example, through major legislative milestones or changes in the behavior of social agents, or was it previously transformed?
- If it has been transformed, can any of the liberalization paths specified in the literature be identified (deregulation, dualization or flexicurity)?
- What macroeconomic developments, before and after the Great Recession, can be observed in the economy?
- Do these developments represent a particular growth model according to the three categories proposed in the literature (debt-led, export-led or domestic demand-led)?
- Has there been any relevant change in the growth model before and after the Great Recession?

Answering these questions will allow us to conclude how institutional structures have evolved, what growth patterns exist and how they have changed. All this makes it possible to establish, within the CPE framework, how the major European countries have evolved.

5 The structure of the book

In particular, this book is focused on the effects of institutional change on growth models. In Chapter 2, the book examines the theoretical framework and in Chapter 3 it considers the position of the European Union. Subsequently, the book includes selected case-study countries, which are based on the following criteria. First, the United Kingdom (Chapter 10) is the archetypal case of a European LME. Second, we look at two Continental CMEs, namely, Germany (Chapter 5) and France (Chapter 4), along with a Nordic CME economy, in this case, Sweden (Chapter 9). Finally, three MMEs are included because there were notable differences between their growth rates after 2008. Spain showed volatile growth (Chapter 8), there was stagnation in the Italian economy (Chapter 7) and a severe recession in Greece (Chapter 6). In addition, the Mediterranean MMEs are compared to an Eastern European MME, in this case, Poland (Chapter 11), in order to emphasize the differences in their growth models.

References

Albert, M. (1993). *Capitalism against capitalism.* Chichester: John Wiley & Sons Incorporated.

Amable, B. (2003). *The diversity of modern capitalism.* Oxford: Oxford University Press.

Aoki, M. (2001). *Toward a comparative institutional analysis.* Cambridge, MA: MIT Press.

Armingeon, K. (2004). Institutional change in OECD democracies, 1970–2000. *Comparative European Politics,* 2 (2), 212–238.

Baccaro, L., & Howell, C. (2018). *Trajectories of neoliberal transformation.* Cambridge: Cambridge University Press.

Baccaro, L., & Pontusson, J. (2016). Rethinking comparative political economy. *Politics & Society,* 44 (2), 175–207.

Barredo, J. (2019). The nature of capitalist money and the financial links between debt-led and export-led growth regimes. *New Political Economy,* 24 (4), 565–586.

Becker, J., & Jäger, J. (2012). Integration in crisis: A regulationist perspective on the interaction of European varieties of capitalism. *Competition & Change,* 16 (3), 169–187.

Becker, U. (2009). *Open varieties of capitalism: Continuity, change and performances.* Berlin: Springer.

Behringer, J., & van Treeck, T. (2019). Income distribution and growth models: A sectoral balances approach. *Politics & Society,* 47 (3), 303–332.

Beramendi, P., Häusermann, S., Kitschelt, H., & Kriesi, H. (Eds.). (2015). *The politics of advanced capitalism.* Cambridge: Cambridge University Press.

Berger, S., & Dore, R. (Eds.). (1996). *National diversity and global capitalism.* Ithaca, NY: Cornell University Press.

Bieling, H.-J., Jäger, J., & Ryner, M. (2015). Regulation theory and the political economy of the European Union. *Journal of Common Market Studies,* 54 (1), 53–69.

Block, F. (2007). Understanding the diverging trajectories of the United States and Western Europe: A neo-Polanyian analysis. *Politics & Society,* 35 (1), 3–33.

Block, F. (2011). Crisis and renewal: The outlines of a twenty-first century new deal. *Socio-Economic Review,* 9 (1), 31–57.

Bowles, S., Gordon, D. M., & Weisskopf, T. E. (1986). Power and profits: The social structure of accumulation and the profitability of the postwar US economy. *Review of Radical Political Economics,* 18 (1–2), 132–167.

Boyer, R. (1990). *The regulation school.* New York: Columbia University Press.

Bruff, I. (2011). What about the elephant in the room? Varieties of capitalism, varieties in capitalism. *New Political Economy,* 16 (4), 481–500.

Bruff, I., & Horn, L. (2012). Varieties of capitalism in crisis. *Competition & Change*, 16 (3), 161–168.

Capoccia, G. (2015). Critical junctures and institutional change. In J. Mahoney & K. Thelen (Eds.), *Advances in comparative historical analysis* (pp. 147–179). Cambridge: Cambridge University Press.

Coates, D. (2000). *Models of capitalism: Growth and stagnation in the modern era*. Cambridge: Polity Press.

Crouch, C. (2005). *Capitalist diversity and change: Recombinant governance and institutional entrepreneurs*. Oxford: Oxford University Press.

Etchemendy, S. (2011). *Models of economic liberalization: Business, workers, and compensation in Latin America, Spain, and Portugal*. Cambridge: Cambridge University Press.

Gordon, D. M., Edwards, R., & Reich, M. (1982). *Segmented work, divided workers: The historical transformation of labor in the United States*. Cambridge: Cambridge University Press.

Gräbner, C., Heimberger, P., Kapeller, J., & Schütz, B. (2020). Is the Eurozone disintegrating? Macroeconomic divergence, structural polarisation, trade and fragility. *Cambridge Journal of Economics*, 44 (3), 647–669.

Hagemejer, J., & Mućk, J. (2019). Export-led growth and its determinants: Evidence from Central and Eastern European countries. *The World Economy*, 42 (7), 1994–2025.

Hall, P. A., & Soskice, D. (Eds.). (2001). *Varieties of capitalism: The institutional foundations of comparative advantage*. Oxford: Oxford University Press.

Hauptmeier, M., & Vidal, M. (Eds.). (2014). *Comparative political economy of work*. London: Macmillan International Higher Education.

Hay, C. (2019). Does capitalism (still) come in varieties? *Review of International Political Economy*, 27 (2), 302–319.

Hein, E., Paternesi Meloni, W., & Tridico, P. (2020). Welfare models and demand-led growth regimes before and after the financial and economic crisis. *Review of International Political Economy*, 1 (1), 1–36.

Heyes, J., Lewis, P., & Clark, I. (2012). Varieties of capitalism, neoliberalism and the economic crisis of 2008. *Industrial Relations Journal*, 43 (3), 222–241.

Iversen, T., Soskice, D., & Hope, D. (2016). The eurozone and political economic institutions. *Annual Review of Political Science*, 19 (1), 163–185.

Jackson, G., & Deeg, R. (2008). From comparing capitalisms to the politics of institutional change. *Review of International Political Economy*, 15 (4), 680–709.

Jackson, G., & Deeg, R. (2012). The long-term trajectories of institutional change in European capitalism. *Journal of European Public Policy*, 19 (8), 1109–1125.

Jessop, B. (1990). *State theory: Putting the capitalist state in its place*. Philadelphia, PA: Penn State Press.

Jessop, B. (2014). Variegated capitalism, das Modell Deutschland, and the Eurozone crisis. *Journal of Contemporary European Studies*, 22 (3), 248–260.

Johnston, A., & Regan, A. (2015). European monetary integration and the incompatibility of national varieties of capitalism. *Journal of Common Market Studies*, 54 (2), 318–336.

Kranendonk, H., & Verbruggen, J. (2008). Decomposition of GDP growth in some European countries and the United States. *De Economist*, 156 (3), 295–306.

Lallement, M. (2011). Europe and the economic crisis: Forms of labor market adjustment and varieties of capitalism. *Work, Employment and Society*, 25 (4), 627–641.

Mahoney, J., & Thelen, K. (2010). A theory of gradual institutional change. In J. Mahoney, & K. Thelen (Eds.), *Explaining institutional change* (pp. 1–37). Cambridge: Cambridge University Press.

Marglin, S., & Bhaduri, A. (1990). Profit squeeze and Keynesian theory. In S. A. Marglin & J. B. Schor (Eds.), *The golden age of capitalism: Reinterpreting the postwar experience* (pp. 153–186). Oxford: Clarendon Press.

Mjøset, L., & Clausen, T. H. (Eds.). (2007). *Capitalisms compared.* Bingley: Emerald Group Publishing Limited.

Molina, O., & Rhodes, M. (2007). The political economy of adjustment in mixed market economies: A study of Spain and Italy. In B. Hancké, M. Rhodes, & M. Thatcher (Eds.), *Beyond varieties of capitalism: Conflict, contradictions and complementarities in the European economy.* Oxford: Oxford University Press.

Nölke, A. (2019). Comparative capitalism. In M. S. L. Timothy, R. Mahrenbach, L. C. Modi, *et al.* (Eds.), *The Palgrave handbook of contemporary international political economy* (pp. 135–151). Basingstoke: Palgrave Macmillan.

Olson, M. (1982). *The rise and decline of nations: Economic growth, stagflation, and social rigidities.* New Haven, CT: Yale University Press.

Palier, B. (Ed.). (2010). *A long goodbye to Bismarck: The politics of welfare reforms in continental Europe.* Amsterdam: Amsterdam University Press.

Palier, B., & Thelen, K. (2010). Institutionalizing dualism: Complementarities and change in France and Germany. *Politics & Society,* 38 (1), 119–148.

Picot, G., & Tassinari, A. (2017). All of one kind? Labor market reforms under austerity in Italy and Spain. *Socio-Economic Review,* 15 (2), 461–482.

Polanyi, K. (1944). *The great transformation: The political and economic origins of our time.* Boston: Beacon Press.

Reale, F. (2019). Comparative institutional advantage: An obituary. *Journal of Institutional Economics,* 15 (4), 569–578.

Rey-Araújo, P. M. (2018). Institutional change in social structures of accumulation theory: An anti-essentialist approach. *Review of Radical Political Economics,* 50 (2), 252–269.

Ryner, M. (2015). Europe's ordoliberal iron cage: Critical political economy, the euro area crisis and its management. *Journal of European Public Policy,* 22 (2), 275–294.

Schneider, M. R., & Paunescu, M. (2012). Changing varieties of capitalism and revealed comparative advantages from 1990 to 2005: A test of the Hall and Soskice claims. *Socio-Economic Review,* 10 (4), 731–753.

Shonfield, A. (1965). *Modern capitalism: The changing balance of public and private power.* Oxford: Oxford University Press.

Stockhammer, E. (2016). Neoliberal growth models, monetary union and the Euro crisis: A post-Keynesian perspective. *New Political Economy,* 21 (4), 365–379.

Streeck, W. (2010). Taking capitalism seriously: Towards an institutionalist approach to contemporary political economy. *Socio-Economic Review,* 9 (1), 137–167.

Streeck, W., & Thelen, K. (2005). Introduction: Institutional change in advanced political economies. In W. Streeck & K. Thelen (Eds.), *Beyond continuity: Institutional change in advanced political economies.* Oxford: Oxford University Press.

Thelen, K. (2014). *Varieties of liberalization and the new politics of social solidarity.* Cambridge: Cambridge University Press.

Tooze, A. (2018). *Crashed: How a decade of financial crises changed the world.* New York: Viking.

Witt, M. A., & Jackson, G. (2016). Varieties of capitalism and institutional comparative advantage: A test and reinterpretation. *Journal of International Business Studies*, 47 (7), 778–806.

Wright, E. O. (2000). Working-class power, capitalist-class interests, and class compromise. *American Journal of Sociology*, 105 (4), 957–1002.

2 Foundations of a growth model perspective

Luis Cárdenas and Javier Arribas

COMPLUTENSE UNIVERSITY OF MADRID AND COMPLUTENSE INSTITUTE FOR INTERNATIONAL STUDIES

1 Theoretical foundations of comparative capitalism

This chapter sets out the theoretical foundations for the growth model perspective, which is part of *comparative political economy* (CPE). To build this theoretical framework, we rely mainly on the proposal by Baccaro and Pontusson (2016), combining the contributions of institutionalist analysis (such as theories of historical institutionalism for institutional change, as well as comparative analysis of capitalisms) with the approaches of schools on the demand side, mainly Kaleckian macroeconomics (which includes Regulation Theory, RT) and post-Fordist growth models.

Baccaro and Pontusson (2016) (hereinafter B&P) proposed a new analytical framework for CPE, called post-Fordist growth models (GMs), which is a demand-side approach and opens up a whole new research agenda (see, among others, Baccaro & Howell, 2018; Baccaro & Benassi, 2017; Behringer & van Treeck, 2019; Hall, 2017). The two major innovations resulting from GMs are, first, moving on from the Varieties of Capitalism (VoC) thesis (Hall & Soskice, 2001), which has been the dominant paradigm in CPE for the past 25 years, and, second, combining institutional analysis within a demand approach (Schwartz & Tranøy, 2019), and in particular Kaleckian macroeconomics. The following subsections discuss both theoretical frameworks.

1.1 Kaleckian macroeconomics

Regulation Theory, which combines macroeconomic and institutional analyses, is part of a broader tradition of macroeconomic research that includes different schools, known as Kaleckian macroeconomics (Blecker, 2016; Hein, 2014; Lavoie, 2017; Lavoie & Stockhammer, 2013; Palley, 2016; Stockhammer & Onaran, 2013; Storm & Naastepad, 2017).

Based on the original thinking of Michał Kalecki, collected in his main writings (Feiwel, 1975; Kalecki, 1971), it was later expanded on by authors such as Steindl (1952) and the so-called "stagnationist models" developed by Asimakopulos (1975), Rowthorn (1981), Dutt (1984, 1987), Taylor (1985), and Lavoie (1995), among others. Since the 1990s, these models have been expanded to include the possibility of a "profit squeeze"-type of crisis (Marglin & Bhaduri, 1990), giving rise to the current state of the literature.

The main characteristics of this tradition are the following. First, the principle of effective demand (the basis of the Keynesian economy) establishes that it is demand supported by the capacity to pay which directs economic activity, i.e., it establishes that supply adjusts to demand as a consequence of the market orientation of production because of the existence of the division of labor and private ownership of the productive factors.

In Kalecki's thinking, investment is the central *pièce de résistance* of macroeconomics since it endogenously determines business cycles through the accelerator-multiplier mechanism. Investment (demand) creates its own supply (savings) automatically to the extent necessary to finance it (Kalecki, 1971). This central role is justified by it being the main variable that leads to business cycles, determines the stock of capital and with it the productive capacities in the medium term, and links the productive sector to the financial system (principle of increasing risk) and the domestic to the foreign side. As the decision to invest is left to companies, it will essentially depend on expected profitability, which in turn is a function of the companies' profits and leverage.

Goods and services markets are generally considered to be in monopolistic competition (firms have some market power) where productive capacity is often not at full utilization. Therefore, the supply of goods is generally elastic (with the exception of some specific markets) and increases in demand will lead to more production rather than just higher prices. However, the scale of profits will depend on the degree of the monopoly, the key socio-institutional variable in determining the functional distribution of income.

Thus, profits are a source of savings and an incentive to invest, so if they are not high enough to meet these profitability expectations, investment is reduced and capital accumulation is thus slowed down. In turn, wages also have a dual character, being, on the one hand, a support for aggregate demand, as the propensity to consume is higher from labor incomes, and, on the other hand, a cost for companies (thus coming into conflict with profits).

These ideas form the basis of two paradoxes. First, the cost paradox implies that a joint wage increase leads to higher capacity utilization, investment and employment. This is because a wage increase translates into higher consumption, which increases the degree of capacity utilization in aggregate terms. This increase also stimulates profitability, which will increase despite an initial reduction in profits, and thus investment and employment.

Second, the thrift paradox argues that an increase in the marginal propensity to save (e.g., by increasing the income of social groups with a higher propensity to save) has a negative effect on the total volume of investment and thus of savings. This is because an increase in savings at the cost of lower consumption can reduce the utilization of installed capacity and, through the accelerator effect, also reduce investment and savings. The corollary of these two characteristics is that lower wages do not reduce unemployment and that an increase in the propensity to save does not necessarily mean an increase in investment.

It follows that there is no *a priori* reason why the economy should aim for full factor utilization, and thus full employment. Rather, in markets with monopolistic competition, firms generally choose to maintain a certain underutilization of productive factors (the desired degree of utilization) in order to be able to adapt to changes in demand. Underutilization is thus an essential feature in both the short term and, by extension, the long term.

Similarly, full employment will only be achieved under certain conditions. As a result, there is generally unemployment due to insufficient aggregate demand. However, the progressive reduction of unemployment leads to faster wage increases as it reduces the disciplinary effect on workers (Boddy & Crotty, 1975; Glyn & Sutcliffe, 1972; Goodwin, 1967; Kalecki, 1943; Weisskopf, 1979). This fact has led some authors to argue in favor of the crisis being a consequence of a "profit squeeze" (Sherman, 1991).

These ideas have been synthesized into several models (Blecker, 1989; Bowles & Boyer, 1988, 1990; Marglin & Bhaduri, 1990), the most common being that presented by Bhaduri and Marglin (1990). This includes the previously mentioned theoretical foundations, such as the principle of effective demand, the centrality of investment in the accelerator-multiplier dynamics and the savings and cost paradoxes, but also the possibility of a "profit squeeze." The main difference between this generation of models and the "stagnationist models" is that in the investment function, profitability (profits in relation to capital stock) is disaggregated into the profit share and the degree of utilization of installed capacity. Following this approach, depending on the marginal effect of the increase in the profit (wage) share, there can be two different types of demand regime (DR): wage-led and profit-led.

In a wage-led DR, the increase in the wage share has a positive marginal effect on economic growth. The increase in real wages leads to an increase in consumption (because the relative propensity to consume is higher for wages), investment (because of the accelerator effect) and production (because of the multiplier effect). Therefore, a wage-led DR is characterized by a propensity to consume that is much higher for labor income than capital income, investment that is not very sensitive to changes in profitability and a strong accelerator effect. Similarly, a high share of public expenditure accompanied by progressive taxation will favor the positive effect of wage growth. In addition, wage-led DR economies tend to have barriers to international trade or a low price elasticity of exported goods and low income elasticity of imported goods. This is because in very open or price-sensitive economies, exports may be reduced in response to wage increases as firms may choose to relocate production or price competitiveness may be lost as a result of those wage increases.

In a profit-led DR, the reduction in the wage share has a positive marginal effect on economic growth. If the profitability effect is high, a reduction in the wage share raises investment because growth expectations are generated, and this raises income and aggregate demand. This positive effect is greater than the negative impact on investment and real production from the fall in wages, due to the weak accelerator effect, offsetting this effect. Thus, a profit-led DR has similar consumption propensities for capital and labor income, investment that is highly sensitivity to profitability and a weaker accelerator effect. They tend to be very open economies with high export price elasticities and high income elasticities for imported goods.

DRs are also linked to institutional factors identified by RT. For example, analyzing the Fordist period in Western economies, Glyn, Hughes, Lipietz and Singh (1990) summarized the factors causing growth during this period into the following elements. First, the international order under the "Pax Americana" provided the context for a Bretton Woods system of international trade and finance, which would gradually eliminate restrictions on the movement of goods but with an exchange rate regime of fixed parities between member states. This would prevent the rapid accumulation of current account deficits or surpluses.

Second, the production system was characterized by the importance of industry and the lesser impact of financial logic. In this sense, the introduction of changes to the organization of work and control and supervision mechanisms is noteworthy. Along with the application of these Taylorist principles, a series of technological innovations, scientific advances and new leading industries took advantage of the expansion of markets, both internationally, as promoted by the existing order, and nationally, as a result of the generalization of demand policies, which strengthened industrial growth. All this allowed for a continued increase in labor productivity.

Third, complementing these productive changes, central to them were the rules of coordination, which are the set of mechanisms for obtaining the required conduct by individual agents. These consisted of collective agreements that made it possible to protect real wages from inflation and to benefit from increases in productivity. In this way, the wage share was either kept constant or increased.

These agreements played a key role because the dual nature of salaries leads to a coordination failure. On the one hand, the wage bill, and therefore a large part of consumer demand, depend on the wages paid by all companies. Consequently, it is in the interest of each individual firm for other firms to pay higher wages so that the wage bill is as high as possible (because consumption and its profits will also be high). At the same time, as wages are a cost, each individual company wants to pay as little as possible. Without coordination rules to harmonize this tension between the micro and macro level, there would be a fall in the wage share that would have a contractionary effect on aggregate demand.

Thus, when such coordination rules exist, in economies with a wage-led DR, wage increases lead to higher investment, production and employment. In order for this wage increase not to lead to inflationary pressures, there must be an expansion of the productive capacity and an improvement in efficiency, which requires a high rate of reinvestment of profits to guarantee the elasticity of supply to changes in income and demand.

The Kaleckian interpretation of the Fordist period considers that the existence of strong unions, centralized wage negotiations and the participation of the labor force in corporate governance guaranteed a wage growth rate equal to or above productivity growth and therefore reduced inequality. As a consequence, the Fordist distributive framework promoted growth based on a sustained increase in private consumption and, with it, investment, encouraged by profit expectations and the high utilization of the production capacity. Additionally, the possible brake on investment (due to the lower profit margin) and exports (due to the appreciation of the real exchange rate) that would result from real wage growth was more than offset by the stimulus to domestic demand.

This virtuous circle reduced unemployment (and its disciplinary effect on wages) which in turn allowed for stronger wage claims, mutually reinforcing the macroeconomic situation through the institutions. In short, during the Fordist period, there was consistency between the positive marginal effect of the increase in the wage share in wage-led economies and the existing coordination rules.

However, Marglin and Bhaduri (1990) consider that during the late 1960s and early 1970s, the positive movement of employment contracted the profit share too much. With the incorporation of new elements (energy prices, the decline in demand growth and the crisis in the international financial system), aggregate demand saw a moderation of its growth or stagnation and the level of employment fell. It is in this context of rising unemployment that the process of liberalization, understood as institutional change aimed at increasing the discretionary power of employers (Baccaro & Howell, 2011), began, along with the tertiarization and deregulation of the financial markets and globalization (Glyn, 2007). On the basis of these processes, the Fordist institutions that had sustained growth (the international order, financial restriction and coordination rules) were weakened or disappeared, leading to a fall in the wage share (Stockhammer, Durand & List, 2016).

Since most empirical studies argue that European economies remain wage-led and the wage share is on a downward trend after the end of Fordism (Lavoie & Stockhammer, 2013), a new research question arises: what are the new sources of aggregate demand growth?

The answer lies in the effect of exogenous factors on income distribution (Hein, Detzer, & Dodig, 2016). International financial liberalization, financialization, and the disappearance of the post-war international monetary order opened up new possibilities for stimulating demand. In particular, Kaleckian macroeconomics has pointed to indebtedness and exports. If there is strong leverage associated with external financing of the net export deficit, we have a debt-led growth in aggregate demand. If, on the other hand, it is based on a surplus of net exports, it is an export-led growth (Hein, 2014).

It should be noted that there is a conceptual difference between the definitions of wage-led/profit-led systems, on the one hand, and debt-led/export-led GM systems, on the other. DRs are defined with respect to the marginal effect on aggregate demand of a change in the wage share, *ceteris paribus*. In contrast, debt-led and export-led GMs are due to exogenous and contingent factors and generally involve relatively unstable dynamics. In short, an economy can have a wage-led/profit-led DR and go through GMs of the debt-led/export-led type, with the financial stimulus compensating for wage stagnation (Stockhammer & Wildauer, 2016).

First, in the debt-led GM, the relationship between private sector debt (households and firms) and aggregate demand is complex, as the link is mediated by rising asset prices and lending creation mechanisms, especially in the presence of real estate bubbles and foreign financing. In this GM, the boom in financialization allows for debt-financed consumption based on the wealth effect. On the one hand, financial liberalization has led to a boom in capital markets and, in many cases, housing prices have generated a wealth effect that has stimulated consumption. On the other hand, deregulation associated with new financial instruments and more lax conditions for financing by commercial banks have made it possible to increase lending to households, especially mortgage lending. Both elements allow consumption to increase at similar rates to aggregate demand, contributing to its growth, but also lead to a deterioration of the external balance. In addition, it leads to greater leverage for households and companies and, therefore, greater financial fragility. Thus, the entire debt-led GM can generate a financial and economic crisis due to the very dynamics of leverage. This implies that in a debt-led model, in the face of stagnant demand that leads to a reduction of the wage share in the functional distribution of income, consumption and investment are first encouraged through indebtedness but are subsequently held back by deleveraging and debt servicing payments.

Second, in export-led GMs, growth is based on a continuous increase in the export surplus that requires either a stimulus to exports or a restriction on increasingly strong domestic demand, which accentuates dependence on foreign markets and can lead to productive weakness in the long term. This is because the main source of external surpluses is actually weak domestic demand associated with low nominal unit labor cost growth and low inflation. However, some authors argue that this GM is counterproductive in wage-led DRs because the increase in net exports is only slightly higher than the depressive effect of the fall in the wage share (Hein, 2014).

1.2 Post-Fordist growth models

According to Baccaro and Howell (2018), in line with the theory of power resources, the weakening of organized labor has meant that employers are freer to act according to their own preferences, regardless of labor preferences and the need to work within shared collective institutions. Second, employers are less likely to have an interest in supporting collective labor relations institutions, and this is a result of the profound changes in GMs over the last three decades that have had the effect of reducing the importance of collective institutions inherited from the earlier Fordist era (Gordon, Edwards & Reich

1982; Glyn, Hughes, Lipietz & Singh, 1990). Thus, with the end of Fordism, institutions that limited the discretion of firms have been weakened in the search for flexibility.

Two ideas arise from this. First, the weakening of labor relations has altered the ability of trade unionism and collective bargaining to stimulate productivity gains and then transfer them to household consumption through increasing real wages. Second, much greater priority than before has been given to flexibility and the ability of employers to respond quickly and in a differentiated manner, both for the manufacturing sector and for the service sector (which is increasingly dominant).

B&P consider that an analysis of the sources of aggregate demand growth based on the Kaleckian approach is better equipped to understand the similarities in the evolution of mixed market economies (MMEs) and liberal market economies (LMEs) and the differences between these two groups of economies. Thus, putting both demand and income distribution at the center of the analysis, B&P emphasize that, faced with the breakdown of the Fordist model of wage-led growth, the fall in the wage share and the increase in wage inequality, OECD countries have had to look for an alternative source of growth to wage-led private consumption. Since then, a number of GMs have emerged that are defined by four factors:

- the relative importance of consumption and net exports in demand;
- the way consumption is financed (wages or debt);
- whether there is a trade-off between consumption and export growth (which depends on the price elasticity of the latter);
- the structure of the inequality (whether it has increased more at the top of the distribution or at the bottom).

B&P identify several GMs: first, growth based on domestic consumption (consumption-led) financed by credit (debt-led)[1] and, second, economic growth guided by exports (export-led). B&P illustrate their approach and categorization by examining the position of the United Kingdom, Germany, Sweden and Italy over the period 1994–2007. B&P consider two paradigmatic cases, the export-led model, represented by Germany, and the debt-led model, of which the United Kingdom is the main exponent. Sweden is a hybrid of both, as there is no trade-off between exports and consumption due to its productive specialization in low price elasticity industries. The last country, Italy, is a failed case, which showed no response to the negative effect of the fall in wages on demand.

As a result of their contribution, a body of literature has been developed which comments on and discusses the advantages and possible nuances of the B&P approach and which, in general, is in line with this perspective. Some of these contributions are discussed below.

First, Streeck (2016) emphasized the virtues of this demand approach, since it makes it possible to explain the common aspects in the transition from the

Fordist stage to neoliberalism of developed economies with different institutional configurations (Mudge, 2008), as well as to identify the differences in the growth of economies belonging to the same group according to VoC. The approach is also dynamic and does not assume the functionalist concept that characterizes VoC. In relation to the latter, Streeck stresses the relevance of rediscovering Kalecki in order to introduce distributive conflict, as opposed to the concept of technocratic disagreement on optimal coordination that is a feature of VoC.

Behringer and van Treeck (2019) explained the institutional foundations of distributive patterns (functional and personal) and how the latter have impacted on growth models, configuring the well-known American debt-led and German export-led models. They defended the persistence of varieties of capitalism in advanced economies and did so by focusing on the behavior of economic agents (companies, families and the state) and their balance sheets abroad. Based on the theory of *consumption cascades*, he explained why LMEs have current account deficits, high levels of 90/50 inequality and a relatively constant and even increasing wage share, while coordinated market economies (CMEs) are characterized by a current account surplus, high 50/10 inequality and a decreasing wage share.

In LMEs, households in the middle of the distribution have responded to the relative fall in their income by reducing their savings and borrowing. The richer households have increased their spending on positional assets and the poorer households, encouraged by deregulated financial markets and fluid labor markets (which do not encourage precautionary saving), have sought to prevent the consumption gap from widening. In addition, the stability of the wage share is explained by the sharp increase in executive salaries. Additionally, in CMEs, the incentives for household indebtedness are lower, since 90/50 inequality is lower, the financial market is more regulated and the labor market is less fluid.

In addition, the corporate sector has reacted to the increase in the profit margin by increasing its savings rather than distributing dividends, thus limiting household consumption. The greater wage coordination of CMEs is also a factor explaining the moderate wage growth of skilled industrial workers, which, together with the expansion of the low-wage sector, explains the sharp fall in the labor share.

Stockhammer (2016) offered a description of the euro crisis based on the idea that despite the increase in the share of profits, growth that is based on a profit-led DR has not been generated. Thus, the neoliberal GMs (equivalent in this context to post-Fordists), after the transformation of social and financial relations in Europe, combine financial bubbles and an increase in household debt (debt-led) or net exports (export-led). These models led to a financial crisis that was amplified by the very architecture of economic policy established in the European Union. In this sense, Stockhammer et al. (2016) identify three different types of European countries, the "East," the "North" and the "South." The "North" follows an export-led GM accompanied by wage restraint and the outsourcing of production to the East where countries have "dependent modernization" which allows for higher wage growth despite the weakening of collective bargaining institutions. Finally, the South mostly follows a debt-led GM with real estate bubbles and high inflation, resulting in large current account deficits.

Hein, Paternesi Meloni and Tridico (2020) apply a methodology to determine the different GMs based on the contributions of each component to aggregate demand growth. Thus, four GMs are identified, with the following characteristics:

- *Export-led mercantilist*: characterized by positive financial balances in the domestic private sector and negative ones in the external sector, with a positive external balance of goods and services and positive contributions to net export growth.
- *Weakly export-led*: characterized by either the same balances as in the export-led GM but with negative contributions to net export growth; or negative but improving domestic private sector financial balances, positive but declining foreign sector financial balances, and negative trade balance but positive contributions to net export growth.
- *Domestic demand-led*: positive or balanced financial balances in all sectors and around a zero contribution to net export growth.
- *Debt-led private demand boom*: negative and positive private sector financial balances in the external sector, with significant contributions to domestic demand growth and negative net exports.

These authors combine these GMs with the different types of capitalism (Welfare models) proposed by Esping-Andersen (1990): Anglo-Saxon/Liberal, Continental European/Corporative, Mediterranean, Scandinavian and Central and Eastern European (CEEC). Combining both classifications, their results point to the fact that in the period before the crisis (2000–2008), continental Europe and Scandinavian economies followed an export-led GM (or weakly export-led), the Anglo-Saxon/Liberal and the Mediterranean economies were debt-led and in the CEECs there was no dominant pattern, but instead the countries showed different GMs.

After the crisis (2009–2016) the Anglo-Saxon/Liberal countries turned to the domestic demand-led GM, the Mediterranean countries, dominated by austerity policies and deflationary stagnation in the eurozone, became weakly export-led, in the CEECs, the export-led mercantilist GM predominated, while the countries following the Continental European/Corporate and Scandinavian model have basically maintained the export-led mercantilist GM. This leads them to conclude that as a general rule, in the post-crisis period there has been a tendency toward export-led models (either mercantilist or weakly).

Looking in more detail at the example of Germany, most studies point to the effect of the strategy of promoting exports as a driver of growth (Höpner,

2019), which has led to a permanent accumulation of current account surpluses (Jacoby, 2020). This strategy, based on the containment of labor costs, has been widely discussed, especially because of its implications for European integration (Höpner & Lutter, 2018; Manger & Sattler, 2020; Regan, 2017; Rhodes, 2014).

However, Hassel (2017) argues that it is actually in an *export-dependency trap*, which implies that its export-led GM is based on the interrelationship of three institutional spheres (the wage bargaining system, the financing of the welfare state, and fiscal federalism), in which a vicious circle has formed because they condition the decisions of agents in the same direction, having the ultimate effect of constraining domestic demand and increasing the economy's dependence on exports.

In the case of the Mediterranean MMEs, Perez (2019) and Perez and Matsaganis (2019) show how the governments of Greece, Portugal, Spain and Italy implemented the liberalization, wage devaluation, and fiscal austerity reforms required by creditor states and EU institutions, in theory to achieve an export-led recovery. However, these policies have failed to produce sustained employment growth because there is no linear relationship between internal devaluation and export growth. Although exports have grown significantly in some countries, this is due in large part to the fall in domestic demand and both labor duality and a weak recovery in demand persist. However, these policies do appear to have led to an increase in inequality (Pontusson & Weisstanner, 2017), which is higher than in other GMs.

For his part, Bohle (2018) analyzed how the economies of Eastern Europe, especially the Visegrád countries and the Baltic countries, responded to the Great Recession. While the Visegrád economies (the Czech Republic, Hungary, Poland and Slovakia) followed a "dependent export-led" growth model, the Baltic countries (Estonia, Latvia and Lithuania) followed a "dependent debt-led" one. In the first group, they depend on foreign direct investment (FDI) for the development of their exports (especially because of their proximity to Germany and their industrial past) but the importance of these as an engine for growth decreased after the Great Recession. In the second group, they have followed a debt-led growth model comparable to that of the Southern European countries, with the same wage devaluation policies being applied in both cases.

With regard to the implications of the existence of different GMs for European integration, it should be borne in mind that export-led GMs can only exist to the extent that other countries absorb their external surpluses, which is why they are actually the other side of the debt-led GM coin (Barredo, 2019). In this way, Fuller (2017) points out that the solution to European divergences is to interrupt the complementarity between export-led and debt-led GMs in Europe.

Finally, there is some debate with VoC. Hope and Soskice (2016) argue that the two GMs identified by B&P actually correspond to traditional VoC categories. The LMEs, like the UK or the US, would have developed a GM based on consumption and debt. On the other hand, GCE is characterized by export-led growth. Their export success is also linked to the institutions identified by VoC, which include strong R&D links between companies, links between the education and corporate systems and coordination in wage setting. Furthermore, they recall that the differences between the Nordic economies (more egalitarian, with high trade union membership and consolidated social protection systems) and the continental ones were already highlighted by the VoC's authors.

However, despite the fact that the authors of the VoC paradigm have tried to adapt their approach to the growth models, these are determined either by the capacity to produce certain goods and services (Hall, 2012; 2017) or by the capacity to control their unit labor costs and thus the evolution of their exports (Hancké, 2013). None of the Keynesian inputs on which B&P is based, such as the role of wages as a source of domestic demand, play a significant role.

In this regard, Soskice (2007) links what he calls "aggregate demand management regimes" (ADMR), an equivalent to growth models, with the nexus of complementarities linking production models to welfare states and political systems. According to his theory, the complementarities of CMEs that link production models with welfare states, political systems and industrial relations systems cushion small adverse shocks, but amplify large ones. This approach is consistent with demand-side approaches, but clearly insufficient because it still rejects the role of endogenous factors in the macroeconomic dynamics themselves.

In short, for decades, demand-side approaches have developed both the spheres of analysis that distinguish between different types of capitalism and their evolution over time (derived from RT), and a macroeconomic theory based on the income distribution effect (wage-led/profit-led DRs) that gives rise to endogenously determined business cycles. This literature has now been linked to CPE, and in particular to the comparative capitalism (CC) approach, which allows a better understanding of the different institutional taxonomies enhanced by a dynamic demand-side approach.

2 A social-structural (SS) approach

This section presents the theoretical approach used in the book, referred to as the "social-structural" analysis. Pulling together the previous sections, this approach is based on considering that the economic and social reality can be explained through a process of structuring, i.e., the formulation of a theoretical system to order the elements of the whole in their essential causal relationships. There are two reasons for this definition.

The first is that the term social is used to emphasize that the behavior of economic agents cannot be interpreted independently from the system of which they form a part, i.e., without considering issues such as the form of production, social class, institutions, existing relations and hierarchies, or culture. To reflect this behavior, it is argued that individuals make decisions based on heuristic rules of behavior, formed as a function of the social environment or preferences developed through cognitive experiences. All institutions are characterized, first, by the interaction between agents and between agents and institutions, and, second, by the fact that they are persistent over time, although subject to change due to the existence of common but continually evolving concepts. As a whole, the psychological, historical and sociological circumstances specific to the economic and social agents are decisive when it comes to defining their behavior; rather than just their functionality.

The second is that the term structural refers to an approach based on the classification of social groups and not explicitly establishing individual foundations.[2] In other words, the subject is collective rather than individual. In this way, there is no fallacy of composition, i.e., the properties of one element differ from the properties of the whole or, in other words, the results expected from the behavior of one element are not representative of the results of the whole. Therefore, it is a particularly suitable approach for macroeconomic analysis.

The methodology used in this approach is based on the structuring of the economic reality and the ordering of the elements that make it up. It applies the following analytical process. First, defining and establishing the geographical limits and time frame of the economic reality to be analyzed. Second, defining the variables and areas of study to be considered. Third, determining and establishing the relationships that functionally coordinate the real elements, subjects and objects grouped in the proposed economic and institutional structure. Fourth, once these fundamental relationships have been obtained and they best represent the economic reality, a typology is constructed that allows for a comparison between the different structures, on either a time or geographical level or a combination of the two.

We should mention that this approach differs from other "structuralist" ones, since in our theory structures do not exist in themselves, so they are not universally objective, but rather have a relationship with the historical moment. They are only a heuristic approach to ordering the elements of the economic reality. With regard to the dynamics, we must consider that there are three levels of analysis:

- *Systemic*: this represents an entity that can be defined independently of the time period in which it is located, i.e., it implies inherent and defining characteristics of the entity studied that exist independently of time. For example, this book studies capitalist economies whose foundations (private ownership of the means of production, division of labor, monetary economy and market-based exchanges) are timeless.
- *Synchronous*: which reflects a situation of some stability. By way of example, the differences between the various taxonomies of capitalism studied by the CC or, in general, the DRs.
- *Diachronic*: which reflects the processes that transform economic reality throughout the course of history, including institutional change and GMs.

According to this approach, the dynamic analysis consists in the recognition of specific historical periods in a geographical area that correspond to a relatively homogeneous stage over a broad and general time period. In these stages, there is a succession of expansion and recession phases, i.e., business cycles, which are determined in an endogenous way, although subject to exogenous shocks. At the same time, some stages are linked to each other since the origin of each one is found in the tensions and dissolution of the previous stage (as RT emphasizes). Thus, the GMs represent a series of regularities that characterize the path of their evolution in a group of countries and these patterns are susceptible to comparison. Each stage will generally be associated with a different type of GM from the one that existed previously.

By way of example, it is clearly the Fordist and post-Fordist stages that give rise to different GMs, so that in the crisis of the Fordist period we find the germ of the characteristics of the post-Fordist period, which through a series of institutional and economic changes (liberalization, tertiarization, financialization, globalization, neoliberalism, etc.) has given rise to a new stage. However, although this post-Fordist stage is common to all European economies, each of them presents GMs with certain differences that allow for the comparison between them.

The GM is defined as the institutional sources of the pattern of aggregate demand growth and how aggregate demand determines the economic situation, income and employment (macroeconomic and employment performance). It therefore combines the macroeconomic structure with the institutional one.

The macroeconomic structure is characterized by how the various components of aggregate demand (private consumption, public and private investment, public expenditure, imports and exports or net exports), income distribution, financial situation and external integration are interrelated. Among these connections, the role of investment can be highlighted since it plays a central role in the evolution of the economy by leading the business cycle in the short term and it also serves as a bridge between the short and the long term, since it is the determinant of the process of capital accumulation and therefore of productive capacities in the medium and long term.

The institutional structure is defined as the set of conventional, hierarchical and historical relationships that make up a certain framework of social coordination, i.e., social, cultural, legal and political elements in which the decisions and behavior of economic agents take place. The main institutional areas are as follows:

1 *Production regime*: institutional aspects of the production of goods and services, inter-company relations, the productive system, structural change, as well as the organization and productive capacities and technical progress. Examples of this institutional environment are the analyses of the "diversified quality production" by Sorge and Streeck (2018), "business systems" (Whitley, 2007), and innovation and governance (Dore, 1986; Lazonick, 1991). The main current trends identified in the

literature are deindustrialization, tertiarization and vertical and horizontal disintegration (outsourcing and offshoring).

2 *Wage–labor nexus*: relations between workers and companies, in particular work organization and the mechanism of wage negotiation (wage dynamics and distribution). It consists, therefore, of the analysis of the system of labor relations and the extent to which this institutional sphere determines the evolution of wages and with it the personal and functional distribution of income. The main transformation in this area has been the decentralization or individualization of labor relations (Baccaro & Howell, 2018).
3 *Labor market institutions*: labor regulations, the forms of hiring, hiring and firing, labor process, the existence of atypical employment and the composition of employment. The most relevant element in this institutional sphere is the process of labor flexibilization or liberalization (Boyer, 1988) with the introduction of flexible production practices.
4 *Financial institutions*: institutions that support the capital markets, including the monetary and financial sphere, which depend on the morphology of the sector (for example, whether it is bank-based or market-based or FDI-dependent) and the financial regulations. Specifically, the financialization process has been identified (Epstein, 2005; Krippner, 2005) as the most important of the changes in this institutional environment.
5 *International institutions*: the entry into international markets for goods and services and capital. This includes the form of opening up to the outside world and specifically globalization, understood as the process of the growing integration of productive (including GVC) and financial processes in the world economy (Glyn, 2007).
6 *Welfare state and public policies*: includes all institutions related to public policies (especially fiscal and monetary), with the development and type of welfare state (Esping-Andersen, 1990). The two major processes in this sense have been, first, neoliberalism, which, as Mudge (2008) points out, has three different aspects (intellectual, bureaucratic and political) and has led to the commodification of society (Howell, 2019), and, second, austerity (Blyth, 2013) as a guiding principle of fiscal policy.

Additionally, in comparative terms, we follow the usual classification of the CPE by distinguishing between three large groups (LME, CME, MME), together with their geographical location (continental, Nordic, Mediterranean and Eastern Europe). As can be seen, there are elements of different taxonomies, which include ideas contributed by VoC and Regulation Theory (Schröder, 2013).

Finally, several strategies have been followed when identifying GMs. In their first study, B&P chose to analyze the growth rates of aggregate demand components and focus on the trade-off between consumption and net exports. In contrast, Hein et al. (2020) questioned their methodology and argued that it is more useful to analyze the contributions to economic growth of each component and not just the growth rate, to which they added the evolution of domestic and external private sector balances. Finally, Behringer and van Treeck (2019) analyzed the sector balances of the economy when identifying each GM. An alternative to these methodologies was presented in Chapter 1.

For the purposes of this theoretical framework, the two main GMs are the debt-financed consumption-led demand regime (debt-led) and the export-driven demand regime (export-led). In the first of these, domestic demand plays the leading role, accompanied by a deterioration of net exports, generating significant debt. If domestic growth does not imply a significant deterioration of net exports, then it is a domestic demand-led model. In the second case, positive net exports generate economic growth, implying a creditor position for these economies:

1 Debt-financed consumption-led demand (debt-led) in the event that there is a trade-off between the evolution of domestic demand and the foreign sector, resulting in strong leverage of the private sector.
2 Export-driven demand regime (export-led) when it is exports that absorb a large part of the economy's added value, leading the overall aggregate demand.
3 Domestic demand-led: if there is growth in domestic demand but no conflict between internal and external growth.

3 Conclusion

A new GM paradigm has begun to develop (Baccaro & Pontusson, 2016; Blyth & Matthijs, 2017; Howell, 2019) which includes both the supply aspects previously emphasized by CPE and the demand aspects typical of Kaleckian macroeconomics. The introduction of aggregate demand and income distribution significantly expands and improves on the approaches used to date. However, for decades, demand-side approaches have developed both the spheres of analysis that distinguish between, first, different types of capitalism and their evolution over time (derived from regulation theory) and, second, a macroeconomic theory based on the income distribution effect (wage-led/profit-led DR) that gives rise to endogenously determined business cycles. This literature has now been linked to CPE, and in particular to the CC approach, to allow a greater understanding of the different institutional taxonomies enhanced by a dynamic demand-side approach. Thus, GMs take into account the institutional sources of aggregate demand, which has given rise to two major groups: debt-led/export-led.

Our social-structural approach, fundamentally based on these demand approaches, systematizes the possible variables in two areas. First, the macroeconomic structure is characterized by how the different components of aggregate demand, income distribution, financial situation and foreign entry are interrelated. Second, the institutional structure is grouped into six spheres: (1) production regime; (2) wage–labor nexus; (3) labor market institutions; (4)

financial institutions; (5) international institutions, and (6) welfare state and public policies. Based on these criteria, a taxonomy of countries can be summarized as follows: LME, Continental CME, Nordic CME, Mediterranean MME and Eastern MME. Finally, we consider three types of GM to be studied: export-led, debt-led and domestic-demand led, which interact with wage-led/profit-led DRs.

From our point of view, this socio-structural approach presents a series of advantages. First, it allows us to explain the common aspects in the evolution of Western economies with different institutional configurations from the Fordist stage and the liberalization paths. Second, we are able to identify the differences in the growth of economies that belong to the same type of capitalism. Third, it combines macroeconomic explanations with institutional foundations in a dynamic way. Finally, it does not assume the functionalist concept of optimal coordination present in other approaches, but rather relies on the existence of institutional change based on conflict and power resources.

Notes

1 As pointed out by Hein et al. (2016) and Stockhammer et al. (2016), the B&P interpretation which emphasizes consumption as an engine of growth is consistent with the usual characterization of a debt-led model.

2 This interpretation includes a wide group of contemporary economic schools of thought such as the (neo-)Marxists, the RT, the institutionalists, the Latin American structuralists, the socio-economists or economic sociologists and the post-Keynesian authors (Kaleckians, Kaldorians, Sraffians, etc.).

References

Asimakopulos, A. (1975). A Kaleckian theory of income distribution. *Canadian Journal of Economics*, 8 (3), 313–333.

Baccaro, L., & Benassi, C. (2017). Throwing out the ballast: Growth models and the liberalization of German industrial relations. *Socio-Economic Review*, 15 (1), 85–115.

Baccaro, L., & Howell, C. (2011). A common neoliberal trajectory: The transformation of industrial relations in advanced capitalism. *Politics & Society*, 39 (4), 521–563.

Baccaro, L., & Howell, C. (2018). *Trajectories of neoliberal transformation*. Cambridge: Cambridge University Press.

Baccaro, L., & Pontusson, J. (2016). Rethinking comparative political economy. *Politics & Society*, 44 (2), 175–207.

Barredo, J. (2019). The nature of capitalist money and the financial links between debt-led and export-led growth regimes. *New Political Economy*, 24 (4), 565–586.

Behringer, J., & van Treeck, T. (2019). Income distribution and growth models: A sectoral balances approach. *Politics & Society*, 47 (3), 303–332.

Bhaduri, A., & Marglin, S. (1990). Unemployment and the real wage: The economic basis for contesting political ideologies. *Cambridge Journal of Economics*, 14 (4), 375–393.

Blecker, R. A. (1989). International competition, income distribution and economic growth. *Cambridge Journal of Economics*, 13, 395–412.

Blecker, R. A. (2016). Wage-led versus profit-led demand regimes: The long and the short of it. *Review of Keynesian Economics*, 4 (4), 373–390.

Blyth, M. (2013). *Austerity: The history of a dangerous idea*. Oxford: Oxford University Press.

Blyth, M., & Matthijs, M. (2017). Black swans, lame ducks, and the mystery of IPE's missing macroeconomy. *Review of International Political Economy*, 24 (2), 203–231.

Boddy, R., & Crotty, J. (1975). Class conflict and macro-policy: The political business cycle. *Review of Radical Political Economics*, 7 (1), 1–19.

Bohle, D. (2018). European integration, capitalist diversity and crises trajectories on Europe's eastern periphery. *New Political Economy*, 23 (2), 239–253.

Bowles, S., & Boyer, R. (1988). Labor discipline and aggregate demand: A macroeconomic model. *The American Economic Review*, 78 (2), 395–400.

Bowles, S., & Boyer, R. (1990). A wage-led employment regime: Income distribution, labor discipline, and aggregate demand in welfare capitalism. In S. A. Marglin & J. B. Schor (Eds.), *The golden age of capitalism: Reinterpreting the postwar experience*. Oxford: Clarendon.

Bowles, S., & Boyer, R. (1995). Wages, aggregate demand, and employment in an open economy: an empirical investigation. In G. A. Epstein & H. M. Gintis (Eds.), *Macroeconomic policy after the conservative era* (pp. 143–171). Cambridge: Cambridge University Press.

Bowles, S., Gordon, D. M., & Weisskopf, T. E. (1986). Power and profits: The social structure of accumulation and the profitability of the postwar US economy. *Review of Radical Political Economics*, 18 (1–2),132–167.

Boyer, R. (1988). *The search for labor market flexibility: The European economies in transition*. New York: Oxford University Press.

Dore, R. (1986). *Flexible rigidities: Industrial policy and structural adjustment in the Japanese economy*. Stanford, CA: Stanford University Press.

Dutt, A. K. (1984). Stagnation, income distribution and monopoly power. *Cambridge Journal of Economics*, 8 (1), 25–40.

Dutt, A. K. (1987). Alternative closures again: A comment on growth, distribution and inflation. *Cambridge Journal of Economics*, 11 (1), 75–82.

Epstein, G. A. (Ed.). (2005). *Financialization and the world economy*. Cheltenham: Edward Elgar Publishing.

Esping-Andersen, G. (1990). *The three worlds of welfare capitalism*. Princeton, NJ: Princeton University Press.

Feiwel, G. R. (1975). *The intellectual capital of Michał Kalecki: A study in economic theory and policy*. Knoxville, TN: University of Tennessee Press.

Fuller, G. W. (2017). Exporting assets EMU and the financial drivers of European macroeconomic imbalances. *New Political Economy*, 23 (2), 174–191.

Glyn, A. (2007). *Capitalism unleashed: Finance, globalization, and welfare*. Oxford: Oxford University Press.

Glyn, A., Hughes, A., Lipietz, A., & Singh, A. (1990). The rise and fall of the Golden Age. In S. A. Marglin, & J. B. Schor (Eds.), *The golden age of capitalism: Reinterpreting the postwar experience*. Oxford: Clarendon Press.

Glyn, A., & Sutcliffe, B. (1972). *British capitalism, workers and the profits squeeze*. Harmondsworth: Penguin.

Goodwin, R. M. (1967). A growth cycle. In C. H. Feinstein (Ed.), *Socialism, capitalism and economic growth*. Cambridge: Cambridge University Press.

Gordon, D. M. (1995). Growth, distribution, and the rules of the game: Social structuralist macro foundations for a democratic economic policy. In G. A. Epstein & H. M. Gintis (Eds.), *Macroeconomic policy after the conservative era.* (pp. 335–384). Cambridge: Cambridge University Press.

Gordon, D. M., Edwards, R., & Reich, M. (1982). *Segmented work, divided workers: The historical transformation of labor in the United States.* Cambridge: Cambridge University Press.

Hall, P. A. (2012). The economics and politics of the Euro crisis. *German Politics*, 21 (4), 355–371.

Hall, P. A. (2017). Varieties of capitalism in light of the Euro crisis. *Journal of European Public Policy*, 25 (1), 7–30.

Hall, P. A., & Soskice, D. (Eds.). (2001). *Varieties of capitalism: The institutional foundations of comparative advantage.* Oxford: Oxford University Press.

Hancké, B. (2013). *Unions, central banks, and EMU labor market institutions and monetary integration in Europe.* Oxford: Oxford University Press.

Hassel, A. (2017). No way to escape imbalances in the Eurozone: Three sources for Germany's export dependency. *German Politics*, 26 (3), 360–379.

Hein, E. (2014). *Distribution and growth after Keynes: A post-Keynesian guide.* Cheltenham: Edward Elgar Publishing.

Hein, E., Detzer, D., & Dodig, N. (Eds.). (2016). *Financialisation and the financial and economic crises.* Cheltenham: Edward Elgar Publishing.

Hein, E., Paternesi Meloni, W., & Tridico, P. (2020). Welfare models and demand-led growth regimes before and after the financial and economic crisis. *Review of International Political Economy*, 1 (1), 1–36.

Hope, D., & Soskice, D. (2016). Growth models, varieties of capitalism, and macroeconomics. *Politics & Society*, 44 (2), 209–226.

Höpner, M. (2019). The German undervaluation regime under Bretton Woods How Germany became the nightmare of the world economy. Max-Planck-Institut für Gesellschaftsforschung Working Paper.

Höpner, M., & Lutter, M. (2018). The diversity of wage regimes: Why the Eurozone is too heterogeneous for the euro. *European Political Science Review*, 10 (1), 71–96.

Howell, C. (2019). Neoliberalism, capitalist growth models, and the state: An agenda for industrial relations theory. *Journal of Industrial Relations*, 61 (3), 457–474.

Jacoby, W. (2020). Surplus Germany. *German Politics*, 29 (3), 498–521.

Kalecki, M. (1943). Political aspects of full employment. *The Political Quarterly*, 14 (4), 322–330.

Kalecki, M. (1971). *Selected essays on the dynamics of the capitalist economy, 1933–70.* Cambridge: Cambridge University Press.

Krippner, G. R. (2005). The financialization of the American economy. *Socio-economic Review*, 3 (2), 173–208.

Lavoie, M. (1995). The Kaleckian model of growth and distribution and its neo-Ricardian and neo-Marxian critiques. *Cambridge Journal of Economics*, 19 (6), 789–818.

Lavoie, M. (2017). The origins and evolution of the debate on wage-led and profit-led regimes. *European Journal of Economics and Economic Policies: Intervention*, 14 (2), 200–221.

Lavoie, M., & Stockhammer, E. (Eds.). (2013). *Wage-led growth: An equitable strategy for economic recovery.* Basingstoke: Palgrave Macmillan.

Lazonick, W. (1991). *Business organization and the myth of the market economy.* Cambridge: Cambridge University Press.

Manger, M. S., & Sattler, T. (2020). The origins of persistent current account imbalances in the post-Bretton Woods era. *Comparative Political Studies*, 53 (3–4),631–664.

Marglin, S. & Bhaduri, A. (1990). Profit squeeze and Keynesian theory. In S. A. Marglin & J. B. Schor (Eds.), *The golden age of capitalism: Reinterpreting the postwar experience* (pp. 153–186). Oxford: Clarendon.

Mudge, S. L. (2008). What is neo-liberalism? *Socio-Economic Review*, 6 (4), 703–731.

Onaran, Ö. (2016). Wage-versus profit-led growth in the context of globalization and public spending: The political aspects of wage-led recovery. *Review of Keynesian Economics*, 4 (4), 458–474.

Palley, T. I. (2016). Wage-vs. profit-led growth: the role of the distribution of wages in determining regime character. *Cambridge Journal of Economics*, 41 (1), 49–61.

Perez, S. A. (2019). A Europe of creditor and debtor states: Explaining the north/south divide in the Eurozone. *West European Politics*, 42 (5), 989–1014.

Perez, S. A., & Matsaganis, M. (2019). Export or perish: Can internal devaluation create enough good jobs in Southern Europe? *South European Society and Politics*, 24 (2), 259–285.

Pontusson, J., & Weisstanner, D. (2017). Macroeconomic conditions, inequality shocks and the politics of redistribution, 1990–2013. *Journal of European Public Policy*, 25 (1), 31–58.

Regan, A. (2017). The imbalance of capitalisms in the Eurozone: Can the north and south of Europe converge? *Comparative European Politics*, 15 (6), 969–990.

Rhodes, M. (2014). It's the labor costs, stupid! Or is it? The complex origins of southern discomfort in the eurozone crisis. *Labor History*, 55 (5), 655–660.

Rowthorn, R. E. (1981). Demand, real wages and economic growth. *Thames Papers in Political Economy*, Autumn, 1–39.

Schröder, M. (2013). *Integrating varieties of capitalism and welfare state research: A unified typology of capitalisms*. Berlin: Springer.

Schwartz, H. M., & Tranøy, B. S. (2019). Thinking about thinking about comparative political economy: From macro to micro and back. *Politics & Society*, 47 (1), 23–54.

Sherman, H. J. (1991). *The business cycle growth and crisis under capitalism*. Princeton, NJ: Princeton University Press.

Sorge, A., & Streeck, W. (2018). Diversified quality production revisited: Its contribution to German socio-economic performance over time. *Socio-Economic Review*, 16 (3), 587–612.

Soskice, D. (2007). Macroeconomics and varieties of capitalism. In B. Hancké, M. Rhodes, & M. Thatcher (Eds.), *Beyond varieties of capitalism* (pp. 89–121). Oxford: Oxford University Press.

Steindl, J. (1952). *Maturity and stagnation in American capitalism*. Oxford: Blackwell.

Stockhammer, E. (2016). Neoliberal growth models, monetary union and the Euro crisis: A post-Keynesian perspective. *New Political Economy*, 21 (4), 365–379.

Stockhammer, E., Durand, C., & List, L. (2016). European growth models and working class restructuring: An international post-Keynesian political economy perspective. *Environment and Planning A: Economy and Space*, 48 (9), 1804–1828.

Stockhammer, E., & Onaran, Ö. (2013). Wage-led growth: Theory, evidence, policy. *Review of Keynesian Economics*, 1 (1), 61–78.

Stockhammer, E., & Wildauer, R. (2016). Debt-driven growth? Wealth, distribution and demand in OECD countries. *Cambridge Journal of Economics*, 40 (6), 1609–1634.

Storm, S., & Naastepad, C. W. M. (2017). Bhaduri–Marglin meets Kaldor–Marx: Wages, productivity and investment. *Review of Keynesian Economics*, 5 (1), 4–24.

Streeck, W. (2016). Varieties of varieties: "VoC" and the growth models. *Politics & Society*, 44 (2), 243–247.

Taylor, L. (1985). A stagnationist model of economic growth. *Cambridge Journal of Economics*, 9, 383–403.

Thelen, K. (2014). *Varieties of liberalization and the new politics of social solidarity*. Cambridge: Cambridge University Press.

Tooze, A. (2018). *Crashed: How a decade of financial crises changed the world*. New York: Viking.

Weisskopf, T. E. (1979). Marxian crisis theory and the rate of profit in the postwar U.S. economy. *Cambridge Journal of Economics*, 3, 341.

Whitley, R. (2007). *Business systems and organizational capabilities: The institutional structuring of competitive competences*. Oxford: Oxford University Press.

3 Institutional reform and changes in the economic governance of the European Union after the economic crisis

Mónica Puente Regidor and Vicente Sánchez Jiménez

COMPLUTENSE UNIVERSITY OF MADRID

1 The impact of the 2008 economic crisis and the process of reforming economic governance in the European Union

The effects of the Greek sovereign debt crisis in 2009 placed in doubt the viability of the European Union's economic and political integration project. The design of the Monetary Union and its inability to cope with the external shock of the financial crisis, originating in the USA in 2008, called into question whether or not it was a viable plan to continue developing the European integration project. Since then, despite evidence that the European Economic and Monetary Union is not an optimum currency area (De Grauwe & Yuemei, 2019), difficulties in managing the crisis due to a lack of effective economic governance by the European Union (Puente Regidor, 2012) and even the exit in 2020 of one of its most powerful members, Great Britain, the process of community integration continues.

The most skeptical voices regarding the Community project's viability, including two Nobel Prize winners in economics (Krugman, 2012; Stiglitz, 2018), consider the European Economic and Monetary Union a "miracle," about to quickly disintegrate. There are reasonable doubts as to whether the costs and benefits of Monetary Union were properly calculated (Puente Regidor, 2012) and the 2009 economic crisis showed that the institutional structure required to reduce the impact of possible external shocks has not been put in place; nevertheless, the European integration project's resilience seems praiseworthy. One of the explanations given for this resilience and which will be established as a fundamental hypothesis in this chapter is that the European Union is a project generated mainly by political leadership. In fact, the European Union's process of integration is one in which economic, political and cultural elements are closely interdependent. While its economic component is significant, leaving aside political, social and cultural aspects, it is also true that, despite its many shortcomings, it continues to enjoy approval from European citizens, even at the most critical times of the economic crisis, as shown in Table 3.1.

Even in Greece, the country most negatively affected by the 2009 sovereign debt crisis, backing for the euro and the development of the European Union

Table 3.1 Support for the euro in Northern and Southern euro area member states (%)

Country	*Nov. 10*	*May 11*	*Nov. 11*	*May 12*	*Nov. 12*	*May 13*	*Nov. 13*	*May 14*	*Nov. 14*	*May 15*	*Nov. 15*	*May 16*	*Nov. 16*	*May 17*
Estonia	63	71	64	71	69	73	76	80	84	83	82	78	81	82
Finland	78	77	72	74	76	75	75	76	75	78	74	75	78	77
Germany	67	63	66	65	69	66	71	74	73	76	73	73	80	81
Greece	64	60	76	75	65	60	62	69	63	69	70	62	68	64
Italy	68	67	57	53	57	59	53	54	54	59	55	54	53	58
Latvia	53	52	42	39	35	43	53	68	74	78	72	78	78	78
Lithuania	51	48	46	42	43	40	40	50	63	73	67	65	67	65
Slovakia	89	82	78	80	72	77	78	74	79	81	78	78	81	89
Spain	62	62	63	55	63	52	56	61	65	61	67	67	71	75
The Netherlands	76	74	71	73	75	68	71	76	75	75	75	77	77	79
Portugal	56	49	54	58	54	52	50	59	58	62	67	69	74	74
EU-28	58	56	53	52	53	51	53	55	56	57	56	56	58	60

Source: European Commission, Public Opinion. ec.europa.eu/COMMFrontOffice/publicopinion/index.cfm

has remained above 50 percent (Table 3.1). In this case, it seems reasonable to say that Greek citizens value more than the project's purely economic aspects. If this were the case, a cost-benefit analysis would have shown that the costs of remaining in the currency integration project and the impossibility of managing the currency were greater than the benefits and, accordingly, the balance for Grexit would be positive (Hishow, Otero-Iglesias, Steinberg & Tokarksi, 2018). However, Greek citizens appreciated the risks of being wholly left out of the currency integration project, taking into account every aspect of the project and balancing possible short-term economic costs against the long-term economic benefits and political advantages of remaining in the European Monetary Union.

The process of European Union as a social phenomenon leads us to analyze the project of monetary integration as a process where economic and political factors are continuously interrelated in its evolution (Granell Trias, 2009). Accordingly, the debate regarding the European Union's structure and institutional reforms is essentially an issue of political economy in which political and economic concerns cannot be separated. The reasons for this interrelationship between economy and politics are highlighted by the declarations made by Jean-Claude Juncker, President of the European Commission (2014–2019), on March 15, 2007 in *The Economist*: "We all know what to do, we just don't know how to get re-elected after we've done it." In Europe, since 2009, we have seen that the toughest structural reforms have been carried out at times "on the brink," when the situation was so serious that the cost of doing nothing would be suicidal (Saka, Campos, De Grauwe, Ji & Martelli, 2019). And politically, the timing of such decisions could mean the difference between winning or losing an election.

The expression of this interrelation of economic, political and cultural factors in the European project is our basis for analyzing the change in the model of economic governance of the European Union after 2010. We start from the concept of economic governance (Puente Regidor, 2012), understood as the set of measures and instruments of an economic, political and financial nature that are institutionalized, with the aim of managing the dynamics of an entity's actions in order to fulfill its objectives. In this respect, the definition of economic governance provided by the European Union on the European Commission's website is particularly relevant: "The European Union's economic governance framework aims to monitor, prevent, and correct problematic economic trends that could weaken national economies or negatively affect other EU countries." This definition is too limited and once again highlights one of the main problems when analyzing the European integration project: the lack of a global vision of processes. This concept disregards the political aspects of the process. Where is the political coordination of governments to put economic measures into practice? Is there a protocol for the political sharing of economic problems? How do we coordinate the political management of the impact of an economic crisis in which millions of Europeans are losing their jobs? One of the weakest aspects of the European project comes from not understanding the process in all its dimensions. Hence, when the famous photo of Angela Merkel and Nicolas Sarkozy on the beach in Deauville in France was published in the international press on November 14, 2010, many European citizens were puzzled by the lack of protocols for action by the European Union in the face of crises. And it showed the lack of political coordination to resolve economic conflicts. The future of the European Union, at that time, a Union made up of 28 member states, 16 of which belonged to the Euro area, ended up operating on the basis of the decisions taken by two politicians from two European Union governments on a beach in France. We can therefore say that the greatest impact of the economic crisis has been political. The economic crisis has swept away a large part of the governments of the European Union. In Table 3.2, we can see that, of the European Union's larger countries, only Germany has managed to support the policies undertaken at the ballot box. The cost has not only been for the Euro area states but also for the European Union as a whole. Both for the Member States who were planning to enter the Euro area soon and for those who were voluntarily outside the group, such as Denmark, Sweden and, above all, Great Britain. In fact, the United Kingdom's exit from the European Union cannot be understood without taking into account the mismanagement of the economic and financial crisis by European governments, which has had a significant impact on the image of the European project's future.

The economic crisis that began to appear in mid-2007 led to a large number of reforms in the international financial system. One of the major challenges for states was the institutionalization in 2009 of the Financial Stability Board (FSB), a working group led by the G20 with the aim of establishing state coordination to develop and promote the implementation of effective supervision and regulation, together with other financial sector policies with the goal of international financial stability. The FSB took into account two premises: (1) global risks require close coordination between states; and (2) there are no national tools to control the global effects of crises, and it attempted to steer policies toward rebuilding the financial system. This working group proposed re-establishing a

Table 3.2 Changes of government in European Monetary Union Member States most affected by the 2008 economic crisis

Country	*Change of government*
Greece	Change of government elections 2009. Victory of the Panhellenic Socialist Movement
Portugal	Change of government elections 2011. Victory of the Social Democratic Party
Ireland	Change of government elections 2011. Victory of the Labour Party
Spain	Change of government elections 2011. Victory of the People's Party
France	Change of government elections 2012. Victory of the Socialist Party
Italy	Change of government elections 2013. Victory of the Italy Common Good Alliance

supervisory and regulatory system by focusing on three main areas: (1) generating transparency; (2) increasing the solvency of financial institutions; and (3) generating effective protection, particularly for small investors.

In 2011, the European Union, as a body in its own right, together with some of its Member States, as members of the G20, took on the challenge of developing measures to generate a supervisory and regulatory system for the financial framework, to be effective and efficient and intended to overcome the effects of the international economic crisis and which in the European Union took shape as a crisis of economic governance in affected countries like Greece, Ireland, Portugal or Spain.

In the early stages of the economic crisis in 2008, when the real scale of the problem was not yet known, stimulus packages were put together on a global level. In order not to repeat a situation like the Great Depression of the 1930s, there was a push for fiscal expansion. The origin of this coordinated movement is taken to be the result of a global process, launched by G.W. Bush at the end of 2008 at the G20 summit in Washington, where financial risks were understood to be global and therefore required cooperation to address financial crises that revealed states' interrelationship. This summit was followed by the G20 meeting in London in April 2009, establishing the need to act through fiscal expansion in a coordinated way. One example of such expansions was Plan E in Spain or Italy's fiscal stimulus programs in 2008 and 2009. However, with the escalation of the sovereign debt crisis in the Euro area from 2010 onwards, a change in thinking occurred regarding political and economic actions based on austerity and control of public finances. At the same time, Germany was the main instigator of these actions which, along with France, led the management of the crisis against a lack of common action protocols which would have allowed coordinated actions to be put into practice. The position of France, represented at the time by President N. Sarkozy, and its support for Germany, may be understood as a way of expressing European leadership in which France played an active role and appeared to public opinion as a "de facto" power in European decision-making. Even so, Chancellor Merkel's German vision of how to address the crisis and that of her French counterpart, Sarkozy, differed in theory, as Germany and France had done since the Monetary Union's establishment. However, differences notwithstanding, the image of October 2010 where Merkel and Sarkozy are walking along Deauville beach marks this coordination of power called "Merkozy," where the first syllable carries the greatest weight. Subsequently, with the arrival of the new French president, Hollande, and a socialist government in the Elysée Palace, in 2012, more favorable to stimuli than to austerity, France posed itself as a counterweight to the German approach, seeking, without losing its prominence, to work alongside the countries of the South, in a position more disposed to expansion and stimuli.

Three types of actions were carried out: (1) that of a financial nature took shape as urgent rescue measures for affected countries such as Greece, Ireland, Portugal and Spain, where community institutions worked together with international bodies such as the IMF (International Monetary Fund); (2) additionally, monetary policy actions were undertaken by the European Central Bank; and (3) a process was instigated to reform the European Union's model of economic governance as an insurance policy against future crises.

2 Economic policy reforms: fiscal policy and monetary policy in the economic governance model as from 2010

The European Union's model of economic governance as from 2010 has sought to strengthen the system of supervision and regulation in the bonds of cooperation between Member States, institutionalizing policies able to respond in unison to the challenges of future crises. For this purpose, reform has focused on three pillars: (1) a more disciplined fiscal policy following a philosophy of austerity led by Germany; (2) a more active monetary policy in which the European Central Bank has shown itself to be a decisive political actor by implementing measures to boost Europe's economy; and (3) a third pillar to reform the European financial system's supervision and regulation, where banking union has been identified as a challenge in the implementation process.

2.1 Reform of the European Stability and Growth Pact

The Stability and Growth Pact (SGP), which came into force in 1997, was introduced by the Maastricht Treaty and the creation of monetary union within the EU. To ensure the Euro area's basic operating requirements, the Delors Plan laid down convergence criteria, also known as "Maastricht criteria," which Member States had to comply with in order to join the European Economic and Monetary Union (EEMU). These criteria referred to four key aspects. First, price stability. It was stipulated that the inflation rate could not exceed 1.5 percent of gross domestic product (GDP), compared with the average of the three European Union states with the lowest inflation over the foregoing three years prior to the state examination for admission to the Euro area. This goal seems essential if the European Central Bank, as the director of the Euro area's monetary policy were to be entrusted with the basic objective of controlling inflation stability. Second, with regard to public finances, two criteria had to be met. On one hand, control of the general government budget deficit, which could not exceed 3 percent of GDP and, on the other, public debt, which could not exceed 60 percent of GDP. Third, with regard to interest rates, the state wishing to be incorporated into the Euro area had to participate in the European Monetary System's exchange rate mechanism and the nominal long-term interest rate had to be no more than 2 percent higher than the average of the three states with the lowest inflation rate during the year prior to assessment. Examination of these criteria was not absolutely exhaustive, but included some political interpretation

(Hernández de Cos, 2010). In other words, if at the time of assessment, the country in question did not meet the deficit criterion, but was expected to do so in the short term, a positive assessment of its compliance was permitted (Wallace et al., 2005). Political reinterpretation of the Maastricht criteria's assessment has been a highly controversial issue. Basically, since the Greek crisis, some authors have attempted to see this flexibility in the compliance with the Maastricht criteria as a basic component of the difficulties in how the Euro area operated (De Grauwe & Asbury, 2017).

In any event, the reason for establishing convergence criteria lies in the origin of the theory of optimum currency areas, proposed by Mundell (1961). The OCA (Optimum Currency Area), on which the Delors Plan was subsequently based, established, among other requirements, that for monetary union to give positive results for its members, there must be aligned macroeconomic variables to avoid excessive distortions and which allow them to have a positive balance among membership, in this case, the Euro area. This criterion could not be merely a matter of entry, but viability had to be found to give it continuity once monetary union was created. Here, it may be seen that since the EMU's origin there had been certain misgivings that it was being set up as an optimum currency union (Mundell & Clesse, 2000).

The price stability goal was ensured, in part, by the ECB's core mandate and monetary policy, although in practice we have seen that despite the central bank controlling a single inflation figure in designing its monetary policy, inflation rates vary widely across the countries that make up the Euro area. However, the question of how to adjust Member States' deficits and public debts was unresolved, because fiscal policy remained in the hands of individual governments. This is where the need arose to create a pact regarding the control of public finances. In the Maastricht Treaty negotiations on how to implement monetary union, two conflicting views were tabled; on the one hand, that of the monetarists, led by France and Belgium, who were confident in the dynamics of belonging to a monetary union as a way of continuing to meet these criteria. In other words, having a common currency strengthens economies with common macroeconomic characteristics and indicators. And, on the other hand, the group of economists, led by Germany and the Netherlands, who did not trust these forces of integration and who considered that some way to control deficit and public debt was essential for the euro area's operation (Dyson, 1999). Behind this need, we may observe the lack of confidence among the group of economists that the euro area would be an optimum monetary union and the destabilization that this implied for its future evolution.

The Stability and Growth Pact is an extension of part of the Maastricht criteria in the light of creating a non-optimum monetary union. Accordingly, some convergence criteria were inherited by the Pact which came into effect in 1997. The SGP is binding on all EU states, not just in the Euro area. For the sake of coherence in the Community integration project, those countries which did not enter the first stage would have to do so in future. Another question is how states' accession to the Euro area was negotiated politically, along with the question of political economy. The SGP was fleshed out at the 1996 Dublin European Council and adopted by the Amsterdam European Council in June 1997. The legal basis for the Pact is to be found in Articles 99 and 104 of the Treaty on European Union (now Articles 121 and 126 of the Treaty on the Functioning of the European Union), as amended in 1993 in Maastricht and subsequent related decisions. The SGP's implementation rests mainly on two pillars: the principle of multilateral surveillance of budgetary positions, and the excessive deficit procedure.

The debate regarding the SGP's methodology began five years after its launch. Discussions focused on the choice between establishing strict or flexible criteria for achieving the Pact's objectives. What was noteworthy at the time was that it was not the countries that had to make an effort to comply with the Maastricht criteria that posed the problem, but rather France and Germany (Figure 3.1) who brought the issue to the table due to the difficulties they had found in meeting the commitments they themselves had undertaken (Varela, 2007).

A debate on the SGP and the commitments to achieve a balanced budget in 2004 took place in autumn 2002. As a result, on the one hand, the European Commission delayed the zero deficit target until 2006 (Evenett & Baldwin, 2009). And, on the other hand, the SGP was reformed, with the introduction of three new items. First, the rule of budgetary balance or surplus which must be adjusted to the situation of the business cycle. Second, the establishment of a surveillance and monitoring procedure for excessive deficits so that states with high levels of debt that were unable to reduce them would be monitored more closely and, in the long run, would automatically be subject to the excessive

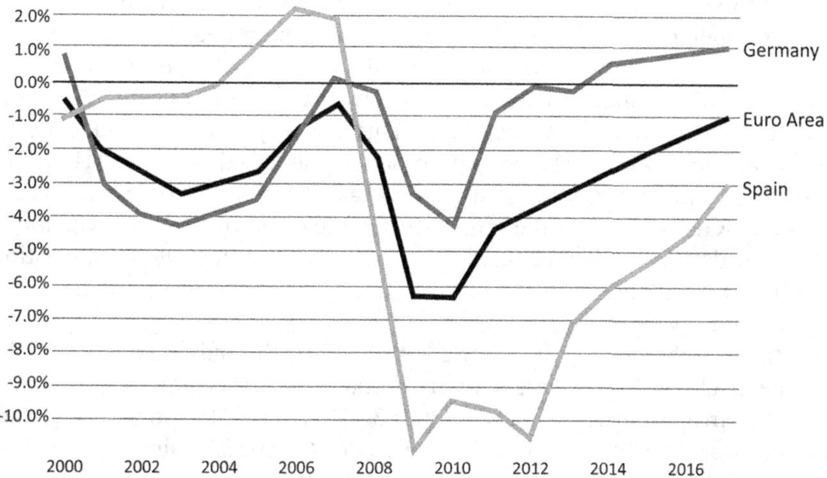

Figure 3.1 Evolution of deficit compared to GDP (%)
Source: Eurostat (n.d.).

deficit procedure. Therefore, compliance with the budgetary balance rule was made more flexible, allowing those states with "healthy" budgetary situations to deviate exceptionally and temporarily from the rule of budgetary balance or surplus, provided that the limit of 3 percent of gross domestic product was not surpassed. In return, they were to be allowed to relax their budgetary position when they were in the expansionary stage of the business cycle.

However, what were the reasons behind those states that promoted the modification of these procedures? The motivations can be understood from common sense, but behind these claims lay a more powerful reason, the strength of the political actors who led this reform, France and Germany. Flexibility may have positive aspects for the project of monetary union; on the one hand, it has less rigidity in compliance with objectives and more flexibility to adapt them to a state's own circumstances or context. Economy is not an exact science, and as we live in such an interconnected world, it is impossible to control every risk. But additionally, one of the most important reasons concerning the reality of the European Union itself was the accession in 2004 of some Eastern European countries. In 2004, the following countries joined the European Union project: the Czech Republic, Cyprus, Estonia, Latvia, Lithuania, Hungary, Malta, Poland, Slovenia and Slovakia. These states had made a very significant effort in their public budget to adapt their institutions and infrastructures to EU standards. And it seemed incongruous to ask these states to make major public investments but at the same time limit their capacity to incur public deficit and debt. However, despite these fairly clear reasons, flexibility in complying with the SGP as opposed to the imperative of its implementation at that time was also a matter of politics. The leading states of the EEMU, France and Germany, were not in a position to meet the criteria they themselves had promoted and they could even be subject to sanctions. This was a sign of the SGP's failure. These changes to the Pact highlight the decision-making power of both countries vis-à-vis the other states. The message was not good: if you are a powerful member, you can adapt the commitments to your own circumstances. In short, the requirements are politically negotiable. This is a very dangerous guideline, as the economic crisis has shown. The problem was whether all EEMU states were in the same position to be able to violate the SGP. If Germany deviates from the SGP targets, is it the same as if Greece does? If there is an economic crisis that destabilizes public finance indicators, are all the states in a position to respond economically in the same way? The answer to these questions can be seen as early as 2009.

With the economic crisis, from 2009 onwards, the public finances of the European Union States were severely destabilized, especially in the case of the Euro area countries (Tables 3.3 and 3.4). The middle and working classes, impoverished by the effects of the economic crisis, required public aid and direct transfers, for example, unemployment insurance, to survive the consequences of the crisis. Therefore, the increase in public debt meant, in many cases and due to the extension in time of the crisis, that the limit set

Table 3.3 Public debt (% GDP)

Area	*2009*	*2010*	*2011*	*2012*	*2013*	*2014*	*2015*	*2016*	*2017*
Euro area (19 countries)	79.2	84.6	86.6	89.7	91.6	91.8	89.9	89.1	86.8
Euro area (18 countries)	79.4	84.7	80.8	89.8	91.7	92	90	89.2	87
EU (28 countries)	73.3	78.8	81.4	83.8	85.7	86.4	84.4	83.3	81.6
EU (27 countries)	73.4	78.9	81.5	83.8	85.7	86.4	84.4	83.3	81.7
Belgium	99.5	99.7	102.6	104.3	105.5	107.6	106.5	106.1	103.4
Bulgaria	13.7	15.3	15.2	16.7	17.1	27.1	26.2	29.6	25.6
Czechia	33.6	37.4	39.8	44.5	44.9	42.2	40	36.8	34.7
Denmark	40.2	42.6	46.1	44.9	44	44.3	39.9	37.9	36.1
Germany	72.6	81	78.6	79.9	77.4	74.5	70.8	67.9	63.9
Estonia	7	6.6	6.1	9.7	10.2	10.5	9.9	9.2	8.7
Ireland	61.5	86	110.9	119.9	119.7	104.1	76.8	73.4	68.4
Greece	126.7	146.2	172.1	159.6	177.4	178.9	175.9	178.5	176.1
Spain	52.8	60.1	69.5	85.7	95.5	100.4	99.3	99	98.1
France	83	85.3	87.8	90.6	93.4	94.9	95.6	98.2	98.5
Croatia	48.3	57.3	63.8	69.4	80.4	84	83.7	80.2	77.5
Italy	112.5	115.4	116.5	123.4	129	131.8	131.6	131.4	131.2
Cyprus	54.3	56.8	66.2	80.1	103.1	108	108	105.5	96.1
Latvia	35.8	46.8	42.7	41.2	39	40.9	36.8	40.3	40
Lithuania	28	36.2	37.2	39.8	38.8	40.5	42.6	39.9	39.4
Luxembourg	15.7	19.8	18.7	22	23.7	22.7	22.2	20.7	23
Hungary	77.8	80.2	80.5	78.4	77.1	86.6	76.6	75.9	73.3
Malta	67.6	67.5	70.1	67.7	68.4	63.7	58.6	56.3	50.9
the Netherlands	56.8	59.3	61.7	66.2	67.7	67.9	64.6	61.9	57
Austria	79.9	82.7	82.4	81.9	81.3	84	84.8	83	78.3
Poland	49.4	53.1	54.1	53.7	55.7	50.4	51.3	54.2	50.6
Portugal	83.6	96.2	114.4	126.2	129	130.6	128.8	129.2	124.8
Romania	22.1	29.7	34	36.9	37.6	39.2	37.8	37.3	35.1
Slovenia	34.6	38.4	46.6	53.8	70.4	80.4	82.6	78.7	74.1
Slovakia	38.3	41.2	43.7	52.2	54.7	53.5	52.2	51.8	50.9
Finland	41.7	47.1	48.5	53.9	56.5	60.2	63.6	63	61.3
Sweden	41.3	38.6	37.8	38.1	40.7	45.5	44.2	42.4	40.8
United Kingdom	83.7	75.2	80.8	84.1	85.2	87	87.9	87.9	87.4

Source: Eurostat (n.d.).

Table 3.4 Public deficit and surplus (% GDP)

Area	*2009*	*2010*	*2011*	*2012*	*2013*	*2014*	*2015*	*2016*	*2017*
Euro area (19 countries)	-6.2	-6.2	-4.2	-3.7	-3.1	-2.5	-2	-1.6	-1
Euro area (18 countries)	-6.2	-6.2	-4.2	-3.7	-3.1	-2.5	-2.1	-1.6	-1
EU (28 countries)	-6.6	-6.4	-4.6	-4.3	-3.3	-2.9	-2.3	-1.7	-1
EU (27 countries)	-6.6	-6.4	-4.6	-4.3	-3.3	-2.9	-2.3	-1.7	-1
Belgium	-5.4	-4	-4.2	-4.2	-3.1	-3.1	-2.5	-2.4	-0.9
Bulgaria	-4.1	-3.1	-2	-0.3	-0.4	-5.4	-1.7	0.2	1.1
Czechia	-5.5	-4.2	-2.7	-3.9	-1.2	-2.1	-0.6	0.7	1.5
Denmark	-2.8	-2.7	-2.1	-3.5	-1.2	1.1	-1.5	-0.4	1.1
Germany	-3.2	-4.2	-1	0	-0.1	0.6	0.8	0.9	1
Estonia	-2.2	0.2	1.2	-0.3	-0.2	0.7	0.1	-0.3	-0.4
Ireland	-13.8	-32	-12.8	-8.1	-6.1	-3.6	-1.9	-0.5	-0.2
Greece	-15.1	-11.2	-10.3	-8.9	-13.2	-3.6	-5.6	0.5	0.8
Spain	-11	-9.4	-9.6	-10.5	-7	-6	-5.3	-4.5	-3.1
France	-7.2	-6.9	-5.2	-5	-4.1	-3.9	-3.6	-3.5	-2.7
Croatia	-6	-6.3	-7.9	-5.3	-5.3	-5.1	-3.4	-0.9	0.9
Italy	-5.2	-4.2	-3.7	-2.9	-2.9	-3	-2.6	-2.5	-2.4
Cyprus	-5.4	-4.7	-5.7	-5.6	-5.1	-9	-1.6	0.3	1.8
Latvia	-9.1	-8.7	-4.3	-1.2	-1.2	-1.5	-1.4	0.1	-0.6
Lithuania	-9.1	-6.9	-8.9	-3.1	-2.6	-0.6	-0.3	0.3	0.5
Luxembourg	-0.7	-0.7	0.5	0.3	1	1.3	1.3	0.6	1.4
Hungary	-4.5	-4.5	-5.4	-2.4	-2.6	-2.6	-1.9	-1.6	-2.2
Malta	-3.2	-2.4	-2.4	-3.5	-2.4	-1.7	-1	0.9	3.5
the Netherlands	-5.1	-5.2	-4.4	-3.9	-2.9	-2.2	-2	0	1.2
Austria	-5.3	-4.4	-2.6	-2.2	-2	-2.7	-1	-1.6	-0.8
Poland	-7.3	-7.3	-4.8	-3.7	-4.1	-3.7	-2.7	-2.2	-1.4
Portugal	-9.8	-11.2	-7.4	-5.7	-4.8	-7.2	-4.4	-2	-3
Romania	-9.1	-6.9	-5.4	-3.7	-2.2	-1.3	-0.7	-2.9	-2.9
Slovenia	-5.8	-5.6	-6.7	-4	-14.7	-5.5	-2.8	-1.9	0.1
Slovakia	-7.8	-7.5	-4.3	-4.3	-2.7	-2.7	-2.6	-2.2	-0.8
Finland	-2.5	-2.6	-1	-2.2	-2.6	-3.2	-2.8	-1.7	-0.7
Sweden	-0.7	0	-0.2	-1	-1.4	-1.6	0.2	1.1	1.6
United Kingdom	-10.1	-9.3	-7.5	-8.1	-5.4	-5.4	-4.2	-2.9	-1.8

Source: Eurostat (n.d.).

by the SGP tended to be exceeded. Faced with the blockade on financing on the international financial markets due to the crisis of confidence, the issue of public debt became "the lifeline of the states" in order to obtain financial resources. Meanwhile, the public deficit was increasing due to the drop in public revenue as a result of cutbacks in production and the closure of companies and the increase in social spending. This imbalance in public finances can be seen especially in the countries that were bailed out by the European Union.

The Euro area countries most affected by the external shock of the international economic crisis could not devalue their currency, so the distortion between public revenues and spending was corrected by issuing public debt, as international financial markets were closed to financing. This is where the ECB's management as a lender of last resort comes into full play, raising many doubts as to its mandate and legitimacy (Puente Regidor, 2012). Less economic activity generates less income and public spending increases due to the need to finance more protection with social policies and unemployment benefits in order to mitigate the effects of the crisis on the population. The conclusion is, in the light of developments, that the transfer of monetary policy to the ECB has a very high cost for the EEMU States. Again, we return to the cost-benefit analysis in creating the EEMU because when the impact of the inability to control monetary policy was assessed, the effort involved in the supranational management of monetary policy was possibly underestimated.

The impact of the crisis on the economies of Greece, Ireland, Portugal and countries of a larger economic scale such as Spain and Italy, as well as the spread of risks to all Member States of the European Union to a greater or lesser extent, led to a reconsideration of the European Union's model of economic governance. This process of reviewing the model in question took place from 2010 onwards and affected fiscal policy control mechanisms, as well as other issues related to the European financial system's supervision. In short, in fiscal terms, an attempt was made to develop monetary and fiscal policy mechanisms that respond to the European Union's objectives. This stemmed from the need to coordinate the different economic policies. Fiscal policy, which is intergovernmental in nature, generates dynamics which affect the objectives of monetary policy, which is supranational in nature. In other words, the management of fiscal policy in the hands of states could threaten the ECB's core mandate. This is particularly true in view of the change in philosophy brought about by amendments to the SGP as from 2005, making it more flexible. Furthermore, monetary policy may create conflicts with states' fiscal policy because the ECB determines a single policy for countries with different fiscal contexts and policies.

The philosophy embodied in the reform of the economic governance model, which was implemented from 2011, with regard to fiscal policy, implied a return to the SGP's initial idea in 1997. In other words, breaking with the flexibility of the 2005 reform pact and returning to the binding nature of commitments (Brunnermeier, James & Landau, 2017). It can be summarized in the phrase "rules rather than discretion." And this is the spirit governing the reformed SGP.

The SGP reform took shape as an initial reform, which came into effect at the end of 2011 with the set of six measures ("the six-pack") and was complemented in May 2013 by regulating the evaluation of draft national budget plans, which is part of the set of two measures ("the two-pack"). These reforms establish the main instruments for monitoring Member States' national budgetary policies and sanctions in the event of non-compliance with these rules (correction of excessive deficit). These amendments are complemented by several opinions of the Economic and Financial Committee on how to understand the flexibility introduced by the November 2015 investment and structural reform clause, endorsed by the February 2016 Economic and Financial Affairs Council and its latest update laid out in the May 2017 EFC agreement. Similarly, the above modifications refer to the margin that should be left to adapt the SGP commitments to economic contexts of growth or crisis.

The SGP's reform as from 2011 ran parallel to the implementation of economic policy measures of austerity to address the situation of economic, financial and political crisis in the most affected states and the European Union as a whole. It was not always so, at the beginning of the crisis, in 2009 and 2010, these economic policy measures were characterized as stimulus policies; however, as from 2011, when the crisis was shown to be deeper and more structural, there was a change of mentality among European leaders. There was a shift in how solutions to the crisis were articulated, from a framework of intervention that focused on the stimulus to establishing austerity policies, especially hard on the populations of states most affected by the crisis. In fact, the SGP's reform as from 2011 strengthened the actions on economic and financial austerity undertaken by the European Union to alleviate the sovereign debt crisis and the aid and rescue programs for affected Member States. This change in philosophy can only be understood from a perspective of Political Economy.

2.2 Monetary policy and the new role of the European Central Bank

Monetary policy and the European Central Bank's role in the new institutional design of the European Union's economic governance have been crucial to understanding the mechanisms for the functioning of the Member States' economic policies after 2010. The economic crisis generated a number of processes in which the worsening of the sovereign debt crises in the Euro area (especially the situation of Greece), the inability of the European Financial Stability Facility to operate and the risk of failure to transfer monetary policy correctly forced the European Central Bank to implement two programs to buy guaranteed bank bonds (the first, mentioned above, in May 2009, and the second in October 2011, for a total value of 100 billion euros), as well as a program to buy sovereign debt securities in the secondary markets. Under the Securities Markets Programme

(SMP), the ECB moderately purchased bonds from the most financially stressed member countries (Greece, Spain, Portugal, Ireland and Italy). The SMP, which was implemented in May–June 2010 and August 2011–January 2012, covered only the level of the country risk premium, while omitting issues of issuer quality, risk, interest and/or maturity when acquiring aid. Furthermore, although indirect debt monetization implied a departure from the spirit of Articles 123 and 125 of its Statute, the ECB sought to accommodate liquidity needs and influence the spending decisions of its final recipients. However, the difficulties faced by the euro area forced the central bank not only to prolong the Securities Markets Programme, but also to take a number of additional measures to mitigate the crisis.

The "dangerous summer" that Spain experienced in 2012, the critical economic situation of the Italian economy and the possible break-up of the euro area prompted the President of the ECB to make the historic declarations on 26 July of that year about safeguarding the stability of the euro area. As a result, the European Central Bank activated the Outright Monetary Transactions (OMT) program, through which it sought to establish financial stability in the euro area. In any event, the OMT, activated at the request of a member country, would proceed with the process of buying and selling the public debt of the states. First, those states previously bailed out by the European Financial Stability Facility or the European Financial Stability Mechanism. And, second, those states that complied with the agreed Memorandum of Understanding and, third, those states that also regained the ability to place their 10-year bonds on the market. Like the Securities Markets Programme, the OMT program was also to be neutralized through liquidity adjustment operations in order to avoid potential inflation. However, with regard to its implementation, the only bailed-out countries able to benefit from its activity so far have been Ireland and Portugal. However, its strict conditionality, the improvement in the markets and the lowering of target countries' risk premiums meant that the OMT program did not come into effect until then.

Furthermore, the publication of the report *Towards a Genuine Economic and Monetary Union* (European Council, 2012), drawn up by the Presidents of the European Council, the European Commission, the Eurogroup and the European Central Bank, and the subsequent report by Herman Van Rompuy, gave a clear impetus to the future completion of EMU. Through a negotiation and legislative process, which took place between 2012 and 2013, it was decided to establish a Community Banking Union with the aim of strengthening the structure of the EU's Economic and Monetary Union and limiting possible financial contagion among the different Member States. Based on two pillars, the Single Supervisory Mechanism (SSM) and the Single Resolution Mechanism (SRM), its structure has been further strengthened by the Harmonised Deposit Guarantee System and a single rulebook. Its main objective is to ensure the soundness and integration of the euro area banking system, as well as to strengthen its financial stability and integrity. Thanks to the SSM, as from November 2014, the ECB became a single banking supervisor, taking on a number of new tasks. Since then, it has directly evaluated the financial viability of all 128 systemic banks, as well as 3,500 non-significant banks indirectly. In the meantime, through the SRM, member countries also established a system for dealing with liquidity problems in the euro area. Backed by the Single Resolution Fund, the Single Resolution Mechanism aims to minimize the costs of potential bank failures.

Finally, in late 2014, the European Central Bank adopted two targeted longer-term refinancing operations (TLTROs) to provide new loans and to limit compliance with previously implemented programs of a similar nature. Additionally, it also re-launched the programs for unsecured bank bonds and securities from securitizations with a total value of 40 billion euros of securities from securitizations. These programs were aimed at buying private debt and operated not only in the primary but also in secondary markets.

Even so, the exhaustion of interest rates as the instrument of monetary policy due to their zero lower bound in September 2014, which limited the effect of easing monetary conditions, the ineffectiveness of actions implemented on the European Central Bank's balance sheet and the goal of price stability in the medium term led to the expansion of its activity by implementing quantitative easing (QE). Using this unconventional measure, as from March 9, 2015, the ECB acquired the debt of public entities from states whose currency is the euro to a value of 60 billion per month. It also purchased bonds of up to 30 years, including those with negative interest rates (maximum -0.2 percent). In order to carry out this activity, in secondary markets, long-term interest rates were leveled out, offering a boost to the economy so as to reactivate it, lower the risk premium of recipient countries, encourage investment, and make credit flow toward the Euro area's actual economy.

The ECB's actions, which on many occasions went beyond the tasks assigned to it by the Treaties and its Statute, have led to a number of criticisms of its mandate and political independence. These doubts about the legitimacy of the ECB's actions raise a number of questions. A central issue is the debate on the need to change its mandate and thus provide it with new instruments and tools to deal with future economic crises. In this respect, some Member States have raised the possibility of giving the ECB a more political role that more realistically reflects the work it carries out. In this respect, countries such as Spain, for example, have sought to reach a consensus and, though with little success so far, lay down a statutory reform of the ECB.

The measures implemented by the ECB as from 2009, such as the QE program, the supervision of banks with greater systemic risk and the indirect financing of member countries, have given the European Central Bank more far-reaching goals than those stipulated by law. In fact, an analysis of the ECB's economic governance model shows that it has become the Community institution that has achieved greatest relevance and power thanks to its active management of the crisis. The lack of determination by Member States to legally grant it these functions seems to reflect their misgivings and distrust of conceding political power from countries to a supranational entity whose political independence is guaranteed and, as one side of the coin, exhibits few instruments of accountability. Reflection on the European Central Bank's role and activity requires a greater understanding of its place within the EU's institutional system (Mongelli, 2008), the principles and objectives it pursues, and the competences it has been assigned in accordance with the Union's general legal acts. Accordingly, the main objective of this section is to briefly analyze the legal basis governing its design, taking into account the provisions of the Treaties.

Adoption of the Maastricht Treaty was of considerable importance in shaping a genuine European monetary policy. In accordance with the provisions of its framework, it gave the go-ahead to a planned three-stage process. The first stage, from July 1, 1990 to December 31, 1993, involved introducing free movement of capital among Member States. The second stage, from January 1, 1994 to December 31, 1998, sought to strengthen cooperation among national central banks and to promote the convergence of Member States' economic policies. Finally, the third stage, which gradually introduced the euro and the implementation of a common monetary policy as from January 1, 1999.

Similarly, through its Article 4a, the European Community laid the foundations to establish the European System of Central Banks and the future creation of the ECB as its cornerstone. Article 105 listed the basis for its main objectives. These included maintaining price stability, defining and implementing the EU's monetary policy, carrying out foreign exchange operations, holding and managing the official foreign reserves of Member States, promoting the proper functioning of payment systems, holding the exclusive right to authorize the issue of banknotes within the Community, backing the Community's general policies, providing advisory functions, and carrying out prudential supervision of credit institutions and the financial system's stability. Additionally, these "Ten Commandments" were also complemented by statistical reporting and international co-operation, both of which are emphasized in the Protocol on the Statute of the European System of Central Banks and of the European Central Bank. Furthermore, Article 106 of the Treaty not only established the structure of the ESCB but also gave the central bank of the Euro area legal personality. Additionally, aspects relating to independence or legal acts to be issued were covered by Articles 107 and 108a of the Treaty. Finally, the Protocol also detailed the monetary functions and operations of the European System of Central Banks. Articles 18, 19, 21 and 23 dealt with conventional measures and external operations and expressly prohibited overdraft facilities and other types of credit facility by the ECB or the national central banks to Community or public institutions or bodies. Subsequently, the Treaty of Amsterdam introduced certain changes with regard to the Treaty on European Union. In regard to monetary policy, not only was there a change concerning the system of internal bodies, but also certain privileges and immunities were granted to their members. This is a necessary step for proper compliance with the work of the European

Monetary Institute (still covered by the Treaties) and the ECB. Moreover, the European Central Bank was exempted from any taxes or charges in respect of its activity, while its headquarters was based in Frankfurt.

The Treaty of Nice, the following amending treaty, did not introduce any major changes concerning the monetary policy of the European Union or the euro area's central bank. By contrast, the Treaty of Lisbon, which consists of the Treaty on European Union (TEU) and the Treaty on the Functioning of the European Union (TFEU), adapts the European community to the reality and development of the integration process by introducing a series of modifications aimed at responding to the challenges of the contemporary world. The legal basis for the common monetary policy, which is provided (mainly) by the new Articles 119–144, 219 and 282–284 of the Treaty on the Functioning of the European Union, together with the new 4th Protocol to the Treaty of Lisbon on the Statute of the European System of Central Banks and of the European Central Bank, underwent a number of important changes.

Article 13 TEU strengthens the role of the European Central Bank by including it among the other Union institutions. Furthermore, Article 127(1) TFEU details its objectives, positioning price stability as its main purpose. At the same time, Article 130 TFEU includes provisions relating to its broad independence. Another change to be highlighted is the assumption of the European Monetary Institute's functions by the European Central Bank, which is detailed in the context of Article 141 TFEU. Article 282 TFEU also differentiates between the European System of Central Banks and the Eurosystem. Accountability and transparency within the Eurosystem and the new voting system are laid down by Articles 284 TFEU and 15 of the Statute and Article 10.2 of the Statute respectively.

Finally, as regards conventional measures for implementing the common monetary policy, we should bear in mind that open market operations (for the purpose of controlling interest rates and managing liquidity on the market, along with indicating the course of monetary policy), permanent facilities (the provision or absorption of liquidity) and the maintenance of minimum reserves are the ECB's only standard mechanisms for action laid down by the Treaty.

In the institutional design for managing the euro in the Maastricht Treaty, the role, characteristics and powers to be legally attributed to the ECB were the focus of much of the negotiation by EU Member States. At that political time, two opposing positions came to the fore, which once again become apparent in the process of reforming the economic governance model in the wake of the crisis. On one hand, the position led by Germany and Luxembourg, the so-called group of "the economists," who proposed a central bank with a limited mandate, highly focused on controlling inflation and being politically independent. And on the other hand, the position led by France and Belgium, who supported a central bank with broad powers that were not restricted exclusively to technical issues, such as inflation control, but which had shared responsibility with other community institutions for fostering economic growth and reducing unemployment as priority objectives of its functions (Torres, 2006). In this case, the ECB's mandate would have a three-fold objective at the same level of relevance: (1) to promote economic growth; (2) to monitor and control inflation; and (3) to combat unemployment in the Euro area. Following this model, the ECB would act as a mostly political institution, with broad powers and with the need to cooperate politically with other Community institutions such as the Commission and the European Council.

Based on the analysis of how its institutional design has evolved, described above, it can be seen that the European Central Bank's actions regarding the negative effects of the crisis have been affected by a number of transcendental factors. The scope of its mandate, the peculiarity of the ESCB, the absence of a single Community government and the ECB's dependence on Member States in implementing fiscal policies, undoubtedly limited its room for maneuver. Through its activity, the ECB has implemented open market operations since the summer of 2007. However, it was not until October 2008 that the major central banks, in a joint operation, reduced interest rates with the aim of preventing the financial crisis from turning into an economic recession. This move was accompanied by the first interest rate cut (to 3.75 percent) by the euro area's central bank. Later, between October 2008 and July 2009, interest rates were reduced up to eight times, and leveled off from 4.25 percent to 1 percent in May 2009. Conversely, in July 2011, the ECB decided to raise them to 1.5 percent due to concerns over inflationary pressures. Finally, in December 2011, it lowered them again to 1 percent, gradually reducing them to 0.05 percent in September 2014.

Although reserved in its approach, there can be no doubt that the European Central Bank reacted quickly. On the basis of its extensive system of collateral, it injected liquidity into the system on a massive scale, taking advantage of different measures through the most appropriate banking channel (González-Páramo, 2012). By providing adjustment and other regular monetary policy operations, it sought to eliminate the mistrust and potential paralysis of the interbank market caused by the bankruptcy of Lehman Brothers. Moreover, by taking on a crucial role in the money market environment, it secured its position as a safe haven without having to significantly change its operational framework. It also reduced the interbank market by incorporating the operations carried out by financial intermediaries on its balance sheet and took on the role of guarantor of last resort. In addition, it implemented a series of extraordinary measures aimed at improving its performance. First, in May 2009, the European Central Bank acquired financial assets known as cover bonds (for a total of 60 billion euros) in order to promote liquidity in the market segment (which had been partially paralysed by the crisis) responsible for providing banks with funds (Ayuso & Malo de Molina, 2011). Second, it temporarily changed the configuration of the long-term refinancing operations (LTROs), injecting (in December 2011 and February 2012) around 1 trillion euros through these non-conventional monetary expansion measures. Provided at a fixed rate (1 percent) and without quantity limits, they had an extended term of three years, in addition to offering an extension to the scale of eligible collateral and/or moderation of admission criteria (Malo de Molina, 2013).

However, we should not forget that the complexity of the crisis forced the Member States to redefine the system of economic surveillance and management within the European Union, with special emphasis on the Euro area. The ECB was involved in designing and implementing the new system of European economic governance and in the process of leveling out the negative effects of the economic crisis, and it proved to be a guarantor for the inclusion of the objective of price stability in the reform and adjustment processes implemented in the different Member States. Accordingly, it sought to support faster consolidation, strengthen more broadly national banking systems, and establish a new framework for macroeconomic surveillance. In any event, the inadequacy of the mechanisms put in place, the worsening of sovereign debt crises in the Euro area, the operational inability of the European Financial Stability Facility (EFSF) or the risk of a failure to transfer monetary policy properly led the ECB to implement not only two covered bank bond purchase programs (in May 2009 and October 2011) for a total value of 100 billion euros, but also to reinforce this with a purchase of sovereign debt securities on the secondary markets. Implemented in May–June 2010 and in August 2011–January 2012, it allowed the European Central Bank to acquire (in moderation) bonds from the member countries under the greatest financial pressure. At this point, we should note that the choice criterion was based solely on the level of the risk premium of the state in question, while conditions relating to issuer status, risk, interest and/or maturity when acquiring aid were ignored.

This indirect monetization of the debt of Greece, Spain, Portugal, Ireland and Italy also implied a departure from the spirit of Articles 123 and 125 of the ECB's Statute, seeking to accommodate the liquidity needs and influence the spending decisions of the end recipients. Insufficient results forced the central bank in question not only to prolong the Securities Markets Programme, but also to take a number of additional measures in order to mitigate the crisis.

This crisis situation led to the activation of the Outright Monetary Transactions program, seeking to establish financial stability within the Euro area. Despite its promotion, the only countries bailed out that were able to benefit from this activity were Ireland and Portugal. In other words, two countries unable to take advantage of this opportunity due to their strict conditionality, the improvement in the markets and the lowering of their risk premium.

At the end of 2014, the ECB additionally adopted two new targeted long-term refinancing operations (TLTROs) with the aim of providing additional loans and limiting compliance with the previously implemented TLTRO programs. It also launched new programs for unsecured bank bonds and securities from securitization (with a total value of 40 billion euros) on both the primary and secondary markets. Nevertheless, the exhaustion of interest rates as the instrument of monetary policy as they approached zero (in September 2014), the limited effect of easing monetary conditions, the ineffectiveness of the actions carried out on the European Central Bank's balance sheet and the goal of price stability in the medium term forced it to expand its activity by implementing QE. When this came into effect in March 2015, the ECB began to purchase the debt of public entities of countries whose currency is the euro for a monthly value equal to 60 billion euros. Accordingly, the non-standard measure in question also involved the purchase of bonds (on secondary markets) of up to 30 years, including those with negative interest rates (maximum -0.2 percent). The aim of this measure was to level out long-term interest rates, providing a boost to the economy so as to reactivate it, lower the risk premium of recipient countries, encourage investment, and help credit to flow to the real economy of the Euro area. Furthermore, although its initial budget was around 1.14 trillion euros, the QE program underwent consequent modifications, due to a historical reduction in interest rates or an increase in funding, in March and April 2016, respectively. In addition, in March 2016, the European Central Bank also adopted new long-term financing operations, thus completing the scope of its actions. In accordance with the ECB's executive decisions (announced in January 2017), the quantitative easing program was scheduled to run until the end of 2017, leaving open the possibility of a further extension in the event of deterioration in economic or financial conditions. By contrast, the scale of its financing (in the period under review) was limited to 60 billion euros per month, while the policy rate remained at 0.0 percent, the deposit facility at -0.4 percent and the marginal lending facility at 0.25 percent. Similarly, the program's funding was reduced accordingly, to 30 billion euros per month between January and September and 15 billion euros per month between October and December 2018.

The ECB is, therefore, the European institution that has emerged most strengthened from this process of reforming the economic governance model, not only thanks to the scope of the measures it implemented to make the economy more dynamic, but also because of the role it plays as a major actor in the decision-making process. We see this again in the design of the banking union, where it also took on a decisive role.

3 The unfinished reform of the European financial system: banking union

Following the far-reaching process of reforming the European Union's economic governance after 2010, it is surprising to see how, in the euro area's first institutional design, European banking supervision depended exclusively on Member States. Only political reasons and the fear of losing competences by states can explain the configuration of a financial union with a single currency and fragmented supervision. The Maastricht Treaty stipulated that each central bank was responsible for supervising its own state's banking system. And this was despite the fact that the EU is structured as a single capital market (Single Act, 1986). In other words, before the reform of the EU's financial supervision system, no EU institution was responsible for overseeing the European financial system. It is true that work had been done regarding a process of greater cooperation between sectoral supervisors: banking, financial markets and insurance, but no EU body had a systemic vision of the European financial system or indeed, sharing a common currency, of the euro area. This circumstance stems from the shortcomings with which the institutional design of European Monetary Union was conceived. The lack of financial macro-supervision in the European context can only be understood in terms of the Member States' lack of trust to relinquish competence in an area that is extremely sensitive to national interests, as are national banking systems, to an institution intended to safeguard the interests of all European banks. Justification for this partial supervision centered on the fact that if Member States withheld the power to supervise their own banks, they could "extinguish fires" within their borders and limit the risk to the rest of the EU's financial systems. This argument, as the 2008 economic crisis showed, cannot be upheld in an increasingly interconnected system. European banks, moving in a European and international context, do not have national borders for risk-taking purposes. As a result, during the crisis, the capacity and competence of national supervisors to act were seriously called into question. It is possible that Member States' supervisors did not have the political objectivity necessary to control banking institutions, nor did they have the instruments necessary to limit risks. It seems totally incongruous and even reckless to maintain a single capital market with fragmented supervision by states. And this is true not only at European level but also relatively well accepted at the international level.

As a consequence of these developments, the process of international and European financial supervision and regulation has undergone a profound change since 2010. Though still unfinished, attempts have been made to correct deficiencies and errors in the original design of the EU's economic governance model. In this brief analysis, we shall comment on three major aspects. First, the philosophy of financial supervision mechanisms in the European context has shifted away from a system inspired by sectoral supervision – banking, financial markets and insurance – to so-called "Twin Peaks" supervision. The "Twin Peaks" system differentiates between surveillance or supervision and the application of sanctions. The objective is to ensure that the institution that carries out the supervisory functions does not contaminate its role by also imposing sanctions on financial institutions (Puente Regidor, 2015).

Second, supervision of the so-called systemic banks, i.e., the largest European banks, becomes the responsibility of the European Central Bank and the financial supervision of smaller banks remains the responsibility of national central banks. And, third, the creation of the European Banking Union, which is a priority if further progress is to be made in the process of financial integration. Although in 2020 the project remains incomplete as there is no responsible agreement on the creation of a Deposit Guarantee Fund, which will be a fundamental aspect of the new financial and banking framework of European financial supervision.

The first regulatory pillars of the banking union were established thanks to the institutional support of the report by the Presidents of the European Council, the Commission, the Eurogroup and the European Central Bank of

June 26, 2012. The European Parliament also backed the creation of the banking union in its July 2010 report on cross-border crisis management in the banking sector, which was endorsed by the Euro area summit on June 29, 2012. In this new design, the ECB's microprudential and macroprudential functions operate closely alongside each other to identify key risks through an exchange of views on risks and vulnerabilities. Macroprudential supervision takes into account macroprudential factors, and microprudential supervision takes into account microprudential factors. Macro factors are taken into account in determining supervisory priorities and in operational planning, in the decision of the supervisory review and evaluation process (SREP) and in monitoring less significant institutions. Macroprudential risk analysis draws on information and signals from microprudential supervision. It can provide early warning of new risks arising from specific systemically important entities, as well as risks arising from changes in business practices or financial innovations. Microprudential and macroprudential tasks are coordinated through a robust governance structure, providing a comprehensive view of how risks are being mitigated in order to achieve complementary, effective supervision in a comprehensive way. This is also necessary to avoid overlaps between micro- and macroprudential instruments and possible double accounting of risks (Sicilia, Fernández & Rubio, 2013).

The banking union is therefore defined as "an integrated financial framework" supported by two policy mechanisms: (1) the single supervisory mechanism; and (2) the single resolution mechanism, underpinned by a single regulatory code which aims to include a third pillar in the future, namely, a common European deposit guarantee scheme. The creation of an institutional structure providing coverage for Community supervision is a major step forward in achieving European financial union (Yiangou, O'Keeffe & Glöckler, 2013). This supervisory framework has three pillars: (1) the European Systemic Risk Board (ESRB); (2) the European Banking Authority (EBA); and (3) the European Stability Mechanism (ESM).

The ESRB is an independent European body responsible for monitoring the risks of the EU financial system as a whole. The ECB supports the Secretariat of the ESRB, and the President of the ECB also chairs the General Board of the ESRB. The ECB is represented by the Vice-President of the ECB on the General Board of the ESRB and participates in the Advisory Technical Committee. Close cooperation between the ECB and the ESRB, allowing for the development of information flows, is mutually beneficial, as it enhances the capacity of the ESRB to effectively identify, analyze and monitor systemic risks across the EU and allows the SSM to draw on the ESRB's expertise, which covers the entire financial system, including other financial institutions, markets and products.

For its part, the European Banking Authority has the task of drawing up draft technical standards, guidelines and recommendations to improve the convergence of supervisory practices and ensure consistency of results throughout the Union. In addition to the EBA, the ECB cooperates with the two other European Supervisory Authorities: the EIOPA (European Insurance and Occupational Pensions Authority) and the ESMA (European Securities and Markets Authority). In the event of a crisis affecting a financial conglomerate, a mixed financial holding company or other financial intermediaries that may spread to or from the financial sector, other cooperation arrangements between the SSM and the other authorities in the European financial supervisory system ensure effective planning, decision-making and coordination with the competent European and national authorities.

Finally, the European Stability Mechanism (ESM) is a mechanism to support stability, set up by Euro area Member States to provide financial assistance to Mechanism members who are facing or at risk of facing serious financial problems, if this is essential to safeguard the financial stability of the Euro area as a whole and its Member States. Among its possible instruments, the ESM may decide to grant financial assistance for financial institutions' direct recapitalization, provided they comply with eligibility criteria and the ESM Regulation, including its provisions regarding internal loss offsetting.

Furthermore, the ECB participates in a number of European and international organizations, and in groups of supervisors organized by multilateral organizations. This participation, which may take various forms, allows the ECB to influence international developments in the field of banking regulation.

4 Summary of the path to banking union

First, the ECB and the National Competent Authorities (NCAs) are responsible for supervisory functions under the SSM. Action by the ECB and NCAs is governed by EU Regulation No. 468/2014 of the European Central Bank of April 16, 2014. This Regulation provides that the SSM is responsible for banking supervision in Member States (Articles 6, 14 and 15 of the Regulation). On one hand, the ECB supervises the institutions classified as significant and the NCAs of those considered less significant, although the ECB reserves the right to assume direct supervision of these institutions should it deem so appropriate. Here we see the ECB's distrust of the NCAs' supervisory capacity due to how these national institutions' supervision was conducted in the 2008 crisis and their lack of independence. The ECB also assumes supervisory competence for cross-border institutions and groups and financial conglomerates following different lines of action. Supervisory decisions by the SSM are prepared by the Supervisory Board, which is made up of the ECB and representatives from the NCAs, and adopted by the Governing Council on a no-objection basis, and directly affect individual institutions. These decisions are subject to an internal review process and may be brought to appeal before the EU Court of Justice. NCAs' decisions concerning less significant entities may be referred to national courts.

The ECB, as mentioned above, has considerably increased its capacity to act in the context of the 2010 institutional reform. Prior to the reform, the issue of the ECB's accountability was a highly controversial aspect of its work, and this strengthening of its power has reignited the debate on how its actions should be monitored and how its monetary policy functions should be separated from these new responsibilities. Accordingly, Article 25 of the Regulation provides that the ECB is accountable for its supervisory activities to the citizens of Europe, through the European Parliament, and therefore its national parliaments, and through the EU Council.

Moreover, one of the issues most debated during the crisis was how to monitor the truth of the data that national financial supervisory institutions made available and sent to the ECB and the financial system as a whole. In this case, the ECB was entrusted with the task of monitoring, and is therefore responsible for verifying the supervisory methodologies of every institution (Articles 43, 62, 67, 70, 96, 97, 98, 99 and 100 of the SSM framework regulation). The ECB's independence is also ensured by financing its activities from its own resources. Accordingly, the ECB covers the costs of its supervisory tasks and responsibilities by charging an annual fee to all supervised credit institutions in the euro area, without prejudice to the right of NCAs to charge fees in accordance with national law. Decision-making is entrusted to the Governing Council, which is set up as the final decision-making body in implementing the ECB's tasks, including supervisory work. (Articles 132, 139 (2)(e) and 288(2) TFEU) and (Article 4 and Chapter III, Section 2 of the SSM Regulation). As explained in the SSM regulation, a supervisory decision is a legal act adopted by the ECB in exercising the tasks and powers conferred on it by the SSM regulation, which is normally addressed to a credit institution. Decisions grant rights or impose obligations which change the recipient's situation and may include other provisions such as time limits, conditions, obligations or non-binding recommendations. Conditions make the decision's effectiveness dependent upon certain events, while obligations are additional requirements that the recipient must comply with, normally within a certain time limit.

The second pillar is the Single Resolution Mechanism (SRM), which centralizes core competencies and resources for managing the failure of any credit institution in participating Member States. The SRM complements the SSM; it ensures that, if a credit institution subject to the SRM is in serious difficulty, its resolution can be managed efficiently with minimal costs to the taxpayer and the real economy. The ECB also cooperates closely with other European institutions and bodies, such as the European Supervisory Authorities, including the EBA and the ESRB, in implementing the EU supervisory, regulatory and resolution frameworks. The ECB also contributes to regulatory and supervisory policy discussions at both international and European level. The availability of adequate, high-quality data is crucial for the supervised institutions and the supervisor. Data quality and risk aggregation capabilities at the level of an institution are prerequisites for sound risk-based decision-making and thus for good risk governance.

And, finally, the deposit guarantee fund. This is the last pillar needed to complete the banking union (Goodhart et al., 2012). A European deposit guarantee scheme would be a way to protect depositors wherever they may be based. Pooling resources would make it easier to manage major shocks or systemic financial crises that exceed national capacities, without resorting to public monies. Such a system would also weaken the bond between banks and their national governments, as banks would be less dependent on public funding in the event of crises. The European Commission proposed that the European system should be introduced in stages. It would take several years for bank contributions to the deposit guarantee fund to meet the target of 0.8 percent of deposits covered. This percentage would be equivalent to approximately 43 billion euros, according to 2011 data. Studies show that this amount would be sufficient to cover disbursements that would have to be made even in situations more severe than the global financial crisis that took place between 2007 and 2009. The current proposals envisage that each bank's contributions to the deposit guarantee fund would be tied to the risks it assumes in comparison with other banks in the banking union, rather than with other banks in its own Member State.

From 2020 onwards, deposit guarantee schemes in Europe have been organized on a national level, although minimum standards have been agreed at EU level, providing for coverage of 100,000 euros per depositor. In some Member States, different rules apply for each category of bank, e.g. savings banks, credit unions, public banks or private banks. This means that, if a national deposit guarantee scheme could not cover depositors' losses in the event of a major bank failure, taxpayers' money might have to be used to cover the necessary amounts, which would be detrimental to public finances (Laroisière, 2009). The financial crisis has shown that banks' problems do not stop at national borders. However, the political negotiations to create a deposit guarantee fund as a final step toward the establishment of the banking union remain unfinished. In November 2019, following the meeting of the euro area finance ministers in November 2019, there was a certain "optimism" that they could finally close the ESM reform and agree on the next steps to be taken to create a Community deposit guarantee fund, after Berlin lifted its blockade of this instrument with a proposal made by its vice-chancellor and head of finance, Olaf Scholz. The main drawback came from Rome, where ESM reform caused a political storm stirred up by the leader of the Lega, Matteo Salvini. The reform provided greater supervisory powers to countries with economic imbalances and included issues such as collective action clauses (CAC). These were intended to facilitate debt restructuring processes by preventing a minority shareholder from blocking the process against the majority. The political problem was that with a debt of 135 percent, critics of such a clause in Italy feared that its inclusion would almost inevitably lead to restructuring, despite the fact that this situation was denied by the European Commission. In December 2019, following the controversy in Italy over a possible restructuring of its debt, tensions within the German government and the enormous differences between the North and the South eventually crushed the chance of progress. Furthermore, the countries of the monetary union also failed to establish a roadmap for the deposit guarantee fund, accompanied by other measures such as legal harmonization to encourage the creation of transnational banking groups and measures to limit the balance of bonds in banks, which, in the opinion of Germany and France, were the means by which sovereign debt crises spread to the financial sector, and vice versa.

In this case, the different positions between Germany and countries such as Spain or Italy are considerable. Germany intended to punish over-exposure to debt by demanding capital buffers above a certain amount of bonds. In this case, Spain, which decouples the creation of the guarantee fund from the banks' exposure to debt, rejected this measure. In view of this situation, the members of the monetary union decided to work on a "roadmap" to advance through the next political cycle. However, the coronavirus crisis has modified the already existing roadmaps and every indication suggests that the banking union's conclusion is still a long way off.

5 The national institutional and political dimension of managing the European Union's economic policies: social policy and different capitalist models

The European Union is a political entity made up of states with heterogeneous economic structures. Ivensen, Soskice and Hope (2016) argue that the EU exhibits a "dual growth model" where the central and northern states are characterized by export-oriented, labor-intensive, skills-based economies with close coordination between the market economy and labor bargaining, while the southern states have demand-driven economies and strong public trade unions.

Mundell (1961) in his article, "A theory of optimum currency areas," argued that the productive diversity of the elements that make up an economic union is a necessary requirement for fostering intra-Community trade through specialization. And this is one of the most relevant advantages of creating an economic and monetary union. In order to maximize this benefit, such productive diversity should be accompanied by a coordinated management among its members, in order to eliminate barriers (administrative, economic, political, etc.) which promote the mobility of productive factors. In practice, this has become one of the advantages of the EU that has generated the greatest benefits for its members. Accordingly, if there is a deficit in a productive factor in one region of the union, the market would redistribute the resources and cover that deficit with resources from another EU region where there is a surplus. If we apply this example to the "goods" productive factor, where the economic union is highly advanced in the common management and elimination of barriers between states, Mundell's advantage is a fact. However, these conditions are not a common denominator for other productive factors, and here we refer to the labor and capital factor. In the case of the labor factor, the economic crisis (2009–2014) and management by EU institutions and states have shown that more complex management is required than for other productive factors for two reasons. First, because of the specific characteristics of the productive factor, the workers, and second, because of the institutional, political and cultural dimension that the labor movement factor implies for the Member States.

As we have seen throughout this chapter, the EEMU model of economic governance has different levels of economic policy management. Monetary policy is managed by a supranational institution, the ECB; fiscal policy is intergovernmental, but with supranational guidelines determined by the Stability and Growth Pact; and finally labor market policy is national and therefore a matter for Member States. The labor market is the market where the least progress has been made toward integration and, therefore, where there exists the weakest Community coordination and management, despite the fact that, as is acknowledged by the existence of a common market (Single Act, 1986), there should be freedom of movement of persons. Barriers of any kind, but especially of an institutional, political and cultural nature, hamper the free movement of workers. One example is the different regulations of the labor markets in the countries of the Union which, faced with uncertainty, obstruct the mobility of workers. The tools for coordinating labor policies have been weak and inconsistent. Since 1997, the European Employment Strategy has endeavored to establish common employment policy objectives with little result so far.

This deficit in coordination between the Member States regarding the labor market highlights the significance of the institutional and political aspects of national labor policy and its importance for Member States, who are reluctant to share management. And this shows through its diversity, the different types of capitalist models at EU level. On the basis of this heterogeneity in the institutional labor systems of Member States, Johnston and Regan (2016) argue that this diversity of capitalist models (two defined models: center and periphery) could generate two trends: on one hand, an integration that promotes convergence toward a neo-liberal system and, on the other, one that gives rise to a system where these differences in capitalist models achieve a balance that allows them to coexist and generate common benefits. However, these authors conclude that the dynamics of the two economic models are incompatible over time.

Regulation of the labor market in the European context and its management is a national political process, where the institutional and labor culture of each country is of considerable importance. Agreements on basic labor issues, such as wage policy, are shaped in national political processes where negotiations between trade unions, employers and government are the focus of basic wage policy guidelines. Therefore, according to Höpner and Lutter (2018), wage policy is a political exchange between different agents which, in the framework of a monetary union, generates tensions over monetary (supranational) and fiscal (basically intergovernmental) policy.

In this respect, the heterogeneity of the EU's political and institutional management in the framework of wage policy (Pérez, 2019) stands as a key element in understanding the tensions that may arise in order to implement a coordinated economic policy in the context of monetary union. And this is one of the most important focuses of institutional reform of the European Union's economic governance model. In this regard, Ryner (2015) analyzes the EU as a product of its own contradictions that has become an "ordo-liberal iron cage."

As a product of the disparity in the wage policies of each Member State, the EU is a project that aims to become a political union with a single voice in monetary policy, but with a lack of coordination at a fiscal level and a disparity in labor markets that distorts the pursuit of common objectives. Countries' public finances are primarily fed by labor income and therefore wage policy should be one of the key objectives of EU integration. And this has implications as relevant for Europeans' social life as the fact that each citizen enjoys a different welfare state depending on where he or she lives. The process of institutional reform of the European Economic and Monetary Union still has a long way to go in the future.

6 Conclusion

We may draw the following conclusions. First, the economic and financial crisis of 2008, with its epicenter in the United States, rapidly spread to the rest of the world, especially Western countries. In this context, the European Union was one of the trade blocs that suffered most from the expansion of the negative economic consequences and the loss of confidence of investors and citizens. The need to take measures at an international level gave rise to debate and discussion forums such as the Financial Stability Board, within the framework of the G20, to share action measures aimed at limiting the costs of the crisis and laying the foundations for a more coordinated financial system with common rules of operation.

Second, in order to address this context of crisis, as from 2010, the European Union undertook a reform of its economic governance model to reconfigure and improve the raft of economic, political and financial measures that ensure the viability of the European project and safeguard the single currency against external shocks. This new model of economic governance revolves around three points: (1) a new framework for Member States' fiscal policy characterized by rigid rules and austerity in its compliance; (2) a highly active monetary policy on the part of the European Central Bank, which becomes a political actor, despite its theoretical independence, whose power is greatly strengthened; and (3) a new institutional and regulatory framework for financial supervision supported by an as-yet incomplete project for a European banking union.

This reform of the EU's economic governance model has neglected one of the policies with the greatest implications and synergies for achieving common goals, namely, wage policy. The divergence of wage policies highlights the existence of different models of capitalism, exhibiting the lack of economic policy coordination and the relevance of the political and institutional aspects of the Member States to the detriment of the Union and in favor of maintaining national competences.

Finally, despite the progress made over the decade following the economic crisis, many issues remain unresolved in the European Union, both as regards the viability of the economic project and the coherence of the philosophy with which the Member States are addressing the political project's implementation. The European Union is a living, dynamic economic and political entity that requires a solid economic governance framework to meet the challenges of the future, which will be not only political and economic but also technological and health-related. Ultimately, a voluntary union such as the European Union will survive if it is perceived by European citizens as part of the solution not only to the problems of individual Member States but also to global dilemmas in the context of the Union. This is the challenge facing the future of the European Union.

References

Ayuso, J., & Malo de Molina, J. L. (2011). El papel de los Bancos centrales durante la crisis financiera. *Papeles de la Fundación*, 42, 49–64.

Brunnermeier, M. K., James, H., & Landau, J. P. (2017). *The euro and the battle of ideas.* Barcelona: Deusto.

De Grauwe, P. (2014). *Economics of monetary union*, 10th edn. New York: Oxford University Press.

De Grauwe, P., & Asbury, A. (2017). *The limits of the market: The pendulum between the government and the market*. Oxford: Oxford University Press.

De Grauwe, P., & Yuemei, J. (2019). Time to change budgetary priorities in the Euro area: Review of European economic policy. *CEPS*, 54 (5), 285–290.

Dyson, K. H. F. (1999). *The road to Maastricht: Negotiating economic and monetary union*. Oxford: Oxford University Press.

European Council (2012). Towards a genuine economic and monetary union. Available at: www.consilium.europa.eu/uedocs/cms_data/docs/pressdata/es/ec/131290.pdf

Eurostat (n.d.). https://ec.europa.eu/eurostat/data/database

Evenett, S., & Baldwin, R. (Eds.). (2009). *The great trade collapse: Causes, consequences and prospects: Crisis-era protectionism one year after the Washington G20 meeting.* London: Voxeu and Centre for Economic Policy Research (CEPR).

González-Páramo, J. M. (2012). La gestión del Banco Central Europeo ante la crisis. *Revista de Economía Mundial*, 30, 83–102.

Goodhart, C., Kashyap, A., Tsomocos, D., & Vardoulakis, A. (2012). An integrated framework for analyzing multiple financial regulations. *International Journal of Central Banking*. Available at: www.ijcb.org/journal/ijcb13q0a5.pdf (accessed January 12, 2020).

Granell Trias, F. (2009). Las medidas contra la crisis, sus problemas y su impacto intergeneracional: La primera crisis global: procesos, consecuencias y medidas. *ICE*, 850, 57–72.

Hernández de Cos, P. (2010). El papel de la política fiscal en la crisis económica. *Presupuesto y Gasto Público*, 59, 39–54.

Hishow, O., Otero-Iglesias, M., Steinberg, F., & Tokarski, P. (Eds.). (2018). The Euro paradox: Explaining the resilience of the single currency. Working Paper RD EU/Europa, 2018/No. 01, January 2018.

Höpner, M., & Lutter, M. (2018). The diversity of wage regimes: Why the Euro area is too heterogeneous for the Euro. *European Political Science Review*, 10 (1), 71–96.

Iversen, T., Soskice, D., & Hope, D. (2016). The euro area and political economic institutions. *Annual Review of Political Science*, 19, 163–168.

Johnston, A., & Regan, A. (2016). European monetary integration and the incompatibility of national varieties of capitalism. *Journal of Common Market Studies*, 54 (2), 318–336.

Krugman, P. (2012). Blog. Available at: https://delong.typepad.com/sdj/2013/04/paul-krugman-2012-economics-in-the-crisis.html (accessed February 22, 2020).

Laroisière, J. (2009). The high-level group on financial supervision in the EU. Available at: http://ec.europa.eu/finance/general-policy/docs/de_larosiere_report_en.pdf (accessed February 12, 2020).

Malo de Molina, J. L. (2013). La respuesta del Banco Central Europeo a la crisis. *Banco de España Boletín económico*, July–August, 115–124.

Mongelli, F. P. (2008). European economic and monetary integration and the optimum currency area theory. *Economic Papers*. Brussels: European Commission.

Mundell, R. (1961). A theory of optimum currency area. *The American Economic Review*, 51 (4), 657–665.

Mundell, R., & Clesse, A. (2000). *The Euro as a stabilizer in the international economy system*. Luxembourg: Springer Science and Business Media.

Pérez, S. A. (2019). A Europe of creditor and debtor states: Explaining the north/south divide in the Euro area. *West European Politics*, 42 (5), 989–1014.

Puente Regidor, M. (2012). *La gobernanza económica de la Unión Europea: Retos y perspectivas de la UEME*. Madrid: Civitas.

Puente Regidor, M. (2015). El marco institucional del nuevo modelo de regulación financiera de la Unión Europea. *Nómadas: Critical Journal of Social and Juridical Sciences*, 39 (3), 133–139. https://doi.org/10.5209/rev_NOMA.2013.v39.n3.48328R.

Ryner, M. (2015). Europe's ordo-liberal iron cage: Critical political economy, the Euro area crisis and its management. *Journal of European Public Policy*, 22 (2), 275–294.

Saka, O., Campos, N., De Grauwe, P., Ji, Y., & Martelli, A. (2019). Blog. Available at: https://voxeu.org/article/financial-crises-and-dynamics-financial-de-liberalisation (accessed February 13, 2011).

Sicilia, J., Fernández, S., & Rubio, A. (2013). Unión Bancaria: Elementos integrantes y medidas complementarias. Análisis económico. BBVA Working Paper No. 13/26. August 2013.

Stiglitz, J. (2018). Blog. June 13. Available at: www.project-syndicate.org/commentary/next-euro-crisis-italy-by-joseph-e–stiglitz-2018-06/spanish?barrier=accesspaylog (accessed January 10, 2020).

Torres, F. (2006). On efficiency-legitimacy trade-off in EMU. *Área científica de Economía*, 36. Aveiro: Universidad de Aveiro.

Varela, P. (2007). *Gobierno de la Unión Europea*. Coruña: Netbiblo.

Wallace, H., Pollack, M. A., & Young, A. R. (2005). *Policymaking in the European Union*. Oxford: Oxford University Press.

Yiangou, J., O'Keeffe, M., & Glöckler, G. (2013). How the ECB's monetary financing prohibition pushes deeper Euro area integration. *Journal of European Integration*, 25 (3), 223–237.

4 France

Low inequality despite poor economic performance in a debt-financed consumption-led model

Julián López

COMPLUTENSE UNIVERSITY OF MADRID AND COMPLUTENSE INSTITUTE FOR INTERNATIONAL STUDIES

1 Introduction

France's variety of capitalism is still a hot topic for discussion. Although it has sometimes been classified as a mixed market economy (MME), some authors consider it a particular type of coordinated market economy(CME). In any case, general agreement exists on characterizing France by some institutional features that point to the power of the state and the existence of high levels of social contestation. The first of these features is the strong French welfare state, which means higher social expenditure and relatively generous benefits but also higher taxes on wages than the Organisation for Economic Co-operation and Development (OECD) average. The second is the high legal protection of labor contracts that has remained stable for the last few decades, implying high protection of regular workers against dismissal as well as legal restrictions on the use of temporary contracts. The third institutional characteristic is the combination of a relatively high minimum wage (MW), a high level of collective bargaining coverage, and, more generally, a significant influence enjoyed by French unions on wage bargaining and national politics.

The point is that these three elements are frequently linked to direct adverse supply effects as well as indirect negative impacts on demand. As a result, what we call Workers' Protection Institutions (WPIs), may represent the institutional foundations of the French debt-financed consumption-led model. The explanation is as follows. As a result of the combination of these three institutional features, both the reservation wages of the unemployed and the labor turnover costs of the employed workers increased and, consequently, workers' bargaining power (particularly of those with typical contracts) was reinforced. Besides, more ambitious redistributive policies mean higher taxes on wages and, therefore, higher non-salary labor costs. Thus, for many economists, although institutional systems with strong WPIs are theoretically protective of vulnerable workers, in practice, these institutional designs can damage their interests: first, because they raise labor market entry barriers for unemployed workers, especially for those with lower skill levels and lower productivity. Second, because they increase employees' unit labor costs, undermining the national and international competitiveness of the economy and, therefore, the basis for stable long-term gross domestic product (GDP) growth.

This perspective is consistent with some recent observations on the French economy that can be grouped into two different problems: The first is the high unemployment and temporary employment rates, which mainly affect young people, but do affect some older population groups as well. The second is France's trade in goods and services deficit that grew at the beginning of the 2000s and has remained stable since the Great Recession. As can be seen below, both features can explain why France's growth strategy is based on internal demand growth and why this growth has been financed by private credit.

Although France shares the sudden unemployment rate increase of the 1970s with other advanced economies, the country's unemployment figures have not returned to previous levels, unlike those of most of the other economically advanced nations. Thus, unemployment rates have remained stable in the range of 8–10 percent during the last three decades. Moreover, there has been an increase in temporary and other forms of atypical employment in France. As a result, a significant proportion of the most vulnerable population is caught between unemployment and short- or very short-term labor contracts. According to some analysts, strong protection of workers with regular contracts can be causing these growing labor market asymmetries.

As for the second problem, the most frequent explanation for France's trade deficit points to the unit labor costs performance. From this point of view, cost competitiveness is mainly driven by the relation between labor compensation and productivity. Whenever the former grows faster than the latter, unit labor costs increase, causing higher prices and damaging the external price competitiveness of the economy. In this sense, WPIs could be negatively affecting France's foreign trade relations by increasing costs and prices (Carcillo, Goujard, Hijzen & Thewissen, 2019; CNP, 2019; Poutvaara, Leithold, Nikolka, Oesingmann & Wech, 2017).

In this context, it is inevitable that one compares the German (Chapter 5 in this book) and the French cases. After the great economic crisis caused by the derived problems of reunification, the German labor market and industrial relations were affected by some important institutional transformations at the beginning of the 2000s. These changes, in turn, were related to the trade surplus and low unemployment rates shown by the economy since then. Germany is therefore seen as a reformist example to be followed. However, when both economies are compared, looking at the policy recommendations made, the possible positive effects of WPIs on income distribution are usually not considered.

This question is particularly relevant when we take into account the differences in earnings disparities between France and other advanced economies, including Germany. Even though it is true that income inequality and the numbers of the poor population increased in France after the Great Recession, their levels remain below those of many economies with lower unemployment rates. From a longitudinal perspective, it can be observed that France's vulnerable population has increased along with the growth of non-standard employment and the increase in short-term as well as long-term unemployment. However, when a cross-sectional perspective is adopted, one can perceive a decoupling between employment and income distribution performance.

Accordingly, some good reasons exist for one to think that the same institutions can represent opposing roles. Even assuming that WPIs have a negative impact on unemployment and external competitiveness, they would explain France's relatively low-income disparities. Indeed, this chapter is about whether or not these differentiated roles of WPIs can explain some of the characteristics of the French model. Based on exploratory analysis, the results point to two insights. First, contrary to some expectations, WPIs seem not to have a significant impact either on total employment and particular forms of employment or on unit labor costs and external competitiveness. Second, stronger WPIs may reduce social and economic inequality, as they imply more ambitious social politics that increase the power of the state to redistribute incomes, as well as stricter laws protecting the most vulnerable workers. I call the former the assumed supply effects of WPIs, while the latter are the hidden redistributive ones.

Thus, the aim of this chapter is to assess the real economic impact of the institutional foundations of the French economic model. To do so, after analyzing WPIs' characteristics and evolution, I will consider their effects on supply, demand, and income distribution. The rest of the chapter is structured as follows: In Section 2, I describe why the three institutional elements previously mentioned (a high collective bargaining coverage, strong employment protection legislation, and ambitious social policies) may explain the existence of strong WPIs in France. Additionally, I will analyze recent legal reforms concerning these institutional aspects and assessing their importance. Section 3 is devoted to analyzing the link between these institutional foundations and some relevant characteristics of the French economic model. Section 4 concludes the chapter.

2 The existence of strong WPIs in France

2.1 An ambitious welfare state protecting vulnerable workers

Like the rest of continental European welfare states, the French social protection system was originally based on a strong link between protection and employment. Even though it was started as a universalist system, in practice, it was restricted to salary earners. Thus, access to social benefits entirely depended on mandatory contributions, and compensation amounts were determined as a function of previous earnings (Palier, 2010). However, as we will see later in this section, since the 1980s, the employment crisis explains, at least partially, the extension of the system to include non-contributory benefits (Palier, 2010; Palier & Thelen, 2010). As a result, despite having a dual bias, the French welfare state is characterized by generous social policies for vulnerable groups. This extended social-protection system has reinforced the redistributive capacity of the state and is linked to the emergence of the so-called new social risks, which are partly derived from labor market changes (Taylor-Gooby, 2004).

This does not mean that there have not been attempts at welfare state retrenchment. In the 1980s, social expenditure increased to alleviate the worst effects of sectoral change and collective dismissals (Palier, 2010; Palier & Thelen, 2010). During the following decade and in the context of Maastricht's budgetary restrictions, fiscal adjustment reforms were adopted to reduce the social security deficit (Bazen & Girardin, 1999). However, these political measures, which impacted on important fields, such as public health, pensions, and unemployment benefits systems, were not just "retrenchment proposals." They were indeed the product of a balance between the preferences of the government and those of the social agents. Thus, along with the adoption of more stringent regulations on access to contributory social benefits, new non-contributory, tax-funded social benefits were created. The aim of these new benefits was to cover those outside of the contributory system because they had recently been excluded as a result of the regulatory changes or simply because they had never been part of it (Hassenteufel & Palier, 2016; Palier, 2010).

As a consequence, the reforms of the 1980s and 1990s did not imply a decreasing welfare state provision but a change in the social protection system's goals and ambitions. The non-contributory part of the system was reinforced at the expense of stricter rules on access to its contributory one. The reasons are both economic and institutional. A strictly contributory welfare state, based on the link between employment and access to protection, cannot maintain social cohesion in a context of high unemployment rates. Indeed, it may increase the income gap between workers with continuous and discontinuous employment trajectories, especially for those permanently out of the labor market as a consequence of structural change (Hassenteufel & Palier, 2016; Palier, 2010).

Among these new forms of social protection adopted by the French welfare state, the *Revenú Minimum d'insertion* (RMI) is particularly important. It was created in 1988 and was replaced in 2009 by a new social benefit, the *Revenú de Solidarité Active* (RSA). This latter was aimed at adults older than 25 years or those younger than 25 having parental responsibilities whose monthly income did not exceed an amount equivalent to the RMI. The RMI consisted of a "differential benefit" because it covered the difference between the benefit recipient's income and the minimum income determined by law. Moreover, since social integration was the main goal of this policy, recipients' commitment to searching for a job was one of the conditions for access, as in the case of RSA. Indeed, despite having a different name, the new RSA and the old RMI are, in practice, the same social benefit. Both put the emphasis on professional reactivation and social integration, making cash transfers dependent on these goals. As for the differences between them, one can consider RSA a more ambitious initiative since the benefit might be extended to every adult younger than 24 years, provided they have worked a certain amount of hours within the last three years (RSA *jeune actif*).

While the conditions for receipt of this benefit are regulated by Articles L. 262–2 to L. 262–12 of the *Code de l'action social et des familles*, the benefit amount has been increased by successive *Décrets* of revaluation from 1988 to 2020. Thus, for a single recipient living alone, it rose from 454.53 euros in 2009 to 564.78 euros in 2020, as established by the first Article of the *Décrets* no. 2009–190 and no. 2020–490. Besides, the amount increases when these factors change. For example, a couple with two children without earnings may receive in 2020 a cash transfer from the French state of 186.04 euros, increasing to 225.91 euros for an additional child. Additionally, the number of recipients has greatly increased in recent years, from fewer than one million in 2009 to almost two million in 2016 (Figure 4.1). This increase can be explained by the rise in the number of economically vulnerable persons during the same period. In a context of crisis, many of them probably

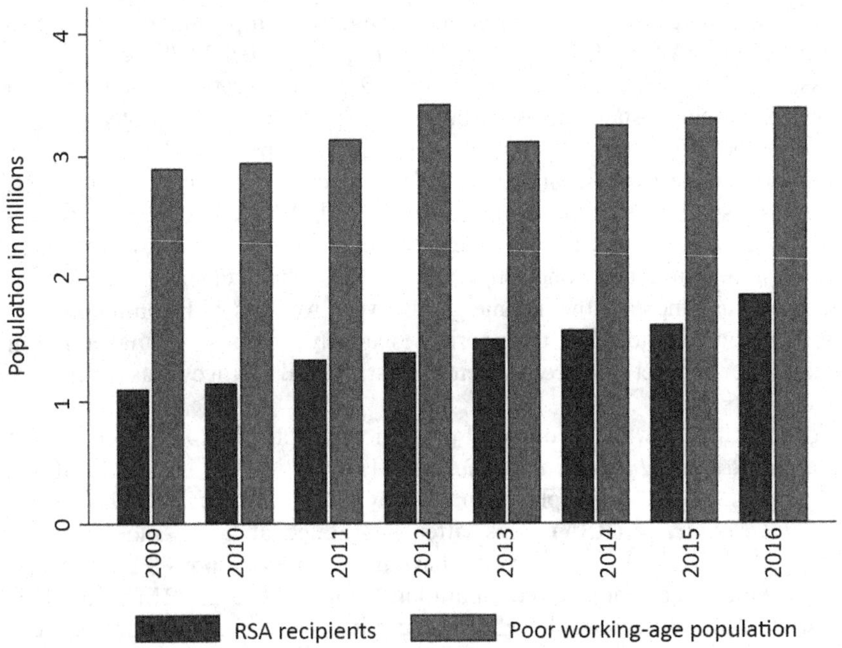

Figure 4.1 RSA recipients and poor working-aged population
Source: OECD SOCR database. www.oecd.org/social/recipients.htm

lost their right to contributory unemployment benefits, thereby becoming dependent on non-contributory benefits. Defining as poor every working-age person living in a household whose earnings are below 50 percent of the median income, we can observe a significant growth in this figure since 2009, but at a slower rate than the growth of recipients of RSA. Accordingly, normalizing the number of RSA recipients by the number of poor working-aged people, a 17 percentage points (p.p.) increase in the RSA coverage ratio is observed. While in 2009, the number of RSA recipients represented 37.8 percent of poor working-aged adults, in 2016, this figure rose to more than 55 percent (Figure 4.1).

As a result, in 2015 (the most recent year for which we could glean internationally comparable data), France's expenditure on social assistance and guaranteed minimum income programs was 0.573 percent of the GDP. This means that these programs received a significant economic effort, one that was even above the efforts made by other countries with strong social protection systems. Thus, expenditure figures are higher in France than in other European continental economies, such as Germany, Austria, and Nordic social democratic economies like Sweden and Norway (Figure 4.2).

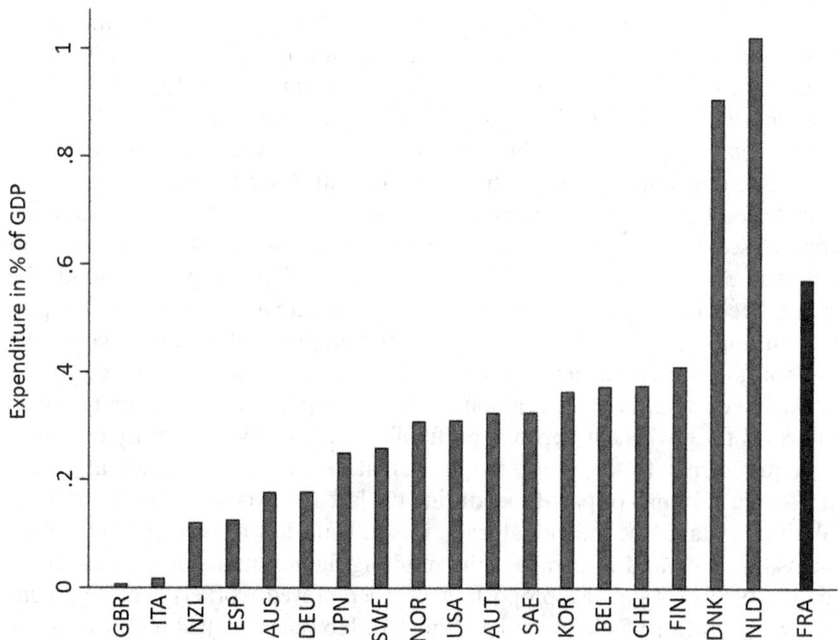

Figure 4.2 Expenditure in social assistance as a percentage of GDP
Notes: GBR Great Britain, ITA Italy, NZL New Zealand, ESP Spain, AUS Australia, DEU Germany, JPN Japan, SWE Sweden, NOR Norway, USA America, AUT Austria, SAE selected advanced economies, KOR Korea, BEL Belgium, CHE Switzerland, FIN Finland, DNK Denmark, NLD the Netherlands, FRA France.
Source: OECD SOCR database. www.oecd.org/social/recipients.htm

Nevertheless, income guarantee and social assistance are only two of the aspects that can explain France's welfare state strength. It is also important to consider the contributory benefits protections for vulnerable workers. In particular, I will focus on the characteristics and recent changes in the two main contributory unemployment benefits, which are the *Allocation d'aide au Retour à l'Emploi* (ARE) and the *Allocation Spécifique de Solidarité* (ASS).

Like many other European countries, France has developed more stringent eligibility criteria for contributory unemployment benefits, putting emphasis on activation (Chevalier & Palier, 2014; Hasenteufel & Palier, 2016; Palier & Thelen, 2010). Thus, ARE recipients must demonstrate they are actively searching for a job by participating in the *Projet Personnalisé d'Accès à l'Emploi* (PPAE). This prerequisite was added to social security contribution requirements in Macron's 2019 reform. After these legal changes, ARE recipients need to have worked 130 days or 910 hours within the last two years, or the same amount of time within the last 35 months in the case of workers more than 54 years old. Furthermore, although some exceptions exist, claimants must be individually or collectively laid-off workers; they do not have the right to access if they have voluntarily left their previous job. The amount and duration of benefits are determined as a function of previous earnings and the number of days worked, differentiating between two age groups. For those older than 53, the minimum duration of unemployment benefits is 182 days, while the maximum is 1095 days, or 913 if they are younger than 55. As for those younger than 53, although the minimum duration is also 182 days, the maximum is restricted to 730 days.

In the case of losing their right to the ARE, the individual can claim the ASS. The ASS shares some elements with other non-contributory benefits. First, it is a means-tested benefit, so the claimant's income is tested by the public administration to see if it is below a certain threshold. Thus, the thresholds are 1182.30 euros per month for a person living alone and 1857.90 euros per month for couples. Second, the benefit amount is not proportional to the recipient's previous earnings but is a fixed, legally established amount, taking into account the household's demographic and economic characteristics. However, it would be a mistake to consider the ASS as a non-contributory payment. The main reason is that access to this benefit depends on fulfilling certain social security contribution requirements. In this sense, the individual needs to have worked at least 5 years (either full-time or part-time) during the last 10 years to claim for the ASS.

Without data at the individual level, it is difficult to measure unemployment benefits coverage and to compare the resulting figures across economies. If we had this type of data, the proportion of unemployed workers receiving contributory payments would easily be estimated. However, we just have two series for each country. One is the average annual number of recipients of unemployment compensation programs, while the other is the average number of persons in unemployment per year. When the ratio of benefit recipients and unemployed persons is calculated, some problems arise, and coverage rates are above 100 percent in some countries. In our view, this is partly the consequence of changes in employment-related benefits systems. During the last decade, along with unemployment risk, underemployment and low-pay risks have been taken into account to design employment-related benefits. As a result, benefits are aimed not only at those in unemployment but also cover some employed workers (OECD, 2018b).

This bias can be overcome by taking into account the number of workers at risk of poverty, to calculate an alternative employment-related compensation coverage ratio. In our view, the resulting ratios are more appropriate to compare different national modern employment-related benefits systems. To do so, the Eurostat in-work at-risk-of-poverty rate indicator is used. Based on the EU statistics on income and living conditions, this indicator shows the share of workers whose disposable income is below 50 percent of the national median disposable income.

The ratio shown in Figure 4.3 consists of the number of employment-related benefits recipients adjusted for the number of workers who are either unemployed or employed in low-pay jobs. It is important to note that this indicator does not measure benefit coverage among this population group. Instead, it is an

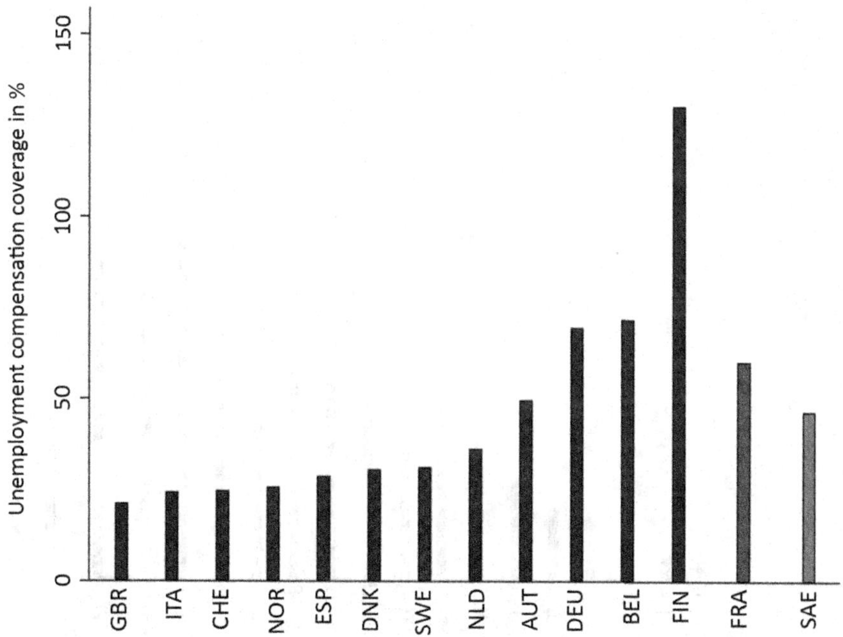

Figure 4.3 Employment-related compensation coverage

Notes: GBR Great Britain, ITA Italy, NZL New Zealand, ESP Spain, AUS Australia, DEU Germany, JPN Japan, SWE Sweden, NOR Norway, USA America, AUT Austria, SAE selected advanced economies, KOR Korea, BEL Belgium, CHE Switzerland, FIN Finland, DNK Denmark, NLD the Netherlands, FRA France.

Source: Based on Eurostat EU-SILC and OECD Social Expenditure database. www.oecd.org/social/recipients.htm

indicator that allows us to compare the employment-related benefits system's capacity to protect vulnerable workers. However, to better capture strictly contributory benefits coverage, I also calculate an alternative indicator that only takes into account contributory benefits protecting workers against unemployment risks (Figure 4.4). As can be seen, France shows, in both figures, values well above the unweighted average of selected advanced economies (SAEs). This gives us an idea of the French social protection system's capacity to protect workers against employment-related risks.

France's benefit coverage rates are, in turn, related to expenditure on passive labor market policies (PLMP). As Figure 4.5 shows, France expended in 2017 almost 2 percent of its GDP on these policies, well above most of the SAEs' spending effort. However, some might state that this higher expenditure is linked to the French higher unemployment rates. To take this fact into account, PLMP expenditure figures are plotted against the unemployment rate figures for the same year. Thus, it could be said that those countries above the fitted line are spending in PLMP more than expected, France being one of them. Indeed, France's expenditure in PLMP is around 0.5 p.p. higher than the expected value.

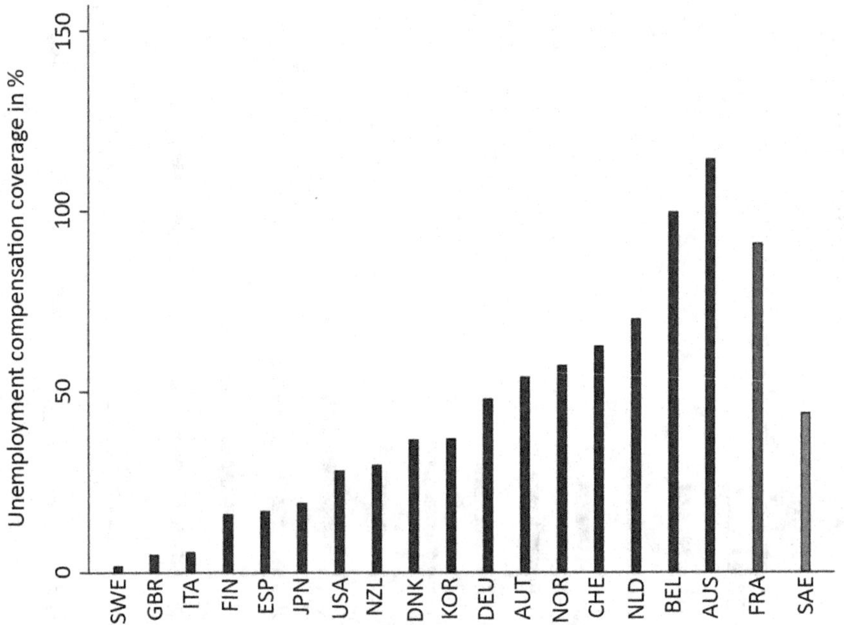

Figure 4.4 Unemployment compensation coverage

Notes: GBR Great Britain, ITA Italy, NZL New Zealand, ESP Spain, AUS Australia, DEU Germany, JPN Japan, SWE Sweden, NOR Norway, USA America, AUT Austria, SAE selected advanced economies, KOR Korea, BEL Belgium, CHE Switzerland, FIN Finland, DNK Denmark, NLD the Netherlands, FRA France.

Source: Based on OECD Social Expenditure and SOCR databases. www.oecd.org/social/expenditure.htm

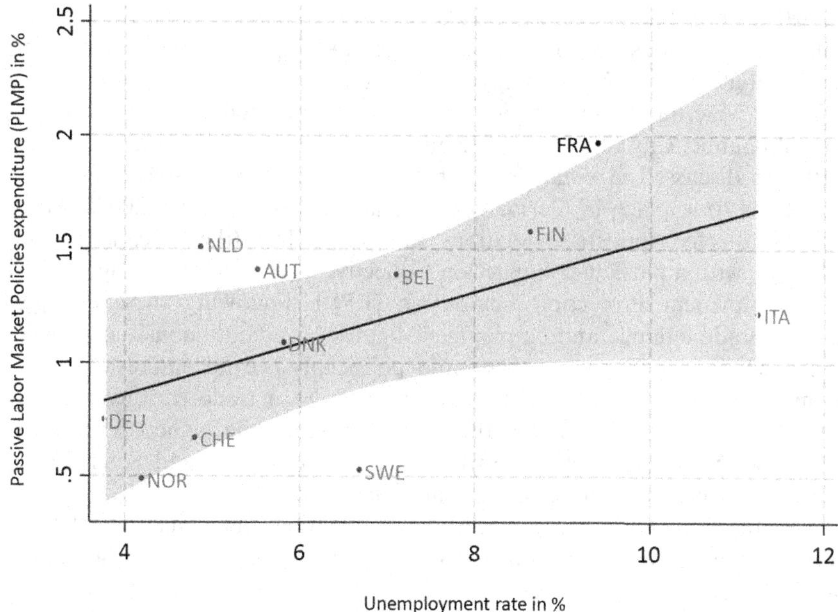

Figure 4.5 PLMP expenditure and unemployment rates
Notes: ITA Italy, ESP Spain, AUS Australia, DEU Germany, SWE Sweden, NOR Norway, AUT Austria, SAE selected advanced economies, BEL Belgium, CHE Switzerland, FIN Finland, DNK Denmark, NLD the Netherlands, FRA France.
Source: OECD Social Expenditure and Short-Term Labor Market Statistics databases. stats.oecd.org/Index.aspx?DataSetCode=STLABOUR

2.2 A high EPL and an extended CBC despite reformist efforts

As has been pointed out on many occasions, French legislation on hiring is characterized by relatively high protection against dismissal, at least when compared with that of other advanced economies (Carcillo, Goujard, Hijzen & Thewissen, 2019; Vlandas, 2013; 2016; 2017). Besides, although union membership rates are very low, French unions' influence on national politics is very significant since the vast majority of workers are covered by collective bargaining agreements (Milner & Mathers, 2013; Poutvaara et al., 2017). After the Great Recession, many political initiatives have tried to change the legal provisions relative to these two institutional features so characteristic of the French economy. Thus, under the presidency of François Hollande (2012–2017) and, later, Emmanuel Macron (2017–), various reforms were proposed. An important proportion of the French population did not support the resulting laws, and massive demonstrations occurred. As a result, both politicians saw their popularity drop and had to change some of their initial plans.

Furthermore, both reformist efforts had the same starting point. First, in both cases, France's competitiveness losses and high unemployment levels were attributed to malfunctioning labor market institutions. Second, Hollande as well as Macron took Germany as an example of good institutional development (Cahuc, Carcillo, Rinne & Zimmerman, 2013; Nikolka & Poutvaara, 2019). As discussed in detail in Chapter 5 of this book, far-reaching transformations took place in Germany in the late 1990s and early 2000s. These changes affected industrial relations and labor law (the so-called Hartz Reforms), with a particular impact on Collective Bargaining Coverage (CBC) and Employment Protection Legislation (EPL). Following these changes, German trade balance and employment figures have continuously improved. This is why many French analysts and politicians became interested in the German case and linked German-type reforms to a trade surplus and low unemployment rates. Proof that this interest reached the highest level is the well-known informal meeting between President Hollande and Peter Hartz, who is considered the father of Germany's labor reforms.

In Section 2.3, I analyze the French labor market and industrial relations reforms to assess whether, as in the German case, they do or do not imply significant changes in EPL and CBC.

2.3 Labor law reforms under Hollande's and Macron's presidencies

In France, hiring is regulated by the Labor Code or *Code du Travail*, which in its Article L. 1221–2, establishes that the open-ended contract or *Contrat à Durée Indéterminée* (CDI) is the normal and general form of the employment relationship. Other types of employment contracts are, therefore, legally considered exceptions. Among them are the apprenticeship contract (Articles L. 6221–1 to L. 6227–12), temporary and part-time agency employment contracts (Articles L. 1251–1 to L. 1252–13), and, the most important of these, the fixed-term contract or *Contrat à Durée Déterminée* (CDD), regulated by Articles L. 1241–1 to L. 1248–11. The use of the CDC is restricted to some particular situations, as established in Article L. 1242–2 of the *Code du Travail.* These situations include the temporary replacement of other employees or professional services regularly provided, jobs linked to short-term increases in demand, and seasonal employment. Furthermore, as established in Article L. 1242–8-1, the total duration of this type of employment contract may not exceed 18 months or 24 months in certain exceptional cases.

Regarding both CDIs and CDDs, French legislation is more restrictive than that of many other advanced economies, first, because of the rules protecting workers against dismissal and, second, due to the restrictions concerning the inappropriate or abusive use of temporary contracts. Moreover, as opposed to other reform trajectories, these characteristics were reinforced during the 1990s. However, as stated by some analysts, some of these restrictions may have been relaxed since 2005, so that year can represent a turning point (Barbanchon & Malherbet, 2013; Vlandas, 2016; 2017). Thus, according to the LABREF database initiative of the European Commission, 22 out of 41 legal changes between 2005 and 2017 (almost 54 percent) represented a decrease in EPL (Turrini, Koltay, Pierini, Goffard & Kiss, 2015). Below, I will discuss these recent reforms in depth and, particularly, those adopted under Hollande's and Macron's presidencies.

Three laws concerning hiring were passed under Hollande's presidency. These were the *2013 Loi relative à la sécurisation de l'emploi* (Law on Employment Security), the 2015 *Loi pour la croissance, l'activité et l'égalité des chances économiques* (Law for Growth, Activity and Equality of Economic Opportunities) and the 2016 Employment Law.

The starting point of the 2013 Act is the January Interprofessional National Agreement or *Accord National Interprofessionnel* (ANI), signed by several business associations (CGPME, UPA, and MEDEF) and major unions (CFDT, CFTC, and CFE-CGC) (see Abbreviations) and transposed into law in July 2013. Before and after this Act, collective dismissals affecting ten or more employees within 30 days required an agreement between employers and unions. However, Article L. 1233–24–4 authorizes firms to unilaterally set the content of the Employment Protection Plan or *Plan de Sauvegarde de l'Emploi* (PSE). Thus, as established in Articles L. 1233–57–3 and L. 1233–57–4, even if there is no agreement, the firm's PSE can be authorized by the French administration within 21 days (the validation deadline is 15 days if an agreement is not signed by the unions).

For its part, the 2015 Law includes a wide range of heterogeneous economic measures that were promoted by Emmanuel Macron, then France's Minister of Economy. By reforming Article L. 1233–58 of the *Code du Travail*, legal conditions for collective dismissal became less stringent. Thus, as established in Article 291 of the Law, even in those cases where the French administration does not validate PSE according to Articles L. 1233–57–2 and L. 1233–57–3, collective dismissal will persist, and workers will remain fired without acquiring compensation rights.

Legal changes introduced by the 2016 Employment Law were also important. The law was criticized by unions and led to massive protests against the government because it decisively impacted the CDI employees' dismissal conditions. After the 2016 Reform, a more detailed legal definition of dismissal for economic reasons was adopted, thereby reducing judges' power to cancel a dismissal order (Carcillo, Goujard, Hijzen & Thewissen, 2019). Because this definition was not particularly strict, firms' capacity to lay off employees in difficult economic contexts increased. As stated in Article L. 1233–3, the economic reasons for dismissal include technological changes, productive reorganization, cessation of activity, or a significant drop in demand or turnover from quarters 1–4, depending on the size of the firm.

In May 2017, Macron was elected. Like his predecessor in office, he considered that some additional changes in regulation on hiring needed to be made. Thus, between September and December of the same year, several *ordonnances* affecting labor relationships were adopted. One of the most important was the September *Ordonnance relative à la prévisibilité et la sécurisation des relations de travail* (Order on Employment Relations Predictability and Security). Under this *Ordonnance*, Article L. 1235–3 of the Code du Travail was reformed, implementing a schedule for the compensation of employees for unfair dismissal. The new schedule establishes a maximum and a minimum compensation amount in terms of months of gross salary, increasing with tenure and firm size (Carcillo et al., 2019). As established in Article L. 1235–3, it is the judge who sets the compensation level within the legal thresholds. To do so, he can take into account additional compensations established by Articles L. 1235–12, L. 1235–13, and L. 1235–15, but not that included in Article L. 1234–9. In any case, total compensation cannot be higher than the maximum amount established by the *Ordonnance*. The September *ordonnance* also reduced the maximum period to claim for unfair dismissal to 12 months. This period had previously dropped from 60 to 24 months due to the 2013 June Law, so the cumulated total decrease is significant.

Additionally, Articles L. 1234–9 and R. 1234–2 of the *Code du Travail*, reformed in the September *Ordonnance*, regulating severance pay requirements and compensation amounts were changed. These changes were, however, favorable to workers. First, the number of months required to qualify for severance pay was reduced from 12 to 8 months. Second, compensation amounts increased both for workers with less than 10 years of tenure and for those with more than 10 years of tenure; thus, severance pay increased from 20 percent to 25 percent of monthly salary per year of tenure for the first group. For the second group, severance pay increased from slightly more than 25 percent of the monthly salary per year of tenure to more than 33 percent of the monthly salary per year of tenure.

In short, legal changes adopted during the presidencies of Macron and Hollande impacted three aspects of France's EPL. The first aspect is the collective dismissal regulation (which is a dismissal affecting more than 10 workers within 30 days, according to French Labor Law). The second comprises the definition of unfair dismissal, as well as the economic consequences for the employer. The third aspect relates to the amount of severance pay in the case of an individual dismissal for economic or personal reasons.

Regarding the first aspect, most legal measures were adopted under Hollande's presidency. Thus, the 2013 and 2015 laws reinforced the power of employers to dismiss 10 employees or more without a previous agreement with the workers' unions. As a result, legal restrictions were relaxed and the power of judges to cancel a dismissal order decreased.

For the second aspect regarding unfair dismissal, the legal changes are similar and share the same aims, despite having taken place under different administrations. First, the 2016 Labor Law introduced a detailed but relaxed definition of dismissal for economic reasons. This new definition gave firms facing economic difficulties greater capacity to dismiss workers and made it more difficult for judges to impose restrictions on these dismissals. Second, the 2013 Law and the 2017 *Ordonnance* reduced the length of the period to claim unfair dismissal, thereby constraining workers' access to corresponding compensation. Third, in the case of unfair dismissal, the 2017 *Ordonnance* implemented a compensation schedule that, in practice, reduced the maximum and minimum compensation amounts. In other words, the 2017 *Ordonnance* not only made unfair dismissal easier but also reduced its economic costs.

Unlike the rest of the legal changes previously reported, the changes affecting severance pay were favorable to CDI employees. Thus, according to the September 2017 *Ordonnance*, job tenure requirements for severance pay were reduced from 12 to 8 months, and compensation amounts increased significantly. These types of changes are even more striking if one takes into account the European context, where many governments were reducing these payments and making access to them more difficult.

Therefore, although some legal provisions adopted under the Macron and Hollande presidencies have increased CDI employees' legal guarantees against dismissals, others have reduced them. This may imply that regular contract workers, who typically have greater employment protection and better working conditions, have been negatively affected by recent reforms (OECD, 2019).

In the following, we will analyze this point by using the OECD's employment protection legislation (EPL) on Regular Contracts index (EPLRC). This indicator measures the level of protection against dismissals for regular contract workers by considering certain legal aspects concerning the regulation on firing, such as the procedural requirements, the length of notice, the amount of severance pay, and the regulatory framework for unfair dismissal as well as their enforcement. Despite having some methodological weaknesses, the OECD's EPLRC index may be used to compare France with other SAEs in two selected years, 2013 and 2019. These years are selected for two simple reasons. First, because the labor market reforms previously analyzed started in 2013 and, second, since 2019 is the last year for which data are available. Accordingly, a change in the indicator may be pointing to the effect of recent legal initiatives. we use the last version of the index, published in 2020 by the OECD. This version includes some significant methodological changes with respect to the previous one, and it is particularly appropriate to capture the effect of recent reforms in France (OECD, 2020).

Before analyzing Figure 4.6, it is important to take into account one methodological caution that minor changes in the index values cannot be significant, as the OECD itself warns (OECD, 2020). However, Figure 4.6 still offers some compelling insights. The first is that the level of EPLRC in France is relatively high, above the non-weighted average of the SAEs and higher than some continental European economies (like Germany or Austria) as well as some Nordic social democratic economies (like Sweden or Denmark). The second is that, although recent reforms seem to have impacted protection levels, index values remain relatively high. Without a doubt, the observed decrease is linked to the more detailed definition of dismissal for economic causes, the reduction in unfair dismissal compensation amount, and

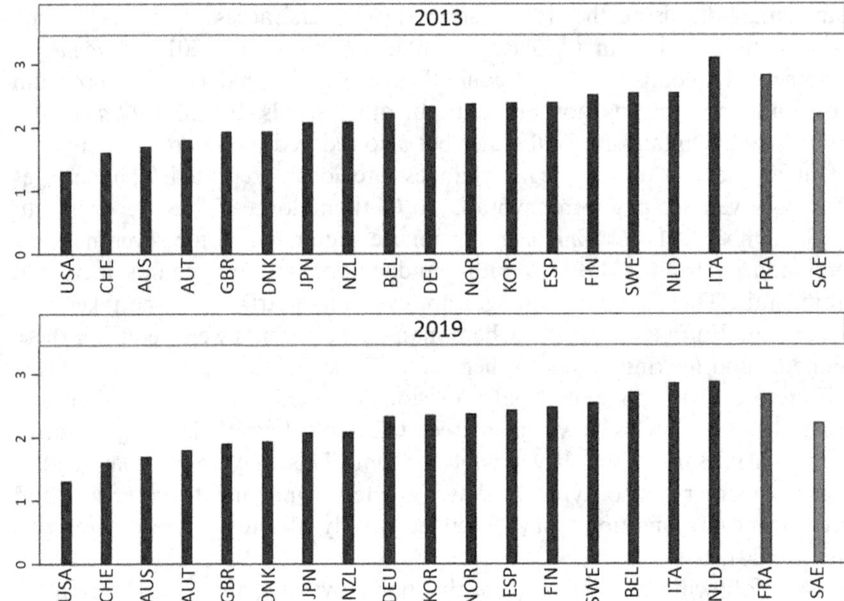

Figure 4.6 EPLRC in selected years, 2013 and 2019

Notes: GBR Great Britain, ITA Italy, NZL New Zealand, ESP Spain, AUS Australia, DEU Germany, JPN Japan, SWE Sweden, NOR Norway, USA America, AUT Austria, SAE selected advanced economies, KOR Korea, BEL Belgium, CHE Switzerland, FIN Finland, DNK Denmark, NLD the Netherlands, FRA France.

Source: OECD Employment Protection Legislation database. www.oecd.org/.../oecdindicatorsofemploymentprotection.htm

the reduction in the maximum time to claim for unfair dismissal. However, this is partly offset by the increase in the amount of severance pay (Carcillo et al., 2019). The third insight points to France's relative position with respect to other economies, which remain stable and are not much different from that of Germany. Indeed, considering the previous version of the OECD's index, it can be noted that EPLRC index values did not change in Germany even in the reformist period of the 2000s when reforms affecting employment regulation were adopted.

The asymmetry between more stringent regulations affecting permanent workers and more relaxed legal provisions concerning the use of fixed-term contracts (OECD, 2018a) is frequently emphasized. Moreover, it is suggested that the asymmetry is increasing, since permanent workers have greater institutional resources and, therefore, greater bargaining power to reinforce their position. In this context, it is a customary assumption that higher EPLRC levels imply higher legal asymmetries concerning employment regulation. However, this is not the case in France (Marx, 2012). Although short-term employment contracts were encouraged after the Great Recession to reduce unemployment (Cahuc & Nevoux, 2017; Carcillo et al., 2019), French labor law is, indeed, particularly restrictive in its use of fixed-term contracts. Besides, unlike other countries, hiring regulations on temporary work have not been significantly reformed in the last few decades (Vlandas, 2013; 2016; 2017).

To analyze this point, we also use one of the indicators provided by the OECD. This time, however, it is the EPL index for temporary contracts (EPLTC), which measures the legal restrictions on hiring temporary workers. There is an important difference between EPLRC and EPLTC indexes. While the former measures the legal protection against dismissal for regular contract workers, the latter measures the constraints in the use of fixed-term or temporary work agency contracts (OECD, 2020). They are calculated differently for three reasons. First, it is assumed that temporary employment relationships end when the deadline established by the contract finishes and not before. Second, dismissal compensation payments for temporary contracts, if any, are lower than the ones for regular contracts. Third, labor law frequently tries to avoid inappropriate or abusive use of temporary work contracts (OECD, 2018a; 2020). Accordingly, by taking these differences into account, one can say that high EPLRC values imply greater indirect incentives for temporary contracts while high EPLTC values imply direct disincentives or restrictions on the use of these contracts. Thus, although labor law may have an influence on the type of contracts used by employers, this influence depends on both direct EPLRC and indirect EPLTC incentives.

This is why the relative performance of France's EPLTC index is important, particularly when it is compared to Germany as a model of successful institutional change. As the contrast between Figures 4.6 and Figure 4.7 shows, the difference between France and Germany is greater when considering the EPLTC index than when considering the EPLRC index. This difference increased during the German reformist period of the 2000s, before the Great Recession, and then remained stable during the 2010s. Therefore, while indirect incentives to temporary contracts did not increase in France, they did in Germany as legal restrictions on the use of this type of contract have been relaxed. In other words, the last changes in labor law may have incentivized atypical employment further in Germany than in France.

2.4 Extensive coverage of sectoral bargaining despite pressures to decentralize

Despite low union density rates, unions in France still have the power to influence labor politics. The reasons are as follows. First, unions' influence is partly based on representing workers in the workplace. Thus, as established by Article L. 2232–12 in the *Code du Travail*, unions can only sign collective agreements if they obtain a minimum share of votes in the workplace elections. More concretely, after the 2016 Labor Law, unions must have obtained 50 percent of the votes in the elections to the main workers' representative institutions (previously, it was 30 percent).

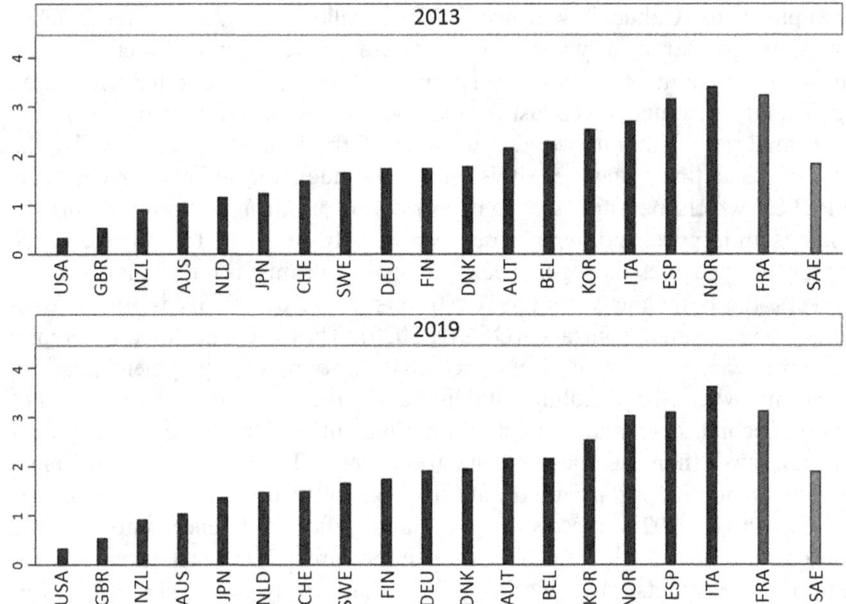

Figure 4.7 EPLTC in selected years (a) 2013; (b) 2019
Notes: GBR Great Britain, ITA Italy, NZL New Zealand, ESP Spain, AUS Australia, DEU Germany, JPN Japan, SWE Sweden, NOR Norway, USA America, AUT Austria, SAE selected advanced economies, KOR Korea, BEL Belgium, CHE Switzerland, FIN Finland, DNK Denmark, NLD the Netherlands, FRA France.
Source: OECD Employment Protection Legislation database. www.oecd.org/.../oecdindicatorsofemploymentprotection.htm

Second, despite the existence of many unions with very heterogeneous views on labor policy and conflicting relations between them, they still have the power to mobilize workers. In France, strikes are not restricted to labor issues; indeed, workers may be called (by unions or by other workers) upon to mobilize for matters different than the ones that can be negotiated within the collective bargaining system. Moreover, unlike some other European countries, like Germany, French workers can strike even during the period of validity of the collective agreement (OECD, 2019; Poutvaara et al., 2017). All these conditions explain why France has more industrial disputes than the rest of the advanced economies. Thus, it is the one where, on average, more days of work per employee were lost between 2008 and 2018 (OECD, 2019).

Third, workplace representation institutions are well embedded in France. Almost 70 percent of French workers have access to representative institutions, well above the European Union average and the rates of other Continental European countries, like Germany or Sweden (OECD, 2019). The September 2017 *Ordonnance* changed the previous system of employee involvement, thereby integrating the works council (*comité d'enterprise*), the union representatives (*délégué syndical, représentant de la section syndicale*), the worker representatives (*délégué du personnel*), and the health and safety committee (*comité de la santé et sécurité au travail*) into one institution, the *Comité Social et Économique* (OECD, 2019).

However, even though all these reasons are important, the design of the industrial relations system still cannot fully explain the influence of French unions on national labor policy. First, because the system is based on the priority conceded to agreements at a higher level between business associations and unions. This is explained by some reasons that will be later discussed and, among them, by the use of administrative extensions of sectoral bargaining, which is almost automatic in France. Thus, Articles L. 2261–15 and L. 2261–15 of the *Code du Travail* confer upon the Labor Ministry the power to extend professional or interprofessional agreements to non-signatory firms and workers (Carcillo, Goujard, Hijzen & Thewissen, 2019; *Ministère du Travail*, 2019; OECD, 2019). Second, due to the role of the central government in the system of collective bargaining, France's labor law is extensive and has detailed legal provisions concerning many issues that, in other countries, are determined by collective bargaining. Moreover, the minimum wage is particularly high (Figure 4.8).

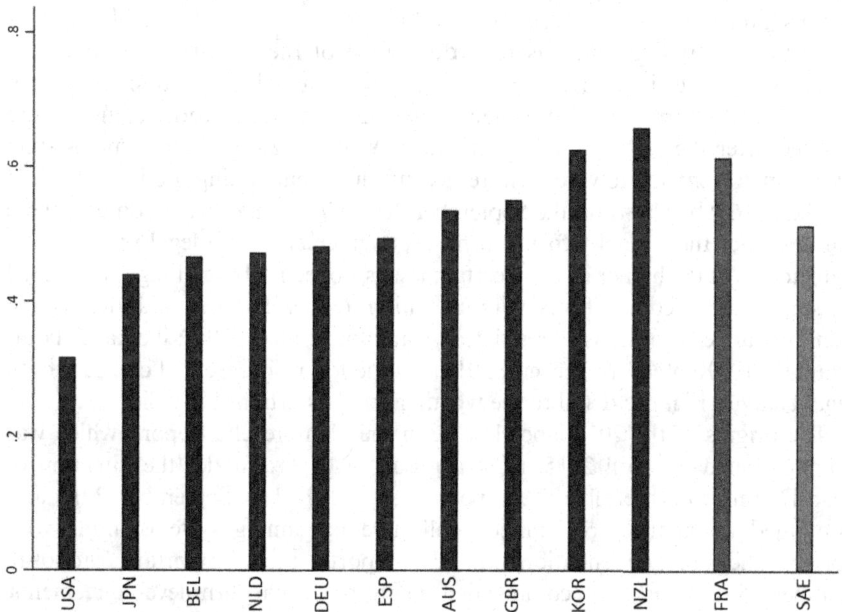

Figure 4.8 Minimum wage relative to the median wages of full-time workers
Notes. Last year for which data are available. GBR Great Britain, ITA Italy, NZL New Zealand, ESP Spain, AUS Australia, DEU Germany, JPN Japan, USA America, AUT Austria, SAE selected advanced economies, KOR Korea, BEL Belgium, CHE Switzerland, NLD the Netherlands, FRA France.
Source: OECD.

This second aspect is in addition to the rule that collective agreement can only improve the terms of employment established by law or by agreements at the higher level (in France, there is the so-called "favorability principle"). As a result, bargaining on a matter as important as wage growth is centralized, and the bargaining range is restricted (Carcillo et al., 2019; Poutvaara et al., 2017; Rehfeldt & Vincent, 2018). Thus, the minimum wage revaluation has a positive effect both on the probability of new wage agreements and on the growth of negotiated wages. Besides, these effects are significant across the entire wage distribution, even though they are particularly high in the lower part of the distribution, with elasticities of 0.5 percent (Fougère, Gautier & Roux, 2018; Groupe d'experts sur le SMIC, 2018).

Nevertheless, legal changes adopted after the Great Recession may have affected both the predominant bargaining level and the role of the French state in the government of the system. During the 2000s, the *Mouvement des entreprises de France* (MEDEF), which is the country's main business association, successfully promoted collective bargaining decentralization.

Thus, in July 2001, the MEDEF reached an agreement with some of the major unions regarding the use of derogation and opt-out clauses in collective agreements. Indeed, after the 2004 law, the *Code du Travail* provides for the possibility of this type of clause in collective agreements being signed by unions and firms at the firm level. However, the labor law still contains important restrictions on this procedure. One of the constraints is that sectoral agreement signatories have the power to avoid derogation of certain provisions by firm-level agreements. In fact, few derogation clauses were applied after the 2004 reform (Rehfeldt & Vincent, 2018). Some studies state that a major change toward a more decentralized bargaining model was made by the 2016 labor law and the September 2017 *Ordonnance.* According to these studies, after these legal reforms, firm-level agreements have legal priority over agreements at the higher level on certain issues, collective bargaining is promoted in small and medium firms without union representatives, and the use of administrative extensions is restricted (Carcillo, et al., 2019; Nikolka & Poutvaara, 2019; Rehfeldt & Vincent, 2018). In the following, we will consider both legal changes in more detail to see whether these assertions are valid.

The origins of the 2016 labor law lie in the Combrexelle Report, which was commissioned in April 2015, from a group of experts under the direction of Jean-Dennis Combrexelle. The report was published in September 2015 and contained an analysis of France's collective bargaining systems along with some policy recommendations. In the report's most important proposal, number 35, the authors recommended giving priority to firm-level agreements. These agreements should be signed by major unions and would be part of what they called the *Accords sur les Conditions et Temps du Travail, l'Emploi et les Salaires* (ACTES). In other words, what the group of experts was suggesting was to decentralize the entire system of collective bargaining (Combrexelle, 2015; Rehfeldt & Vincent, 2018; Poutvaara et al., 2017). The proposals from the Report were so well received by the French government that the February

2016 draft of the Labor Law included the majority of them. Moreover, it also included a reduction in unfair dismissal compensation amounts. As expected, this draft was unanimously contested by the five major unions.

After some negotiations between the government and one of them, the CFDT, important changes were introduced with respect to the draft of February (Rehfeldt & Vincent, 2018). The result was the 2016 June Labor Law. This law no longer included the reduction in unfair dismissal compensations and gave legal priority to firm-level agreements in even fewer matters than the ones included previously. Thus, restrictions on the use of derogation clauses in Article L. 2253–3 were extended to new issues. Regarding this point, sectoral bargaining was reinforced instead of being undermined.

Indeed, despite the turmoil, the more important changes concerning collective bargaining were not caused by the 2016 Labor Law, but by the September 2017 *Ordonnance* under the presidency of Macron. First, because this *Ordonnance* facilitates collective agreement at the firm-level. Thus, it makes collective agreements possible for firms with less than 20 employees without union representatives, provided the agreement has been approved by two out of three workers in a referendum. For its part, from that moment on, agreements reached by firms having between 20 and 50 workers are valid, even though they are not signed by union representatives.

Second, because some of the *Ordonnance*'s legal provisions may have important effects on sectoral bargaining coverage. To better analyze this point, one should take into account the three elements explaining the high coverage rates of sectoral bargaining and, more in general, of collective bargaining in France (Figure 4.9). The first element is the high share of workers employed in firms that are part of business associations. Figures are around 80 percent, which is above that of other European countries, such as Denmark, Portugal, and Germany (OECD, 2019). The second element, which is linked to the first one, is the frequent application of clauses to extend collective agreements to all the employees working at signatory firms and not only the members of the signatory unions. The third element is the almost automatic use of the administrative extensions of sectoral bargaining, as explained above.

The third of these elements is affected by some legal provisions reformed by the September 2017 *Ordonnance*. Thus, the *Ordonnance* adds two restrictions to the use of administrative extensions. First, to be extended, sectoral agreements must either contain particular clauses for firms with less than 50 workers or explain why those clauses are not included (Articles L. 2261–23–1 and L. 2232–10–1 of the *Code du Travail*).

Second, sectoral agreements will not be extended if they might have a negative effect on most vulnerable workers and firms. Moreover, the *Ordonnance* provides for the creation of a group of experts to assess the economic and social impact of extensions (Carcillo et al., 2019). As a result of these changes, extension procedures have become more complex, thereby increasing the average delay of an agreement extension by 56 percent. The number of

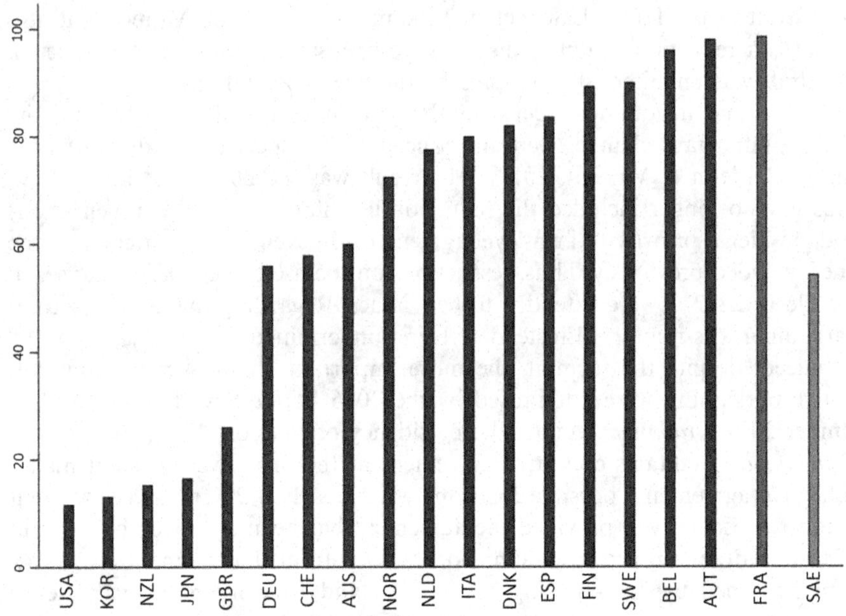

Figure 4.9 CBC in France and the SAEs

Notes. Last year for which data are available. GBR Great Britain, ITA Italy, NZL New Zealand, ESP Spain, AUS Australia, DEU Germany, JPN Japan, SWE Sweden, NOR Norway, USA America, AUT Austria, SAE selected advanced economies, KOR Korea, BEL Belgium, CHE Switzerland, FIN Finland, DNK Denmark, NLD the Netherlands, FRA France.

Source: OECD.

working days from the start of the procedure to the official publication of the agreement extension increased from 122 days in 2017 to 190 days in 2018. The Ministry itself recognizes that legal changes adopted in 2017 may explain this increase. Besides, despite a 34 percent increase in the number of extension requests, the number of extended agreements decreased by 25 percent. All of these figures point to a significant effect of the *Ordonnance*, at least in the short term (Ministère du Travail, 2019).

However, we should not consider the 2016 Labor Law or the 2017 September *Ordonnance* as turning points in the French collective bargaining system, as the studies previously cited suggest. To begin with, as has been previously shown, legal changes adopted in 2016 and 2017 introduced new restrictions on the use of derogation clauses. Additionally, the number of professional branches was reduced, grouping the smallest or most inactive and, therefore, reinforcing the system's centralization. Meanwhile, the March 2014 and August 2016 laws provided a regulatory framework for employer representativeness, thereby strengthening what in France is called the *couverture patronale*, that is, the share of workers employed in firms that are part of a business association or the density of employer's organization (Langevin, 2017).[1] Finally, unlike other advanced economies, such as Spain, France did not remove the principle of ultra-activity in the period after the Great Recession. This means that in France collective agreements are valid beyond their completion date, so they remain applicable until their replacement by a new agreement.

3 Explaining France's debt-financed, consumption-led model from WPIs' potential economic effects

3.1 Impacts on demand

Whenever the inflationary effects of WPIs relative to unit labor costs (ULC) are assumed, one can point to WPIs in France reducing export competitiveness and, therefore, constraining one of the possible sources of GDP growth. Thus, the characteristic institutional features of the French model may explain why, unlike other continental European economies such as Germany, France's growth model is not based on an export strategy but on internal demand growth. Besides, in the context of growing competitive pressures and high investment volatility, these institutions do not promote internal demand or stable growth. Although it is true that WPIs may contribute positively to raise annual and hourly permanent employee wages, they can also encourage non-standard employment forms, which typically involve lower wages. Indeed, they can make access to employment harder for most vulnerable workers and thus have a negative impact on employment levels. As a result, the total impact of WPIs on the wage bill may be negative.

Accordingly, strong WPIs would not be compatible either with an export-led growth strategy or with a consumption-led strategy based on wage growth. Therefore, the French model's characteristic institutions might explain why GDP growth in France is based on consumption financed by private credit. In other words, WPIs are the institutional foundations of France's consumption-led, debt-financed model.

This hypothesis is supported by two macroeconomic facts. First, as Figure 4.10 shows, most external demand contributions to quarterly GDP growth were negative during the 2000s and 2010s due to the trade imbalances. This trade in goods and services deficit, which started in the late 1990s, may have been caused by both a higher import growth and a slowdown in export growth. However, export performance is what is important here, as can be concluded from the comparison of France with other advanced economies. Thus, the trade deficit grew in the period 2000–2007, when France's import growth was no higher than the SAEs' unweighted average,[2] but France's export growth rates were lower than those of other continental European economies like the Netherlands, Germany, and Austria (Figure 4.11). In other words, since the decline in France's export market share coincided with the country's growing trade deficit, it may be reasonable to explain the latter through the former.

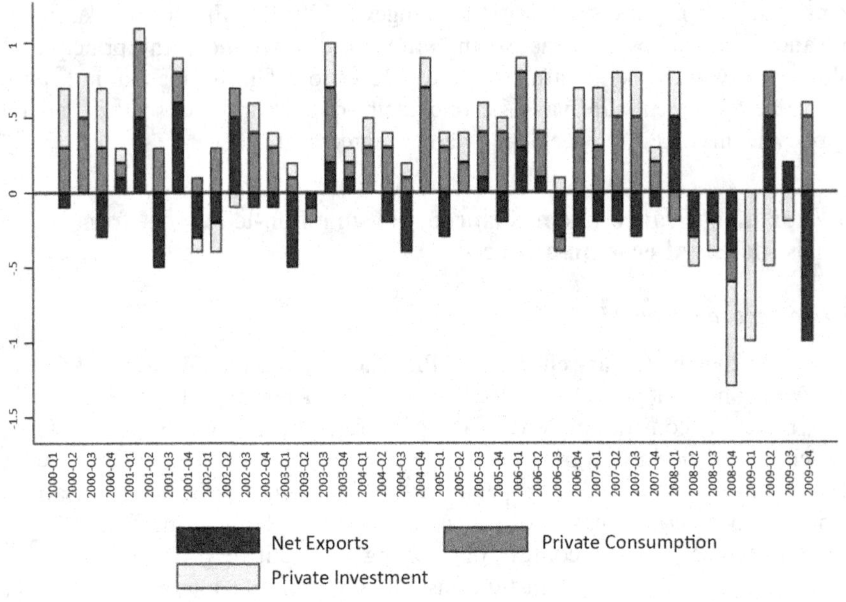

Figure 4.10 Contributions of aggregate demand components to quarterly GDP growth rates: (a) 2000s; (b) 2010s.

Source: OECD quarterly national accounts. www.stats.oecd.org/index.aspx?queryid=350

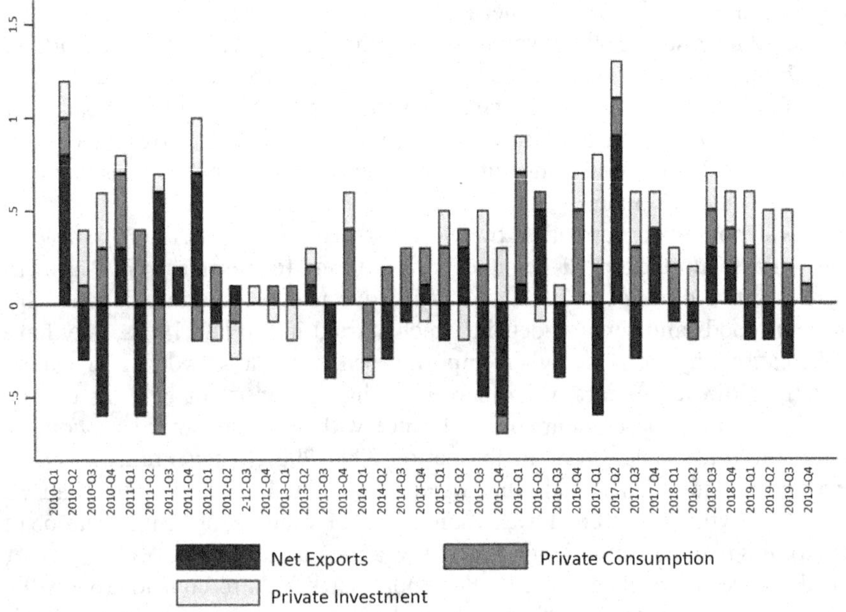

Figure 4.11 Export growth rates before and after the Great Recession

Note: Average annual growth rates by country.

Source: OECD System of National Accounts. www.oecd.org/sdd/na

Second, France's average wage bill growth rate is lower than the SAEs' unweighted average, particularly after the Great Recession (Figure 4.12). This performance, explained by both a lower than average hourly wage growth rate and relatively low employment growth, is hardly compatible with an internal demand fueled by wages. Instead, private credit to households has probably been the main source of consumption growth over the last two decades. In this sense, despite France's ratio of household debt to GDP being still relatively low compared with other advanced economies, it has increased since the early 2000s. Indeed, unlike what happened in most advanced economies, the ratio continued to grow in France after the Great Recession. However, the link between these observed facts and WPIs depends on the existence of certain supply effects attributable to the latter. To be correct, this institutional explanation of France's growth model assumes that WPIs contribute to rising unemployment rates and unit labor costs. Section 3.2 is devoted to the analysis of these assumed effects.

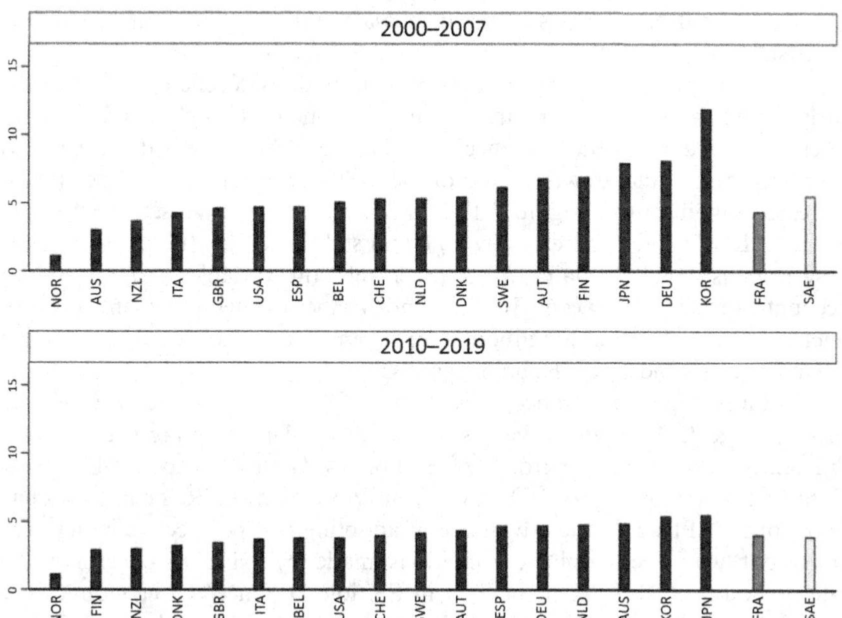

Figure 4.12 Labor compensation growth rates before and after the Great Recession; (a) 2000–2007; (b) 2010–2019

Notes. Average annual growth rates by country. GBR Great Britain, ITA Italy, NZL New Zealand, ESP Spain, AUS Australia, DEU Germany, JPN Japan, SWE Sweden, NOR Norway, USA America, AUT Austria, SAE selected advanced economies, KOR Korea, BEL Belgium, CHE Switzerland, FIN Finland, DNK Denmark, NLD the Netherlands, FRA France.

Source: OECD System of National Accounts. www.oecd.org/sdd/na

3.2 The assumed supply effects

3.2.1 Potential impacts on unemployment and temporary employment rates

As has been frequently emphasized, some of the WPIs might have a negative impact on employment levels. For example, some researchers state that high minimum wages and generous benefits may raise unemployment rates, particularly among low-skilled workers. In this sense, they maintain that high minimum wages can indeed harm low-productivity workers because this policy can raise their wages above their efficiency levels, thereby reducing their job opportunities. Likewise, higher amounts and a longer duration of unemployment benefits are seen as increasing reservation wages and, therefore, discouraging employment search.

However, the institution most frequently related to the existence of high unemployment rates is legislation protecting the regular contracts of workers against dismissals, which can be captured by OECD's Employment Protection Legislation on Regular Contracts (EPLRC) index. Higher values of EPLRC might imply a stricter definition of dismissal, higher severance payments, or greater procedural requirements. This means, in turn, greater guarantees for permanent contract workers facing dismissals and, therefore, higher employment substitutions costs.

At first glance, this perspective is congruent with the French case. Since the early 1990s, the French economy has shown particularly high unemployment rates compared with other advanced economies. Although this difference had decreased during the growth period of the 2000s, after the Great Recession, it increased significantly (Figure 4.13). Moreover, as we have seen in Section 2.2.1, EPLRC values are relatively high and stable despite after-crisis reforms. However, as I will explain, when other relevant variables are taken into account, the link between EPLRC and France's unemployment rates is unclear, either from a longitudinal or from a cross-sectional perspective (Vlandas, 2016 and 2017; Heimberger, 2020).

To address this issue, France, as well as the SAEs, are grouped according to their average EPLRC index values in the 2010s. The resulting classification differentiates between two groups of economies, High Protection on Regular Contracts Economies (HPRCE) and Low Protection on Regular Contracts Economies (LPRCE). One advantage of adopting this perspective is that it is congruent with methodological cautions made by OECD concerning the interpretation of EPLRC (explained in Section 2). Once the economies are classified, GDP growth rates are isolated to better estimate whether EPLRC significantly influences unemployment performance. Thus, Figure 4.14 plots France's and SAEs' average GDP growth rates and average unemployment rates in 2010–2019. Whenever the economy is above the fitted line, it means that the unemployment rate is higher than the one predictable (following a linear prediction) according to GDP performance. If this happens, unobserved factors must be contributing to the unemployment increase. Thus, provided EPLRC has explained the differences in unemployment rates and

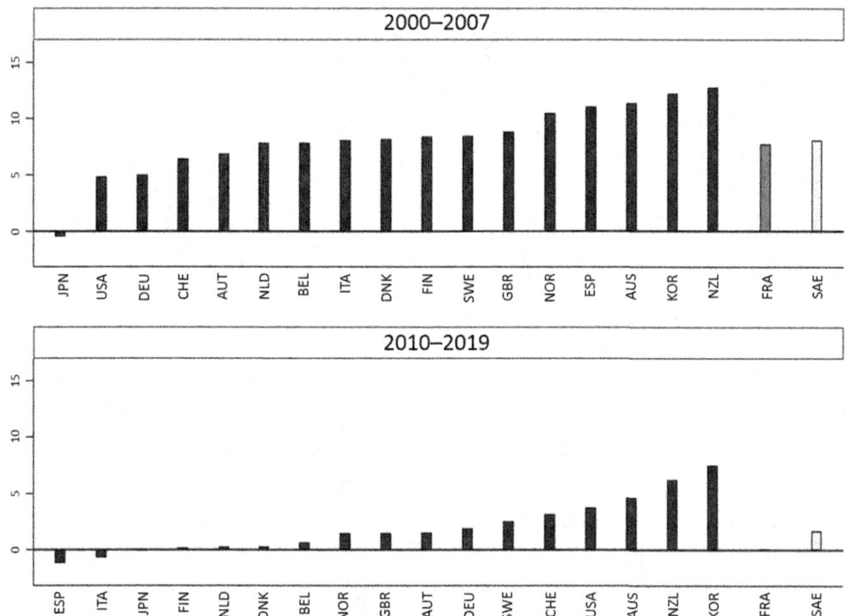

Figure 4.13 France's and SAEs' unemployment rates (a) 2000–2007; (b) 2010–2019
Source: OECD short-term labor market statistics database. www.stats.oecd.org/Index.aspx?DataSetCode=STLABOUR
Notes: GBR Great Britain, ITA Italy, NZL New Zealand, ESP Spain, AUS Australia, DEU Germany, JPN Japan, SWE Sweden, NOR Norway, USA America, AUT Austria, SAE selected advanced economies, KOR Korea, BEL Belgium, CHE Switzerland, FIN Finland, DNK Denmark, NLD the Netherlands, FRA France.

was, therefore, one of those not-observed factors, most HPRCE would be above the fitted line, while most LPRCE would be below it. However, Figure 4.14 does not show such a distribution. Although it is true that the economies most positively deviated from the fitted line, including France, are HPRCE, the results of this simple exploratory analysis are far from conclusive.

However, one can maintain that France's regulatory framework does not affect employment levels as much as the type of employment. Thus, particularly protective labor legislation might explain why temporary employment figures are higher in France than in other advanced economies.

Without a doubt, high temporary employment rates, which have remained stable over the last several decades, are one of the distinct features of the French labor market. However, as Table 4.1 suggests, institutional coherence prevails in France, as in most of the SAEs. This means that relatively high levels of EPLRC coincide with relatively high levels of EPLTC. While all the economies with higher-than-average temporary employment rates can be classified as HPRCE, most of them have more stringent legislations concerning the use of temporary contracts.

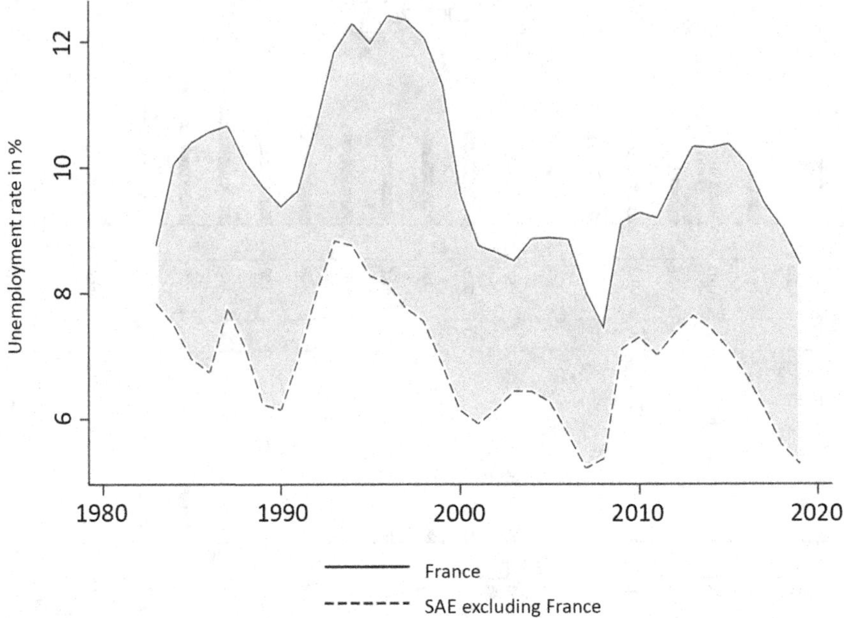

Figure 4.14 Average unemployment rates and GDP growth rates
Notes: GBR Great Britain, ITA Italy, NZL New Zealand, ESP Spain, AUS Australia, DEU Germany, JPN Japan, SWE Sweden, NOR Norway, USA America, AUT Austria, SAE selected advanced economies, KOR Korea, BEL Belgium, CHE Switzerland, FIN Finland, DNK Denmark, NLD the Netherlands, FRA France.
Source: OECD short-term labor market statistics database and system of national accounts. www.stats.oecd.org/Index.aspx?DataSetCode=STLABOUR

In other words, in France, as in most of the HPRCE, the effects of EPL on the type of labor contracts are ambiguous. Certainly, French legislation contains indirect incentives with regard to the use of temporary contracts, since regular contract workers are relatively well protected against dismissals. Nonetheless, some legal provisions provided by the French legislation directly disincentivizes temporary employment, as they restrict the use of that type of contract.

3.2.2 Effects on unit labor costs

The growth of French and German unit labor costs are frequently compared. Thus, the contrast between the stagnant ULC of Germany during the 2000s and 2010s and the growing ULC of France in the same period has been emphasized. Besides, these differences in ULC performance are attributed to the differences in wage bargaining systems previously analyzed in Section 2.4. As explained above, France's bargaining system is concentrated at the higher level because of administrative extensions and is politically conditioned by minimum wage setting. This is why some researchers state

Table 4.1 Temporary employment rates, EPLRC and EPLTC levels in France and the SAEs

Country	*Temporary employment rates*	*EPLRC*	*EPLTC*
USA	3.95	Low	Low
Australia	5.38	Low	Low
United Kingdom	6.00	Low	Low
New Zealand	7.96	Low	Low
Norway	8.34	High	High
Austria	9.15	Low	High
Belgium	9.24	High	High
Denmark	9.85	Low	High
Switzerland	13.08	Low	Low
Germany	13.27	High	Low
Japan	13.72	Low	Low
Italy	14.40	High	High
Finland	15.77	High	Low
France	*16.07*	*High*	*High*
Sweden	16.82	High	Low
the Netherlands	20.27	High	Low
Korea	22.38	High	High
Spain	25.14	High	High

Source: OECD LFS and EPL databases.

that French bargaining institutions give firms little room to negotiate more flexible labor conditions so that they can adapt to changing competitive environments (Carcillo et al., 2019; CNP, 2019; Poutvaara et al., 2017).

However, a detailed analysis of the data presents a more nuanced vision. First, German ULC growth before the Great Recession is unusual when compared with ULC growth in most of the SAEs over the same period. The picture significantly changes when Germany is excluded from the comparison, because French ULC average growth rates are lower than the unweighted average of the SAEs in that period. Second, after the Great Recession, France's unit labor costs growth is very modest, less than those of Germany and most of the SAEs.[3] Third, although French employees' wages are relatively high when compared with average wages in the SAEs, the same can be said about French employees' relative real productivity.

Thus, in the last year for which we have data, the hourly nominal labor compensation of a French worker represented a 102.76 percent of the SAEs' average hourly labor compensations, while his or her hourly real productivity was equivalent to a 104.95 percent of the SAEs' average hourly real productivity.

3.3 The hidden effects on income distribution

Generally, conventional explanations of the rise in inequality have pointed to skill-biased technological change, trade openness, and offshoring, while less conventional views have emphasized the role of institutions like the financial regulation, the collective bargaining system, or the welfare state redistributive policies (Acemoglu & Autor, 2011; Esping-Andersen & Myles, 2011; Jaumotte & Osorio, 2015; Kristal & Cohen, 2017). However, in the last decade, this opposition has been somewhat blurred as leading scholars and organizations have adopted some of these alternative institutional hypotheses to explain rising income inequalities (OECD, 2019; Philippon & Reshef, 2013; Stansbury & Summers, 2020).

This change of focus accompanies a growing concern about income disparities, which, in turn, is caused by recent methodological improvements in inequality measurement. Thus, the Gini coefficient is now considered an insufficient indicator to capture new trends in global and national inequality. Two reasons why may be adduced. First, this coefficient can hardly measure the distributional impact that derives from the top earners' income rise. Second, by using the Gini coefficient, one can reliably assess whether below the last decile inequality has increased over time or is greater in certain countries but one cannot discern the type of distributional asymmetries.

As shown by recent studies, different patterns of inequality at the national level can be detected when considering alternative indicators. Some countries can perform relatively well in some indicators (meaning low levels of inequality) but not in others, and this may be related to certain economic or institutional features (Baccaro & Pontusson, 2016; Behringer & van Treeck, 2018; 2019). Thus, it is important to take into account the difference between functional and personal income distribution or between the lower and upper half of the distribution, as well as other indicators of income polarization, as top income shares or poverty rates.

Following this methodological caution, Table 4.2 displays the average values of four income polarization indicators in France, the SAEs, and some selected economies for the 2010s. These four indicators are the Gini coefficient, the P50/P10 and P10/P50 interdecile ratios, and the poverty rates. While the Gini coefficient captures more general differences in income disparities across economies, the P10/P50 interdecile and the poverty rates measure income disparities affecting the most vulnerable individuals.

As the figures show, for all the indicators, and particularly those related to lower incomes, France's values are below the SAEs' average. This may be surprising in view of the poor economic performance of the country, since a context of high unemployment rates and low GDP growth rates typically affects the vulnerable population more because low-income earners are more likely to be dismissed and since employment-loses impact them more as their income sources are less diversified. However, we contend that the observed low inequality is not a striking fact but instead the predictable outcome of the

Table 4.2 Income distribution indicators

Country	*Gini coefficient*	*P50/P10 interdecile*	*P90/P50 interdecile*	*Poverty rate*
Denmark	0.261	1.8	1.7	12.6
Norway	0.262	1.9	1.7	14.5
Belgium	0.264	2.0	1.7	18.4
Finland	0.269	1.8	1.7	13.4
Sweden	0.275	1.9	1.7	16.6
Austria	0.275	1.9	1.8	15.2
the Netherlands	0.285	1.9	1.8	15.0
Germany	0.289	2.0	1.8	16.1
France	*0.292*	*1.9*	*1.8*	*14.4*
Switzerland	0.299	1.9	1.9	15.5
SAEs	*0.310*	*2.1*	*1.9*	*18.1*
Australia	0.325	2.2	2.0	20.4
Spain	0.333	2.4	2.0	22.1
Italy	0.334	2.4	2.0	20.2
Japan	0.339	2.5	2.0	21.7
New Zealand	0.349	2.1	2.1	19.6
Korea	0.355	2.8	2.1	23.2
United Kingdom	0.366	2.1	2.1	18.2
USA	0.390	2.7	2.3	25.0

Source: OECD Income Distribution Database. www.oecd.org/social/income-distribution-database.htm

French model's institutional features. Although further research is needed, the hypothesis is that strong WPIs reinforce vulnerable workers' bargaining, thereby protecting them against labor market risks.

4 Conclusion

This chapter has shown why France is characterized by policies and legislations that are part of what is called Workers' Protection Institutions (WPIs). This term is used to classify those institutions that give workers some protection against several risks linked to the labor market, such as unemployment, underemployment, or low earnings. Throughout the chapter, the focus is put on three of these institutions because of their particular importance in a French context. First, the contributory and non-contributory benefits systems' relative generosity implies both higher expenditure effort and higher coverage ratios regarding most of the advanced economies. Second, French legislation contains greater legal guarantees against dismissal for regular contract workers and stricter legal provisions regulating the use of temporary contracts.

Third, wage-setting institutions are concentrated at the higher level and politically conditioned as a result of the combination of three elements: (1) a relatively high minimum wage; (2) extensive collective bargaining coverage; and (3) a significant influence of unions on national politics. As indicated in Section 2, most of the legal changes adopted in the last two decades have not had a significant impact on the three institutional features mentioned earlier. Indeed, in some cases, recent reforms seem to have reinforced them.

During the same period, poor performances from international trade relations and the labor market were observed. Thus, the trade deficit rose to 3 percent of GDP in the 2000s and remained stable during the following decade, despite the minor adjustment after the Great Recession. Likewise, unlike other advanced economies, such as that of Germany or the United Kingdom, France's unemployment figures did not decline significantly after the Great Recession. While the unemployment rates in these economies are at their lowest levels in decades, in France, they have been in the range of 7–10 percent since their increase in the early 1970s.

The coincidence of both facts has led some analysts to maintain that WPIs might be introducing disrupting effects to France's competitiveness and market efficiency. These effects, in turn, impact supply conditions, thereby affecting employment and trade balance negatively. In this sense, the absence of reforms is, therefore, seen as the main factor causing trade deficits and high unemployment rates (Carcillo et al., 2019). In short, provided some supply effects are assumed, strong WPIs may explain why France's growth model is based on internal demand growth funded by private debt. In other words, they can be seen as the institutional foundations of France's consumption-led, debt-financed growth model.

In any case, before blaming those institutions for the weaknesses of France's growth model, the assumed effects on supply need to be proved. Nonetheless, as a preliminary exploratory analysis of Section 3.2 shows, it is unclear whether WPIs can explain high unemployment and temporary employment rates as well as the trade deficit. To begin with, WPIs' influence on unemployment or temporary employment rates is ambiguous once the relevant variable performance is isolated. Likewise, WPIs' impact on France's international competitiveness depends on WPIs' inflationary effect on ULC. However, both before and after the Great Recession, France's ULC growth rate was, indeed, lower than that of the SAEs.

Moreover, even assuming that WPIs cause supply and demand imbalances, effects on the income distribution of these institutions should be taken into account to fully complete the picture. As some recent studies state, WPIs can reinforce vulnerable workers' bargaining power, both within workers' representative institutions and within firms. This might explain why, despite persistent high unemployment rates, France is characterized by low income disparities and relatively low incidence of the population at risk of poverty, at least compared with other advanced economies. This does not mean that inequalities did not increase in France after the Great Recession, as they did in many other

European economies. What it means is that France's income disparities and shares of the vulnerable population are still lower than other advanced economies. In short, France's strong WPIs cannot explain the increase of inequalities over the last decade, but they do explain the observed relatively low rates of poverty when a cross-sectional perspective is adopted.

Consequently, this chapter proves that WPIs can also benefit most vulnerable workers and not only those with better working conditions, as is frequently suggested in both theoretical and applied analysis. Despite having some possible disruptive effects, these institutions can also guarantee relatively low income disparities. This last feature is one of the defining characteristics of France's economic model and may explain the country's resistance to adopting more liberalizing reforms.

Notes

1 This is important because in France agreements are frequently extended for all workers employed by signatory firms. The higher the density of employer's organizations, the greater the probability of a given worker being employed by a sectoral bargaining signatory firm and, therefore, of being covered by sectoral agreements.

2 France's import average growth rate was 5.6 percent in 2000–2007, while the SAE non-weighted average was 6.1 percent during the same period.

3 Before the Great Recession, in the 2000s, ULC in France had grown on average at 1.83 percent per year, while ULC average growth rates were 0.21 percent in Germany, but the same figures are 3.39 percent in Spain, 2.03 percent in the Netherlands or 2.77 percent in the United Kingdom. After the Great Recession, in the 2010s, the French ULC average annual growth rate (0.74 percent) was lower than the SAEs' and Germany's averages (0.99 percent and 1.53 percent). Data are averages of OECD yearly figures on ULC growth rates.

References

Acemoglu, D., & Autor, D. (2011). Skills, tasks and technologies: Implications for employment and earnings. In D. Card & O. Ashenfelter (Eds.), *Handbook of labor economics*, vol. 4B (pp. 1043–1171). Amsterdam: Elsevier.

Baccaro, L., & Pontusson, J. (2016). Rethinking comparative political economy: The growth model perspective. *Politics & Society*, 44 (2), 175–207.

Barbanchon, T., & Malherbet, F. (2013). An anatomy of the French labour market. ILO Employment Working Paper No. 142.

Bazin, S., & Girardin, E. (1999). France and the Maastricht criteria: Fiscal retrenchment and labour market adjustment. In D. Cobham & G. Zis (Eds.), *From EMS to EMU: 1979 to 1999 and beyond* (pp. 95–128). London: Palgrave Macmillan.

Behringer, J. & van Treeck, T. (2018). Income distribution and the current account. *Journal of International Economics*, 114, 238–254.

Behringer, J., & van Treeck, T. (2019). Income distribution and growth models: A sectoral balances approach. *Politics & Society*, 47 (3), 303–332.

Cahuc, P., Carcillo, S., Rinne, U., & Zimmermann, K. (2013). Youth unemployment in old Europe: The polar cases of France and Germany. *IZA Journal of European Labor Studies*, 2 (1), 1–23.

Cahuc, P., & Nevoux, S. (2017). Inefficient short-time work. *IZA-Institute of Labor Economics*, 11010.
Carcillo, S., Goujard, A., Hijzen, A., & Thewissen, S. (2019). Assessing recent reforms and policy directions in France implementing the OECD Jobs Strategy. OECD Social, Employment and Migration Working Papers No. 227.
Chevalier, T., & Palier, B. (2014). The French welfare state system: With special reference to youth unemployment. In C. Aspalter (Ed.), *The Routledge international handbook to welfare state systems* (pp. 216–228). London: Routledge.
CNP (2019). *Productivité et compétitivité: Où en est la France dans la zone euro? Premier Rapport*. Paris: Conseil National de Productivité.
Combrexelle, J. D. (2015). La négociation collective, le travail et l'emploi. In *Rapport au Premier ministre*. Paris: France Stratégie.
Esping-Andersen, G., & Myles, J. (2011). Economic inequality and the welfare state. In B. Nolan, W. Salverda, & T. M. Smeeding (Eds.), *The Oxford handbook of economic inequality*. Oxford: Oxford University Press.
Fougère, D., Gautier, E., & Roux, S. (2018). Wage floor rigidity in industry-level agreements: Evidence from France. *Labour Economics*, 55, 72–97.
Groupe d'experts sur le SMIC (2018). Salaire Minimum Interprofessionnel de croissance. Rapport du groupe d'experts. Paris: SMIC.
Hassenteufel, P., & Palier, B. (2016). The French welfare system. In R. Elgie, E. Grossman, & A. G. Mazur (Eds.), *The Oxford handbook of French politics* (pp. 60–78). Oxford: Oxford University Press.
Heimberger, P. (2020). Does employment protection affect unemployment? A meta-analysis. *WIIW Working Paper* No. 176.
Jaumotte, F., & Osorio, C. (2015). Inequality and labor market institutions. *IMF Staff Discussion Notes*, 15/14.
Kristal, T., & Cohen, Y. (2017). The causes of rising wage inequality: The race between institutions and technology. *Socio-Economic Review*, 15 (1), 187–212.
Langevin, G. (2017). Adhésion aux organisations patronales: une mesure de la couverture patronale: Une utilisation conjointe des résultats de l'audience patronale, des DADS et de la Base des minima de branche. *Document d'études de la direction de l'animation de la recherche, des études et des statistiques*, 228.
Marx, P. (2012). Labour market dualisation in France: Assessing different explanatory approaches. *European Societies*, 14 (5), 704–726.
Milner, S., & Mathers, A. (2013). Membership, influence and voice: A discussion of trade union renewal in the French context. *Industrial Relations Journal*, 44 (2), 122–138.
Ministère du Travail (2019). *La négociation collective en 2018*. Paris: Ministère du Travail.
Nikolka, T., & Poutvaara, P. (2019). Labour market reforms and collective bargaining in France. *IFo DICE Report*, 16 (4), 44–49.
OECD (2018a). Non-regular employment, job security and the labour market divide. In OECD (Ed.), *OECD employment outlook* (pp. 141–209). Paris: OECD Publishing.
OECD (2018b). Unemployment-benefit coverage: Recent trends and their drivers. In OECD (Ed.), *OECD employment outlook* (pp. 185–210). Paris: OECD Publishing.
OECD (2019). Collective bargaining systems and workers' voice arrangements in OECD countries. In OECD (Ed.), *Negotiating our way up: Collective bargaining in a changing world of work* (pp. 22–104). Paris: OECD Publishing.

OECD (2020). Recent trends in employment protection legislation. In OECD (Ed.), *OECD employment outlook 2020: Worker security and the COVID-19 crisis.* Paris: OECD Publishing.

Palier, B. (2010). Ordering change: Understanding the 'Bismarckian' welfare reform trajectory. In B. Palier (Ed.), *A long goodbye to Bismarck? The politics of welfare reforms in continental Europe* (pp. 19–44). Amsterdam: Amsterdam University Press.

Palier, B., & Thelen, K. (2010). Institutionalizing dualism: Complementarities and change in France and Germany. *Politics & Society*, 38 (1), 119–148.

Philippon, T., & Reshef, A. (2013). An international look at the growth of modern finance. *Journal of Economic Perspectives*, 27 (2), 73–96.

Poutvaara, P., Nikolka, T., Leithold, D., Oesingmann, K., & Wech, D. (2017). Comparative study about the powers and the representativeness of employee representatives in French and German enterprises. *IFo Forschungsberichte*, 84.

Rehfeldt, U., & Vincent, C. (2018). The decentralisation of collective bargaining in France: An escalating process. In S. Leonardi & R. Pedersini (Eds.), *Multi-employer bargaining under pressure: Decentralisation trends in five European countries* (pp. 151–184). Brussels: European Trade Union Institute.

Stansbury, A., & Summers, L. H. (2020). The declining worker power hypothesis: An explanation for the recent evolution of the American economy. NBER Working Paper No. 27193.

Taylor-Gooby, P. (2004). New risks and social change. In P. Taylor-Gooby (Ed.), *New risks, new welfare: The transformation of the European welfare state* (pp. 1–28). Cambridge: Cambridge University Press.

Turrini, A, Koltay, G., Pierini, F., Goffard, C., & Kiss, Á. (2015). A decade of labour market reforms in the EU: Insights from the LABREF database. *IZA Journal of Labor Policy*, 4 (1), 1–33.

Vlandas, T. (2013). The politics of temporary work deregulation in Europe: Solving the French puzzle. *Politics & Society*, 41 (3), 425–460.

Vlandas, T. (2016). Labour market developments and policy responses during and after the crisis in France. *French Politics*, 15 (1), 75–105.

Vlandas, T. (2017). Labour market performance and deregulation in France during and after the crisis. In A. Piasna & M. Myant (Eds.), *Myths of employment deregulation: How it neither creates jobs nor reduces labour market segmentation*. Brussels: European Trade Union Institute.

5 The mechanics of German capitalism

Dualism and inequality in an export-led economy

Daniel Herrero

COMPLUTENSE UNIVERSITY OF MADRID AND COMPLUTENSE INSTITUTE FOR INTERNATIONAL STUDIES

1 Introduction

The transformation of German capitalism has been widely analyzed by political economists (Baccaro & Benassi, 2017; Carlin & Soskice, 2009; Hall & Soskice, 2001; Streeck, 2009). The interest in the topic is due to two related factors: on the one hand, the process of institutional change by which the labor market and industrial relation arenas were progressively liberalized, and, on the other, the country's macroeconomic performance, which was very weak during the 1990s and the early 2000s, and quite positive from 2007 onward. Since then, the German economy has been growing steadily through the external sector, which has been accumulating large commercial surpluses since the beginning of the 2000s. Furthermore, despite the moderate growth rates, Germany reached a situation close to full employment (3 percent in 2019).

The country was considered the sick man of Europe at the end of the 1990s,[1] but after the liberalizing reforms undertaken and the successful performance during the Great Recession (the 2008–2009 global crisis), it was widely praised by multilateral institutions (Hüfner & Klein, 2012), and was held up as an example to follow for other European economies. Nonetheless, the deregulation of the labor market and the erosion of the industrial relations (IIRR) system have resulted in a dual model, in which high employment protection standards and the coverage of the dual system of IIRR (the combination of collective agreement and work councils) are concentrated in a small section of workers, who enjoy good working conditions and high wages. On the contrary, an increasing share of employees are located on the periphery or in a secondary segment of the economy, where precarious work is spread thinly and the IIRR system is barely present, so working conditions have deteriorated and wages have dramatically fallen. The shape adopted by these liberalizing reforms was due to the prevailing interest of the dominant social bloc, the exporting manufacturing sector, which is composed of workers with *insider* status and exporting firms in advanced manufacturing industries (Baccaro & Pontusson, 2016). This social bloc has managed to preserve the traditional institutions of the German model to work for them, while promoting (or at least not opposing) liberalization on the margins of the economy (Hassel, 2014).

Since the formation of the eurozone, macroeconomic management in Germany has been characterized by the repression of domestic demand through sharp wage moderation (achieved by the reform of labor institutions) and a conservative fiscal stance, with the aim of fostering the trade balance. Such an extreme export-led growth regime is still registered after the global crisis, although a certain rebalancing can be seen. From 2010 onward, the contribution of domestic demand to output growth has been greater and both real wages and the wage share have grown at a faster pace, since they have been stimulated by the low unemployment rate and a slight re-institutionalization process at the margins of the labor market (in which the major milestone was the introduction of a statutory minimum wage in 2015).

However, after the Great Recession, the German economy still shows similar patterns to the pre-crisis period. The *production regime* is characterized by the central role of the manufacturing sector, whose relative weight on total output and employment is still high, and has a critical influence on the development of service industries. Two trends are observed regarding these latter industries. On the one hand, dynamic service industries are an important vector of employment growth because they supply inputs to exporting manufacturing firms, and at the same time export part of their production. On the other hand, the production of non-dynamic service industries is predominantly oriented toward the domestic market, therefore experiencing the pervasive consequences of the wage restraint.

On the *demand side*, Germany exhibits a strong economic dependence on the external sector to grow, and a *trade-off* between the domestic and the external demand, which reflects the country's extreme export-led growth regime. Furthermore, we detect a dysfunctional relationship between the wage-led demand regime and the growth model. More specifically, the focus of the macroeconomic management on the squeeze on domestic demand via wage repression has been detrimental to economic growth and has fostered the growth of inequality.

In sum, Germany is a case of a segmented or dual coordinated market economy. We claim that macroeconomic dynamics are determined by the development of the institutional framework. Concretely, the dualization of labor institutions has served to solve the problem of unemployment (currently at a historic low), but at the cost of higher levels of inequality. Additionally, since the mechanisms for wage moderation imply restraint on domestic demand, the employment creation policy basically consisted of the distribution of working hours via part-time work contracts. Furthermore, this equilibrium between low unemployment and high inequality levels is by no means an economic trade-off, but a political decision determined by the dominance of the interests of the manufacturing social bloc. Finally, not surprisingly, descriptive evidence, as well as the estimations that we refer to, suggest that the export-led growth model would not be negatively affected by higher wage growth and a more expansionary public spending stance, and that economic growth and economic equality would benefit from these political decisions.

2 The production regime: the predominant role of manufacturing and the weakness of the service sector

2.1 The central role of manufacturing

The German economy has faced difficulties in growing and creating employment throughout the last 20 years. In fact, since 2000, total working hours in the economy have almost stagnated, and, when looking at the private sector, the average annual growth has even been negative (-0.06 percent, see Table 5.1). Overall, such weak growth has been compensated for by the distribution of working hours, undertaken through the reduction of the weekly working time of standard contracts, and, especially, by the deregulation of the labor market and the expansion of precarious part-time work (see the discussion of the development of part-time and marginal employment in Section 4). Thus, by deregulating the margins of the labor market, it was possible to achieve and maintain the difficult equilibrium between a dominant and highly productive manufacturing sector, a relatively underdeveloped service sector and low levels of unemployment from 2010 onward. The particular features of Germany are better captured in comparison with other advanced economies, in the present case, the UK and Sweden, the paradigmatic cases of a liberal market economy and a Nordic coordinate market economy, respectively (Table 5.1).

First, the most prominent aspect of the German production regime is the development of manufacturing output and employment. This sector has led the country's value-added growth. Moreover, in terms of employment, it can be appreciated that Germany managed to successfully contain deindustrialization, while both the UK and Sweden performed worse. Interestingly, this is due to the remarkable performance of high technology or advanced manufacturing industries, which are also the most productive industries. This pattern is unique among advanced economies and is explained by the extraordinary development of export demand. Actually, these industries accounted for 65 percent of total exports between 2000 and 2018 (calculations based on Comext, Eurostat). These results are in stark contrast not only with the UK's figures, where the deindustrialization process has been profound, but also with Sweden's figures, where industrial exports have grown at a high rate too.

Regarding the service sector, it has led the growth of employment, although the growth rates displayed are low. On the one hand, employment growth in dynamic service industries has been similar to Sweden, measured in both people and total hours worked. Nonetheless, productivity growth is much weaker. The development of this type of services is partly explained by their connection to manufacturing industries. In fact, a large part of this service category is made up of the knowledge-intensive business services (KIBS),

Table 5.1 Average growth of real value added, employment and productivity by sector (2000–2015) (%)

	Value added	*Persons employed*	*Hours worked*	*Hours worked per employee*	*Productivity*
Germany					
Total economy	1.08	0.47	0.10	-0.37	0.98
Private economy	1.07	0.35	-0.06	-0.40	1.12
Manufacturing	1.50	-0.26	-0.40	-0.14	1.90
• High-technology manufacturing	2.26	0.04	-0.14	-0.17	2.39
• Middle-low and low technology manufacturing	0.25	-0.50	-0.61	-0.12	0.86
Services	1.04	0.97	0.59	-0.37	0.44
• Dynamic services	1.35	1.15	0.81	-0.34	0.53
• Non-dynamic services	0.72	0.98	0.51	-0.47	0.21
United Kingdom					
Total economy	1.53	0.81	0.65	-0.16	0.88
Private economy	1.53	0.57	0.38	-0.19	1.15
Manufacturing	-0.35	-2.54	-2.61	-0.07	2.26
• High-technology manufacturing	0.02	-2.72	-2.84	-0.12	2.86
• Middle-low and low technology manufacturing	-0.69	-2.46	-2.50	-0.04	1.81
Services	1.96	1.39	1.33	-0.06	0.62
• Dynamic services	2.57	1.48	1.28	-0.21	1.30
• Non-dynamic services	1.78	1.40	1.49	0.09	0.29
Sweden					
Total economy	1.91	0.70	0.58	-0.12	1.33
Private economy	2.42	0.66	0.38	-0.28	2.05
Manufacturing	1.78	-1.52	-1.66	-0.15	3.45
• High-technology manufacturing	0.95	-1.58	-1.78	-0.20	2.73
• Middle-low and low technology manufacturing	1.66	-1.47	-1.58	-0.11	3.24
Services	1.53	0.97	1.03	0.06	0.50
• Dynamic services	1.80	0.92	1.14	0.22	0.66
• Non-dynamic services	2.34	0.97	1.25	0.28	1.09

Source: Author's calculations based on EUKLEMS, EU Growth and Productivity Accounts.

which provide expert knowledge and technical support to other companies, thus promoting innovation and technical progress (Castaldi, 2009; Den Hertog, 2000; Tomlinson, 2000). Comparative empirical studies agree that the integration of KIBS into manufacturing productive strategies is quite high in Germany (Ciriaci & Parma, 2016). Indeed, this is a traditional feature of German manufacturing. For instance, Windrum and Tomlinson (1999) find that, in comparison with other service-intensive economies like the UK or the Netherlands, KIBS were highly developed and strongly integrated with other economic activities during the 1980s and the 1990s. Other country-specific studies point out that business services have contributed to the successful export performance of manufacturing (Franke & Kalmbach, 2005; Herrero, 2020). Moreover, apart from the connection to domestic industries, KIBS are tradeable activities, and they were part of the exporting boom of the economy.

The reason for the sclerotic employment creation lies in the performance of non-dynamic services (a main vector for employment growth in advanced economies). This category essentially comprises consumer and personal services, which are particularly labor-intensive and present low levels of capitalization. Therefore, the development of non-dynamic service employment is very sensitive to the business cycle, and, in turn, to changes in domestic demand, since they produce for the domestic market. In comparison to the UK and Sweden, hours worked in these services have increased very little, whereas the number of people employed has grown much faster (at the same rate as Sweden) (see Table 5.1). As will be argued in Section 5.3, this result is partly explained by the slow growth of private consumption demand, because of the stagnant average real wages, which hampered the increase in disposable income of households (Baccaro & Pontusson, 2016; IMF, 2019). On the other hand, the expansion of non-standard employment (particularly marginal part-time work) has been concentrated in these industries, therefore driving down the average hours worked per employee.

However, the central role of the manufacturing sector in the German productive structure is better captured when using a subsystem or vertical integrated sector approach to the input-output analysis (Passinetti, 1973). A vertical integrated sector (VIS) or subsystem represents all the domestic activities that directly or indirectly satisfy the final demand of a particular commodity. Thus, each VIS is a completely independent production system, in which every domestic input required to meet the final demand is included.[2] Table 5.2 compares the size of the manufacturing sector when applying the traditional approach to the economic analysis (that classifies commodities according to the industry that produces them, therefore implicitly assuming that each industry is an autonomous unit of production) and when using the subsystem approach.

According to the former method, manufacturing activities represent 23 percent of total nominal value added and around 18 percent of employment. Nonetheless, when considering the manufacturing sector as a VIS, its size is 10 percentage points (pp) larger. Moreover, the share of vertically integrated

Table 5.2 Size of the manufacturing sector: differences between traditional and subsystem approach, selected years (%)

	2000	*2008*	*2014*
Value-added (VA) (subsystem approach)	31.0	33.1	31.6
VA (traditional approach)	23.0	22.5	22.6
Employment (subsystem approach)	27.3	28.2	27.1
Employment (traditional approach)	19.6	18.3	17.5

Source: Author's calculations based on World Input-Output Database. www. wiod.org

manufacturing employment reduces much less. Thus, all service employment destined for intermediate uses of manufacturing is taken into consideration. This is particularly important in capturing the pervasive use of outsourcing by German manufacturing companies (Goldschmidt & Schmieder, 2017) and the increasing demand of KIBS that requires the modern production of manufactured goods (Ciriaci & Parma, 2016).

It should be noted that, no matter which approach is followed, Germany stands out as the advanced economy that has managed to better contain the deindustrialization process. To gain insight into this pattern, it is useful to follow the comparative analysis performed by Peneder and Streicher (2018). According to these authors, there are two main drivers of deindustrialization (measured as the development of the manufacturing value added share in total value added at current prices): (1) *the economic development effect*; and (2) *the competitiveness effect*. The economic development effect comprises two sub-effects: (1) the income effect captures the fact that the increase of income per capita leads to changes in domestic demand patterns. As the income per capita grows, the income elasticity of the demand of different goods and services changes, affecting sector shares (historically, agricultural commodities have displayed declining shares in favor of manufacturing and service ones; this is the income effect or Engel's law); and (2) the price effect captures the change in relative prices due to the faster productivity growth in the manufacturing sector relative to the rest of the economy, by which manufacturing prices tend to decrease more than those of the other industries, thus reducing the manufacturing share in total nominal value added. This latter effect has been identified as the main driving force behind the shift in productive structure from manufacturing to services in advanced economies.

Concerning the effect of international competitiveness, naturally, changes in this variable determine output and the employment growth of the manufacturing sector. An increase in manufacturing competitiveness relative to other countries has a positive effect on the sector's nominal value added share, thanks to international trade. Now we focus on the specific results captured by Peneder and Streicher (2018) for Germany. First, the negative contribution of domestic demand patterns to manufacturing value added share is lower than that of the rest of advanced economies. Furthermore, the development of relative prices is less favorable to services than one might expect, given the existing differentials in productivity, i.e. prices in services are much lower than in neighboring economies. Second, the amount of induced value added by external demand (i.e. the sector's competitiveness) is greater than that of other developed economies and almost compensates for the negative effect of the domestic induced value added.

All in all, the centrality of the manufacturing sector in the German productive structure is due to the combination of its international competitiveness, which drives output and employment up, thanks to the remarkable development of the external demand (see Appendix Table A5.1). But it is also explained by the low level of development of the service industries, predominantly the less dynamic ones. Moreover, as further discussed below, wage restraint, particularly tough in services, has slowed down prices, real value added and employment growth in these industries, therefore, contributing to the above-mentioned development of relative prices and the high share of manufacturing in total output and employment.

2.2 Productive links between manufacturing and services

The German production regime had been characterized as a diversify quality production model (DQP) (Sorge & Streeck, 1987; Streeck, 1991). It consisted of a set of institutional constraints on employers' preferences that, in combination with the new production technologies for the modularization of production, allowed German firms to remain highly competitive in international markets by offering high quality goods at relatively high prices. The main institutional features of the DQP model were the cooperative relations between small and large companies in technological creation and transfer, a large number of high-skilled employees in firms' workforces or the coordinated system of IIRR, which promoted high wages and good working conditions across the entire economy. In contrast, during the last 20 years, competitive relations among supplier firms and assemblers have become more common (Silvia, 1997; Silvia & Schroeder, 2007), as well as the outsourcing of non-core competences to other firms (Doellgast & Greer, 2007) and the offshoring of most labor-intensive activities (mainly to Eastern Europe) (Herrigel, 2015) due to cost-saving reasons.

One of the main channels of labor segmentation and wage restraint in Germany has been outsourcing or vertical disintegration. By this process, workers who used to work in large manufacturing firms, with long-term and well-paid job contracts, are transferred to a more deregulated segment of the economy, where unions are weak and the coverage of IIRR institutions is low, thus damaging wages and working conditions. The result of the value chain is that the labor cost structure is compressed, allowing firms to offer lower prices or to increase their profit margins. Furthermore, firms also gain flexibility in the face of demand shocks and in the overall decision-taking procedure.

One way to empirically approximate outsourcing is the subsystem approach to input-output, employing as proxy the development of service employment in manufacturing subsystems (Montresor & Vittucci Marzatti, 2007; Sarra, Di Bernardo, & Quaglione, 2018). We have performed this estimation, and Figures 5.1 and 5.2 represent the development of different types of service employment integrated in manufacturing VIS by their R&D intensity. The proportion of service employment has grown 3.4 pp and 4.3 pp in high technology and low technology manufacturing subsystems, respectively. This is mainly due to the relative increase in business services and, to a lesser extent, personal services employment.

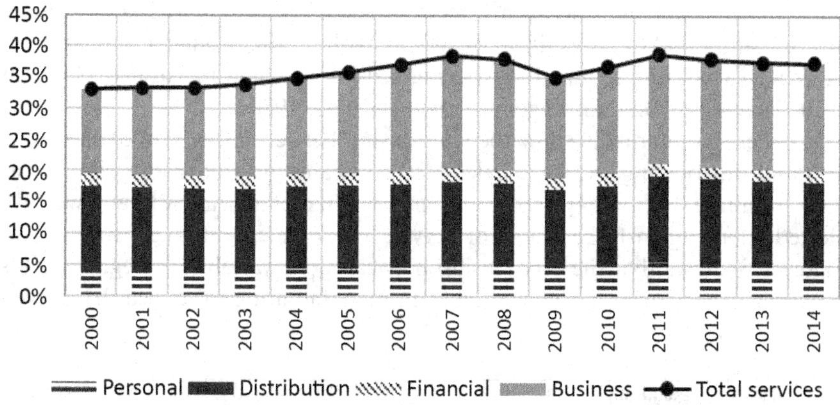

Figure 5.1 Service employment in high and medium-high technology manufacturing VIS
Source: Author's calculations based on World Input-Output Database. www. wiod.org

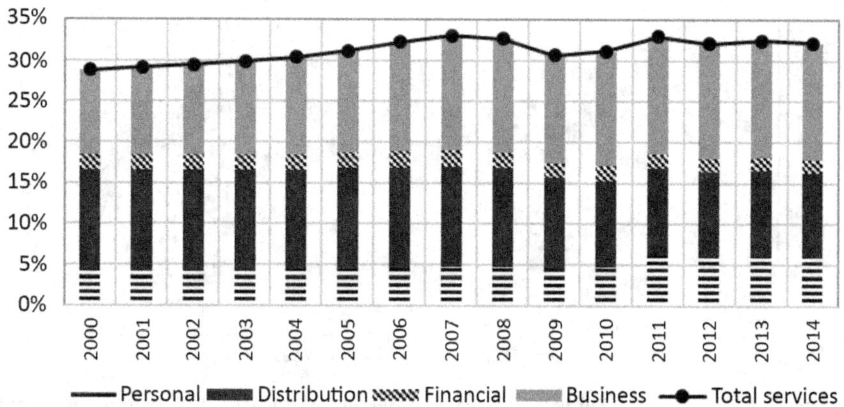

Figure 5.2 Service employment in medium-low and low technology manufacturing VIS
Source: Author's calculations based on World Input-Output Database. www. wiod.org

As explained above, the high employment growth in dynamic services is partly due to the links of KIBS with manufacturing. The growing demand of these sorts of advanced intermediate services is a channel for their development in Germany.

Moreover, productive relations have also been a source of growth for less dynamic services. For instance, the personal services category comprises activities such as retail, company canteens or cleaning services. A large part of the wage restraint has been concentrated in these activities through outsourcing from large manufacturing firms. This way, many workers were excluded from collective agreements that ensure good working conditions, and became part of the deregulated segment of the economy, where trade unions and IIRR are weaker. In this sense, recent work by Goldschmidt and Schmieder (2017) reports that the wage penalty of outsourcing is between 10 percent and 15 percent in logistics, cleaning, security and food services in comparison with non-outsourced similar jobs. Moreover, according to this study, outsourced jobs account for around 9 percent of the increase in German wage inequality since the 1980s.

In order to empirically show the relationship between labor cost competitiveness and outsourcing, we have calculated vertically integrated unit labor costs (ULC)[3] in high technology and low technology manufacturing VIS and we have plotted them against the share of service employment in these subsystems. Figure 5.3 shows that the relationship between both variables is negative, thus supporting the view that outsourcing from manufacturing to services has served to save labor costs.

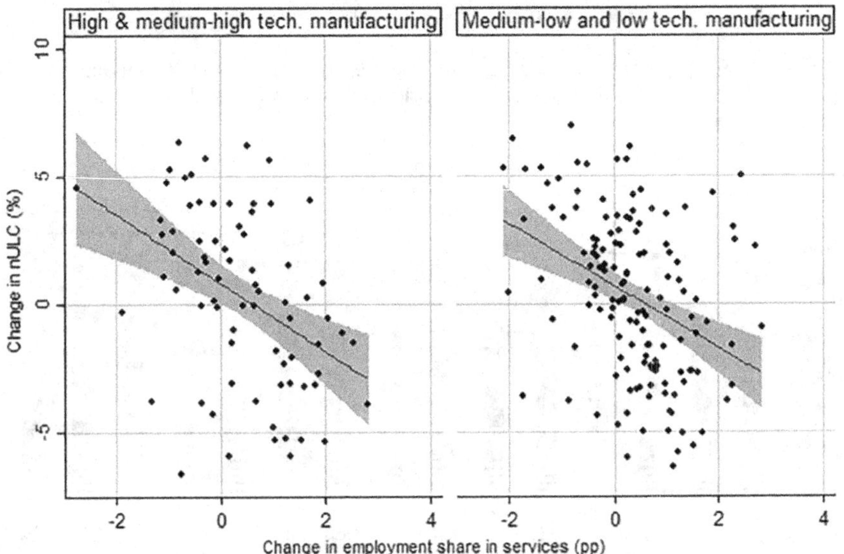

Figure 5.3 Relationship between service employment and vertically integrated nominal ULC

Source: Author's calculations based on World Input-Output Database. www. wiod.org

In sum, the manufacturing sector is still at the center of the German production regime. Those services connected with these industries or that are oriented toward the external market have performed relatively well in terms of output and employment. Nonetheless, precisely due to the central role of exporting manufacturing, which imposes wage restraint policies across the entire economy, less dynamic services are relatively underdeveloped. These service industries depend upon the growth of private consumption demand (which in turn is a function of wage growth) and they are one of the main vectors of employment creation of modern economies.

3 The consequences of 20 years of an extreme export-led regime

3.1 Income distribution and the evolution of the aggregate demand

The German growth model is widely categorized as export-led since, at least, the introduction of the euro. This is because of both the remarkable growth in exports and the vast size of the commercial surplus, and its contribution to output growth.

Historically, Germany has been marked by its exporting strength and has tended to accumulate current account surpluses (Höpner, 2019; Lindlar & Holtfrerich, 1997). However, their size and duration have never been so large. Since the early 1990s, the country has displayed an almost chronic commercial surplus (Figure 5.4). In spite of the growing importance and economic dependence of the exporting sector, most empirical works suggest that the demand regime is still wage-led (Hein & Vogel, 2008; Naastepad & Storm, 2006; Onaran & Galanis, 2011; Stockhammer et al., 2011), i.e. the GDP shows a positive response to increases in the wage share.

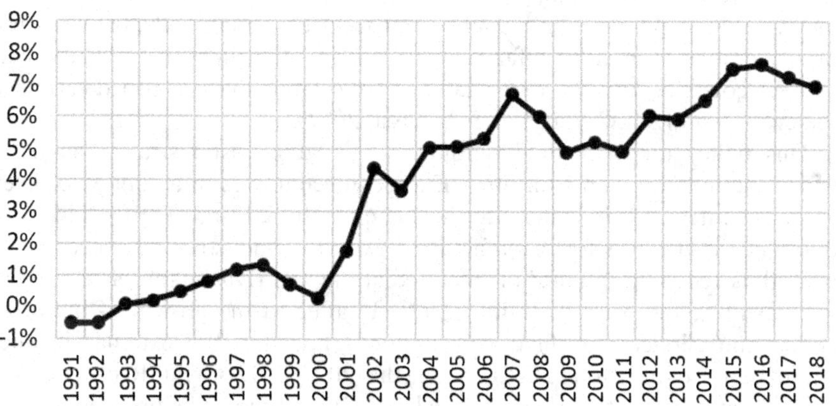

Figure 5.4 Nominal net exports (% GDP)
Source: Author's calculations based on www.OECD.stats

This result is quite problematic, since the macroeconomic management during the last 25 years has been oriented toward the control of the real effective exchange rate (REER) through the restraint of nominal wages and the implementation of a conservative fiscal policy, thus repressing domestic demand (mainly the private consumption demand), and with net exports being the main driver of economic growth. Put differently, what was observed in the previous section from the supply side (the central role of high-technology manufacturing), is explained by the behavior of the aggregate demand components: manufacturing exports became the first source of economic growth at the price of squeezing domestic demand, thus harming total output and employment growth. In the academic field of political economy, there is some consensus that this sort of macroeconomic management is a result of the influence exerted by the manufacturing social bloc, which is able to impose across the board its goals of wage moderation and price stability (Baccaro & Howell, 2018).

Macroeconomic policy orientation in Germany has always prioritized price stability and ULC contention to manage REER trends against its neighboring economies, and the institutional reforms undertaken since the mid-1990s have exacerbated the country's ability to restrain wages. In fact, Germany has always had institutional tools to control ULC growth. The coordinated model for wage-setting – the *pattern bargaining* [4] – in combination with the non-accommodative monetary policy of the Bundesbank, has been traditionally focused on controlling nominal wage growth, thus contributing to keep prices and unemployment under control (Franzese & Hall, 2000). After the onset of the euro, the negotiated wage growth in collective agreements experienced a drastic moderation (see Section 5.1, and see Figure 5.10). Furthermore, the reforms of the IIRR system allowed economic agents to decentralize the wage bargaining to workplaces, where work councils (in those establishments where they exist) and firm managers exchanged internal flexibility measures for investment compromises and employment security. Additionally, the weakness of the unions in non-manufacturing industries, the drop in collective bargaining coverage and the deregulation of the labor market also determined the evolution of ULC (Baccaro & Benassi, 2017).

This policy for price moderation through labor cost restraint sought to widen the inflation gap with other European economies in a context of fixed exchange rates to gain competitiveness (Cesaratto & Stirati, 2010). This way, domestic input prices for manufacturing exporting industries were cheaper as well, thus reducing imports of intermediate inputs (Dustmann et al., 2014). Furthermore, the wage restraint negatively affected the growth of imported goods and services for final consumption, boosting the external balance (European Commission, 2010). After the 2008–2009 Great Recession, the main German export markets changed and China became its first commercial partner. Thus, in spite of the crisis (which hit the rest of European countries much more severely), Germany managed to keep its commercial surplus, and exports recovered rapidly. The other key element in this policy is the adoption of a conservative fiscal policy stance. Continuous primary fiscal surpluses were obtained through weak public spending during the phases of economic expansion (this is the well-known *black zero rule* or *Schwarze Null*). Concretely, the fiscal policy stance of Merkel's center-right government has been guided by this principle. However, it should be pointed out that, during the moments of economic downturn (as in 2009 and 2010), the government launched a series of fiscal stimulus measures, incurring deficits and increasing public debt. Immediately after, it returned to the path of fiscal consolidation.

It is worth highlighting that, in spite of ULC repression, investment did not increase very much. According to most econometric estimations, this variable is wage-led too, i.e. is more responsive to demand growth than to the increase in the profit share (Hein & Vogel, 2008; 2009; Naastepad & Storm, 2006; Onaran & Obst, 2016; Stockhammer, Hein, & Grafl, 2011). Naturally, given that it is a centerpiece of the economic dynamic, this pattern is an additional factor explaining the weak economic growth and employment creation.

Table 5.3 displays the trajectory of the aggregate demand and its components, and illustrates the existing trade-off between domestic and external demand. Until the Great Recession, when wage restraint was harsher, economic growth was modest. The growth in private domestic demand was rather low due to the growth of both private consumption and investment, which grew below total spending. On the other hand, external demand grew at a high pace, led by advanced manufacturing industries as well as dynamic services.[5] Therefore, the main beneficiaries of this style of growth have been exporting manufacturing companies, which strengthened their position against foreign competitors and, at the same time, managed to amplify their profit margins.

After the crisis, this style of growth has been stable, in the sense that one can still observe the above-mentioned trade-off. However, it is also possible to note that the macroeconomic model is more balanced. From 2010 onward, both private consumption and investment start to grow much faster. Additionally, public consumption displays higher growth rates, particularly at the beginning of the period, when fiscal stimulus measures were applied to soften the negative effects of the crisis. Since 2011, fiscal consolidation has been in force again and the public sector has moderated its spending. Overall, the contributions to economic growth of these variables are much greater than in previous periods, when they remained almost stagnant. The main drivers of this rebalance were both the wage share, which experienced a substantial recovery (it grew 2.5 pp between 2008 and 2013), as well as the effect of fiscal stimulus.

Thus, the German growth model reflects the interests and political influence of the exporting manufacturing social bloc, which benefits from a sort of macroeconomic management that aims at stabilizing price growth, thus containing the real exchange rate and the cost of domestic inputs. Despite this "deflationary" context possibly being positive for exporters, the literature is far from reaching a consensus about the effect of price competitiveness, in general, and labor costs, in particular on German exports. For instance, Storm and Naastepad (2015) estimate that the impact of ULC is not

Table 5.3 Evolution of the aggregate demand components and the wage share

	Year-to-year growth				*Contributions to GDP growth*				*Share on nominal GDP*			
Years	2000–2003	2004–2008	2009	2010–2018	2000–2003	2004–2008	2009	2010–2018	2000–2003	2004–2008	2009	2010–2018
GDP (%)	0.9	1.9	-5.9	2.1	100.	100	100	100				
Domestic demand (%)	0.0	1.1	-1.5	1.8	4.2	61.8	34.4	87.2	96.5	93.4	95.7	93.4
Consumption	0.6	0.7	0.7	1.5	47.6	32.7	-11.7	59.1	75.4	73.7	76.4	73.2
Private consumption (%)	0.5	0.6	-0.1	1.4	27.3	18.5	1.2	39.0	56.2	55.3	56.4	53.6
Government consumption (%)	1.0	1.3	3.1	1.9	20.3	14.3	-13.1	20.0	19.1	18.4	20.0	19.6
GFKF (%)	-2.1	2.6	-9.9	2.8	-43.4	29.2	46.0	28.1	21.1	19.7	19.3	20.2
External demand (5)	62.1	16.8	-45.1	5.2	95.8	38.2	65.6	12.8	2.5	5.7	5.0	6.3
Exports (%)	6.1	7.9	-15.4	5.0	194.7	139.6	145.2	95.6	32.0	40.5	38.1	45.9
Goods (%)	6.0	7.8	-18.3	4.9	163.3	118.0	146.5	78.3	27.5	34.5	31.5	38.0
Services (%)	6.7	8.2	-0.3	5.1	31.5	21.6	0.5	17.3	4.5	6.0	6.6	7.8
Imports (%)	3.5	6.4	-10.2	4.9	98.8	101.4	79.5	82.8	29.6	34.7	33.1	39.5
Goods (%)	3.8	7.2	-10.7	5.0	81.3	84.3	64.5	65.0	22.5	27.3	25.7	30.8
Services (%)	2.4	3.8	-8.2	4.6	17.1	15.5	14.4	17.8	7.1	7.4	7.4	8.7
Wage share *	-1.0	-2.2.	-2.9	-2.2								
Wage share (%)			.		71.2		65.5		68.4		67.4	

Note: * The growth of wage share is the total difference between the last and first year of the period expressed in percentage points (it is not a growth rate).
Source: Author's calculations based on Ameco (https://ec.europa.eu/info/business-economy-euro/indicators-statistics/economic-databases/macro-economic-database-ameco_en) and Wirtschafts- und Sozialwissenschaftliches Institut (2019).

statistically significant. Furthermore, taking into account that ULC are a small proportion of total costs and assuming a complete pass-through onto prices, if the effect had been significant, the estimated elasticity of ULC exports would be -0.25, a rather small effect to explain the German export boom. On the other hand, most studies report a significant effect. For instance, Stockhammer et al. (2011) estimate an elasticity of -0.29, whereas Baccaro and Benassi (2017) offer -0.4. In a recent study, we report a growth rate elasticity of -0.13 for the period 2000–2014, using a panel of manufacturing VIS as observations (Herrero, 2020). Although we are not going to discuss this issue further, it should be emphasized that by no means can the growth in wage costs explain the export performance of the economy. Moreover, most empirical studies capture an Incomplete pass-through onto prices, which is not surprising when looking at the growth in profit margins. Furthermore, the ULC and export price elasticity captured vary quite a lot among studies, and depend on the estimation technique used and the time scope. Besides, those models based on export and import prices tend to capture a higher coefficient than those based on relative labor cost measures (our literature review reports a non-weighted average elasticity of -0.67 and -0.30, respectively; Herrero, 2020). In sum, it can be said that the reduction of wages and non-wage cost of the exporting industry did contribute to boosting the commercial balance, although the main driver of it was the ability of German firms to hook into global demand, thus leaving non-price factors at the center of the exporting success.

Given the available evidence, one can ask whether the wage restraint process has been beneficial or not to the economic growth. Put differently, the question is whether the existing relationship between the wage-led demand regime and the export-led growth model has fostered or harmed the overall economic performance. Following Stockhammer et al. (2011) or Onaran and Obst (2016), among others, it seems that the weak growth of consumption and investment demand due to the drop in the wage share has not been compensated for by the positive effect of this variable on net exports. In this sense, it is worth highlighting the econometric results of the Keynesian IMK (the Macroeconomic Policy Institute of the Hans Böckler Foundation) model (Horn et al., 2017). The estimations for the period 2001–2015 suggest that, if a *macroeconomic-oriented wage policy* [6] had been applied, ULC would have been 14 percent higher at the end of the 15-year period than their effective value. Nonetheless, the negative impact on net exports (in current prices) would have been negligible (-6 percent relative to its effective level in 2015) and the positive effect on private consumption (+5.4 percent) and investment (+0.7 percent) would have increased tax revenues (+11.4 percent), thus widening the room for public spending and having a positive impact on output growth (+1.7 percent).

3.2 Sectoral balances and the current account

The interactions between the development of the external sector and income distribution dynamics can be addressed from the point of view of the economic agents, since the current account balance is equal to the sum of the financial balances of corporations, households, and the government. The financial balance of each sector is defined as the difference between its income and its expenditure (Figure 5.5).

A set of recent papers by Behringer and van Treeck (2018a; 2018b; 2019) has explained in a satisfactory manner the evolution of these variables. First of all, the household balance has been positive since (at least) 1995. This result is in stark contrast with what is usually displayed in liberal economies, where households tend to present a net debtor position. Regarding the German case, two factors explain the positive balance of this sector: (1) top-end inequality is low in comparison with Anglo-Saxon economies, therefore *expenditure cascades* or consumption imitation effects are much lower (i.e. the decrease in savings for the acquisition of positional goods – goods that indicate social status – by low- and middle-income households, following the consumption patterns of high-income ones); (2) additionally, certain positional goods are public (such as health and higher education), so the need to decrease savings (or increase debt) of German households when high-end inequality rises is lower; and, finally, (3) the precautionary saving motive of households is stronger in Germany, because the cost of losing one's job is high for the worker, since the national labor market is rigid (relative to liberal economies) and the share of workers with industry-specific skills (normally more exposed to long-term unemployment) is bigger.

Regarding the corporate sector, since 2002, net exports have ballooned, and the position shifted from a net borrowing to a net lender one. Such a rise in corporate savings is explained by both the growth of the profit share and the

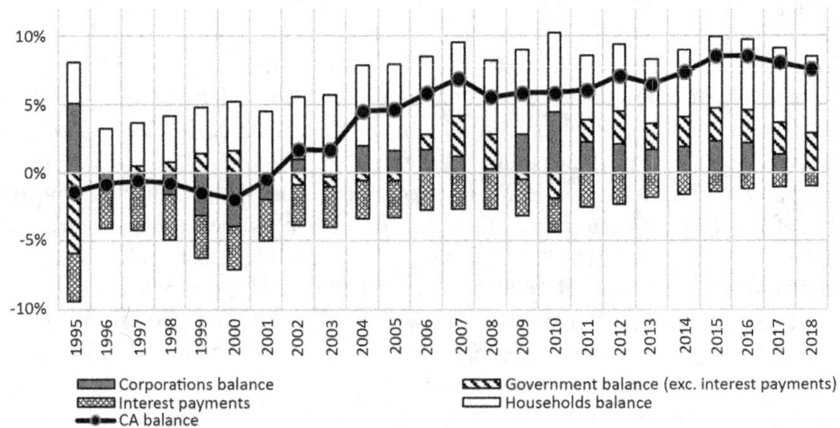

Figure 5.5 Current account and sectoral balances
Source: Author's calculations based on Ameco https://ec.europa.eu/info/business-economy-euro/indicators-statistics/economic-databases/macro-economic-database-ameco_en

disincentives for private investment due to the weak domestic demand growth, derived from the growth in households' disposable income. Furthermore, this excess in corporate savings has not been transferred to families due to the specific ownership structure of the German corporate sector, in which the *Mittelstand* (family-owned firms) constitutes a large proportion of firms in the economy[7] and shareholder-orientation strategies remain a minority. These companies have less incentive for profit-sharing since the owner and the manager are frequently the same person and the firm property is passed from one family generation to the next. In addition, the literature stresses that taxes on retained profits are comparatively low in relation to taxes on distributed profits, thus encouraging the increase in corporate savings rather than profit-sharing. In sum, corporate profits, instead of being channeled to the domestic economy via profit distribution or top-management wage growth, have led to an increase in corporate savings, thus constraining households disposable income and consumption demand growth.

Turning to the issue of the effects of the drop in the wage share in a wage-led economy, Braun and Deeg (2020) showed that the investment rate of non-financial corporations (NFCs) has remained stable throughout the period 2000–2018, and its development has not been influenced by the evolution of the (growing) profit margin. That is to say, the increasing profits thanks to the widening in the profit share have not been fully reinvested, neither distributed among shareholders nor top managers. Likewise, following these authors' results, NFCs' financial wealth has grown as well, including that of small and medium companies. As pointed out by Keller (2018), part of the increase in the NFCs' financial wealth is driven by precautionary reasons. After the Great Recession and the approval of Basel III, banks faced stricter equity requirements and the borrowing conditions for companies (particularly for small and medium-sized enterprises, SMEs) were tighter. All of this has further increased companies' saving motive, since they seek to become less dependent on external finance in general, and commercial banks in particular (which had traditionally been at the heart of the German model). Therefore, the rise in retained profits has served to finance investment, and due to the low investment levels, the corporate sector shows a net lender position.

Finally, as previously argued, the government's primary balance (excluding interest payments) indicates that the main goal of the fiscal policy was budgetary stability. Thus, during periods of economic upswing, the public sector displays a net lender position.

In conclusion, the extreme export-led German growth regime, which is based on a regressive income distribution pattern and a conservative fiscal stance, can also be understood from a sectoral balance perspective. When using this approach, the most remarkable issue is the net lender position of the corporate sector, which is explained by the wage restraint policies undertaken, the disincentives for investment as well as the institutional features of the country's specific ownership structure.

4 The evolution of the labor market

Germany has experienced certain difficulties in creating employment since the early 1990s because of the weak economic growth. Directly after reunification, the economy registered a short upswing, and subsequently passed through a decade of stagnation, when the traditional problems for employment creation became sharper. The logical result of these patterns was the rise in both the unemployment and the long-term unemployment rates (Figure 5.6).

As has been argued in previous sections, unemployment trends are partly explained by the scarce level of development of non-dynamic labor-intensive services (affected by the weak domestic demand growth) and by the high productivity of the manufacturing sector, which accounts for a large share in total employment. Since the reactivation of domestic demand growth would have required higher wage growth across the economy and an expansive fiscal policy, the policy response of the government and social agents to the problem of unemployment was the distribution of working hours by deregulating the labor market.

In this context, the institutional reforms undertaken at the margins of the labor market should be understood. The use of fixed-term (1997) and part-time (2001) contracts, as well as the activity of temporary agencies (1997 and 2001), were progressively liberalized. In parallel, IIRR institutions were eroded throughout the decade, in a process characterized by the

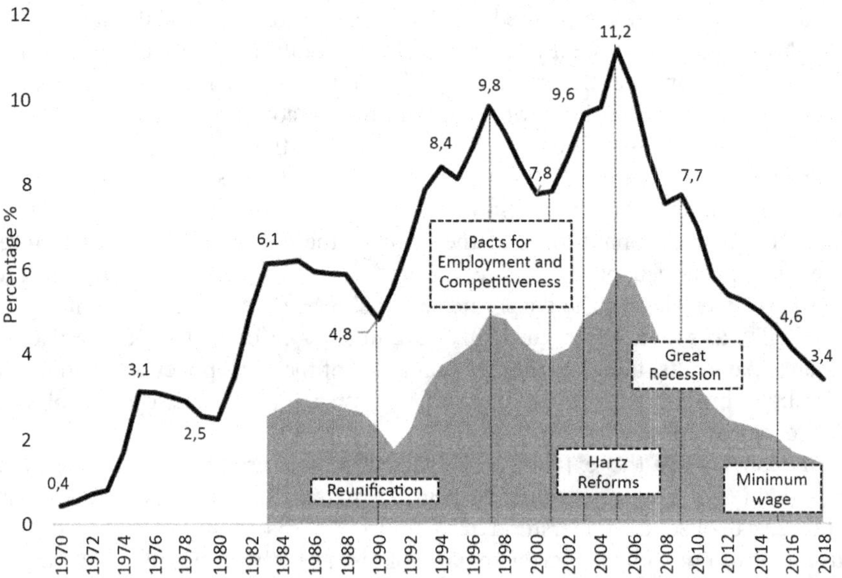

Figure 5.6 Evolution of the unemployment rate and structural unemployment
Source: Author's calculations based on OECD Statistics.
Note: * The gray area represents structural unemployment.

decentralization of the wage-setting negotiations and the fall in coverage of both collective agreements and work councils (see Section 5).

As is well known, the Hartz Reforms (2003–2005) were the last and most paradigmatic stage in this liberalizing trajectory. They introduced profound changes in labor regulation and constituted a shift in the non-interventionist attitude of the German state in labor relations. They consisted of the following four packages of measures:

- *Hartz I*: this comprises the full liberalization of agency work, by removing the maximum length of this type of contract.
- *Hartz II*: this reformed marginal part-time employment, i.e. the minijobs and midijobs contracts (with a wage threshold of €400 (nowadays €450) and € 800 (nowadays €850), respectively). This package abolished the maximum of 15 hours per week for these contracts.
- *Hartz III*: this implied the reorganization of the Federal Employment Agency and reinforced active labor market policies.
- *Hartz IV*: this controversial package consisted of the reduction of the duration of unemployment benefit and the introduction of means-tested social assistance for the long-term unemployed, with the aim of reducing the reservation wage.

As a consequence of this process of institutional liberalization, atypical employment expanded rapidly (around 10 pp between 1997 and 2007), but the unemployment rate experienced a progressive decrease from 2007 onward. In other words, in recent years the employment creation difficulties due to output growth still exist, but the liberalization of the labor market has promoted the creation of many reduced-hours jobs. That is to say, in a context in which working hours have grown at an average rate of 0.1 percent between 2000 and 2015, the distribution of them was the main policy to attack unemployment levels.

The deregulation of the margins of the labor market has allowed firms to increase the share of atypical workers on their books, and different forms of precarious part-time and temporary work (in which working conditions are set outside sectoral collective bargaining), expanded across the whole economy. The case of temporary workers is particularly flagrant. They are subcontracted employees and perform the same task as directly employed workers, but their wages and working conditions are much lower, because they are based on different agreements (normally, in the business services agreement), negotiated by weak unions. Figure 5.7 illustrates that approximately 25 percent of the workforce are non-standard workers. Naturally, the number of working hours and the institutional conditions regulating the job are determinants of wages. Thus, this sort of working time distribution strategy constitutes one of the main vectors of wage and income inequality in the country. Stated differently, in Germany a *trade-off* between inequality and unemployment exists.

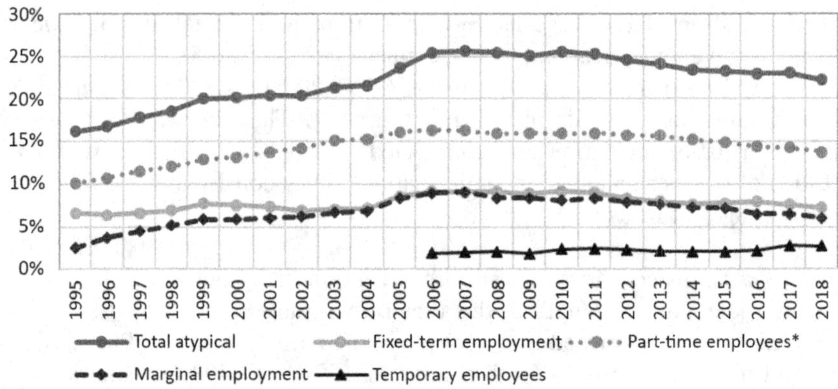

Figure 5.7 Evolution of atypical employment (% of wage earners)
Source: Author's calculations based on Destatis www.destatis.de/EN
Note: * Only part-timers who worked ≤ 20h per week.

Nonetheless, the flexibilization at the margins is in stark contrast with the stability at the core. Contrary to economies like Sweden, Italy or Spain, in Germany, labor market reforms did not affect the employment protection legislation of standard contracts. The OECD's employment protection legislation index (EPL) remained stable throughout the period 1995–2013, while this same index for temporary contracts suffered one of the steepest falls among advanced economies. Germany is, therefore, a textbook case of a dual labor market.

4.1 The labor market "miracle" during the Great Recession

Labor market reforms provoked a pronounced change in the relationship between output and unemployment growth (the so-called Okun coefficient, Figure 5.8). From 2006 onward, the evolution of the unemployment rate became less responsive to economic growth. Interestingly, this change did not imply high levels of unemployment; on the contrary, the unemployment rate decreased as a consequence of the policies for distribution of working time implemented.

Such (relative) independence of unemployment from the business cycle was evidenced during the Great Recession. In 2009, Germany was hit by the crisis like the rest of Europe. Exporting firms were particularly affected (exports fell 18.3 percent), since the demand from the main commercial partner at that time, the eurozone, dropped sharply. However, in spite of the negative output growth, the rise in unemployment was negligible (0.7 pp between the fourth quarter of 2008 and the third quarter of 2009), and from 2010 onward this variable continued declining at the same pace as previous years.

Despite multilateral institutions praising the liberalizing reforms undertaken (Hüfner & Klein, 2012), the successful crisis management in Germany is

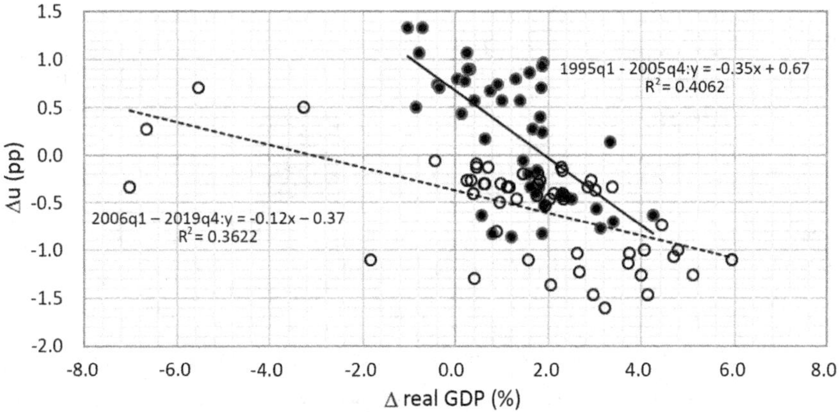

Figure 5.8 Okun's law before and after the Hartz reforms
Source: Author's calculations based on Ameco https://ec.europa.eu/info/business-economy-euro/indicators-statistics/economic-databases/macro-economic-database-ameco_en

mainly explained by the implementation of some institutional tools that already existed, and that are at the core of its traditional corporative IIRR system (Herzog-Stein, Lindner & Sturn, 2018a; Reisenbichler & Morgan, 2012). This set of tools comprises the well-known short-time work schemes (*Kurzarbeit*), as well as other instruments non-statutorily defined but agreed between individual businesses, workers and collective actors in the context of social concertation, such as paid overtime hours, working-time accounts and temporary deviation from regular working hours through opening clauses. During the Great Recession, each of the four types of instruments was employed in a similar proportion by companies. According to estimations by Herzog-Stein et al. (2018a), thanks to the reduction in hours worked per employee, 1.27 million jobs were safeguarded, while 1.35 million were preserved due to the drop in labor productivity.

Our results agree with these estimations. Figure 5.9 illustrates that the 2009 economic shock was absorbed equally by the reduction of the hours worked per employee (-2.96 percent) and labor productivity (-3.06 percent). In this manner, the number of people employed that year remained constant (0.15 percent).

As mentioned above, exporting firms were the most affected by the economic downturn. However, they evidenced their willingness to undertake labor hoarding, because they had previously invested in their formation, and between 2005 and 2007 they experienced difficulties in finding skilled workers, with industry-specific skills (Möller, 2010; Reisenbichler & Morgan, 2012). At the same time, it should be pointed out that economic expectations also played an important role in explaining the "miracle." Exporting firms envisioned that world demand would recover rapidly, and, therefore, they would need a supply of skilled workers to handle it. An illustrative example of the role played by expectations is that companies kept recruiting apprentices, who, after finishing

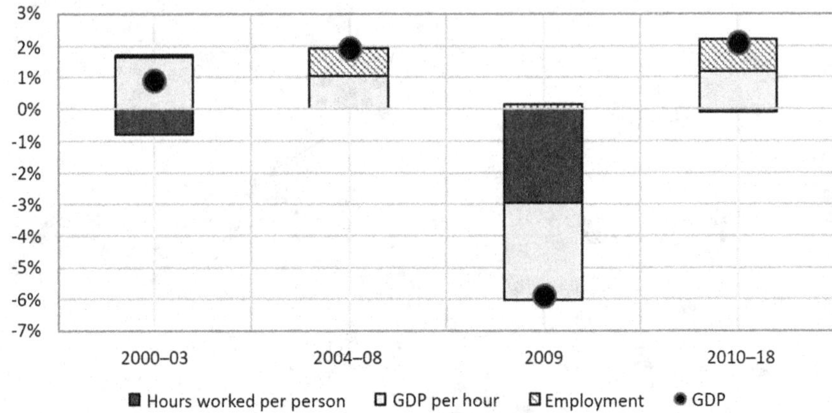

Figure 5.9 GDP growth and its components
Source: Author's calculations based on Ameco https://ec.europa.eu/info/business-economy-euro/indicators-statistics/economic-databases/macro-economic-database-ameco_en

their training, were hired in a standard labor contract (Bosch, 2011). Indeed, world demand recovered over the following three years, and the German export basket quickly recovered thanks to the economic growth in China and the US. Since then, the eurozone has stopped being the first destination of the country's exports and German firms are still main actors in the international market.

Nonetheless, it is worth mentioning that dualization dynamics had a significant presence in the crisis management. As Figure 5.10 shows, non-standard workers bore the bulk of the external flexibility measures (layoffs) undertaken, since layoff costs of these types of contracts are lower, while aggregate standard employment did not suffer the shock. Interestingly, temporary agency work is the most common form of atypical employment in manufacturing industries, and its marked decrease in 2008–2009 reflects the gap in bargaining power between core and peripheral workers, and the different adjustment channels used by firms. However, all types of employment show a rapid recovery right after the crisis.

5 The wage-labor nexus: dualism and inequality

The development of wages and working conditions in Germany is fundamentally explained by institutional factors. Moreover, the ability of the exporting manufacturing sector to influence wage policies across the entire economy has been a determinant of the process. The literature has widely discussed the transformation of the IIRR system (Eichhorst, 2015; Hassel, 1999; 2014; Silvia, 2013; Streeck, 2009) and has highlighted the following tendencies (which are summarized in Table 5.4).

First, as in the rest of European economies, both trade unions and employers' association density have declined significantly. In the German case, this trend

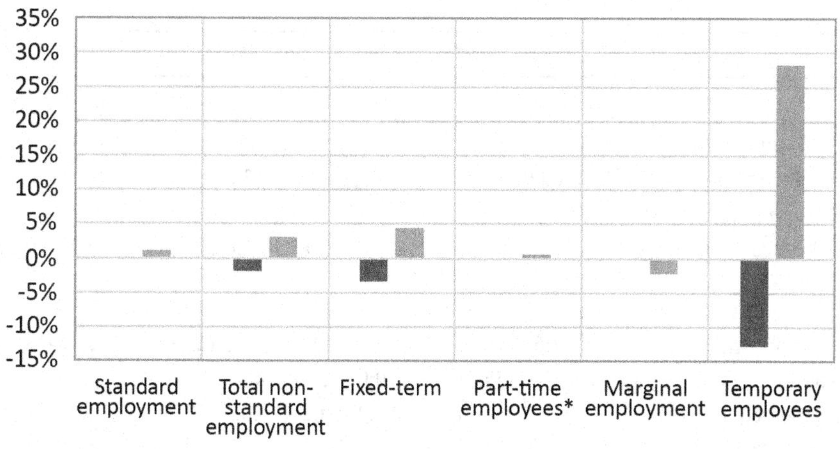

Figure 5.10 Growth rates of standard and non-standard employment during the Great Recession

Source: Author's calculations based on Destatis www.destatis.de/EN

Note: * Only part-timers who worked ≤ 20h per week.

began just after reunification (Silvia, 1997). At present, the bulk of union affiliates are concentrated in the manufacturing sector, as well as firm members. Collective actors are still strong in this sector, and especially in metalworking and the chemical industries, where the main unions are IG Metall and IG BCE, and the most important business' associations are Gesamtmetall and BAVC. In the rest of the economy, collective representation is much weaker and individual work relations dominate (Schulten & Bispinck, 2018).

Traditionally, the German system of collective bargaining was characterized by encompassing sectoral agreements and a high level of coordination among industries to set wages. Nevertheless, the coverage of collective bargaining has dramatically fallen since the mid-1990s. Currently, only 56 percent of employees in western federal states and 46 percent in the East are covered by collective agreements. When looking at the share of workplaces covered, the numbers are even smaller (29 percent and 20 percent, respectively). Such a fall has been driven by several factors. In the first place, by the decrease in affiliation of businesses' associations, since it is compulsory for standard members to comply with the sectoral agreement. Furthermore, in order to prevent the loss of their members, in 1993, employers introduced a special membership status (*Ohne Tarifbindung*), which relieves firms of the duty of following the collective agreement, while providing them with the rest of the association services. This way, the drain on membership slowed down partially, but the fall in coverage continued. Additionally, the coverage rate of work councils, with information, consultation and co-determination rights, decreased as well. Between 1996 and 2015, the share

Table 5.4 Evolution of IIRR indicators: workers and establishments covered (in brackets)

	1999–2008		*2009–2018*	
	Average (%)	*Growth**	*Average (%)*	*Growth**
Trade union density	22.3	-6.3	17.8	-2.3
Employers' org. density**	63.0	-	43.0	-
Western federal states				
Collective bargaining coverage	68.0 (44.4)	-10.0 (-9.0)	60.0 (32.8)	-9.0 (-10.0)
• Sectoral	60.4 (41.5)	-10.0 (-9.0)	52.4 (30.7)	-7.0 (-9.0)
• Firm	7.6 (2.9)	0.0 (0.0)	7.6 (2.2)	-2.0 (-1.0)
Not covered	32.0 (55.7)	10.0 (11.0)	40.1 (66.9)	8.0 (10.0)
• Oriented	16.2 (23.0)	6.2 (6.0)	20.4 (27.8)	4.0 (5.0)
• Non-oriented	15.8 (33.5)	3.8 (5.0)	19.7 (39.1)	4.0 (5.0)
Eastern federal states				
Collective bargaining coverage	54.3 (24.7)	-5.0 (-3.0)	47.8 (20.6)	-5.0 (-3.0)
• Sectoral	42.5 (20.6)	-6.0 (-2.0)	36.1 (17.6)	-3.0 (-2.0)
• Firm	11.8 (4.1)	1.0 (0.0)	11.7 (3.0)	-2.0 (-1.0)
Not covered	46.0 (75.2)	5.0 (2.0)	52.1 (79.4)	6.0 (3.0)
• Oriented	23.2 (31.3)	1.0 (-2.0)	25.0 (31.9)	0.0 (-2.0)
• Non-oriented	22.8 (43.9)	4.0 (4.0)	27.1 (47.5)	6.0 (5.0)

Notes: * The growth of each variable is the total difference between the last and first year of the period expressed in percentage points. ** Employers' organization density represents the number of workers and salaried employees in private sector firms organized in the employers' association as a share of the total workforce in the private sector. Data available only for years 2002 and 2013.
Source: Wirtschafts- und Sozialwissenschaftliches Institut (2019) and author's calculations based on AIASS dataset.

of employees represented in a work council dropped 10 pp, reaching 44 percent in western federal states and 37 percent in the East (Oberfichtner & Schnabel, 2019). Consequently, this factor, along with the general weakening of unions, directed the trend of the sectoral agreements coverage, since workers' representatives have not been strong enough to force many employers into collective bargaining, and could not stop the individualization of the wage setting agreements. As a result, the traditional dual system of IIRR (i.e. the joint presence of collective agreement and work councils) covered 39.6 percent of workers (9.4 percent of workplaces) in 2015 (Oberfichtner & Schnabel, 2019). This is quite relevant, since the dual system has always been the core of the German cooperative or coordinated IIRR. It has long been documented that the division of functions, by which distributional issues were settled outside of workplaces, while work councils mainly focused on organizational and productive matters, encouraged a climate of cooperation between the workforce and the firm's management at the plant level and has led companies to obtain positive economic outcomes regarding innovation, productivity, or even total profits (Freeman & Lazear, 1995; Jacobi et al., 1992; Müller & Stegmaier, 2017). Thus, German labor relations became much more conflicted and individualized.

Not only did the IIRR coverage decrease, but the content of the agreements also became more flexible. During the late 1990s, in the context of the *Pacts for Employment and Competitiveness* (*Bündnisse für Arbeit und Wettbewerbsfähigkeit*), a broad concessionary bargaining process among collective actors, opening clauses in collective agreements were generalized. These clauses were originally designed for companies with economic difficulties (mainly in the East), but in practice they are used by healthy firms to adjust the content of sectoral agreements to their specific situation, allowing them to cut wages or reorganize working time (Seifert & Massa-Wirth, 2005). This way, the decision process on wages and working conditions has been progressively decentralized to workplaces, in which work councils (when they do exist), have tended to exchange internal flexibility measures and wage restraint for employment protection, investment compromises, and training for workers.

Nonetheless, it should be stressed that these agreements have not covered most workers. What characterizes the transformation process of German labor institutions is that it has been driven by a coalition between employers and the core workers of large exporting manufacturing firms (Baccaro & Pontusson, 2016; Palier & Thelen, 2010). Work councils and unions, in which the main affiliates are core workers, did not oppose liberalization of atypical employment nor the increase in temporary agency workers in the company staff in order to preserve their own working conditions. At the same time, industrial firms were able to recover their profit margins and regain competitiveness by the reduction of ULC (Eichhorst, 2015; Hassel, 2014).

Third, outsourcing strategies undertaken by manufacturing and large service firms also contributed to the drop in the collective bargaining coverage. Subcontracting of (mainly) low-level service activities contributed to the rise of a secondary segment comprised of workers on the margins of IIRR institutions, where wages are much lower and unions and work councils are weak (Doellgast & Greer, 2007; Holst, 2014).

As a result, bargaining on wages and working conditions of a large proportion of the workforce became increasingly individualized. The erosion and decentralization of collective bargaining, in combination with the above-mentioned reforms on the margins of the labor market, created the conditions for the coexistence of a secondary segment or periphery of workers, with an inferior status in terms of salaries and employment protection, that provide external flexibility to the labor market, alongside another core segment that enjoy high wages and working conditions.

Both processes are the basis of two important developments: (1) the sharp wage restraint across the whole economy (especially strong until the Great Recession); and (2) the rise in income inequality.

5.1 Wage moderation

The period of sharpest wage restraint in Germany was before the Great Recession, when the main institutional reforms of the labor market and the IIRR system were implemented. During those years, along with the institutional factors, the gradual increase in the unemployment rate harmed workers' bargaining capacity. Consequently, the average mean wage decreased 4.6 percent and the wage share dropped 7.9 pp between 1995 and 2007 (Figure 5.11).

As mentioned above, the trend followed by wages was driven by a double process. On the one hand, the moderation of wages agreed between trade unions and business' associations in collective bargaining was extended across the whole economy through the system of pattern bargaining (negotiated wages grew 0.8 percent per year). In turn, new bargaining rounds at the firm level between work councils and management contributed to squeeze wages even more. Here, core workers exchanged employment stability for investment compromises. On the other hand, the deregulation on the margins of the labor market, the rise in non-standard work and the overall erosion of the IIRR system boosted the wage restraint as well.

Scholars in political economy have pointed out that both processes are just "two sides of the same coin" (Thelen, 2014: 51). The core workforce not only protected their working conditions through externalizing the toughest consequences of the wage restraint to the periphery of the labor market. Additionally, the wage moderation in the periphery has been passed onto

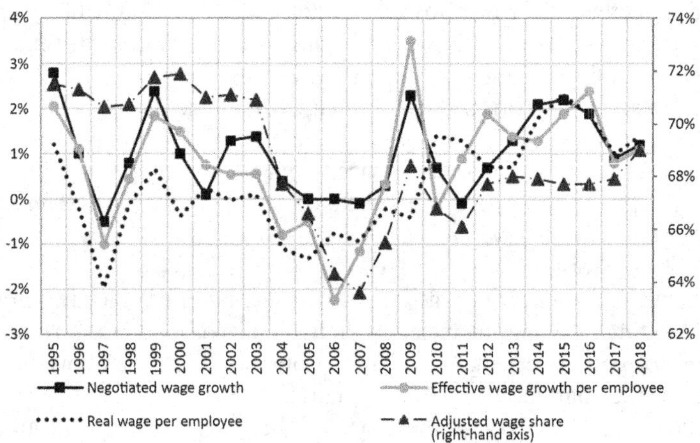

Figure 5.11 Annual growth rates of the negotiated and effective wage and evolution of the wage share

Source: Author's calculations based on Wirtschafts- und Sozialwissenschaftliches Institut (2019).

Note * The large rise in actual earnings in 2009 is due to special factors during the Great Recession, such as the reduction of positive balances on working time accounts with no cut in remuneration (Deutsche Bundesbank, 2018).

domestic prices, thus improving the real wages of core workers. Due to this particular trend, Germany is the only European economy, along with Austria, in which wages in services grew less than in manufacturing (Hassel, 2014). This is a quite remarkable fact given that services are more sheltered from international competition.

Furthermore, Figure 5.11 shows that the formal principle of favorability[8] in collective bargaining has been eroded with the transformation of the IIRR system. It can be appreciated that the average agreed wage growth fell below the effective wage growth per employee, i.e. it stopped acting as a wage "floor" (as in the traditional German model) to become a mere reference for economic agents at the firm level. Put differently, the wage drift (differences between the rates of variation of the average real wage and the average agreed wage) was negative in most years during this period, and remained this way during phases of both economic growth and recession. It is also possible to observe in Figure 5.11 that after the Great Recession, average wages slowly recovered (mean real wage increased 1.1 percent per year) and the labor share increased 3.5 pp. Despite unemployment having reached an all-time low and labor shortages for highly skilled jobs, social agents keep negotiating low wage growth and, at the same time, the high rates of atypical employment acted as a barrier to wage increases on the margins of the labor market.

5.2 The growth of wage inequality

Since the mid-1990s, a distinguishing feature of coordinated market economies (CMEs) in general and Germany in particular has been the growth in income inequality, particularly at the lower end of the distribution, due to the erosion of labor institutions and the above-mentioned dualization dynamics (Baccaro & Pontusson, 2016; Behringer & Van Treeck, 2019; Dustmann et al., 2009). As previously argued, the wage squeeze in Germany has been unequal due to the specific features of the institutional change. Social agreement has always been oriented toward the moderation of the nominal wages in core industries, and top management remuneration is less dependent on financial goals, so top wages have grown less than in other economies, particularly the Anglo-Saxon ones. Therefore, the rise in wage inequality is due to the sclerotic growth rates of lower wages relative to the median wage, rather than the sharp growth of higher wages.

After the Great Recession, this sort of dualization dynamics is still in place. As a result of these trends, the German low-wage sector is one of the largest among advanced economies. According to our results, based on OECD data (Figure 5.12), the low-wage segment increased 5 pp before the crisis, and has remained stable since then. In 2017, its size was 18.3 percent. However, research based on the German Socio-Economic Panel (SOEP) estimates that it is much larger: around 23 percent of the salary earners in 2017 (including atypical workers) and 24.5 percent of total job contracts belong to this segment (Gräbka & Schröder, 2019). Actually, Gräbka and Schröder also show that

Figure 5.12 Evolution of low and high pay incidence (3 years moving average)
Source: Author's calculations based on OECD.stats.

higher real wage deciles were barely affected by the crisis. On the contrary, the last three deciles of the real wage distribution were the most hard-hit, and, although they have started to grow again since then, they experienced a total decrease of between 5 percent and 10 percent over the period of 1995–2017.

However, what the literature has not highlighted enough is the change in inequality patterns after the Great Recession, when high-end inequality started to grow progressively. Overall, high-pay incidence has increased 2 pp since the crisis (Figure 5.13). Furthermore, in comparative terms, it can be appreciated that the relationship between decile 9 and decile 5 of the income distribution of

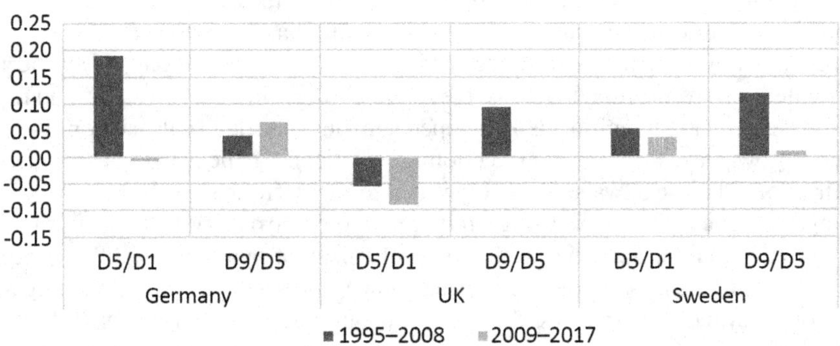

Figure 5.13 Change in high and low-end inequality (gross earnings full-time employees; 3 years moving average)
Source: Author's calculations based on www.OECD.stats
Note: D5/D1 is the ratio between the median wage (5th decile) and the 1st decile of the wage distribution; D9/D5 is the ratio between the 9th decile and the median wage.

full-time employees has increased much more in Germany than in the UK or Sweden. The elite of core workers and top management have benefited more from the economic recovery than the median worker. Although further evidence is needed, the evolution of top-end inequality might be related with the recovery of the wage share from 2009 onward. As in liberal market economies, the ongoing growth of top wages more than compensate the weak evolution of the lower ones, thus boosting average wage growth above productivity (Behringer & van Treeck, 2018a).

A brief note on the growth of income inequality might be appropriate here. Several papers point out that this sort of inequality (as well as wealth inequality) is underestimated in Germany due to the "corporate veil hypothesis." The story is based on the very institutional foundations of the German growth model. The hypothesis holds that companies retain a significant portion of their profits, instead of passing them onto private households in the form of higher salaries for top management. Therefore, the degree of income inequality would be much greater if firms had acted similarly to their Anglo-Saxon counterparts (Behringer et al., 2020; Behringer & van Treeck, 2019; IMF, 2019). This behavior is explained by the following institutional factors: on the one hand, shareholder orientation strategies are less common in Germany than in liberal countries. Moreover, family-owned companies or *Mittelstand* constitute a large proportion of the firms in the economy. As previously argued, these companies have less incentives for profit-sharing. On the other hand, the relatively high taxes on distributed profits encourage the increase in corporate savings, rather than profit-sharing. Therefore, in the case of the *Mittelstand*, the law incentivizes the use of corporations as piggybanks (Ruscher & Wolff, 2012, cited in Behringer & van Treeck, 2019: 15). These particularities contribute to explaining why the wage share has fallen sharply while high-end inequality and top incomes have increased very little in comparison with other advanced economies. In the absence of these institutional mechanisms, one would expect higher top incomes than the actual ones.

5.3 *An ongoing process of dualization?*

In spite of the dynamics described above, it is worth highlighting that institutional change should not be understood as an irrevocable process toward liberalization. Usually, periods of deregulation alternate with others in which re-regulation dominates. In the German case, this occurs due to the existing relationship between the core and the periphery of the model, which are not self-contained areas. On the contrary, as the dualization process advances, competing relationships emerge and intensify between both segments, and public opinion on inequality also changes (Eichhorst & Marx, 2011; Marx & Starke, 2017). In dynamic terms, the process of dualization generates endogenous dynamics that make dominant social blocs react and correct some of its most pernicious consequences.

At some point, for instance, in manufacturing, the expansion of temporary agency work negatively affected core skilled workers, which are part of the dominant social bloc (Benassi, 2016). At first, workforce segmentation strategies in Germany are marked by classical variables, i.e., the skill level of the worker and the job routine. This way, once labor institutions weaken and the employment relationship becomes increasingly liberalized, workers who are less skilled, as well as those who perform routine tasks, are primarily affected. However, the weaker the IIRR institutions, the easier it would be for employers to use non-standard job contracts and the higher the number of workers who would be affected by dualization. As dualization has moved forward, wage competition dynamics between skilled core workers and others with the same skill level (usually younger workers and with less labor market experience) and employed in temporary agencies increase (Eichhorst, 2015). Thus, due to the extreme deregulation of the periphery of the labor market, core employees see their working conditions threatened by more and more workers and the manufacturing social bloc narrows gradually.

For these reasons, trade unions have paid more attention to the situation of peripheral workers and have exerted growing pressure for the re-regulation of the secondary segment of the labor market. In this sense, IG Metall has led several campaigns to improve collective bargaining and wages of temporary agency workers (Benassi & Dorigatti, 2015; 2018). For instance, laws on minimum wages were passed in several industries, and the union made it so that after 24 months working for the same subcontractor, temporary workers have to be directly hired by the client.

Likewise, the increase in inequality has affected public opinion, which has become more critical of institutional dualization. Thus, there are incentives for trade unions and political parties to defend the institutional reorganization of the labor market, i.e. rewards in terms of both affiliates and electoral votes (Béland, 2010; Marx & Starke, 2017). This tendency accounts for the emergence of new initiatives that, *a priori*, are against the logic of dualization. The most important one is the introduction of a statutory minimum wage in 2015 (€8.5 per hour; and increased to €8.87 in 2017), which naturally affects less protected employees and implies an important landmark mainly for mini-job holders. In an assessment report of this policy, Herzog-Stein et al. (2018b) estimate a positive impact on wages and salaries, as well as a structural shift away from marginal work to employment involving mandatory social security contributions, thus entailing more rights for workers (e.g. unemployment insurance), while changes in the volume of total hours worked were insignificant. Furthermore, the approval of a statutory minimum wage implied a change in the German collective bargaining model. The principle of autonomy of collective bargaining is constitutionally guaranteed. It establishes that social agents are the only ones with the competences to bargain and take decisions on topics related to industrial relations. Because of this, manufacturing trade unions have traditionally been reluctant to accept the introduction of a national minimum wage, since it implies the political intervention in a field (more or less) dominated by them. Nonetheless, an increasing section of their own affiliates, as well as service unions and public opinion in general, pressed for the introduction of this policy, persuading both manufacturing unions and business' associations of the suitability of this policy.

Furthermore, these processes of re-regulation on the margins were accompanied by the reduction of unemployment, resulting in a slight recovery of the bargaining capacity of peripheral workers. As a consequence, low wages have slightly recovered during the last 10 years, although they are still below the mid-1990s levels (Gräbka & Schröder, 2019). This trend in low wages may have contributed in some way to the recovery of the wage share. Therefore, one might think that the slight rebalancing of the German growth model since 2010, thanks to domestic demand growth, is partially grounded in these events.

Lastly, it is worth mentioning that the conservative fiscal policy stance and the concern with budgetary stability have been at the center of the political debate in 2019. In 2019, Germany displayed low growth rates due to the slowdown of the world trade and the commercial war between the US and China. During that year, discussions among policy-makers on the need to implement a more expansive fiscal policy intensified. In 2020, due to the COVID-19 crisis, the goal of budgetary stability has been cast aside and the country has launched the largest stimulus package among European economies. Once more, Germany showed that, in spite of its traditional obsession with fiscal consolidation, when required, the government will respond more vigorously than its European partners.

6 Conclusion

This chapter examined the extreme export-led German growth model from 2000 onward. Our analysis points to the centrality of the exporting manufacturing social bloc in properly understanding most aspects of the economic and institutional dynamics. The whole story is summarized in Figure 5.14.

Advanced manufacturing industries (i.e. medium-high and high technology ones) are the main drivers of output growth. However, wage restraint and domestic price control policies, boosted by the dominant social bloc, are detrimental to output growth. On the one hand, those industries that are able to produce for the external market, as well as those ones with links to manufacturing, are not particularly harmed by these policies, as in the case of dynamic services. On the other hand, those economic activities that depend upon domestic market growth are badly affected by wage moderation (this is the case of non-dynamic services).

The institutional reforms undertaken in the labor market and the IIRR system led to an overall but also unequal wage moderation. Although exports have grown a lot, the empirical results of much of the specialized literature suggest that the link between ULC and international competitiveness is rather weak in the German case. It seems quite clear that the drop in ULC was not

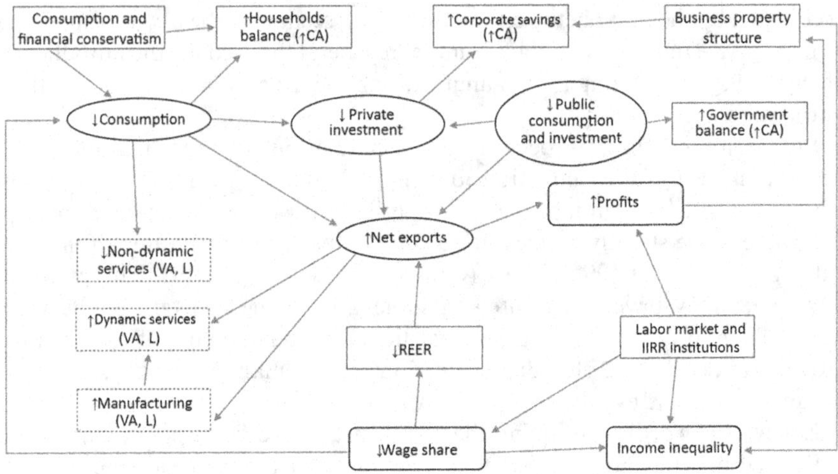

Figure 5.14 The mechanics of German capitalism

completely passed onto prices, resulting in larger profit margins for exporting firms. Wage cuts have not been compensated for by higher household indebtedness levels, so domestic demand grew at a slow pace and, as a result, net exports ballooned. Since the Great Recession in 2009, wages have slightly recovered thanks to the low unemployment rate and certain re-regulation of the labor market, which partially reversed the pre-crisis liberalizing reform path. However, the slight recovery of both wages and the wage share were not strong enough to drive domestic demand growth up and encourage the development of non-dynamic services. Furthermore, the obsession with budgetary stability of the German federal government dampened demand growth as well (with the exception of the management of the Great Recession, when the fiscal impulse was large).

Regarding sectoral balances, the interaction between labor market duality, weak domestic demand and disincentives for investment, and the high proportion of family-owned businesses are the reasons behind the positive corporate balance since 2002. Moreover, the household sector and the government display a net lender position as well (the latter in all years except during the Great Recession). Thus, the chronic current account surplus of the country is due to institutional factors too.

In a context in which the macroeconomic management is oriented toward the achievement of commercial surpluses and price control, the main strategy to fight against unemployment was the distribution of work time through the reduction of working hours of standard contracts and, especially, the widespread embracing of part-time atypical work. On the other hand, the evolution of wages was unequal. While they dropped at the lower end of the distribution, they grew slowly at the high end. These trends are reflecting a trade-off between inequality and employment growth.

All in all, it can be said that the German growth model, which is unbalanced and dependent on the evolution of international markets, and whose economic management is largely influenced by the interests of the manufacturing social bloc, is dysfunctional for the overall economic growth and the growth of income inequality.

Notes

1 *The Economist*, June 3, 1999: www.economist.com/special/1999/06/03/the-sick-man-of-the-euro
2 A vertically integrated variable is built by multiplying the diagonalized vector of production by the Leontief inverse matrix, and by the diagonalized vector of final demand. This operator, usually known as operator B, is in turn multiplied by the diagonalized vector of the variable that one wants to vertically integrate, such as the value added or employment (in such a way, the matrix commonly known as C is derived). Further information about this methodology can be found in Montresor and Vittucci Marzetti (2007).
3 To that end, the vertically integrated nominal wage is divided between vertically integrated real value added and vertically integrated real productivity. This indicator captures the mean wage costs directly or indirectly needed to produce one unit of a certain commodity in constant prices.
4 Through this informal coordination mechanism, the collective agreement reached in electrical and metalworking engineering between IG Metall and Gesamtmetall in Baden-Württemberg set the reference pace for other economic branches and regions. In this way, wage growth was coordinated among industries and the required price stability for an export-oriented economy was achieved.
5 The composition of German exports remained more or less constant throughout the period 2000–2018. Around 65 percent are high and medium-high technology goods, 27 percent are medium-low and low technology goods and the remaining 9 percent are service exports (based on Comext, own calculations).
6 A macroeconomic-oriented wage policy is defined as a wage growth rate across the whole economy of 2.65 percent. This implies that wage setters make full use of the distributional space arising from trend productivity growth and the inflation target of the European Central Bank (Horn et al., 2017)
7 According to data presented by Behringer and van Treeck (2019), nowadays the *Mittelstand* still accounts for 65 percent of total companies, 35 percent of total sales and 59 percent of employment.
8 The favorability principle or *Günstigkeitsprinzip* establishes that departures from collectively agreed norms at the workplace level could only be concluded in the employees' favor.

References

Albu, N., Joebges, H., & Zwiener, R. (2018). Increasing competitiveness at any price? A dispute with Dustmann et al. (2014). IMK Working Paper No. 192.

Baccaro, L., & Benassi, C. (2017). Throwing out the ballast: Growth models and the liberalization of German industrial relations. *Socio-economic Review*, 15 (1), 85–115.

Baccaro, L., & Howell, C. (2018). *Trajectories of neoliberal transformation*. Cambridge: Cambridge University Press.

Baccaro, L., & Pontusson, J. (2016). Rethinking comparative political economy: The growth model perspective. *Politics & Society*, 44 (2), 175–207.

Behringer, J., Kowall, N., Theobald, T., & van Treeck, T. (2020). Inequality in Germany: A macroeconomic perspective. *German Politics*, 29 (3), 479–497.

Behringer, J. &van Treeck, T. (2018a). Income distribution and the current account. *Journal of International Economics*, 114, 238–254.

Behringer J. van Treeck, T. (2018b). Varieties of capitalism and growth regimes: The role of income distribution. IMK Working Paper No. 194.

Behringer J. van Treeck, T. (2019). Income distribution and growth models: A sectoral balances approach. *Politics & Society*, 47 (3), 303–332.

Béland, D. (2010). Reconsidering policy feedback: How policies affect politics. *Administration & Society*, 42 (5), 568–590.

Benassi, C. (2016). Liberalization only at the margins? Analysing the growth of temporary work in German core manufacturing sectors. *British Journal of Industrial Relations*, 53 (3), 533–555.

Benassi, C., & Dorigatti, L. (2015). Straight to the core – explaining union responses to the casualization of work: The IG Metall campaign for agency workers. *British Journal of Industrial Relations*, 54 (3): 597–622.

Benassi, C., & Dorigatti, L. (2018). The political economy of agency work in Italy and Germany: Explaining diverging trajectories in collective bargaining outcomes. In V. Doellgast, N. Lillie, & V. Pulignano (Eds.), *Reconstructing solidarity: Labour unions, precarious work, and the politics of institutional change in Europe* (pp. 124–143). Oxford: Oxford University Press.

Bosch, G. (2011). The German labour market after the financial crisis: Miracle or just a good policy mix? In D. Vaughan-Whitehead (Ed.), *Work inequalities in the crisis? Evidence from Europe* (pp. 243–277). Cheltenham: Edward Elgar.

Braun, B., & Deeg, R. (2020). Strong firms, weak banks: The financial consequences of Germany's export-led growth model. *German Politics*. https://doi.org/10.1080/09644008.2019.1701657.

Carlin, W., & Soskice, D. (2009). German economic performance: Disentangling the role of supply-side reforms, macroeconomic policy and coordinated economy institutions. *Socio-Economic Review*, 7 (1): 67–99.

Castaldi, C. (2009). The relative weight of manufacturing and services in Europe: An innovation perspective. *Technological Forecasting and Social Change*, 76, 709–722.

Cesaratto, S., & Stirati, A. (2010). Germany and the European and global crises. *International Journal of Political Economy*, 39 (4): 56–86.

Ciriaci, D., & Palma, D. (2016). Structural change and blurred sectoral boundaries: Assessing the extent to which knowledge-intensive business services satisfy manufacturing final demand in Western countries. *Economic Systems Research*, 28 (1), 55–77.

Den Hertog, P. (2000). Knowledge-intensive business services as co-producers of innovation. *International Journal of Innovation Management*, 4, 491–528.

Deutsche Bundesbank (2018). Wage growth in Germany: Assessment and determinants of recent developments. *Monthly Report*, April 2018.

Doellgast, V., & Greer, I. (2007). Vertical disintegration and the disorganization of German industrial relations. *British Journal of Industrial Relations*, 45 (1), 55–76.

Dustmann, C., Fitzenberger, B., Schönberg, U., & Spitz-Oener, A. (2014). From sick man to economic superstar: Germany's resurgent economy. *Journal of Economic Perspectives*, 28 (1), 167–188.

Dustmann, C., Fitzenberger, B., Schönberg, U., Spitz-Oener, A., Ludsteck, J., & Schönberg, U. (2009). Revisiting the German wage structure. *The Quarterly Journal of Economics*, 124 (2), 843–881.

Eichhorst, W. (2015). The unexpected appearance of a new German model. *British Journal of Industrial Relations*, 53 (1), 49–69.

Eichhorst, W., & Marx, P. (2011). Reforming German labour market institutions: A dual path for flexibility. *Journal of European Social Policy*, 21 (1), 73–87.

European Commission (2010). The impact of the global crisis on competitiveness and current accounts divergences in the euro area. *Quarterly Report on the Euro Area*, 9 (1).

Franke, R., & Kalmbach, P. (2005). Structural change in the manufacturing sector and its impact on business-related services: An input-output study for Germany. *Structural Change and Economic Dynamics*, 16, 467–488.

Franzese, R. J., & Hall, P. A. (2000). Institutional dimensions of coordinated wage bargaining and monetary policy. In T. Iversen, J. Pontusson, & D. Soskice (Eds.), *Unions, employers and central banks: Macroeconomic coordination and institutional change in social market economies* (pp. 173–204). Cambridge: Cambridge University Press.

Freeman, R. B., & Lazear, E. P. (1995). An economic analysis of work councils. In J. Rogers & W. Streeck (Eds.), *Work councils: Consultation, representation and cooperation in industrial relations* (pp. 27–52). Chicago: University of Chicago Press.

Goldschmidt, D., & Schmieder, J. F. (2017). The rise of domestic outsourcing and the evolution of the German wage structure. *The Quarterly Journal of Economics*, 132 (3), 1165–1217.

Gräbka, M. M., & Schröder, C. (2019). The low-wage sector in Germany is larger than previously assumed. *DIW Weekly Report*, 14.

Hall, P. A., & Soskice, D. (Eds.). (2001). *Varieties of capitalism: The institutional foundations of comparative advantage*. Oxford: Oxford University Press.

Hassel, A. (1999). The erosion of the German system of industrial relations. *British Journal of Industrial Relations*, 37 (3), 483–505.

Hassel, A. (2014). The paradox of liberalization: Understanding dualism and the recovery of the German political economy. *British Journal of Industrial Relations*, 52 (1), 57–81.

Hassel, A.(2017). No way to escape imbalances in the Eurozone? Three sources for Germany's exports dependency: industrial relations, social insurance and fiscal federalism. *German Politics*, doi:10.1080/09644008.2017.134281.

Hein, E., & Vogel, L. (2008). Distribution and growth reconsidered: Empirical results for six OECD countries. *Cambridge Journal of Economics*, 32 (3), 479–511.

Hein, E., & Vogel, L. (2009). Distribution and growth in France and Germany: Single equation estimations and model simulations based on the Bhaduri/Marglin model. *Review of Political Economy*, 21 (2), 245–272.

Herrero, D. (2020). Productive linkages in a segmented model: Analyzing the role of services in the exporting performance of German manufacturing. ICEI Working Paper No. 05/20. Available at: www.ucm.es/icei/file/wp0520.

Herrigel, G. (2015). Globalization and the German industrial production model. *Journal of Labor Market Research*, 48 (2), 133–149.

Herzog-Stein, A., Lindner, F., & Sturn, S. (2018a). The German employment miracle in the Great Recession: The significance and institutional foundations of temporary working-time reductions. *Oxford Economic Papers*, 70 (1), 206–224.

Herzog-Stein, A., Logeay, C., Nüß, P, Stein, U., & Zwiener, R. (2018b). The positive impact of the statutory minimum wage. *IMK Report*, 141e, September.

Holst, H. (2014). Commodifying institutions: Vertical disintegration and institutional change in German labour relations. *Work, Employment and Society*, 28 (1), 3–20.

Höpner, M. (2019). The German undervaluation regime under Bretton Woods: How Germany became the nightmare of the world economy. *MPIfG Discussion Paper*, 19 (1).

Horn, G., Lindner, F., Stephan, S., & Zwiener, R. (2017). The role of nominal wages in trade and current account surpluses: An econometric analysis. *IMK Report*, 125e, June.

Hüfner, F., & Klein, C. (2012), The German labour market: Preparing for the future. *OECD* Economics Department Working Paper No. 983. http://dx.doi.org/10.1787/5k92sn01tzzv-en.

IMF (2019). IMF Country Report No. 19/214, July.

Jacobi, O., Keller, B., & Muller-Jentsch, W. (1992). Germany: Codetermining the future. In A. Ferner & R. Hyman (Eds.), *Industrial relations in the new Europe* (pp. 218–270). Oxford: Blackwell.

Keller, E. (2018). Noisy business politics: Lobbying strategies and business influence After the financial crisis. *Journal of European Public Policy*, 25 (3), 287–306.

Lindlar, L., & Holtfrerich, C. L. (1997). Geography, exchange rates and trade structures: Germany's export performance since the 1950s. *European Review of Economic History*, 1 (2), 217–246.

Marx, P., & Starke, P. (2017). Dualization as a destiny? The political economy of the German minimum wage reform. *Politics & Society*, 45 (4), 559–584.

Möller, J. (2010). The German labor market response in the world recession: De-mystifying a miracle. *Journal for Labour Market Research*, 42 (4), 325–336.

Montresor, S., & Vittucci Marzetti, G. (2007) Outsourcing and structural change. What can an input-output analysis say about it? *Economia Politica*, 14, 43–78.

Müller, S., & Stegmaier, J. (2017). Why is there resistance to work councils in Germany? An economic perspective. *Economic and Industrial Democracy*. https://doi.org/10.1177/0143831X17734296.

Naastepad, C. W. M., & Storm, S. (2006). OECD demand regimes (1960–2000). *Journal of Post Keynesian Economics*, 29 (2), 211–246.

Oberfichtner, M., & Schnabel, C. (2019). The German model of industrial relations: (Where) does it still exist? *Journal of Economics and Statistics*, 239 (1), 5–37.

Onaran, Ö., & Galanis, G. (2011). Is aggregate demand wage-led or profit-led? National and global effects. In *Conditions of Work and Employment Branch*. Geneva: ILO.

Onaran, O. & Obst, T. (2016). Wage-led growth in the EU15 member states: The effects of income distribution on growth, investment, trade balance, and inflation. Post Keynesian Economics Study Group, Working Paper No. 1602.

Palier, B., & Thelen, K. (2010). Institutionalizing dualism: Complementarities and change in France and Germany. *Politics & Society*, 38 (1), 119–148.

Passinetti, L. (1973). The notion of vertical integration in economic analysis. *Metroeconomica*, 25, 1–29.

Peneder, M., & Streicher, G. (2018). De-industrialization and comparative advantage in the global value chain. *Economic Systems Research*, 30 (1), 85–104.

Reisenbichler, A., & Morgan, K.J. (2012). From 'sick man' to 'miracle': Explaining the robustness of the German labor market during and after the financial crisis 2008–09. *Politics & Society*, 40 (4), 549–579.

Sarra, A., Di Bernardo, C., & Quaglione, D. (2018). Deindustrialization and the technological intensity of manufacturing subsystems in the European Union. *Economia Politica*, 36, 205–243.

Schulten, T. (2018). The role of extension in German collective bargaining. In S. Hayter & J. Visser (Eds.), *Collective agreements: Extending labour protection* (pp. 65–92). Geneva: ILO.

Schulten, T., & Bispinck, R. (2018). Varieties of decentralisation in German collective bargaining. In S. Leonardi & R. Pedersini (Eds.), *Multi-employer bargaining under pressure: Decentralisation trends in five European countries* (pp. 105–149). Brussels: ETUI.

Seifert, H.,& Massa-Wirth, H. (2005). Pacts for employment and competitiveness in Germany. *Industrial Relations Journal*, 36 (3), 217–240.

Silvia, S. J. (1997). German unification and emerging divisions within German employers' associations: Cause or catalyst? *Comparative Politics*, 29 (2), 187–208.

Silvia, S. J.(2013). *Holding the shop together: German industrial relations in the postwar era*. Ithaca, NY: Cornell University Press.

Silvia, S. J., & Schroeder, W. (2007). Why are German associations declining? Arguments and evidence. *Comparative Political Studies*, 40 (2), 1433–1459.

Sorge, A., & Streeck, W. (1987). *Industrial relations and technical change: The case for an extended perspective*. Berlin: Wissenschaftszentrum.

Stockhammer, E., Hein, E., & Grafl, L. (2011). Globalization and the effects of changes in functional income distribution on aggregate demand in Germany. *International Review of Applied Economics*, 25 (1), 1–23.

Storm, S., & Naastepad, C. W. M. (2015). Crisis and recovery in the German economy: The real lessons. *Structural Change and Economic Dynamics*, 32, 11–24.

Streeck, W. (1991). On the institutional conditions of diversified quality production. In E. Matzer & W. Streeck (Eds). *Beyond Keynesianism: The socio-economics of production and full employment* (pp. 21–61). Cheltenham: Edward Elgar.

Streeck, W. (2009). *Re-forming capitalism: Institutional change in the German political economy*. Oxford: Oxford University Press.

Thelen, K. (2014). *Varieties of liberalization and the new politics of social solidarity*. New York: Cambridge University Press.

Tomlinson, M. (2000). The contribution of knowledge-intensive services to the manufacturing industry. In B. Andersen, J. Howells, R. Hull, I. Miles, & J. Roberts (Eds.), *Knowledge and innovation in the new service economy* (pp. 36–48). Cheltenham: Edward Elgar.

Windrum, P., & Tomlinson, M. (1999). Knowledge-intensive services and international competition: a four country comparison. *Technology Analysis & Strategic Management*, 11, 439–445.

Wirtschafts- und Sozialwissenschaftliches Institut (2019). WSI-Tarifarchiv 2019, June, Düsseldorf: WSI.

Appendix

Table A5.1 Classification of economic activities (ISIC revision 4)

1. Manufacturing

1.1 High and medium-high technology

C20, C21, C26, C27, C28, C29, C30

1.2 Medium and medium-low technology

C10, C11, C12, C13, C14, C15, C16, C17, C18, C19, C22, C23, C24, C25, C31, C32, C33

2. Services (see Table 5.1)

2.1 Dynamic services

45, 46, J, K, L, M, N

2.2 Non-dynamic services

47, I, P, Q, S, T

3 Services (see Figures 5.1 and 5.2)

3.1 Business services

J62, J63, M69, M70, M71, M72, M73, N74, M75, N

3.2 Personal services

G47, I, P85, Q, R, S

3.3 Distribution

G45, G46, H49, H50, H51, H52, H53

3.4 Financial

K64, K65, K66, L68

6 The impact of the institutional change on the economic growth path in Greece

Juan Rafael Ruiz and Oana Cristian

COMPLUTENSE UNIVERSITY OF MADRID AND COMPLUTENSE INSTITUTE FOR INTERNATIONAL STUDIES

1 Introduction

In this chapter, we analyze the different growth patterns of the Greek economy between the period before joining the eurozone to the last decade, from a socio-structural perspective (Chapter 2). Despite the small size of its economy compared to that of other EU countries, Greece has made decisions of great importance which have generated debates and controversies that still remain open within the European Union. During the period of analysis, a profound transformation of the Greek economic structure took place, consisting of: (1) a process of deindustrialization, privatization and tertiarization; (2) the liberalization of financial markets, together with important modifications in the financing of economic agents; (3) the privatization of public companies and a clear commitment to contain public spending; (4) correction of the current account deficit; and (5) increased inequality, loss of workers' rights and liberalization of labor market institutions.

Greece is an outstanding example in the mixed Mediterranean economies, where several waves of privatizations took place and with an anomalous labor market where self-employed workers have an excessive weight. The institutional changes and reforms have been profound and have sometimes involved traumatic processes through which the Greek socio-economic structure has been deeply modified. The liberalization plan for Greece's entry into the euro was similar to that of other Mediterranean economies and was based on massive privatizations at the same time as the economy was opening up to competition with other euro zone countries. Despite failing to meet the Maastricht criteria, these eventually were relaxed so that Greece could become part of the select club of countries to take part in the euro project which, to some extent, represented a point of no return. As is well known, these criteria were not eased when decades later the structural problems of Hellenic growth surfaced. Greece embraced the eurozone free trade while being faced with an uncompetitive production structure and lost its currency devaluation as a means to maintain competitiveness.

In the following sections, we analyze the different growth patterns of the Greek economy and the extent to which the structural reforms based on implementing an export-led model have been successful, in which necessary adjustments were made through the flexibility of prices and wages to restore economic growth, In Section 2, the main political objectives and economic reforms that took place in Greece between 1990 and 2000 are discussed. Section 3 presents the main changes in the economic structure of the Hellenic country from its entry into the euro area until the beginning of the international financial crisis. Section 4 analyzes the 2010–2018 period, marked by a deep crisis caused by the negative effects of the structural deficiencies that had dragged on for decades, together with those induced by the imposed contractionary policies of aggregate demand. Finally, Section 5 present the conclusion.

2 Before Greece's entry into the EMU, 1990–2000

Although Greece was eventually accepted as a member of the Economic and Monetary Union (EMU) in 2001, the decade of the 1990s was a tumultuous period in Greek history. It was a period marked by reforms, adjustment plans and privatizations at the same time as the country benefited from the EU Structural and Cohesion Funds. Reforms carried out during this time failed in their objective to meet the Maastricht convergence criteria, however, the outcome was a "successful" one, as Greece had finally joined the select club of the Monetary Union member countries, adopting the euro as its official currency. This was, however, a controversial issue that led to multiple views on the wisdom of this decision.

The International Monetary Fund (IMF) data show the difficult situation in Greece at the beginning of the 1990s. That same year Greece registered the highest inflation rate in the EU reaching 23 percent, with a 13 percent deficit and 71 percent of GDP debt. In the year immediately prior to EMU entry, inflation had notably been contained (3.7 percent), although the deficit was 4 percent, and the debt was 104.9 percent of GDP, well above the 60 percent target established in the Maastricht Treaty. During the first half of the decade, Greece experienced very low growth rates, although this situation reversed during the second half, when Greece's growth actually exceeded the euro area average. Despite the high growth, however, structural problems remained: low wage-employed job creation, high inflation, government deficit, negative current account balance and increasing indebtedness.

To understand the characteristics of the Greek economy before the adoption of the euro, we must analyze the policies carried out during the preceding stage, the labor market developments, the role of the foreign sector, the funds received from the EU and the financial situation of the country. As Featherstone and Papadimitrou (2008) indicate, Greece is a southern or peripheral economy, which is difficult to fit into the tight categories of Varieties of Capitalism of Hall and Soskice (2001). Other approaches such as Amable (2003) seem to be better suited since they offer new categories such as South European capitalism systems (see Chapter 2).

Interesting contributions in this respect were made by Gambarotto and Solari (2015) who consider European countries to be a set of asymmetrically integrated Varieties of Capitalism and they also introduce the dynamics of institutional change to offer an explanation of the difficult role of the southern countries in Europe. As Pagoulatos (2003) reports, major political changes took place during this period. The Greek economy, as well as its regulatory framework, underwent profound transformations, as the liberalization process following the indications of the EU was initiated, aiming to reduce the weight of the public sector via labor market deregulation combined with privatizations of Greek companies.

2.1 The labor market

The unemployment rate increased progressively, going from 6.4 percent in 1990 to 9.2 percent in 1995, and reaching 11.2 percent in 2000. At the same time, the numbers of long-term unemployed grew to reach 53 percent of total unemployment, while the European Union average was 8 points lower. But what gives a different dimension to the problem of employment in Greece is the large proportion of self-employed workers. In 1995, the ratio of self-employed to total employed workers was 68 percent compared to 19 percent in the eurozone. At the end of the period, although there is a small correction in the ratio, Greece continued to record much higher values than the average, being the country in the European Union where the self-employed represented the highest proportion (61 percent) of the total employed workers. Of the total self-employed workers, the "only self-employed" type in Greece represented between 80–75 percent of the total, compared to a much lower European average, of around 60 percent. This feature is important when it comes to understanding the smallholding nature of private companies in Greece.

Social consensus is difficult to achieve in Greece. As Featherstone and Papadimitriou (2008) point out, employers considered that the high unit costs and the rigidity of the labor market hindered competitiveness and contributed to the inability of the Greek economy to create employment at a faster rate. Trade unions, on the other hand, argued that the cost of employment in Greece was one of the lowest in the European Union and that more investment to boost productivity was needed in order to raise competitiveness, instead of walking the easy path of labor market deregulation, which was already considered to be very flexible. It is a fact, however, that in the years prior to joining the euro, wages in Greece were among the lowest in the entire EU. In 1995, the compensation of employees per hour worked in purchasing power standard in Greece was 8 euros, while the eurozone average stood at 16. In 2000, the compensation per hour worked was 11 euros in Greece and the Euro area average was 19. Nonetheless salaries grew systematically above productivity during this period. A comparison with Germany between 1995 and 2000 shows that the difference between wages and productivity in Greece was 3.8 percentage points for the former, while in Germany wages lost 0.1

points against productivity. However, it is important to emphasize that in Greece the employee compensation was at very low levels compared to the EU average, and in addition, the wage share represented 29.2 percent of GDP in 1995, while the average in the eurozone countries was 49.3 percent. At the end of the period, Greece only reduced the eurozone average by 2.6 points.

We should highlight that this pattern did not lead to a better distribution of wealth, since the 1990s were characterized by a process of concentration where the richest 1 percent went from accumulating 6.6 percent of national wealth in 1990 to 9.3 percent in the year 2000 (Figure 6.1). The richest decile also saw its share increase from 26 percent to 33 percent, while the bottom 50 percent saw its share decrease from 31.6 percent to 23.6 percent.

The labor market underwent profound reforms in the years prior to Greece joining the euro. At the same time there were high tensions between the employers' association and trade unions and increasing unemployment rates. In 1998, the government passed the Law 2639/98, whose key points are highlighted by Featherstone and Papadimitriou (2008) as:

> the calculation of working time on a three and six month basis based upon union consent, introduction of territorial employment pacts, improvements in the regulation of 'atypical' and part-time employment, introduction of part-time employment in state-controlled enterprises, creation of private employment agencies, and medical and pharmaceutical coverage for the young (under 29) and long-term unemployed.

In December 2000, a new labor reform was approved, introducing:

- the annualized calculation of working time, based on union consent and linked to a 38-hour week;
- increases in the cost of overtime;
- reduction of employers' National Insurance contributions for newly recruited staff;
- small increase for the wages of part-time employees.

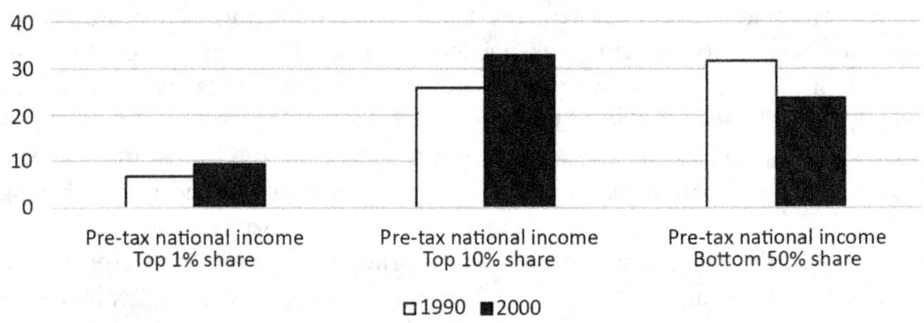

Figure 6.1 Income inequality in Greece
Source: Eurostat. www.ec.europa.eu/eurostat

2.2 Structural policy, the cohesion policy and a privatization plan that did not stop the deficit

When the Maastricht Treaty was signed in 1992, one of the pillars of the EU was launched: the Cohesion Fund created to help Member States whose GNP per capita was less than 90 percent of the EU average. Spain, Ireland, Portugal and Greece would benefit the most from its creation. The main objective was to help countries adapt to the challenges of economic and monetary union by co-financing projects in the fields of the environment and trans-European transport infrastructure. The EU structural assistance budget for Greece for the period 1994–1999 amounted to €19,271,000 to which an additional €2,836,000 of Cohesion Funds were added. Greece became thus one of the main beneficiaries of the cohesion policy, but despite the funds disbursed, regional disparities persisted and convergence did not improve substantially. In 1990, the GDP per capita of Greece was €14,745 and in 2018 it stood at €17,765, just 20 percent higher. In Germany, the GDP per capita increase in the same period was 47 percent, a measure according to which the distance from the most important country in the union is greater than at the beginning of the process. There are multiple analyses (Bradley, Morgenroth, & Untiedt, 2003; Karvounis & Zaharis, 2015; Katseli, 2001) discussing the role that these funds played.

Two main plans were introduced during the 1990s: The first Community-support Framework 1989–1993 and the Second Community-support Framework 1994–1999. According to Karvounis and Zaharis (2015), the former was characterized by the wide dispersal of funds to small structure projects with a strong focus on infrastructure, but no productive restructuring strategy was adopted to support an economy with major issues in this regard. The Second Community-support Framework 1994–1999 placed greater emphasis on large infrastructure projects. Preparing the country to join the Economic and Monetary Union was the priority of this plan. Heinz-Jürgen (2015) analyzes the suboptimal performance of the effects of the cohesion policy and finds important reasons which are exogenous to the design of common policy in his explanation, such as: corruption, clientelism, ineffective administration, low absorption rates and decreasing competitiveness, in addition to the low economic impact on growth that these investments had.

At the same time as the process for designing the EU cohesion policy was taking place, a long process of privatization began. As Wright and Pagoulatos (2001) point out, this was a slow and erratic process as it was met with fierce political opposition. The New Democracy government during 1990–1993 had an aggressive privatization plan that the Panhellenic Socialist Movement (PASOK) strongly disputed while in opposition, although it was none other than PASOK that carried it forward once they returned to power in 1993 with the election of Papandreou. Around 100 companies had been privatized by the end of 1995 and $1 billion was raised, a figure much lower than originally anticipated, while half of the income came from the controversial sale of the cement industry AGET. Despite the extraordinary income that came from privatizations, the deficit did not meet the provisions of the convergence criteria, although the privatizations served to restrain it. Table 6.1 reflects the development of the deficit and debt in Greece during this stage, and we can observe that, although the deficit went from an alarming 13 percent in 1990 to just above 4 percent in 2000, it systematically stood above 3 percent. Despite the deficit being contained, the debt grew from 73 percent in 1990 to more than 100 percent in 2000. All this, in spite of the fact that Greece registered higher growth rates than the eurozone average during the second half of the decade. This was due to the weight of the debt service, as well as the interest on the bonds, which were much higher in Greece during this period. The data show debt service in Greece was moving in the range of 6.9–10.7 percent of GDP, while in the eurozone the interest burden registered significantly lower values, between 3.8–5.4 percent. Regarding the risk premium of the Greek bonds, the average difference against the German bond was 4.7 percent.

2.3 Economic growth in Greece

One of the main features of the Greek economy is that consumption has a great weight on growth due to its internal market focus, reaching almost 11 points more than the Eurozone average. Figure 6.2 shows that consumption is the element that contributed the most to economic growth prior to joining the Monetary Union, while gross fixed capital formation (GFCF) was the second main contributing component, which started growing from the middle of the decade, although less than consumption. The trade balance, however, tended to contribute negatively to growth, which would eventually become a source of concern.

The current account deficit became a structural problem as the trade balance reached a staggering -11 percent of GDP in 2000. OECD data show that, despite

Table 6.1 Greek deficit, growth and debt, 1990–2000 (%)

	1990	*1991*	*1992*	*1993*	*1994*	*1995*	*1996*	*1997*	*1998*	*1999*	*2000*
Deficit/ GDP	13.1	9.5	10.5	11.3	8.4	9.7	8.2	6.1	6.3	5.8	4.1
Debt/ GDP	73.2	74.7	80	100.3	98.3	99	101.3	99.5	97.4	98.9	104.9
Greece GDP growth	0	3.1	0.7	-1.6	2	2.1	2.9	4.5	3.9	3.1	3.9
Euro area GDP growth	3.6	2.6	1.4	-0.7	2.5	2.4	1.7	2.7	3.0	3.0	3,9

Source: Eurostat. www.ec.europa.eu/eurostat

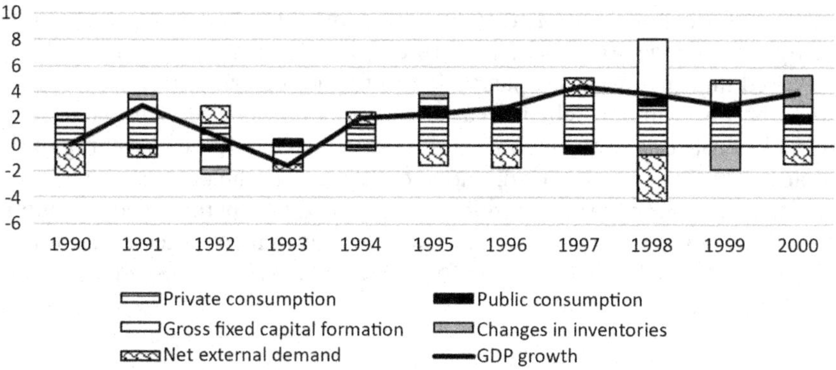

Figure 6.2 Contribution to the increase in GDP at constant prices
Source: AMECO. https://ec.europa.eu/info/business-economy-euro/indicators-statistics/economic-databases/macro-economic-database-ameco_en

the negative contribution to growth, there is a slight improvement in the technological content of the Greek exports. Exports classified as low and medium technological content accounted for 90 percent of exports at the beginning of the 1990s, while the remaining 10 percent comprised 8 percent for medium-high technological content and 2 percent for the high technological content category. During the 1990s, the proportion of exports classified between low and medium technological content decreased by 10 percentage points, reaching 80 percent, while the medium-high and high technological content categories increased their weight by the same proportion.

More precisely, exports with a high technological content came to represent 8 percent, when previously they were only 2 percent, while medium-high exports rose from 8 percent to 13 percent. This was a major improvement considering that Greece was the EMU country that registered the lowest levels of exports with a high technological content over total exports. For Petrakis (2013), the liberalization of the Greek economy is evidence of the drawbacks of neoliberal policies in non-competitive economies. Unrestricted opening up to international trade can only benefit countries whose exports are able to face foreign competition. In a weakly competitive and consumerist economy like the Greek one, international liberalization presents major economic challenges. Domestic producers are displaced by the entry of new foreign products, which has an impact on investment and job creation. To maintain the level of consumption, it is necessary to resort to foreign loans that increase debt, while production and savings that should finance consumption are reduced.

To conclude, we can state that during this period Greece experienced a weak wage-led pattern. The wage share rose, as real wages grew above productivity, GDP growth rates were also higher than the Euro area average during the second half of the decade. However, the labor market was characterized by an anomalous structure where self-employment gained disproportionate importance.

Employment suffered as registered unemployment levels were higher than the European average and inequality rose. The balance of the trade deficit increased and the external opening led to further deterioration. At the same time, the government debt increased sharply and debt servicing started to play a key role due to the high interest rates registered at the beginning of the decade. The Cohesion Funds did not close the gap in the productive structure with the main European economies. The privatization plan helped to contain the deficit, but the collection of revenues was less than expected and both the deficit and the debt remained far from the objectives established within the Maastricht Treaty.

3 Joining the eurozone: the beginning of the debt-led growth

At the political level, joining the Monetary Union was viewed as a great success. At that time the conversion was agreed at 340.75 drachmas/euro. At the economic level, however, there were conflicting opinions. As explained by Kotios et al. (2011), those who made this positive reading expected price stability to set in, due to political pressures coming to an end and the reduction of transaction costs. The latter, coupled with the elimination of the uncertainty created by the exchange rate regime that had previously existed, would boost trade and production, while monetary stability would increase the propensity to invest due to lower interest rates and greater liquidity. But the loss of control of monetary policy concealed important challenges for the economy as a new scenario was emerging, where the opportunities to issue debt increased substantially, at the expense of losing the possibility to devalue the national currency as a way to increase competitiveness (Petrakis, 2013).

Greece remained in the group of countries with a GNP per capita less than 90 percent of the EMU average and therefore continued to benefit from funds coming from the European budget. These investments, however, were not able to put a stop to the tertiarization of the economy. This was because the plans maintained their focus on infrastructure projects, and especially those related to transport. The main criticism of this policy design concerned in particular the emphasis on basic infrastructure, to the detriment of those interventions supporting primarily productive activity (Plaskovitis 2006). During this growth stage, the share of industry and manufacturing on GDP continued to decline, with their combined contribution dropping from 29 percent to 25 percent. At the same time the service sector, which in the previous period accounted for almost 64 percent, rose to 70 percent. As Gambarotto and Solari (2015) point out, Greece never managed to fully develop its industry sector, which placed the country in the group of semi-peripheral countries where regulation and protectionism helped to maintain the profitability of sectors that otherwise would not have survived external competition. In addition, two other factors must be considered. First, the size of the informal economy was considered to be the largest in the euro area and stood at 28.5 percent of GDP (Schneide,r 2007). And the second factor refers to the size of the companies, since small and medium-sized enterprises (SMEs) with few employees proliferate, which makes it extremely difficult to achieve increases in productivity and take advantage of economies of scale (Hyz & Gikas, 2012).

Table 6.2 shows the macroeconomic profile of Greece. We observe that unemployment was eventually corrected, dropping from 10.8 percent in 2001 to 7.8 percent in 2008. Despite systematically exceeding the 2 percent target, inflation moved toward acceptable levels around 3–4 percent, far from the extreme figures of the 1990s. Growth was higher than that registered in the eurozone, except for 2005, and we observe that on average the Greek economy grew 2 points above the monetary union average. Although the deficit continued to be higher than the eurozone average, registering values that ranged between 5–8 percent annually, the weight of public debt on GDP could be contained during this period due to the decline of interest rates on public debt as Greece joined the single currency, combined with high nominal growth rates.

Regarding contributions to growth, consumption continued to be the main element that explained the country's growth during this period. Its contribution during this stage stood at 2.5 percent, while the second main contributor was GFCF, with an average of 1 percent. But the combination of high levels of consumption and trade deficit implied the need to resort to foreign loans. In this way, private debt with the exterior grew and become a major issue, without any kind of intervention from the national or the European institutions in order to contain the associated risks.

3.1 The labor market

During this stage the high levels of unemployment were reduced and youth unemployment was also partially corrected, dropping from 14.6 percent to 11.6 percent, which positioned the ratio 3 points below the eurozone average.

Table 6.2 Macroeconomic profile, 2001–2008 (%)

	2001	*2002*	*2003*	*2004*	*2005*	*2006*	*2007*	*2008*
Inflation, end of period consumer prices	3.5	3.5	3.1	3.1	3.5	3.2	3.9	2.2
Gross domestic product, constant prices	4.1	3.9	5.8	5.1	0.6	5.7	3.3	-0.3
Unemployment rate	10.8	10.4	9.8	10.6	10.0	9.0	8.4	7.8
General government net lending/borrowing	-5.5	-6.0	-7.8	-8.8	-6.2	-5.9	-6.7	-10.2
General government gross debt	107.1	104.9	101.5	102.9	107.4	103.6	103.1	109.4
Current account balance	-6.9	-6.3	-6.3	-5.5	-7.3	-10.9	-13.9	-14.5

Source: Eurostat. www.ec.europa.eu/eurostat

The percentage of young people who neither studied nor had a job decreased by 5 points and the long-term unemployment was also corrected by 10 points. Finally, the percentage of freelancers over employed workers was still at very high levels as the 51 percent ratio shows, a figure that was 10 points lower in the previous period, but nonetheless very far from the eurozone average, which stood at 18 percent. The wage share had a positive shift as well, increasing from 24 percent of GDP in 2001 to 28 percent in 2009, allowing Greece to reduce the gap with the eurozone average by 3 points (Figure 6.3). During this period, wages grew again above productivity, this time by 2.6 points.

After joining the Monetary Union, the increase in unit labor costs (ULCs) in Greece was greater than in most of the eurozone countries. During the 2001–2009 period, ULCs surged by 11 points, while the eurozone trend was toward a strong containment of ULCs, especially in countries like Germany, which during this period significantly contained theirs. In Greece, this increase attempted, combined with the lack of investments by the state and the private sector, to promote a significant change in the productive structure, which accounted for the country's specialization in lower productivity sectors, such as services, where tourism played a significant role. This is one of the problems deeply rooted in the Greek productive structure. In this sense, it is important to note that research & development (R&D) investment during this stage in Greece was barely 0.55 percent of GDP, while the EU average was 1.8 percent of GDP and in Germany it was 2.4 percent, more than four times higher.

Regarding the regulatory framework of the labor market, two important legislative reforms took place. In December 2000, reform 2874/00, known as Giannitsis's labor market law, was approved. Featherstone and Papadimitriou (2008) point out the key points of this reform:

- the annualized calculation of working time, based on union consent and linked to a 38-hour week;
- increases in the cost of overtime;

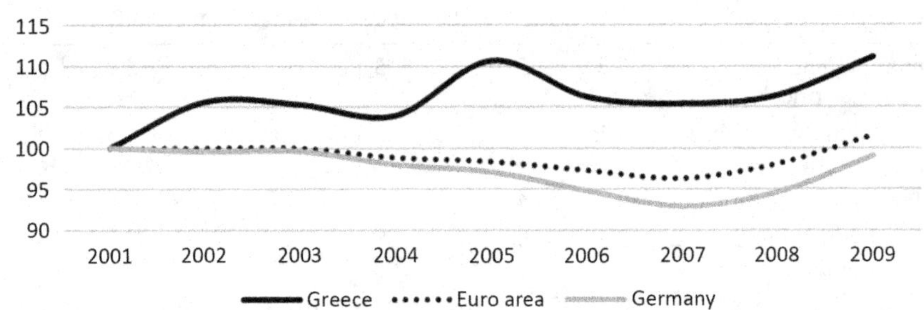

Figure 6.3 Real unit labor costs: total economy (ratio of compensation per employee to nominal GDP per person employed)

Source: AMECO. https://ec.europa.eu/info/business-economy-euro/indicators-statistics/economic-databases/macro-economic-database-ameco_en

- small reduction of limits on collective redundancies for medium-sized businesses;
- reduction of employers' national insurance contributions for newly recruited staff;
- increase in the wages of part-time employees.

Later, in 2005, Panagiotopoulos's labor market law (Law 3385/05) was enforced, which would imply a deterioration of the working conditions of workers and a breakthrough in the neoliberal agenda. The key points were that the cost of overtime declined to levels prior to 2000, the calculation of working time on a four-month basis, based on a 40-hour week, and it allowed small businesses to negotiate individual agreements with their employees.

3.2 The trade balance deteriorates and private debt grows

The trade balance continued to deteriorate and the gap between exports and imports grew after Greece joined the euro. The deficit rose sharply from €16,075,000 in 2001 to €30,507,000 in 2008. Despite the deterioration of the trade balance, during this period the technological content of exports improved. The sum of exports of high and medium-high technological content went from 21 percent in 2001 to 28 percent in 2007. However, the share of exports of low and medium-low technological content continued to weigh more than 50 percent on the total.

This time the need for external financing was not centered on the purchase of government securities. Government debt to GDP remained most of the time below the levels of the preceding decade, although these were quite high as discussed in Section 3.1. Once again, the high nominal growth, combined with the lower interest rates registered during this period, allowed the government debt to be kept under control, despite recording unwavering deficits above 3 percent. As Figure 6.4 shows, the long-term debt rates of Greece after it joined the euro remained on par with those of the German government

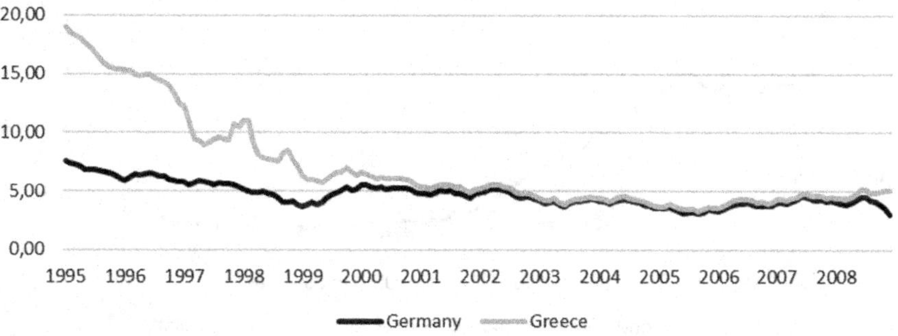

Figure 6.4 Long-term government bond yields
Source: Eurostat. www.ec.europa.eu/eurostat

until 2008. But one must consider that inflation in Greece was higher than in Germany throughout this period, and therefore the real rates were even lower than those of the reference bond. This combination of low interest rates and high nominal growth even allowed a decrease in debt to GDP for some years despite the fact that deficits have constantly been maintained above the 3 percent Maastricht limit.

Despite the fact that during this stage the public debt did not mount significantly, a clear debt-led pattern can be observed in what refers to private debt since the private sector's indebtedness rose sharply. As Lapavitsas et al. (2010) explain, the enforcement of the common monetary policy caused the interest rates to drop to those of German levels, while inflation was higher in the periphery, so that real interest rates tended to be lower. This created a more attractive scenario for borrowers and banks were able to meet the growing domestic demand for credit on relatively cheap terms. If we take the ATHIBOR (Athens Interbank Offered Rate) as a reference, we can see that in the period prior to the Monetary Union, its values were high and systematically above inflation (Figure 6.5). However, with the single currency, this relationship was disrupted between 2001 and 2006, constituting a favorable scenario for the debtor's appetite. In addition to the above, freedom of capital movements brought a new dimension to transnational financial flows and lax policies on the part of borrowers, creating a scenario with all the necessary ingredients for debt to guide growth and imbalances to accumulate in the financial system. For Kotios et al. (2011), the asymmetries in the monetary policy of the European Central Bank (ECB) aggravated the situation. Given that inflation in Greece had constantly been above the imposed ceiling of 2 percent, a restrictive monetary policy with higher interest rates than those applied would have been required under the ECB statutes. However, due to the circumstances of the main European economies like Germany and France, monetary policy worked in a procyclical manner, thus facilitating indebtedness.

During this stage, private debt was the engine of the country and, as of 2001 the inflow of financial capital corresponding to loans and portfolio

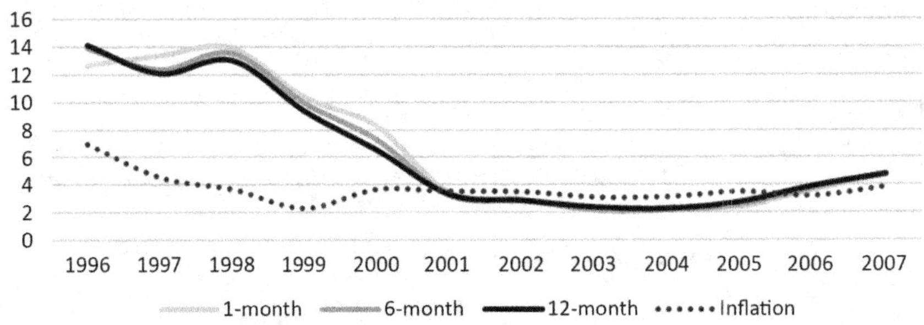

Figure 6.5 ATHIBOR (1996–2000), EURIBOR (2001–2007) and inflation
Source: Bank of Greece.

investments grew firmly, while the foreign direct investment (FDI) remained stagnant. Most Greek debts were held by French, German, Italian, Belgian, Dutch, Luxembourg, and British banks (Lapavitsas et al., 2010), and the loans granted by foreign banks grew six-fold. The distribution of credit underwent a major shift during this period, as Figure 6.6 shows: credit to the government declined from 46 percent of total credit in 2001 to 16 percent in 2008, while credit to non-financial companies rose from 36 percent to 42 percent and loans to individuals and private non-profit institutions increased as well from 17 percent to 38 percent. This new debt pattern constituted the most remarkable change during this period.

The accumulating imbalances led to a sharp deterioration in Greece's net investment position. As illustrated in Figure 6.7, Greece strongly increased its

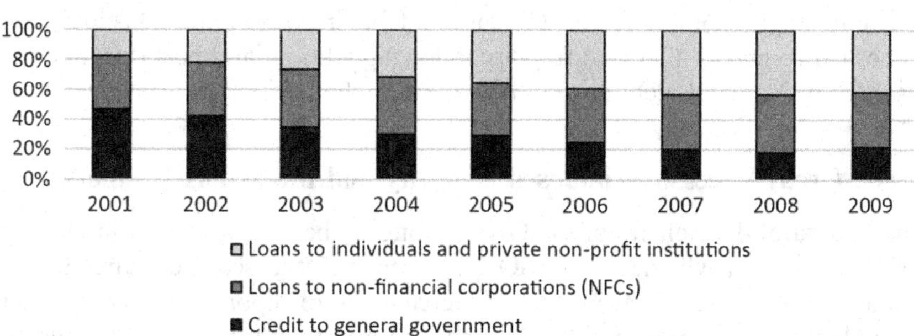

Figure 6.6 Credit to domestic public and private sectors by domestic monetary financial institutions
Source: Bank of Greece.

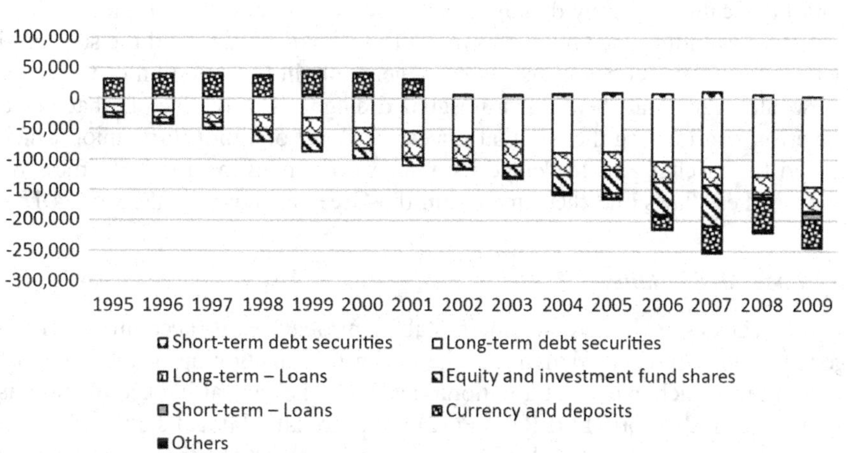

Figure 6.7 Financial statements for the aggregate economy (million euros)
Source: Bank of Greece.

net debtor position vis-à-vis the rest of the world. This new dimension of debt financed by foreign capital in the context of the single currency is the main difference that took place with respect to the previous growth period and would condition the policies carried out in Greece from this moment on.

We can conclude that this stage of growth in Greece was marked by a debt-led pattern that allowed large imbalances to accumulate in the private sector. The high indebtedness served to sustain consumption, but not to modernize the increasingly tertiary production regime dominated by SMEs that allowed little productivity gains. Meanwhile the trade balance continued to deteriorate. The financial liberalization and the end of the exchange risk that came with the euro fostered the boom in the capital markets and facilitated the entry of foreign capital, on which the Greek economy increasingly grew more and more dependent. These factors, coupled with a scenario where very low interest rates and lax financing conditions by commercial banks proliferated, allowed credit to rise to unprecedented levels. The high indebtedness of households and companies led to greater financial fragility following a boom and bust dynamic that resulted in the Greek debt crisis, which marked the beginning of the next stage.

4 The Great Recession: imposed austerity and the export-led model

The structural deficiencies of the Greek economy became apparent in October 2009 when the newly elected PASOK government released the figures for the country´s public deficit: from the 3.6 percent figure reported by the previous New Democracy government to 12.8 percent and then further to 13.6 percent in 2010 (Frangakis, 2011; Katsimi & Moutos, 2010; Prodromidou, 2018: 189). That exposed the previous Greek government's ploy before the international community, consenting to falsifying statistics, and rendered the country's statistical data completely unreliable. Moreover, top officials publicly recognizing data falsification severely damaged the image of the Greek government.

Notwithstanding the Greek government's mismanagement and the structural deficiencies of the Greek economy more generally in the gestation of the crisis, we would argue that there was a misguided diagnosis of the factors that led to the crisis, overlooking the fact that Greece was part of a monetary union which lacked the mechanisms to defend its weaker economies in turbulent times. We address these flaws and their impact on the Greek economy in tSection. 4.1.

4.1 EMU design failures

The EMU design lacked two main stabilizing features to account for endogenous boom and bust dynamics inherent in the functioning of the capitalist system and which existed at a national level: (1) the central bank's function as a lender of last resort (LOLR); and (2) the automatic budget stabilizers.

The ECB was established with one primary objective: that of preserving price stability, while financial stability has been disregarded (De Grauwe, 2013; Dourakis, 2013) until after the crisis. Preserving financial stability implies that the central bank will act as a LOLR in times of distress, as it has infinite capacity to buy government bonds and is thus the only institution capable of preventing panic from spreading in the sovereign bond markets. However, from its foundation, the ECB was created under a mandate that prohibits direct purchase of sovereign debt instruments. The central bank was thus stripped of its LORL function in order to avoid moral hazard and risk sharing, but started to exercise it in 2012 when it launched the OMT (Outright Monetary Transactions) program (De Grauwe, 2013), as the sovereign debt crisis led to a banking crisis affecting the core financial institutions of the eurozone. This is when the ECB's no lending policy came into direct conflict with the decision to finance rescue packages for the troubled banks of the eurozone by indirectly buying sovereign debt instruments mainly held by those banks in the secondary markets. In reality, the ECB could not provide liquidity directly to the governments but it could do so for the banking sector. The ECB's inability to guarantee to provide liquidity in times of crisis to governments, who were issuing debt in a currency they did not control, was one of the reasons for the liquidity crisis that the Greek government suffered and which eventually led to its incapacity to service its debt at reasonable interest rates.

The second element in the flawed design of the EMU concerns the budget stabilizers. In times of crisis, when the private sector is in need to deleverage, it will do so in two ways: (1) by selling assets, and (2) by increasing savings in order to obtain liquidity to repay its debt. This can set in motion a debt deflation process explained by Fisher (1933), whereby, when all agents try to deleverage at the same time, it can lead to a generalized fall in asset prices or a currency revaluation, implying that the real value of unpaid debt is actually increasing even as the nominal debt is being reduced. Therefore, nobody succeeds in improving their solvency, leading to Fisher's paradox that the more debtors pay, the more they owe. The only institution able to prevent this deflationary spiral from happening is the government, provided it is willing to do the exact opposite, that is to attempt to save less, or increase its spending and debt levels, putting a floor on asset price falling.[1] However, instead of counteracting the private sector's deleveraging, the EU leadership forced all debtor governments – starting with Greece – into a prolonged austerity program built on spending cuts and tax hikes, in order to repay what was thought to be an unsustainable public debt that had presumably been the main factor causing the crisis. This was a misguided diagnosis, as Section 3 showed that the high indebtedness levels were mainly a reflection of the private sector's rising debt in the context of low relative interest rates.

There is also a third, more structural element contributing to the EMU's flawed design, which refers to the lack of a supranational authority in charge of implementing a common fiscal policy (De Grauwe, 2013; Dourakis, 2013; Frangakis, 2011). The EMU is a monetary union with a single currency but lacking a political and fiscal union able to manage a proper European budget. The fiscal arrangements in the EMU rely mostly on peer pressure and severe discipline which involve adhering to the rules laid out in the Stability and Growth Pact, while the EU budget is minimal, barely amounting to around 1 percent of EU GDP, and roughly seven times lower than that of the US (Frangakis, 2011). As such, the EMU lacks a redistribution function capable of balancing out the disequilibria emerging from the different nature of its economies, i.e. surplus and deficit ones. As a result of the crisis, most adjustment has been done by debtor countries in the form of internal devaluations/ deficit reductions, with harsh consequences in terms of economic growth and social inequalities, as we will analyze further, however, no internal revaluations/ surplus reductions were imposed on the creditor countries.

The EMU´s design thus excluded any form of risk sharing or transfer mechanism for fear of moral hazard, and refused to account for the imbalances which would inevitably emerge as a result of sharing a common currency. Such imbalances are actually exacerbated at a national level as a result of the single interest rate imposed by the ECB, too low for booming countries and too high for countries in recession (De Grauwe, 2013). When economies like Spain, Greece, or Ireland started to grow at higher rates than the eurozone average, inflation picked up, leading to a lower real interest rate that fostered indebtedness and attracted vast amounts of capital inflows, thus aggravating the boom. The opposite occurred in countries experiencing lower inflation or higher real interest rates, where growth was lower or where there was a recession.

The EU leadership, particularly the European Commission, the ECB and the German government, however, refused to acknowledge the existence of any of the structural deficiencies mentioned above, and Greece's crisis was blamed on a dramatic diagnostic failure focusing on the government's profligacy, a low productive and uncompetitive economy geared toward consumption and high wage policy setting and an inflated public sector. That led to several years of inaction where the EU leadership did "too little, too late" (Galbraith, 2016; Gkasis, 2018; Guzman, Ocampo, & Stiglitz, 2016) and during which Greece experienced severe speculative attacks in the financial markets, it became unable to service its debt at non-prohibitive interest rates, and faced a fiscal crisis of enormous magnitude, which would spread to other European countries and could potentially threaten the very existence of the single currency.

It was not until the core of the eurozone's financial sector came under threat in 2012, several years after the outbreak of the sovereign debt crisis, that the ECB decided to take action and perform a somewhat limited LOLR function. As numerous eurozone banking institutions and main holders of Greek sovereign bonds viewed their stability threatened, the ECB started to provide liquidity directly and exclusively to the banking institutions (De Grauwe, 2013; Frangakis, 2015; Gkasis, 2018). The need for public debt monetization. however, was never acknowledged, due to fears of hyperinflation that did not materialize at any point in time: the average EU area harmonized indices of consumer prices (HICP) inflation rate from 2009 to 2019 stood at just 1.25 percent, far below the ECB's objective of 2 percent. Indebted governments instead entered programs by which they were only allowed to obtain bailout funds from the European Financial Stabilization Mechanism/European Stability Mechanism conditioned to austerity measures, and in Greece's case, such conditions were even harsher, given that by that time it was considered to be an insolvent state. The first financial assistance program started in February 2010 and granted an initial amount of €52.9bn loan from the euro area member states. An additional €20.1 billion were disbursed by the IMF. Two other programs followed from 2012 to 2018, disbursing an additional €204 billion, provided mainly by the ESM. The second program lasted from March 2012 until June 2015, where the ESFS disbursed €141.8 billion and the IMF an additional €12 billion, amounting to a total of €153.8 billion. The third and last assistance program started in 2015 and ended in 2018, where the total amount disbursed was €45.9 billion provided mainly by the ESM (ESM, 2017).

The assistance programs came with stringent conditions attached in the form of contractionary aggregate demand policies, targeting fiscal and current account deficits,[2] as a result of the misguided diagnosis described above, which focused on the government's profligacy and the refusal to acknowledge the EMU's design flaws. The policies that were implemented from 2010 to 2018 relied on two main pillars (Perez & Matsaganis, 2018): the first one aimed to eliminate the public debt and deficit by means of tax increases and cutting public spending; and the second focused on current account deficit reductions via an internal devaluation wage reduction process in order to gain competitivity in the international markets. We will analyze both in the rest of this chapter, to determine the growth pattern in Greece and discuss its evolution during this stage.

4.2 Achieving a balanced fiscal budget

Greece entered the crisis with a two-digit budget deficit, however, the fiscal problems the country was facing were not primarily the result of excessive public spending, which had historically been, with a few exceptions, just below the euro area average in the pre-crisis period, but the lack of revenues, which was in part as a result of systematic tax evasion (Dourakis, 2013; Katsimi & Moutos, 2010). As can be noted in Figure 6.8, fiscal deficit was eventually eliminated in 2016 and Greece registered a slight surplus of around 1 percent of GDP thereafter. However, this was achieved by severely cutting government expenditure from 2008 to 2014, as a result of the structural reforms imposed by the EU authorities, without increasing public revenues. During this period, government spending was reduced by an annual average of 5 percent and by 1 percent thereafter. Not surprisingly, as a full-blown crisis emerged, and unemployment experienced an unprecedented rise, from less than 8 percent in 2008 to 27.5 percent in 2013, reducing the state's capacity to collect taxes, government revenues actually decreased by 3 percent on a yearly average during the same period.

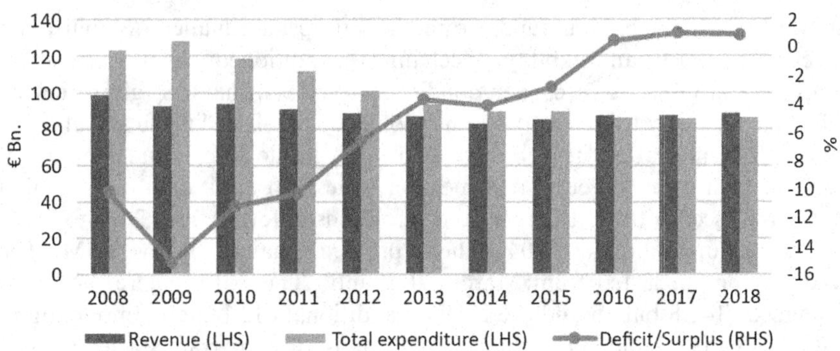

Figure 6.8 General government fiscal position, 2008–2018 (€bn and %)
Source: World Economic Outlook. www.imf.org/en/Publications/WEO/weo-database/

Reducing public spending, however, does not automatically lead to a decrease in fiscal deficit, as expenditure cuts tend to have a negative impact on GDP and taxable income, and may thus indirectly reduce tax revenues. In the case of Greece, the latter experienced a dramatic fall of 12 percent, from €73 billion in 2009 to €64.3 billion in 2014, accumulating six consecutive years of negative growth. This was mainly due to a significant decline in social security contributions of 23 percent, which continued to decrease the following year, due to high unemployment. Another important component of tax revenue, taxes on income, profits and capital gains also fell by 15 percent during the same period.

The misguided diagnosis repeatedly circulated in the mainstream media suggested that one of the main factors leading to the Greek crisis was profligacy and the government's over-indebtedness at unsustainable levels, as highlighted above (Kouretas & Vlamis, 2010). General government debt to GDP was indeed already far from the Maastricht levels of 60 percent when the crisis hit, and it had been so for almost two decades, from 1993 to 2008. As explained above, a combination of relatively high nominal growth and low real interest rates in the decade of the 2000s had allowed government debt levels to remain stable around these levels. Therefore, the debt to GDP ratio in Greece, even though high, had been stable throughout the decade of the 2000s and what rose significantly was the private sector debt (households, firms and banks), as argued in Section 3. Public debt to GDP in Greece started to rise sharply, however, only from 2008 to 2011, as Figure 6.9 shows, experiencing an unprecedented increase to almost 180 percent. This was due to the combined effect of GDP decline and surging debt levels in nominal terms, precisely as the government was stepping in to rescue large segments of the private sector in need of deleveraging. Even though debt/GDP declined to 160 percent in 2012, it rose back up to 180 percent the following year and even exceeded this level in 2018.

As the US subprime crisis started to unravel and rapidly extended to European economies, international investors channeled large amounts of capital

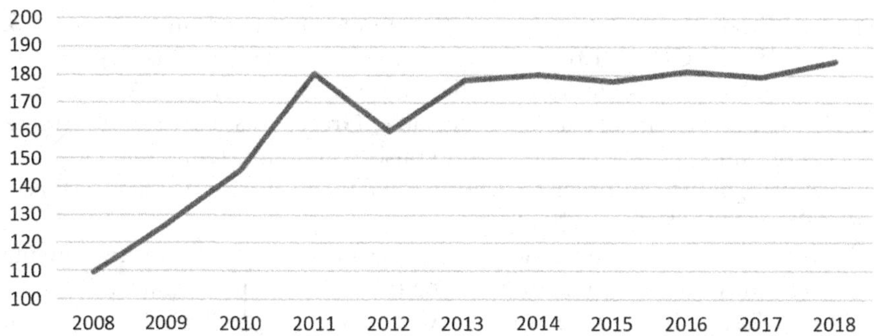

Figure 6.9 General government gross debt to GDP, 2008–2018
Source: World Economic Outlook. www.imf.org/en/Publications/WEO/weo-database/

toward safer assets, and doubts were arising about the ability of certain sovereign states to face their debt payment obligations. This was a direct consequence of one of the design flaws of the EMU mentioned previously: in a monetary union where member states issue debt in a currency they have no control over, the unwillingness of the ECB to act as a LORL in times of distress renders sovereign states susceptible to default and thus prone to speculative attacks (De Grauwe, 2013). Greece was the first country to experience severe surges in its risk premia as speculation began to mount about the government's ability to service its debt. From 2008 to 2011, interest payable on the general government debt rose from 4.8 percent to 7.5 percent of GDP, a staggering 56 percent increase in the cost of debt. As debt service costs became prohibitive, the Greek government was indeed faced with the possibility of defaulting. However, one can argue that Greek debt only became unsustainable as a consequence of the speculative attacks in the markets, leading to extreme increases in the bonds' spreads, and which were as a result of the ECB's unwillingness to provide a LOLR guarantee.

Moreover, the structural programs implemented in Greece which required stringent fiscal austerity and internal devaluation never achieved a reduction in public debt because these are two conflicting objectives (Kouretas & Vlamis, 2010). If the aim to increase competitivity by pursuing real devaluation proves successful, that implies an induced deflation in the form of lower nominal incomes and prices which will actually increase the real value of debt owed. Debt reduction therefore cannot be achieved via internal devaluation. Nonetheless, this was the second main policy pursued in Greece, as part of the structural adjustment programs. We address this analysis in Section 4.3.

4.3 The export-led model: gaining competitivity via internal devaluation

The rationale behind the austerity measures implemented in Greece was mainly based on the idea that "wage rises had outpaced productivity gains," according to the ESM, the main European institution that devised the structural adjustment plans for Greece during the last decade (ESM, 2017; Greek

National Productivity Board, Centre of Planning and Economic Research, & Kepe, 2019; OECD, 2013). In their view, Greece had lost its capacity to compete with other countries on the international markets. As currency devaluation in a monetary union is unviable, Greece was forced to undergo a process of "internal devaluation," that consisted of wage reduction and labor market deregulation in order to achieve a balanced current account (Afonso, 2019; Perez & Matsaganis, 2019).

Figure 6.10 shows the evolution of wage growth from 2010 onwards, giving a first insight of the outcome of the structural adjustment programs. Between 2010 and 2016, the average wage growth in Greece declined by 6 percent whereas the European average wage grew by 2 percent. In the same period and for three consecutive years, from 2011 to 2013, negative wage growth rates were higher than -10 percent in Greece, whereas the European average growth never entered negative territory. It is a fact that wage growth in Greece has been substantially higher than in Europe in the previous decade, 7 percent in the former and 4 percent in the latter, which was the argument used to enforce internal devaluation (Perez & Matsaganis, 2019). However, the wage share to GDP during 2000–2009 in Greece stood at 26.2 percent compared to 36.6 percent in the euro zone. What is more, during the next decade, from 2010 to 2018, the Euro zone wage-to-GDP share increased to 37.1 percent whereas the Greek share decreased to 25.1 percent.

As a result of wage contention policies applied during the crisis period, the compensation of employees per hour worked in purchasing power standard further decreased in Greece while it was rising in the Euro zone or in countries like Germany. As Figure 6.11 shows, while compensation of employees in Greece decreased from €14.2 to €13.5 during 2010–2016, the EU average increased from €23.2 to €25.8, which accounts for a total reduction of -5 percent in Greece compared to an 11 percent increase for the Euro zone. This implies that, while in 2010, the Greek compensation per employee represented barely 61 percent of the EU average, by 2016, it had decreased to 52 percent.

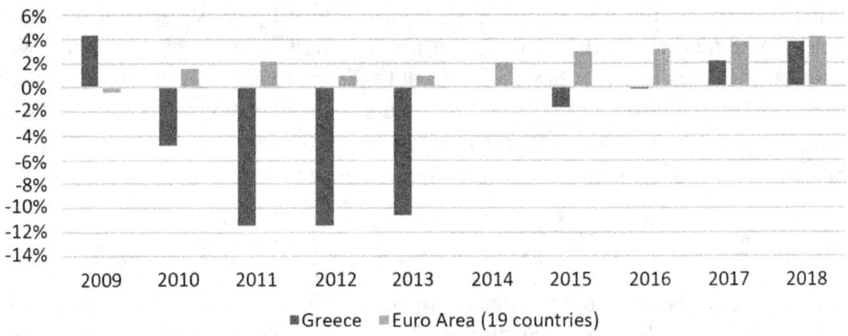

Figure 6.10 Growth of wages and salaries, 2009–2018 (%)
Source: Eurostat. www.ec.europa.eu/eurostat

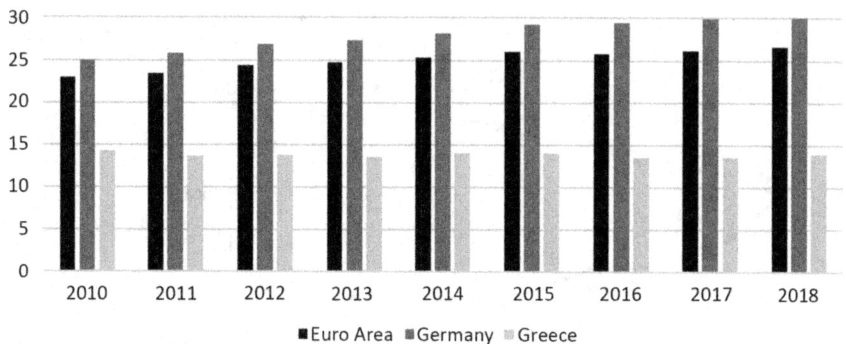

Figure 6.11 Compensation of employees per hour worked (purchasing power standards, PPS)
Source: Eurostat. www.ec.europa.eu/eurostat

The argument underpinning such rampant wage reduction has consistently converged on the same idea among the mainstream ideologues: the institutional framework for wage policy setting during the pre-crisis period contributed substantially to eroding Greece's competitiveness (EMS, 2017; Greek National Productivity Board, Centre of Planning and Economic Research, & Kepe, 2019; OECD, 2013). As such, it shielded domestic economic sectors and left the sectors producing international tradeable goods and services in an unfavorable position. The temporary improvement in earnings and standards of living during this period was thus unsustainable, because higher wages setting policies were not accompanied by lower labor costs and higher productivity levels, undermining the country′s international competitiveness. Productivity growth was thus the prerequisite for wage increases and the only way to gain competitiveness without undermining growth. An automatic relationship has been established between wage increases that cause inflation, in the absence of productivity improvements, thus decreasing competitiveness and reducing exports. According to the conventional wisdom, the only factor affecting competitiveness of a country seem to be wage increases. The reasonable outcome of this analysis cannot thus be other than implementing generalized wage contention policies, an argument which, by now, has been proven to be erroneous in the relevant literature (Lavoie & Stockhammer, 2013; Perez & Matsaganis, 2019).

However, no policy has been put in place in order to achieve a reduction in labor costs via a meaningful increase in productivity levels instead of wage contention. As explained in Section 3, Greece's specialization in low productivity sectors such as services with an important weight of tourism is one of the structural problems of the Greek production regime. As Figure 6.12 shows, Greece's real labor productivity levels decreased with respect to 2010 during the entire decade, having had the worst performance when compared with other European countries. Among its peers, only Italy and Greece

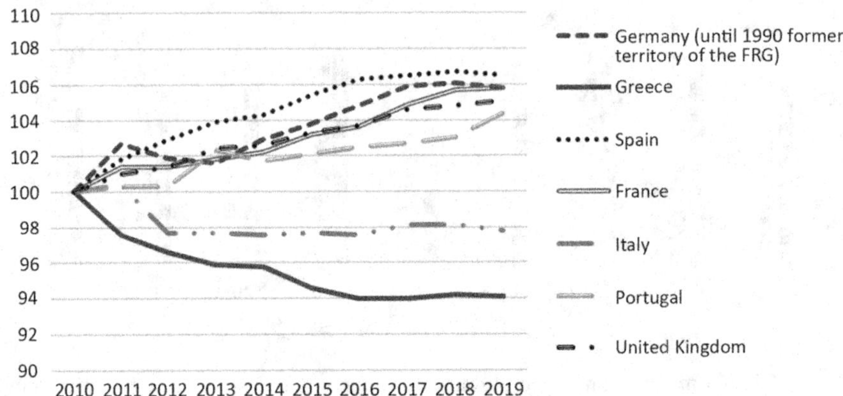

Figure 6.12 Real labor productivity per person employed
Note: 2010 = 100.
Source: Eurostat. www.ec.europa.eu/eurostat

experienced an all-time decline in productivity with respect to 2010 levels. Real labor productivity growth in Greece registered negative rates during most of the decade, as high as -3 percent in 2010, with a positive growth of 0.2 percent only in 2018 (Figure 6.12).

What is more, while it has been widely argued that Greek wages increased above productivity, the fact is that the relative wage levels are still lower than their relative productivity when compared to the eurozone average levels, as Figure 6.13 shows. We plot the nominal labor productivity and compensation of employees per hour worked calculated as a percentage of EU27 at purchasing power standards (PPS). We notice that both variables decrease in time, however, compensation per employee consistently lags behind productivity levels. This suggests that wage levels in Greece are not only far

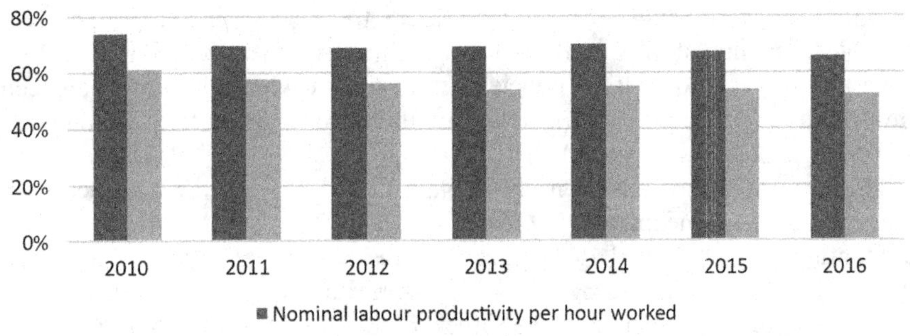

Figure 6.13 Wage and productivity levels as a percentage of eurozone levels
Source: Eurostat. www.ec.europa.eu/eurostat

below the EU average in absolute terms, as discussed previously, but also in relation to their productivity levels. And this has been a constant feature in the Greek economy since the 1990s, questioning thus the validity and necessity of wage contention policies implemented in Greece during the last decade.

Mainstream economists, therefore, argued that Greece did not have a proper strong and developed productive basis to allow for the salary increases experienced during the 2000s. And currently, there seems to be widespread agreement around the fact that wage reduction from 2010 to 2016 has been the main factor behind Greece's regained competitiveness in the international trade markets. The subsequent analysis of the trade account position will allow us to assess the accuracy of this statement.

The sharp current account deficits from the pre-crisis period have been significantly mitigated, in line with the structural adjustment programs agreed with the EU authorities. This was achieved by a mix of falling imports and rising exports with the latter rising faster than the former fell, From 2010 to 2014, imports decreased on average by 1.8 percent, while exports rose by 5.2 percent on a yearly average (see Figure 6.14). This allowed a rapid reduction in the trade deficit to occur, from 8.6 percent of GDP to 2.4 percent in the same period, even leading to a small 0.1 percent surplus the following year. However, deficits returned from 2016 to the present, although below 1 percent of GDP, as both imports and exports in goods and services experienced a sharp rise of 23 percent and 25 percent respectively.

Despite this rapid surge in exports of goods and services that closed up the trade deficit in record time, the technological content of Greek exports

Figure 6.14 Trade account (€ million and % of GDP)
Source: Eurostat. www.ec.europa.eu/eurostat

actually worsened with respect to the pre-crisis levels. If in 2008 the high and medium high R&D-intensive activities rose to 28 percent from 21 percent of the total in 2000, by 2018, they were down at 20 percent and had been as low as 17 percent in 2013 (such a low figure had not been registered since 1995). The low and medium low R&D-intensive activities, on the other hand, rose from 58 percent of the total in 2008 to 65 percent in 2018, also similar to levels seen prior to the decade of 2000s.

To sum up, trade deficits in Greece were eliminated during a convulsive decade of implementing wage contention policies underpinned by the dogma of internal devaluation. According to mainstream economists, due to wage increases which had surpassed productivity gains in the previous decade, labor costs increased, leading to a similar increase in relative domestic prices, and causing inflationary pressures that would in turn lead to weaker exports, thus undermining international competitiveness. A deterministic relationship between wage increase and loss of competitiveness was thus established, that required wage contention policies to be put in place. We argued that this was an unnecessary policy which inflicted much social pain and came at a great cost for the Greeks, for various reasons: (1) wages were already low in Greece compared with the European average in absolute terms; (2) the relative wage levels are still lower than their relative productivity levels when compared to the EU average, suggesting that wages in Greece are lagging behind the EU average also in relation to their productivity levels; and (3) no policies were devised in order to lower unit labor costs via increases in productivity.

Internal devaluation achieved a rapid elimination of the trade deficit via increased exports mainly in low and medium low R&D-intensive activities, but there is no evidence of increased competitivity gains. The productivity levels in Greece are still the lowest among other EU countries, and have experienced higher decline during the post-crisis period.

4.4 The result of the export-led pattern

We can thus identify an export-led growth pattern in Greece during the 2010–2018 period, given that the main component contributing positively to GDP growth was net external demand, particularly from the 2009–2013 recessionary period (see Figure 6.15). During this time both consumption and GFCF made a negative contribution to growth due to the contractionary demand policies applied, consisting in eliminating the public deficit via severe spending cuts, on the one hand, and eliminating the trade deficit via wage contention measures, on the other. As a consequence, the Greek economy entered a profound recession, with GDP falling by 5.9 percent on a yearly average during the same period. From 2014 to 2018, while still experiencing two consecutive years of negative growth, Greek GDP average growth was 0.7 percent, far below the growth rates of 3–4 percent experienced during the previous decade.

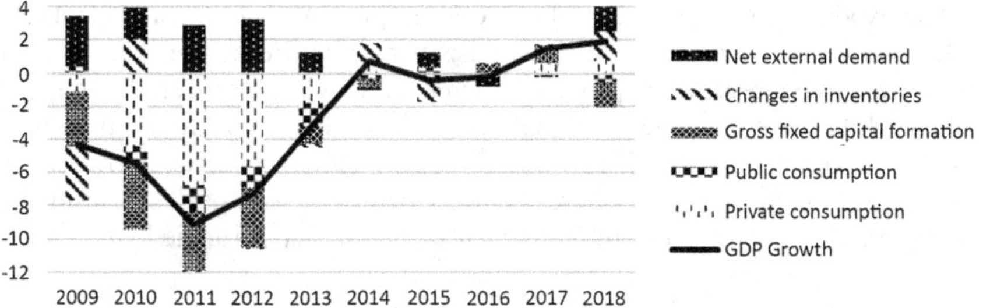

Figure 6.15 Contribution to GDP growth by aggregate demand category
Source: AMECO. https://ec.europa.eu/info/business-economy-euro/indicators-statistics/economic-databases/macro-economic-database-ameco_en

As far as the other GDP components are concerned, the decade of austerity implemented in Greece has severely dampened consumption and investment too. As discussed before, the impetus for reducing the wage share in Greece was underpinned by the mainstream conventional wisdom that the pre-crisis wage-led growth increased unit labor costs, negatively affecting net exports and thus resulted in a loss of competitiveness in Greece. Consequently, as a result of wage contention policies, the wage share dropped significantly from 28 percent to 25 percent of GDP from 2010 to 2018 (compared to an EU average of more than 10 percentage points higher, as seen in Section 4.3). However, a higher wage share is likely to be associated with increased private consumption expenditure since wage incomes are usually associated with higher consumption propensities. Private consumption therefore makes up the largest part of aggregate demand and real wages falling behind productivity levels or stagnating will have a negative effect on consumption (Lavoie & Stockhammer, 2013; Stockhammer, Onaran & Ederer, 2009; Storm & Naastepad, 2017).

Indeed, the figures for Greece are clear in this respect: household consumption growth suffered eight consecutive years of negative growth, from 2009 to 2016, while the Euro zone consumption average grew by 1.2 percent. Negative rates in Greece were as high as 8 percent in 2011 and 2012. In turn, this depressed future investment prospects, hampering future productivity growth. GFCF in Greece collapsed by 64 percent during 2008–2015, from roughly €60 billion to €20 billion and remained at those levels up to the present day. Productivity levels, far from improving, have dropped significantly with respect to 2010 levels, compared with other European countries, as shown in Figure 6.12. Unemployment as percentage of total labor force increased sharply from 12.7 percent to 27.5 percent between 2010–2013 and then decreased only gradually to 19.3 percent in 2018, quite far from pre-crisis levels around 7 percent. The Greek experience stands as proof that regaining competitiveness in the international markets should not be based on a low wage policy stance.

The export-led pattern did not lead to an improvement in income inequality either. As Figure 6.16 shows, the post-crisis period in Greece was characterized by a wealth concentration process, whereby the wealthiest 1 percent group increased its share of pre-tax national income[3] by 53 percent, from 7 percent to almost 11 percent between 2009 and 2016. At the same time the richest 10 percent also increased their share from 28 percent to 31 percent during the same period, while the bottom 50 percent saw their share decline by 6 percent.

5 Conclusion

In this chapter we analyzed the different economic growth patterns in Greece from the 1990 to the present date and their interactions with the institutional changes that took place during this period. As such, we divided our analysis into three parts and identified the corresponding growth patterns: the first, comprising the time previous to Greece´s entrance to the Monetary Union from 1990 to 2000 was characterized by a weak wage-led pattern, in the second, from 2000 to 2010, we find that Greece´s growth experienced a debt-driven regime, and the third period from 2010 to 2018 was characterized by an export-led demand pattern.

During the first period, growth in Greece experimented a weak wage-led growth, as the wage share and real wages grew faster than productivity, and GDP growth rates were superior to those of the Euro zone average during the second half of the decade. However, the labor market was characterized by an anomalous structure with a disproportionate importance of freelance contracts. Income inequality was on the rise, and unemployment was higher than the EU average. The already significant trade deficit was exacerbated by the capital account liberalization at the same time as the public deficit was on the rise, given the high interest rates at the beginning of the decade. The privatization plans that took place during this time helped to contain the public deficit to a certain extent, however, tax revenues were lower than expected and thus both deficit and public debt in Greece remained far from the Maastricht established criteria.

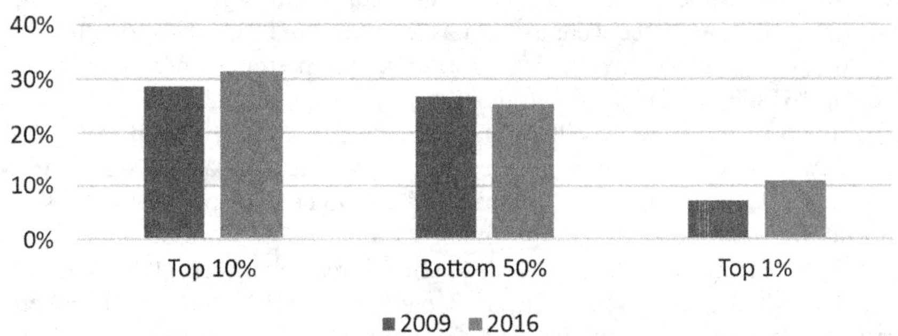

Figure 6.16 Share of pre-tax national income
Source: World Inequality Database. www.wid.world

Despite this fact, Greece was eventually accepted into the EMU in 2000 and the decade was marked by a debt-led growth model which allowed great disequilibria to accumulate in the private sector. The public debt grew unabated and served to sustain consumption but not to modernize the productive structure of the country, characterized by the predominance of SMEs which allowed scarce productivity gains. The adoption of the single currency brought financial liberalization of the capital accounts as well as the end of exchange rate risk, facilitating constant capital entry flows, on which the Greek economy grew more and more dependent. In a context of low interest rates coupled with looser loan conditions from commercial banks, this fueled credit growth to unprecedented levels. Higher indebtedness of firms and households led to an increased financial fragility which surfaced in the next decade, once the Greek public debt crisis broke out.

The 2010–2018 period was marked by a profound crisis in Greece, partly caused by the structural deficiencies of the Greek economy that had been built up during the previous decades, and partly induced by the aggregate demand contractionary policies that were imposed by the EU leadership. On the one hand, spending cuts policies were undertaken in order to eliminate fiscal deficit and reduce public debt and, on the other, trade deficit elimination was pursued via wage contention policies, thought to be the only alternative, given the impossibility of currency devaluation. However, to the extent that the goal of increasing competitivity by pursuing real devaluation proved successful, induced deflation in the form of lower nominal incomes and prices occurred, *de facto* increasing the real value of owned debt. An export-led growth pattern has been identified during this period, given that net external demand is the only positive component driving growth in Greece. Trade deficit has been eliminated in record time via an extreme ramp-up of exports, as real wages remained stagnant or declined during the decade, in line with conventional economic theory which establishes a deterministic relationship between wage increase and loss of competitiveness. However, wages in Greece were not only much lower than the EU average in absolute terms, but also in relation to their productivity levels, during the previous decade, which questions the validity of the widely used argument to enforce wage reduction policies: that wage increases had outpaced productivity gains. What is more, no policy was put in place to achieve a meaningful reduction in the unitary labor costs by improving the productive layer of the country.

The contractionary policies implemented in Greece during this period proved ineffective and inflicted great harm, as income inequality rose, and the country plunged into a deep recession in the first half of the decade, only to experience meagre growth thereafter.

Notes

1 Increasing debt levels do not need to become unsustainable as long as the central bank stands firm to support the currency from speculative attacks, by effectively acting as a LOLR and this was a mechanism well implemented at a national level, before the EMU came into being (see De Grauwe, 2013).

2 For a detailed account of the reasons why austerity policies which contract aggregate demand have been the preferred policy stance, see Dourakis (2013).
3 Defined as the sum of pre-tax labor income and pre-tax capital income.

References

Afonso, A. (2019). State-led wage devaluation in Southern Europe in the wake of the Eurozone crisis. *European Journal of Political Research*, 58 (3), 938–959. https://doi.org/10.1111/1475-6765.12317.

Amable, B. (2003). *The diversity of modern capitalism*. Oxford: Oxford University Press.

Bradley, J., Morgenroth, E., & Untiedt, G. (2003). *Macro-regional evaluation of the Structural Funds using the HERMIN modelling framework*. Paper presented at the 43rd Congress of the European Regional Science Association, 27–31 August, Finland.

de Grauwe, P. (2013). Design failures in the Eurozone—Can they be fixed? In *European economy—economic papers 2008–2015*, No. 491. Brussels: Directorate General Economic and Financial Affairs (DG ECFIN), European Commission. Available at: https://ideas.repec.org/p/euf/ecopap/0491.html.

Dourakis, G. (2013). Doomed to failure: The EU's role in the Greek debt crisis. In B. Temel (Ed.), *The great catalyst: European Union project and lessons from Greece and Turkey*. New York: Lexington Books.

ESM (2017). ESM annual report 2017 | European Stability Mechanism, Programme country experiences: Greece. Available at: www.esm.europa.eu/publications/esm-annual-report-2017.

Featherstone, K., & Papadimitriou, D. (2008). *The limits of Europeanization: Reform capacity and policy conflict in Greece*. London: Palgrave.

Fisher, I. (1933). The debt-deflation theory of the Great Depression. *Econometrica*, 1 (3), 337–357.

Frangakis, M. (2011). The public debt crisis in Greece: Roots, policies, outlook and alternatives. Available at: www.academia.edu/1084354/The_public_debt_crisis_in_Greece_Roots_policies_outlook_and_alternatives.

Frangakis, M. (2015). Public debt crisis, austerity and deflation: The case of Greece. *Review of Keynesian Economics*, 3 (3), 295–313. https://doi.org/10.4337/roke.2015.03.02.

Galbraith, J. K. (2016). *Welcome to the poisoned chalice: The destruction of Greece and the future of Europe*. New Haven, CT: Yale University Press.

Gambarotto, F., & Solari, S. (2015). The peripheralization of Southern European capitalism within the EMU. *Review of International Political Economy*, 22 (4), 788–812, doi:10.1080/09692290.2014.955518.

Gkasis, P. (2018). Greece and European Monetary Union: The road to the demise of the Greek economy. In O. Parker & D. Tsarouhas (Eds.), *Crisis in the Eurozone periphery: The political economies of Greece, Spain, Ireland and Portugal* (pp. 93–110). Cham: Springer. https://doi.org/10.1007/978-3-319-69721-5_5.

Greek National Productivity Board, Centre of Planning and Economic Research, & Kepe, N. (2019). *Annual report 2019: The productivity and competitiveness of the Greek economy*. Available at: https://ec.europa.eu/info/sites/info/files/economy-finance/el.2019-final.pdf.

Guzman, M., Ocampo, J. A., & Stiglitz, J. E. (Eds.). (2016). *Too little, too late: The quest to resolve sovereign debt crises*. New York: Columbia University Press.

Hall, P.A., & Soskice D. (2001). *Varieties of capitalism: The institutional foundations of comparative advantage.* . Oxford: Oxford University Press.

Heinz-Jürgen, A. (2015) Greece not competitive in spite of European subsidies: the EU should rethink its cohesion policy. In P. Liargovas, S. Petropoulos, N. Tzifakis, & A. Huliaras (Eds.), *Beyond 'absorption': The impact of EU Structural Funds on Greece.* Berlin: Konrad-Adenauer-Stiftung e.V.

Hyz, A., & Gikas, G. (2012). The SME sector in Greece: Financial gap during the crisis. *Agrarna Ekonomika*, 1–2, 43–49.

Karvounis, A., & Zaharis, N. (2015) Greece and EU structural funds: What do the choices made by Greece regarding the allocation of Structural Funds over the past three decades imply for the developmental model of the country? In P. Liargovas, S. Petropoulos, N. Tzifakis, & A. Huliaras (Eds.), *Beyond 'absorption': The impact of EU Structural Funds on Greece.* Berlin: Konrad-Adenauer-Stiftung e.V.

Katseli L.T. (2001). The internationalization of Southern European economies. In H. D. Gibson (Ed.), *Economic transformation: Democratization and integration into the European Union.* London: Palgrave Macmillan.

Katsimi, M., & Moutos, T. (2010). EMU and the Greek crisis: The political-economy perspective. *European Journal of Political Economy*, 26 (4), 568–576. https://doi.org/10.1016/j.ejpoleco.2010.08.002.

Kotios, A., Pavlidis, G., & Galanos, G. (2011). Greece and the Euro: The chronicle of an expected collapse. *Intereconomics*, 46, 263–269.

Kouretas, G. P., & Vlamis, P. (2010). The Greek crisis: Causes and implications. *Panoeconomicus*, 57 (4), 391–404. https://doi.org/10.2298/PAN1004391K.

Lapavitsas. C., Kaltenbrunner, N., Lambrinidis, G., Lindo, D., Meadway, J., Michell, J., Painceira, J. P., Pires, E., Powell, J., Stenfors, A., & Teles, N. (2010). The Eurozone between austerity and default. Research on Money and Finance, occasional report.

Lavoie, M., & Stockhammer, E. (2013). Wage-led growth: concept, theories and Policies. In M. Lavoie & E. Stockhammer (Eds.), *Wage-led growth: An equitable strategy for economic recovery* (pp. 13–39). Basingstoke: Palgrave Macmillan. https://doi.org/10.1057/9781137357939_2.

OECD (2013). OECD economic surveys: Greece 2013. Text 9789264206403 (PDF). Available at: www.oecd-ilibrary.org/economics/oecd-economic-surveys-greece-2013_eco_surveys-grc-2013-en.

Pagoulatos, G. (2003). *Greece's new political economy: State, finance, and growth from postwar to EMU.* Basingstoke: Palgrave Macmillan.

Perez, S. A., & Matsaganis, M. (2018). The political economy of austerity in Southern Europe. *New Political Economy*, 23 (2), 192–207. https://doi.org/10.1080/13563467.2017.1370445.

Perez, S. A., & Matsaganis, M. (2019). Export or perish: Can internal devaluation create enough good jobs in Southern Europe? *South European Society and Politics*, 24 (2), 259–285. https://doi.org/10.1080/13608746.2019.1644813.

Petrakis, P. E. (2013). Greece and the Eurozone: Staying or leaving? In B. Temel (Ed.), *The great catalyst: European Union project, lessons from Greece and Turkey.* New York: Lexington Books.

Plaskovitis, I. (2006). The evolution of regional policy objectives in Greece: Twenty years of regional development programmes. European Regional Science Association, ERSA conference papers.

Prodromidou, A. (2018). Continuity and change in Greek politics in an age of austerity. In O. Parker & D. Tsarouhas (Eds.), *Crisis in the Eurozone periphery: The political economies of Greece, Spain, Ireland and Portugal* (pp. 181–201). Cham: Springer. https://doi.org/10.1007/978-3-319-69721-5_9.

Schneider, F. G. (2007). Shadow economies and corruption all over the world: What do we really know? *Economics The Open-Access, Open-Assessment E-Journal*, 1 (5), 1–29.

Stockhammer, E., Onaran, Ö., & Ederer, S. (2009). Functional income distribution and aggregate demand in the Euro area. *Cambridge Journal of Economics*, 33 (1), 139–159. https://doi.org/10.1093/cje/ben026.

Storm, S., & Naastepad, C. W. M. (2017). Bhaduri–Marglin meet Kaldor–Marx: Wages, productivity and investment. *Review of Keynesian Economics*, 5 (1), 4–24. https://doi.org/10.4337/roke.2017.01.02.

Wright, V., & Pagoulatos, G. (2001). The comparative politics of industrial privatization: Spain, Portugal and Greece in a European perspective. In H. D. Gibson (Ed.), *Economic transformation, democratization and integration into the European Union*. Basingstoke: Palgrave Macmillan.

7 Italy and the global financial crisis

The fallacy of debt-led growth through moderation, austerity, and populism

Andrea Carrera

NEBRIJA UNIVERSITY

1 Introduction

Over the last 25 years, Italy has faced economic and social changes that have been significant in the aftermath of the global financial crisis of 2008. The advent of the euro led to an increase in the general price level that was negatively perceived by most of the population. The official unemployment rate varied from 11 percent in 2000 to 6 percent in 2007, from 13 percent in 2015 to 11 percent in 2018. Youth unemployment increased from 20 percent in 2007 to more than 40 percent in 2014. Despite a net trade surplus since 2012, the gross domestic product (GDP) has been growing relatively slowly. Also, public and sovereign debts appear to be worrisome. Public debt increased, for instance, from 104 percent in 2007 to 135 percent in 2019. Moreover, poverty increased sharply between 1995 and 2020: as of 2019, 4.6 million individuals were at risk of poverty. These economic and social changes have gone hand in hand with three institutional phases and the relative changes in the Italian economic growth model, which can be defined as debt-led: (1) the period of the moderate coalition of Forza Italia and Lega Nord in the 1990s–early 2000s; (2) the technocrat, pro-austerity government of the crisis years, whose Pension Reform and Job Act Law were very unpopular (deregulation); and (3) the nationalist coalition of Lega and Cinque Stelle. The aim of this chapter is to show the fallacy of the debt-led growth model of Italy over the last 25 years. First, the real economy has not benefitted from the debt increase as one would have expected. Second, the sovereign debt appears to have increased beyond any justifiable reason. Indeed, the sovereign debt of Italy is higher than the justifiable indebtedness of Italy's residents. The explanation for this would appear to be found in the unaccomplished architecture of the international monetary system.

The Italian economic and institutional framework shares a number of similarities with other European countries. For instance, in spite of different electoral systems – proportional in Italy, whereas majoritarian in Greece, Portugal, and Spain – Southern countries share the same variety of capitalism. Indeed, following Molina and Rhodes (2007: 232), Italy, as well as Spain for instance, is a case of a mixed market economy (MME):

> Italy and Spain … share numerous institutional features: similar structural cleavages that derive from their MME production regimes; certain common characteristics in their Bismarckian-type social protection systems; and similar (fragmented) forms of interest-group organization. State involvement in the economy has been pervasive in both.
>
> (Molina & Rhodes, 2007: 233)

The origins of Italy's contemporary capitalism dates back to the 1970s, when the peninsular economy had been rebuilt on the ashes of World War II. Italy, by that time, had become an active member of international trade and politics. Italy's capitalism, which came to be known as "dysfunctional" (see Della Sala, 2004; Rangone & Solari, 2012: 1202), "had the merit of distributing income in a way that enabled growth via the expansion of consumption" (Rangone & Solari, 2012: 1202). The last three decades of the twentieth century were characterized by a low degree of government intervention, according to the neoliberal policies that clearly took the form of privatizations in the early 1990s. "The 1980s–2000s have largely been characterized by policy stagnation punctuated by sporadic, consensus-based reform" (Molina & Rhodes, 2007: 242).

The 1980s were a fundamental turning point in Italy's political and institutional systems, due to major facts somewhat interrelated to each other: (1) the dismantling of the masonic lodge *Propaganda 2*, according to many, the Italian arm of NATO's Operation Gladio (e.g. see Williams, 2015); (2) corruption trials that led to the fall of the First Republic – *Mani Pulite* or *Tangentopoli*; and (3) the end of the Cold War, which paved the way to the current international economic and institutional system. The current economic path of Italy and Southern Europe started with those countries' access to the Economic Monetary Union (EMU) in the early 1990s, "despite apparently intractable initial imbalances" (Molina & Rhodes, 2007: 232). The one-Europe-one-currency project emerged a few years later through the eurozone, in spite of the fact that not all European countries met the entry requirements set out in the European Treaty. Italy and other countries such as Spain also share other features of a certain importance: "the consolidation and re-organization of collective bargaining systems that have resisted pressures for decentralization, a gradual loss of trade union strength notwithstanding; and renegotiation of the welfare state without delivering across-the-board retrenchment and substantial cuts in benefit entitlements" (Molina & Rhodes, 2007: 232). All these features constitute the current economic-institutional system of the Mediterranean country.

Italy, between the 1970s and the late 1990s, following a continental European pattern, concentrated mainly on the de-regulation of so-called non-standard or atypical employment relations for particular groups within the labor market – basically labor market entrants – but left "standard" employment and existing work contracts largely unchanged. This process has been referred to as "partial and targeted deregulation" (Esping-Andersen & Regini, 2000). In consequence, atypical employment grew from about 5 per cent in north and central Italy and about 7 per cent in southern Italy in 1970 to about 17–19 per cent in both parts, about 30 years later (Barbieri & Scherer, 2009: 1).

Institutional changes have occurred in Italy since the downfall of left-wing parties in the early 1990s to the present time. Three broad institutional phases and relative economic changes can be identified in Italy's last quarter of a century: (1) the advent of right-wing moderation; (2) austerity measures in the wake of the financial crisis of 2008; and (3) the time of uncertainty and populism. No government, in any of these phases, was able to fix the structural economic and social problems that have been afflicting the Italian peninsula since the late 1990s and especially since the crisis of 2008, from high levels of unemployment to the soaring sovereign debt.

Sixteen governments have been formed between the beginning of Legislature XII on April 15, 1994 and the current legislature (XVIII), which started on March 23, 2018. The following legislatures and governments have run the country over the past 25 years (Government of Italy, 2020):

1 Legislature XII, April 15, 1994–February 16, 1996: Berlusconi I; Dini.
2 Legislature XIII, May 9, 1996–March 9, 2001: Prodi; D'Alema; D'Alema II; Amato II.
3 Legislature XIV, May 30, 2001–April 27, 2006: Berlusconi II; Berlusconi III.
4 Legislature XV, April 28, 2006–February 6, 2008: Prodi II.
5 Legislature XVI, April 29, 2008–December 23, 2012: Berlusconi VI; Monti.
6 Legislature XVII, March 15, 2013–March 22, 2018: Letta; Renzi; Gentiloni.
7 Legislature XVIII, March 23, 2018–present: Conte; Conte II.

A moderate coalition of right-wing parties – *Forza Italia* and *Lega Nord* (now *Lega*) – was in power in the late 1990s till the early 2000s. At that time, the "progressive liberalization of NSE, especially project work and fixed-term contracts [was implemented,] such as the controversial 2003 *Biagi reform* adopted by a right-wing government" (Picot & Menendez, 2017: 13–14).

When the new right came to power in 2001 it took advantage of labor to further deinstitutionalize labor relations to keep profits high – general economic stagnation notwithstanding. The consequence is that any recent attempt to increase competitiveness has been made only by the precarization of labor and without serious policies to increase productivity. Therefore, Italy can be said to have enjoyed increased laissez-faire rather than better market co-ordination (Rangone & Solari, 2012: 1203).

Over the 2000s, Italy faced significant economic and social turmoil, in particular due to the global financial crisis of 2007–2008, which forced, together with other reasons, the Prime Minister, Silvio Berlusconi, to resign. The advent of the euro led to an increase in the general price level that was negatively perceived by most of the population. Despite the official unemployment rate falling from 11 percent in 2000 to 6 percent in 2007, Italy's economic and social problems have never been completely removed, not even in the 2010s, when different measures were adopted to deal with the aftermath of the crisis. For instance, youth unemployment increased from 20 percent in 2007 to 45 percent in 2014. Moreover, poverty increased between 1997 and 2018, mostly affecting the South: as of 2019, 4.6 million individuals were living at poverty risk, according to the Italian National Statistical Institute (2020).

The technocrat, pro-austerity government of the crisis years, led by Mario Monti, aimed to avoid the worsening of major economic indicators and, with that aim in mind, adopted a pension reform and Job Act Law which have been very unpopular. In the following years, other center or left-wing governments, such as the one led by Matteo Renzi, implemented a number of reforms in an attempt to increase employment levels. In the Renzi era,

> The major reform [was] clearly the Jobs Act, which [aimed] to alleviate the dualism of the Italian labor market. It [followed] in the footsteps of the Fornero labor market reform of 2012 in its objective to recalibrate Italian labor market policy and in its disregard for involving the unions.
>
> (Picot & Tassinari, 2015: 136)

Between 2012 and 2018, the governments led by Mario Monti (November 2011–April 2013), Enrico Letta (April 2013–February 2014), Matteo Renzi (February 2014–December 2016), and Paolo Gentiloni (December 2016–June 2018) carried out a series of "welfare measures alongside retrenchment and liberalisation" (Vesan & Ronchi, 2019: 2). The unemployment rate fell from 13 percent in 2015 to 11 percent in 2018, yet public debt increased from 100 percent of GDP in 2007 to 135 percent in 2019 (National Statistical Institute, 2020).

The reforms facilitated a rapidly rising share of temporary workers, even if since the late 2000s it stabilized around the West European average. The share of part-time work has also risen and is high in international comparison (20 percent in 2013). Unemployment protection is strongly segmented in Italy and often insufficient for non-standard workers (Berton, Ricchiardi, & Sacchi, 2012; Picot, 2012). Overall, these developments have led to precarious labor (*lavoro precario*) being a frequent term in public debate (Picot & Menendez, 2017: 14).

The years of Renzi as Prime Minister determined a fracture with the austerity measures imposed by major international and national monetary authorities. "The slow recovery of the Italian economy pushed Renzi to incorporate counter-austerity measures, although only in some social policy areas" (Vesan & Ronchi, 2019: 20–21). In particular, Renzi introduced a series of measures aiming to change the fiscal, educational, and pension systems, by removing certain restrictions imposed by the Monti government.

The end of austerity and the institutionalization of populism came in 2018, when a time of political pacts began between *Cinque Stelle* (the Five Stars Movement), a new populist political party, and *Lega* (the former *Lega Nord* or Northern League, now a nationalist party). The political alliance between the two parties did not last long. In fact, it was replaced by the second government led by Giuseppe Conte (*Governo Conte II*), a political coalition between the Five Stars Movement, the Democratic Party, and other minor parties. Yet, the 2018 election marked the clear rise of an anti-establishment culture promoted, in particular, by major populist members of the right-leaning party.

In spite of the political effort and different kinds of policies implemented in the last two decades and, in particular, since the global financial crisis of 2008, the economy has never fully recovered:

> At a local level, SMEs and their networks cooperate in a flexible and neo-voluntaristic way to produce territorial competitive advantages: a networked economy based on relational capacities. However, the success of local economies has delayed the adjustment of public policies at a central level. In the last decade, this process has endangered economic development, while Italian firms were challenged by increasing globalization.
>
> (Trigilia & Burroni, 2009: 630)

Globalization is a challenging issue. Indeed, despite a net trade surplus since 2012, Italy's finances have not benefitted from international trade as one would have expected to happen. Indeed, sovereign debt appears to be worrisome, and has reached levels which have never been so high, both in absolute and in relative terms. With a soaring sovereign debt and slow GDP growth, Italian institutions, as well as those of other European countries, are called to dig deeper so as to understand the formation of the monetary and financial problems that affect the eurozone. As shown in this chapter, the way international payments are carried out, indeed, appears to be at the crossroads, since it appears to give rise to sovereign debts. The indebtedness of Italy's residents – households, firms, and the state – appears indeed to be partly unjustified. It will be shown that a structural problem has never been the focus of the Italian institutional eye. In fact, data show that the Italian banking system turns out to be indebted to foreign countries, even though Italian importers always pay for their purchases – and trade surpluses notwithstanding.

Over the last 25 years and more, the Italian economy has been managed through a debt-led growth model. Data show, however, that the high debt increase – unjustified to a certain extent – was accompanied by economic stagnation. Therefore, as opposed to Baccaro and Pontusson (2016), who describe the Italian case as an indeterminate growth model, this chapter shows that the economic growth of Italy has been limited by the high increase in the sovereign debt. In particular, Italy's debt accumulation cannot be fully ascribed to the bad performance of the real economy. Indeed, it will be argued that the international financial system played – and still does play – a major role in the overaccumulation of Italy's sovereign debt. A fallacy in the architecture of the international monetary system leads to the over-indebtedness of the country, subtracting financial resources that could be used for investment purposes.

The following investigation deals, at first, with the current account balance, the foreign exchange reserves, and the gross external debt position of Italy since the creation of the eurozone. Comparative statistics will help explain the extent of the Italian sovereign debt together with the indebtedness of other Southern European countries. Data also show the presence of statistical discrepancies that have rarely been studied by the public authorities – not even by the monetary institutions. Such discrepancies between actual debt data and the expected ones show the existence of the unjustified indebtedness of Italy. The chapter then deals with the explanations of such an anomaly, focusing on the current international payment system and the role played by national monetary institutions in the international arena. In particular, it will be argued that national institutions should allow for the creation of international central banking practice to carry out monetary transfers and net commercial imports in a sound way.

2 The macroeconomy of Italy in historical perspective: major trends

Reaching about US$2 trillion in 2019, the GDP of Italy has almost doubled the level of 1995. According to the Italian National Statistical Institute (2020), the Italian service sector is the largest in terms of created value (about 1.3 trillion euros in 2019 compared to 1.1 trillion euros in 1995). The industrial system represents the second largest national sector (its products were worth about 0.25 trillion euros in 2019, that is the same as in 1995). The contribution of the construction sector to the GDP has been decreasing since the global financial crisis, reaching 1960 levels in 2015–2016 (about 0.07–0.08 trillion euros), with a sector average value fluctuating around 0.1 trillion euros over the past 25 years. Current account balances of the country have been positive since 2013, which means a strong performance by Italy on the international markets (a thorough analysis of Italy's balance of payments will be developed in Section 3).

The relatively significant increase in GDP over the last 25 years, however, has not been constant, and it must be understood by looking at three time periods: 1995–2000, 2001–2008, and 2009–2019 (see Figure 7.1 and Figure 7.2). In the second half of the 1990s, the Italian GDP growth experienced a fall from 3 percent to 1 percent between 1995 and 1996, recovered to about 2 percent from 1997 to 1999, and reached a peak of 4 percent in 2000. The early months of the twenty-first century marked the beginning of a quite sensitive growth of absolute GDP. Yet, the growth rate started declining fast and never recovered above 2 percent per year. Indeed, the largest GDP in recent Italian history was produced in 2007–2008, reaching approximately US$2.5 trillion. In those two years, which are known as the start of the global financial crisis, the Italian economy entered a recession which pushed the GDP growth rate to fall to as low as -5 percent in the aftermath of the crisis. Despite an economic recovery in 2010 (2 percent growth rate of GDP), national production dropped to -3 percent in 2012. The GDP started growing then until 2017, when the growth rate started falling once more.

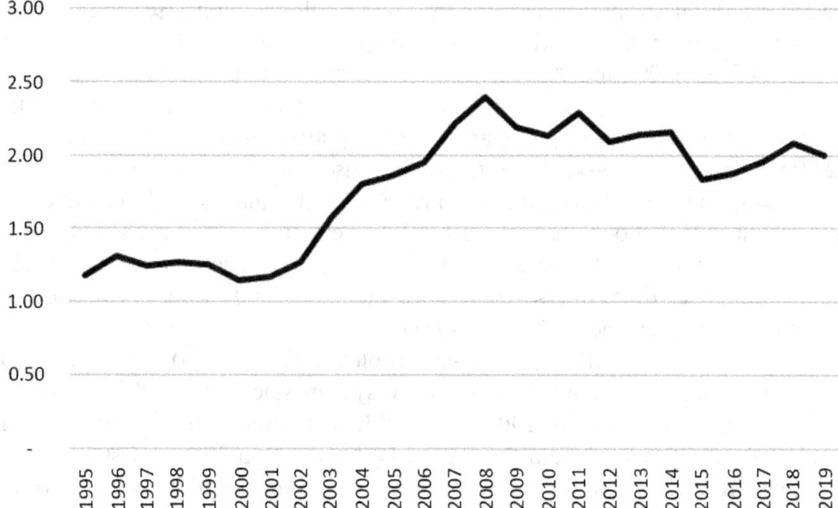

Figure 7.1 Italy's GDP (US$ trillion), 1995–2019
Source: Adapted from World Bank (2020b).

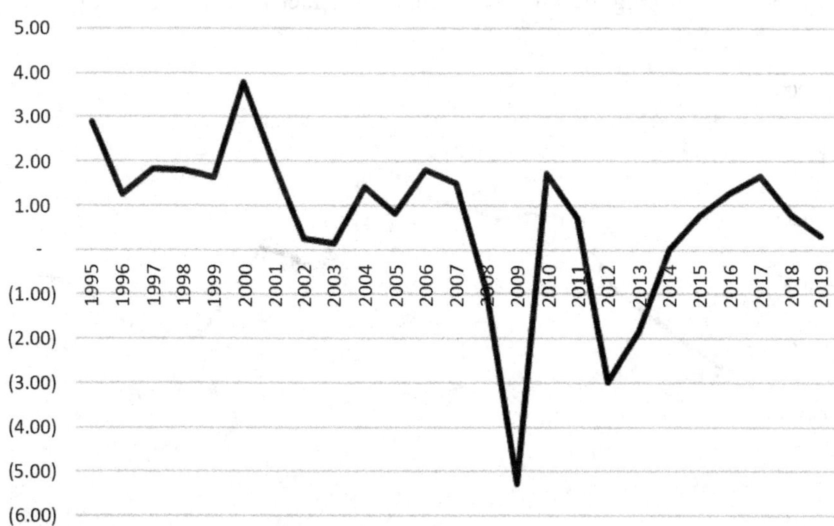

Figure 7.2 Italy's GDP growth (yearly %), 1995–2019
Source: Adapted from World Bank (2020b).

The financial crisis of 2007–2008 and the subsequent economic recession gave rise to a relatively fast decrease in Italy's GDP per capita (see Figure 7.3). Per-capita yearly product, indeed, had increased from about US$39,000 in 1995 to almost US$46,000 in 2007. After the crisis, the annual GDP per head went down to US$40,000 in 2014, which is almost the same as 20 years before. The second half of the 2010s was characterized by an increase of more than US $2,000 in per-capita product. Yet, a comparison of the GDP per capita at purchasing power parities of Italy, France, Germany, and the UK (Heimberger & Krowall, 2020) shows that, if the GDP per capita of Germany is held constant, the economic performance of the other three countries has comparatively deteriorated over time, in particular since the early 2000s. Italy is the country that has experienced the worst fall in GDP per capita.

By focusing on the GDP per person employed (Figure 7.4), one can grasp the deterioration of the Italian productive system since 2000–2001. With the exception of recoveries in 2007 and 2011, the annual product per head employed has decreased from more than US$118,000 in 2000 to less than US $110,000 in 2019. Over the last 20 years, the Italian economy has not been able to follow the constant growth path it started in the second half of the 1990s. In 2019, indeed, the GDP per person employed was equal or slightly less than its 1995 level.

It must be observed that the annual production of any Italian worker (Figure 7.4) is much higher than the yearly GDP per head, considering the total population (Figure 7.3). This reflects the fact that a large share of the

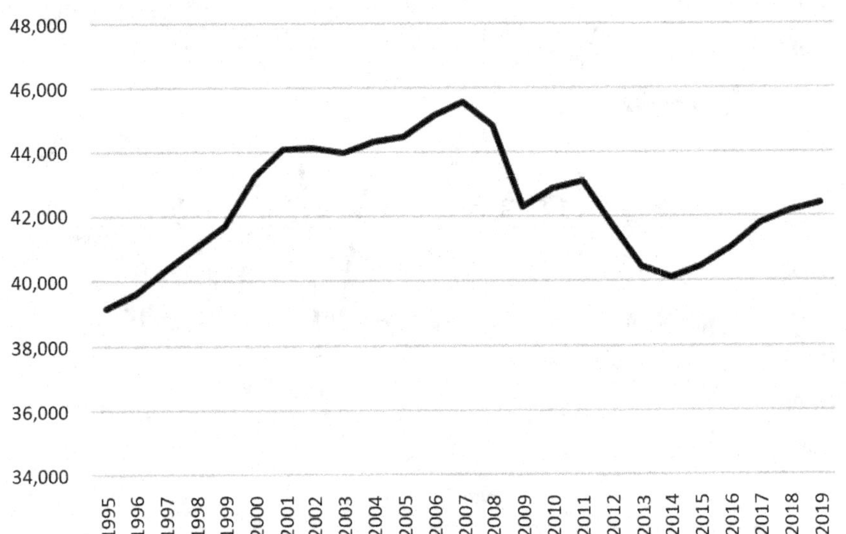

Figure 7.3 Italy's GDP per capita, 1995–2019
Note: PPP (constant, 2017, US$).
Source: Adapted from World Bank (2020b).

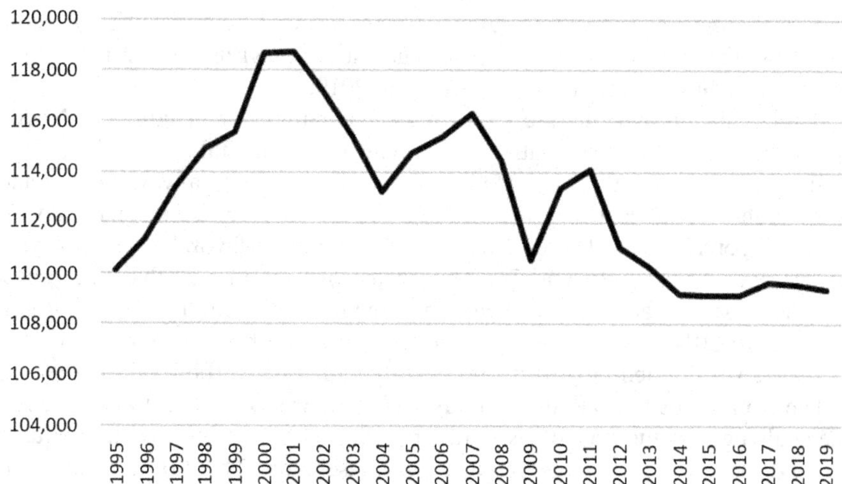

Figure 7.4 Italy's GDP per person employed, 1995–2019
Note: PPP (constant, 2017, US$).
Source: Adapted from World Bank (2020b).

population is not active, because they are either retired or unemployed (see Figure 7.5, which depicts total unemployment in Italy from 1995 to 2019). Total unemployment in Italy decreased by a half between 1995 and 2007, from 12 percent to 6 percent respectively. The good result of those years' policies and economic conditions was erased between 2007 and 2014–2015,

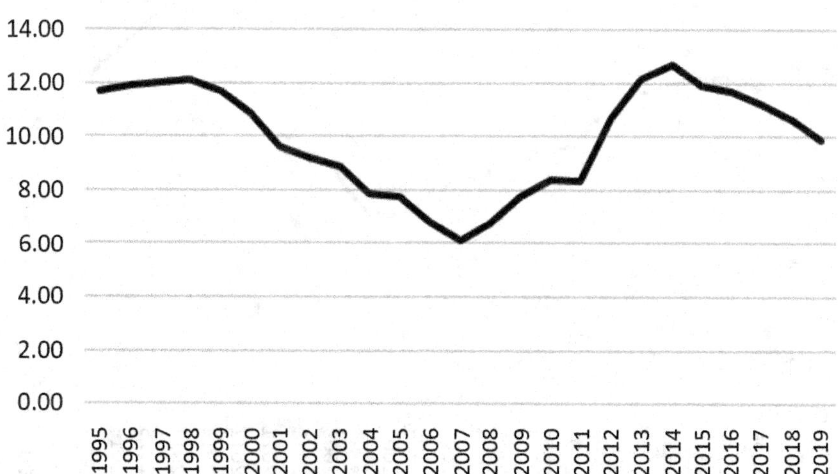

Figure 7.5 Total unemployment in Italy, 1995–2019
Note: Total labor force (%)
Source: Adapted from World Bank (2020b).

with a soaring unemployment rate that went above 12 percent. Future data will show the effects of public policies against coronavirus on the unemployment rate, which had reached 10 percent in 2019.

If total unemployment rate seems high, compared, for instance, to North American standards, the youth unemployment rate in Italy is much higher. Youth unemployment in the Mediterranean country has always been relatively high over the last 25 years (see Figure 7.6). In 1995, for instance, it was about 35 percent. Yet, the years up to 2007 were more favorable to employed people aged between 15 and 24. The unemployment rate in that age range had decreased in fact to 20 percent when the crisis started. The situation got worse until 2014, when about 42 percent of the youth was unemployed. By 2019, the youth unemployment rate in Italy had reached the level of 1995.

The troubles of the Italian economy and its slowness to adjust and react to the challenges of the post-crisis years are reflected by the increase in inequality and poverty of a large number of households. The GINI index, for instance, changed from 33 to 36 (out of 100) between 2007 and 2017–2018, in contrast to the pre-crisis trend (Figure 7.7). This means that, over the last few years, inequality has been rising. According to Eurostat (2019), 20.3 percent of the Italian population was at risk of poverty in 2017. After benefitting from social transfers, this rate fell to 19 percent of the total population, and amounted to 12.2 percent of employed individuals, 24.7 percent of total non-employed persons, 42.2 percent of the unemployed population, 12.7 percent of retired people, and 30.3 percent of all other non-active individuals. In 2019,

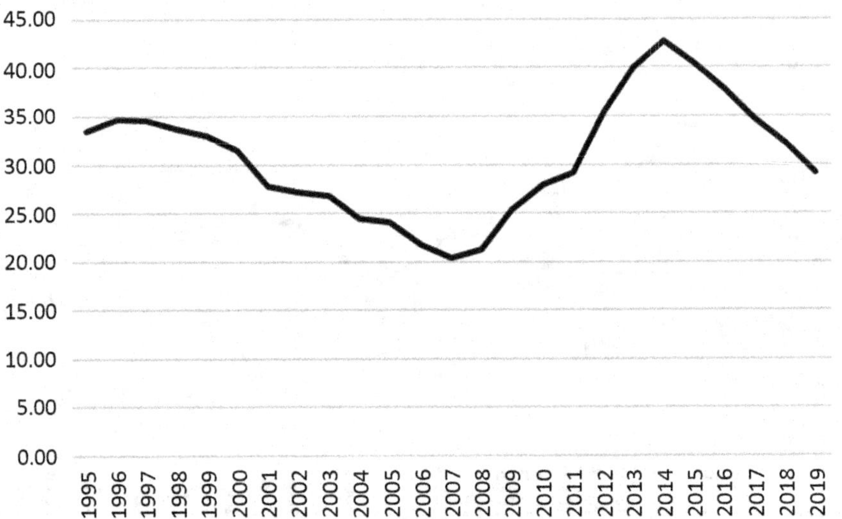

Figure 7.6 Youth unemployment in Italy, 1995–2019
Note: Percentage of total, 15–24 years old.
Source: Adapted from World Bank (2020b).

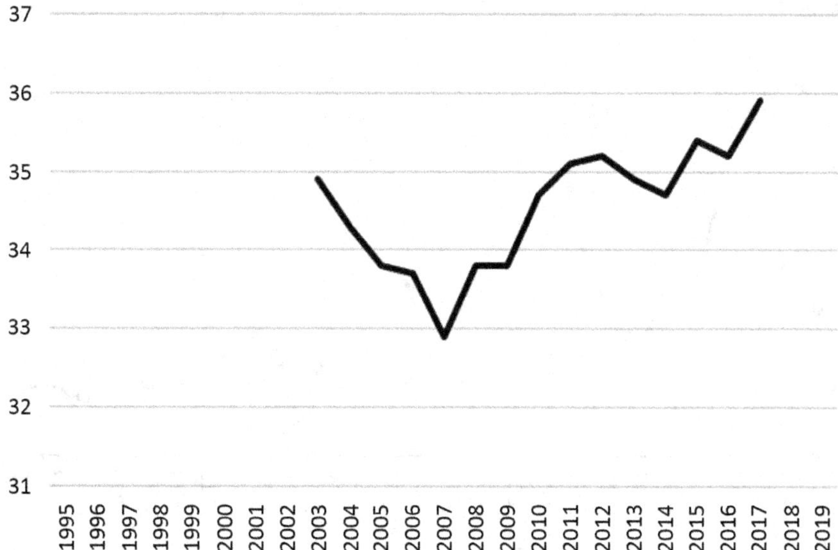

Figure 7.7 GINI index in Italy, 1995–2019
Source: Adapted from World Bank (2020b).

4.6 million people (6.4 percent of total households) lived below the poverty line, which was 7.7 percent of total population (National Institute of Statistics, 2020), compared to 8.4 percent of total individuals (7 percent of total households) in 2018.

As regards the price level, inflation has followed a downward trend since 1995, despite a few recoveries between 1999 and 2002, 2005 and 2007, 2010 and 2011 (see Figure 7.8). It must be observed that the early years of the twenty-first century are still remembered by the Italian population as a time in which the cost of living increased significantly as a consequence of Italy joining the eurozone. The population indeed has often attributed the price increase to the replacement of the Italian lira by the euro. Nevertheless, the global financial crisis brought about a sharp decrease in prices to such an extent that national and international monetary authorities – such as the European Central Bank – started dealing with the possibility of deflation.

Italy's public debt varied from about 120 percent of GDP in 1995 to about 135 percent in 2019, with a low of 104 percent of GDP in 2007 (World Bank, 2020b). Thus, the debt-GDP ratio is far above the 60 percent ratio established by the international stability pact and, significantly, in 2019–2020 it had increased by more than 30 percent compared to the crisis years. The increase has never been stopped, not even through the austerity measures of the post-crisis era. In particular, the sovereign debt of Italy has not decreased – rather the opposite, indeed –, despite the many attempts and recommendations from national and international authorities to lower it in order to achieve sound

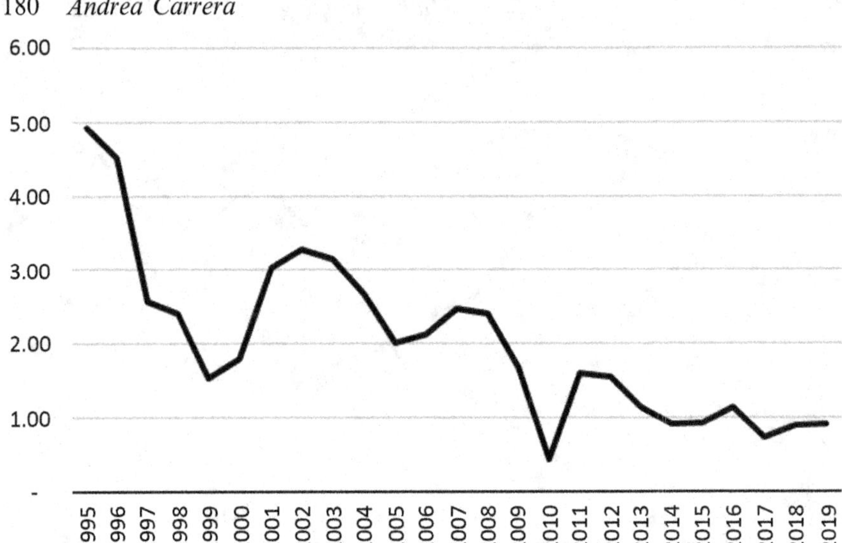

Figure 7.8 Inflation in Italy, 1995–2019
Note: GDP deflator (annual %).
Source: Adapted from World Bank (2020b).

national finances. Also, the increase in the debt of Italy does not seem to have spurred the economic growth so much sought by Italian residents. Section 3 is devoted to the analysis of the gross external debt position of Italy, its current account balance, and foreign exchange reserves in comparative perspective. It will be observed that the economic growth model of Italy, which can be called debt-led, has not been as successful as expected. In particular, statistical discrepancies show that the debt position of the country can only partly been explained by the traditional analysis. Indeed, the amount of debt contracted by Italy's firms, households, and the state appears to be far above their financing needs.

3 Current account balance, foreign exchange reserves, and gross external debt position: the case of Italy

3.1 Italy's increasing debt: comparative statistics

Italy has been a member of the eurozone since the adoption of the euro as the new official currency of a number of European countries. Over the years, the gross external debt position of Italy has varied, following a gradual increase from US$ million 1,117,911.67 in the last quarter of 2002 to US$ million 2,443,010.93 in 2018. The debt change amounted to US$ million 1,325,099.26. At the same time, the current account deficits of Italy turned into current account surpluses from 2013 to 2018. Total reserves of foreign exchange reserves and gold had been increasing substantially around 2007 and 2012, from US$ million 75,773.3 to US$ million 181,670.32 in 2012. The variation in reserves between the last quarter of 2002 and 2018 amounted to US$ million 96,740.21.

Any current account balance, as defined by the World Bank (2020b), "is the sum of net exports of goods and services, net primary income, and net secondary income." The current account balances of Italy between 2002 and 2018, as shown in Figure 7.9, increased until reaching their maximum value in 2010 and then decreased until turning into current account surpluses in 2012.

The current account (CA) balance of Italy has improved over time. Compared to the most indebted European countries since the crisis of 2007–2008, the Italian current account surplus is the highest. Indeed, in 2018, the United Kingdom had a CA deficit of US$ million 123,105,58, Greece has a CA deficit of US$ million 6,248,52, Ireland a CA surplus of US$ million 40,900.55, Italy a CA surplus of US$ million 53,839.13, Portugal a CA surplus of US$ million 956.88, and Spain a CA surplus of US$ million 27,306.63.

Foreign exchange reserves (FERs) are defined by the World Bank as those claims of national monetary authorities on non-residents. These include foreign currencies, deposits, and securities. "Total reserves include: monetary gold, special drawing rights, reserves of IMF members held by the IMF, and holdings of foreign exchange under the control of monetary authorities" (World Bank 2020b). Between 2002 and 2018, Italy's total reserves increased constantly until reaching their highest amount in 2012. They have never gone down to pre-crisis levels (see Figure 7.10).

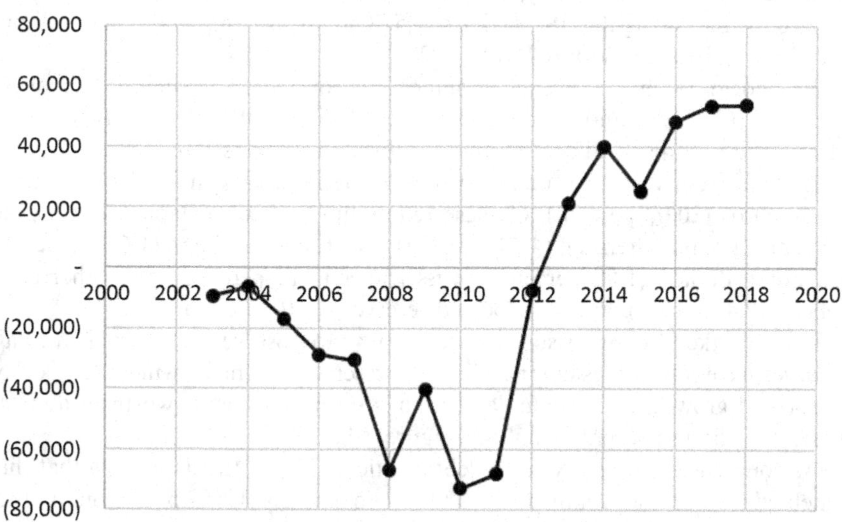

Figure 7.9 Italy's current account balances, 2002–2018 (US$ million)
Source: Adapted from World Bank (2020b).

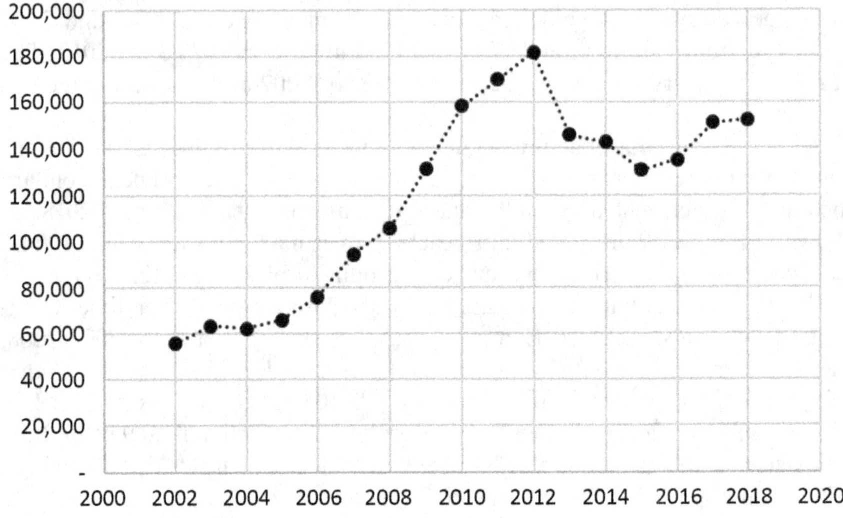

Figure 7.10 Italy's total reserves, 2002–2018 (US$ million)
Source: Adapted from World Bank (2020b).

Compared to the other most indebted countries in the European continent, Italy is the country that has accumulated the largest foreign exchange reserves (including gold), being surpassed by the United Kingdom in 2018 (see Figure 7.11). From largest to smallest, 2018 total reserves amounted to US$ million 172,657.75 in the United Kingdom, US $ million 152,361.94 in Italy, US$ million 70,633.19 in Spain, US$ million 24,920.34 in Portugal, US$ million 7,578.50 in Greece, and US$ million 5,222.68 in Ireland (World Bank, 2020c).

As shown by the Currency Composition of Official Foreign Exchange Reserves (COFER) and by the International Financial Statistics (IFS), total reserves are made of allocated and unallocated reserves (see Table 7.1).[1] In 2019, total reserves were made up of allocated reserves in US$ (61.78 percent), euros (20.07 percent), Chinese renminbi (2 percent), Japanese yen (5.6 percent), pounds sterling (4.44 percent), Australian dollars (1.67 percent), Canadian dollars (1.89 percent), Swiss francs (0.15 percent), and other currencies (2.4 percent), and unallocated reserves (6.29 percent).

For the sake of comparison, it is interesting to observe that European total reserves have low values compared to the reserves of China, which, thanks to export-led growth, has accumulated claims on non-residents worth of almost US$3.5 trillion in recent years (see Figure 7.12).

As concerns the gross external debt position of Italy, the data show that the indebtedness of the country reached approximately US$2.5 trillion in the crisis year of 2007 (World Bank, 2020b). The position has not improved, and it is 2.5 times the amount of Italy's debt in 2002 (see Figure 7.13).

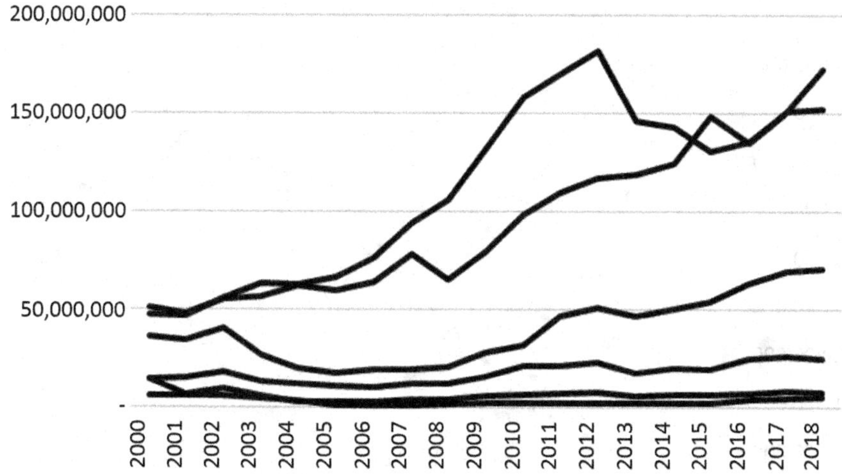

Figure 7.11 Total reserves (includes gold, current US$ million), 2000–2018: Great Britain, Greece, Ireland, Italy, Portugal, and Spain

Note: Lines, from highest to lowest, refer respectively to Italy, Great Britain, Spain, Portugal, Greece, and Ireland.

Source: Adapted from World Bank (2020c).

Table 7.1 World total foreign exchange reserves, 2019

Foreign exchange reserves	*US$ billion*
Allocated reserves	10927
Claims in US$	6751
Claims in euros	2193
Claims in Chinese renminbi	219
Claims in Japanese yen	612
Claims in pounds sterling	485
Claims in Australian dollars	183
Claims in Canadian dollars	206
Claims in Swiss francs	16
Claims in other currencies	262
Unallocated reserves	733
Total foreign exchange reserves	11660

Source: Based on IMF (2020).

In 2018, Italy's debt was the third highest, of the six most highly indebted countries during the crisis of 2007–2008. Gross external debt positions (all sectors, all maturities, all instruments in US$ million) between 2000 and 2018 amounted to US$8,424,581.45 in the United Kingdom, US$2,729,696.03 in

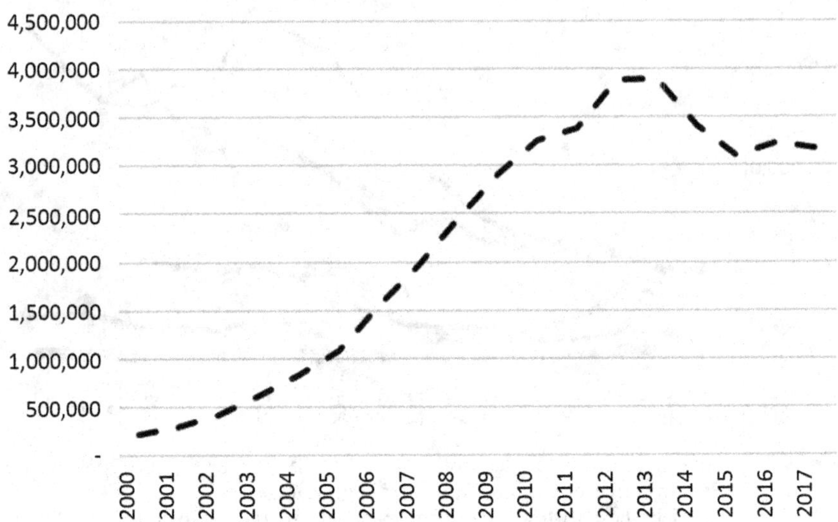

Figure 7.12 Chinese total reserves (includes gold, current US$, millions)
Source: Adapted from World Bank (2020c).

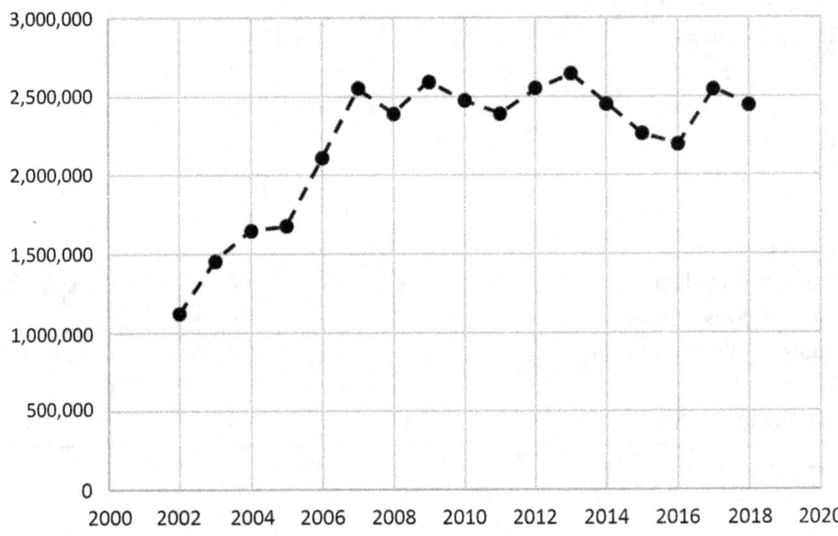

Figure 7.13 Italy's gross external debt position, 2002–2018 (US$ million)
Source: Adapted from World Bank (2020b).

Ireland, US$2,443,010.93 in Italy, US$2,305,339.97 in Spain, US$,329.89 in Greece, and US$472,616.96 in Portugal (see Figure 7.14).

As observed hereafter, Italy's indebtedness increased greatly, despite the good performance of the current account balance since the end of 2012. A contradiction is shown, indeed, between the positive behavior of the real economy – international trade – and the increasingly worse financial indebtedness of the country.

3.2 Statistical discrepancies: the unjustified indebtedness of Italy

The increase in Italy's debt was significant between 2005 and 2009, during the crisis which began in 2007–2008. Despite a slight reduction in 2015 and 2016, the debt of the country has never dropped down to the pre-crisis levels. The missed reduction in the gross external debt position of the European country is at odds with the fact that the current account balance has been positive for six consecutive years since the crisis. Indeed, all things being equal, a reduction in current account deficits should have led to a decrease in debt. Schmitt (1973; 1984; 2009) and Cencini (2015; 2017) have advanced the hypothesis that a

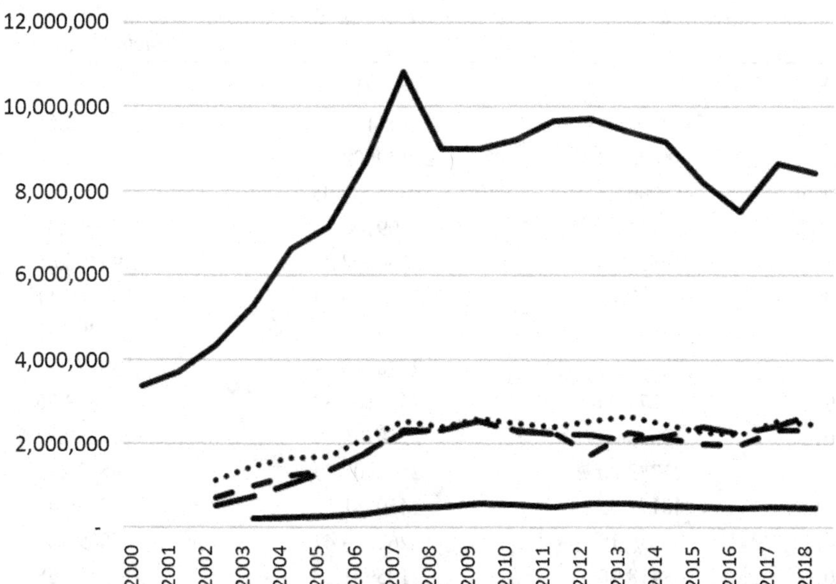

Figure 7.14 Gross external debt positions (all sectors, all maturities, all instruments, US$ million), 2000–2018: Great Britain, Greece, Ireland, Italy, Portugal, and Spain

Note: Lines, from highest to lowest on left side, refer respectively to Great Britain, Italy, Spain, Ireland, Portugal, and Greece. Lines relative to Portugal and Greece almost overlap in the graph.

Source: Adapted from World Bank (2020c).

certain amount of the Italian gross external debt position is unjustified, and they have also provided an explanation of that phenomenon.[2]

As shown in Table 7.2, the variation in Italy's debt from the last quarter of 2002 to 2018 amounted to US$ million 1,325,099.26. The change in total reserves in the same period amounted to US$ million 96,740.21. The sum of current account balances equaled US$ million -105,323,000.66, representing a current account deficit from 2003 to 2018.

As reported by French and Swiss economists Schmitt and Cencini to an investigating panel from the International Monetary Fund and the World Bank in Washington, DC, a discrepancy can be observed by studying the balance of payment of net importing countries like Italy.

The justified increase of any net importing country's debt is due to the total amount of current account deficits being accumulated over a certain number of years. In fact, the increase in debt is justified because it represents the need to finance current account deficits. The increase in the gross external debt position is also justified by the increase in foreign exchange reserves, which, in

Table 7.2 Italy's CA balance, total reserves, and gross external debt position, 2002–2018 (US$ million)

	Current account balance	*Gross external debt position*	*Total reserves (includes gold)*
2002		1117911.67	55621.73
2003	-9309.29	1453165.37	63263.65
2004	-6476.88	1649008.45	62386.14
2005	-17000.91	1676763.05	65954.01
2006	-28764.14	2109100.89	75773.33
2007	-30521.26	2550407.37	94108.65
2008	-66827.46	2389910.74	105649.11
2009	-40358.96	2589631.20	131496.92
2010	-72993.79	2470715.31	158478.31
2011	-68277.00	2390165.83	169872.36
2012	-7328.07	2550156.11	181670.32
2013	21282.00	2642900.34	145724.51
2014	40172.05	2450881.82	142756.49
2015	25379.13	2262635.41	130592.43
2016	48418.40	2195981.23	135133.28
2017	53443.39	2543780.06	151120.44
2018	53839,13	2443010.93	152361.94
	-105323,66 (sum)	1325099,26 (change)	96740.21 (change)

Source: Based on World Bank (2020b).

Note: Gross external debt position includes all sectors, all maturities, and all instruments.

the case of any net importing country, must be financed through foreign loans to its national banking system. Therefore, one expects the increase in the debt of net importing countries to be equal to the sum of current account deficits and the variation in total reserves. Yet, such is not the case.

By replacing the values of the total current account balance and total reserves change in the following identity, we expect to find the variation in the gross external debt position from the last quarter of 2002 to the last quarter of 2018:external debt change = total current account balance + reserves changeCA sum + reserves change = 105,323,66 + 96,740,21 = US $202,063,000.87The debt variation of US$ million 202.063,87 is not the one expected, i.e. US$ million 1,325,099.26. Thus, we conclude that a large part of the actual external debt position of Italy cannot be justified by referring to the current account balance and the change in total reserves. The amount of the unjustified change in the indebtedness of Italy from the end of 2002 to the end of 2018 is US$ million 1,123,035.39:Statistical discrepancies like the one found above show that the Italian monetary statistics cannot fully explain the huge increase in the Italian gross external debt position. It is interesting to observe that this does not hold true only in the case of Italy, but also in the case of all other indebted countries. Statistical imbalances, indeed, are also documented, for instance, in the cases of the United Kingdom, Greece, Italy, Portugal, and Spain (see Carrera, 2020; Cencini, 2015; 2017).

Between 2005 and 2006, the indebtedness of Italy increased from US $1,656,763.05 to US$2,109,100.89. Table 7.3 shows that the debt has increased ever since. The debt has never reduced to its lower levels that preceded the financial crisis of 2007 and 2008.

It is interesting to observe that between the last quarters of 2005 and 2018, the unjustified debt of Italy amounted to US$ million 607,303.37, while actual debt change was US$ million 766,247.88. That means that almost the entire amount of the debt of Italy was unjustified.

It is likely that national statistical imbalances are part of the international monetary discrepancies that have been under the scrutiny of the world monetary institutions over the last three decades or more. Indeed, national imbalances as in the case of Italy remind us of the imbalance in the world current account, which was discovered by the Working Party of the IMF back in 1987. The imbalance in the CA of the global balance of payments (BoP) has gone down in economics literature as the *mystery of the missing surplus* (see Krugman & Obstfeld, 2003). The same imbalance has transformed into a proper *mystery of the missing deficit* (see Cencini, 2015). As shown by the International Monetary Fund (IMF, 1992), an imbalance also takes place in the global financial and capital account – a phenomenon that has been labeled by Cencini (2015) as the *mystery of the missing capital outflow* or the *mystery of missing capital inflow*. Both discrepancies in the world balance of payments are shown in Table 7.4.

The International Monetary Fund has come to believe that global statistical discrepancies cannot be justified by mere errors and omissions in collecting

Table 7.3 Italy's CA balance, total reserves, and gross external debt position, 2002–2018 (US$ million)

	Current account balance	*Gross external debt position*	*Total reserves (includes gold)*
2005		1676763.05	65954.01
2006	- 28764.14	2109100.89	75773.33
2007	- 30521.26	2550407.37	94108.65
2008	- 66827.46	2389910.74	105649.11
2009	- 40358.96	2589631.20	131496.92
2010	- 72993.79	2470715.31	158478.31
2011	- 68277.00	2390165.83	169872.36
2012	- 7328.07	2550156.11	181670.32
2013	21282.00	2642900.34	145724.51
2014	40172.05	2450881.82	142756.49
2015	25379.13	2262635.41	130592.43
2016	48418.40	2195981.23	135133.28
2017	53443.39	2543780.06	151120.44
2018	53839.13	2443010.93	152361.94
	- 72536.58	766247.88	86407.93

Source: Adapted from World Bank (2020b).

Note: Gross external debt position includes all sectors, all maturities, and all instruments.

Table 7.4 World BoPs discrepancies

	2000	*2002*	*2004*	*2006*	*2008*	*2010*	*2012*
World capital account	-175,8	-135	-2,6	203	183,9	305,4	341,9
World financial and capital account	251,5	161	-208,6	-80	55	175,7	203,4

Source: Adapted from Cencini (2015: 353).

Note: Values are in US$ billion.

BoP data. Indeed, the IMF has also started looking for the causes of such imbalances by studying debt interest payments. The only explanation of national monetary discrepancies, instead, has been advanced by Schmitt (1973; 1984; 2009) and Cencini (2015; 2017). According to the French and Swiss economists, the lack of a multilateral system of settlement and clearing gives rise to monetary disturbances both in net importing countries and in net exporting countries. The next section delves into the monetary disturbances that afflict Italy and that probably are the source of the unjustified increase in its gross external debt position.

The high indebtedness of Italy does not seem to be due to the worsening of the current account, which has indeed been positive for almost a decade. The increase in the indebtedness of Italy's residents – firms, households, and the state – has not led to a proportional positive performance of macroeconomic indicators, in contrast to other countries, such as the United Kingdom or Spain, the indebtedness of which has gone along with a relatively sustained economic growth over the last few years. Section 4 suggests some explanations for the unjustified increase in Italy's sovereign debt and sketches the foundations of a reform of the system of international payments that would stop the over-accumulation of the country's indebtedness.

4 The current international payment system and national monetary disorders: the case of Italy

This section deals with the architecture of the current monetary system, aiming to show the disturbances that afflict Italy's payments system, and it also sketches the principles of the monetary reform that, through an international system of payments settlement and clearing (ISPSC), would eliminate the burden of Italy's unjustified indebtedness.

4.1 International monetary transactions

The composition of foreign exchange reserves shows that the US dollar is, at present, the national currency that is most widely used in international transactions. The US dollar, indeed, followed by the euro, is the currency that, more than any other, is used to make international purchases. Moreover, in the absence of an international central bank, payments between countries are carried out directly by national monetary authorities with no intermediation in-between. Section 4.1.1 shows how the system works and the monetary disturbances arising from it.

4.1.1 International monetary transfers

Table 7.5 sketches how monetary payments in euros and in dollars are made between Italy and the rest of the world (RW). Suppose that clients of Italy's banks transfer their deposits to other bank accounts in the rest of the world and that clients of the banks in the rest of the world transfer money to bank accounts in Italy. Entry 1a represents a situation in which Italy's bank clients hold deposits amounting to €100. Entry 2a is symmetrical to entry 1: bank clients in the rest of the world hold deposits to an amount of $100. Once Italy's bank clients transfer their deposits to the banking system of the rest of the world (entries 2a and 2b), Italian clients are debited by Italy's banking system and are credited by the banking system of the rest of the world (RW); at the same time, RW's banking system is credited by Italy's banking system and Italy's banking system is debited by RW's banking system. Symmetrical

Table 7.5 International payments

Italy's banking system				*RW's banking system*			
Assets		*Liabilities*		*Assets*		*Liabilities*	
(1a) Firms (Italy)	€100	Clients from Italy	€100	(1b) Firms (RW)	$100	RW's clients	$100
(2a) Clients from Italy	€100	RW's banking system	€100	(2b) Italy's banking system	€100	Clients from Italy	$100
(3b) RW's banking system	$100	RW's clients	€100	(3a) RW's clients	$100	Italy's banking system	$100
(4a) Firms (Italy)	€100	RW's clients	€100	(4b) Firms (RW)	€100	Clients from Italy	$100

Source: Adapted from Cencini & Rossi (2015).

operations take place once the clients of RW's banking system transfer their deposits from RW to Italy (entries 3a and 3b). Entries 2b and 3b also show that, as a consequence of international payments, credits in euros and in dollars are formed, respectively, in the rest of the world and in Italy. These credits in euros and in dollars constitute foreign exchange reserves held by RW's banking system and by Italy's banking system, respectively. As a result of reciprocal transfers, the titularity of monetary deposits is exchanged from the hands of Italy's clients to RW's clients and vice versa (entries 4a and 4b).

Whenever Italy pays the rest of the world in dollars, euros are never lost to Italy's banking system. In broader terms, no country ever loses a single cent of its national currency as a consequence of international transactions, either to transfer money abroad or to import foreign products (see Cencini, 2015; Mishkin, 2019; Rueff, 1964; Schmitt, 1973). The deposits level in the Italian banking system does not suffer any variation from international monetary transfers and this is due to current international banking practice. Indeed, when a payment order is made by one bank client on a foreign bank, a debit-credit relationship arises between the two national banking systems that prevents domestic deposits (or demand) from falling. As shown in Table 7.5, Italy's banking system is indebted to RW's banking system (creditor) and RW's banking system is indebted to Italy's banking system (creditor). Accordingly, there is no fall in national monetary deposits (or demand).

Table 7.5 shows how monetary transfers are processed by Italy and the rest of the world. An exception is made, for instance, by a certain amount of payments carried out within the eurozone through the use of the Trans-European automated Real-time Gross-settlement Express Transfer system (TARGET2). TARGET2 is a bilateral payment system that settles and clears a number of payments between eurozone member countries, but not all of them. As argued hereafter, the current international monetary system is such that, whenever imports and exports take place, an unjustified debit-credit relationship exists between countries, even though their residents have paid and have been paid. Moreover, inflation rises in the payee's country.

4.1.2 Net commercial imports

Table 7.6 sketches the way in which balanced imports and exports are carried out between Italy and the rest of the world. Suppose the exchange rate is on a par (€1 = $1). Entries 1a and 1b show the availability of bank deposits in euros and in dollars, respectively. Entries 2a and 2b represent the payment by Italy's income-holders (importers) to RW's income-holders (exporters); importers are debited, and exporters are credited. The two entries also show the credit-debit relationship of Italy's and RW's banking systems; foreign exchange reserves constitute a new credit in euros in the rest of the world. Entries 3a and 3b are symmetrical to the first ones, but in the opposite direction, as they represent the payment of income-holders in Italy (exporters) by income-holders in the rest of the world (importers). RW's banking system is debited in Italy and Italy's banking system is credited in the rest of the world. Italy's reserves in dollars increase as a result of the debit-credit relationship between the two banking systems. As a result of the reciprocal exports and imports by the residents of Italy and the rest of the world, national real productions have been exchanged and the debit-credit relationships between the two banking systems have been extinguished.

Even though balanced imports and exports may seem to be carried out in an orderly way, the current international banking practice leads to the formation of monetary disorders in both exporting and the importing countries.

Table 7.6 The equality of imports and exports

Italy's banking system				*RW's banking system*			
Assets		*Liabilities*		*Assets*		*Liabilities*	
(1a) Firms (Italy)	€M100	IHs (Italy)	€M100	(1b) Firms (RW)	$100m	IHs (RW)	$100m
(2a) IHs (Italian importers)	€M100	RW's banking system	€M100	(2b) Italy's banking system	€M100	IHs (RW's exporters)	$100m
(3b) RW's Banking System	$M100	IHs (Italian exporters)	€M100	(3a) IHs (RW's importers)	$M100	Italy's banking system	$100m

Source: Adapted from Cencini & Rossi (2015).

A first monetary disorder in net exporting countries is inflation. The exchange of national real productions would be carried out in an orderly way if money were used as a neutral means of payments, that is, as a vehicle of national products from one country to another without creating any monetary disturbance. Whenever monetary transactions are made at the international level, however, inflation occurs in the exporting country. Indeed, as shown by entries 3b and 2b in Table 7.6, as soon as national exporters are credited, bank deposits rise by an amount equal to the value of exports. In the example of Italy and the rest of the world, deposits double from €M100 to €M200 and from $M100 to $M200. The increase in deposits is not justified by any increase in real national production and, thus, it is inflationary.

On the other hand, in any exporting country, inflation is due to the very formation of Eurocurrencies. Any net exporting country enjoys an amount of foreign currencies that accrues to the official reserves account held by its central bank, or to private reserves, and that is invested in the Euromarket. As shown in entry 2b of Table 7.6, the structure of the current international monetary system is such that, when Italy pays in euros, foreign exchange reserves in euros in the rest of the world (exporter) increase by an amount equal to the value of Italy's imports. Eurocurrencies constitute a duplication of euros that have never left Italy's banking system. Thus, Eurocurrencies are a flawed product of the current international payments system, a purely monetary capital that feeds a speculative bubble in net exporting countries like China, which owns the largest amount of Eurocurrencies in the world.

A second monetary disorder takes place in net importing countries and consists in their unjustified indebtedness. Let us observe the issue through Table 7.7, which depicts the case of the United States, which is a net

Table 7.7 Net imports from the rest of the world

US banking system				*RW's banking system*			
Assets		*Liabilities*		*Assets*		*Liabilities*	
(1a) Firms (US)	$100	IHs (US)	$100	(1b) Firms (RW)	€100	IHs (RW)	€100
(2a) IHs (US importers)	$5	RW's banking system	$5	(2b) US banking system	$5	Firms (RW's exporter)	€5
(3a) Firms (US)	$100	IHs (US) RW's banking system	$95 $5	(3b) Firms (RW) (3b) US banking system	€95 $5	IHs (RW)	€100

Source: Adapted from Cencini & Rossi (2015).

importing country *par excellence.* Entries 1a and 1b show the bank deposits in the hands of income-holders in the United States and in the rest of the world, respectively. Entries 2a and 2b show US income-holders' purchase of products coming from the rest of the world. Once the payment is processed, importers and exporters have paid and have been paid, respectively. Yet, the US banking system is still indebted toward the rest of the world. This unjustified indebtedness is also shown in entries 3a and 3b.

As Section 4.2 shows, the creation of international central banking, through an international system of payments settlement and clearing would allow for the neutrality of money in the international monetary space. Ultimately, thanks to an international monetary intermediary, monetary disturbances in net importing and net exporting countries would cease to exist (Cencini, 2015; 2017; Schmitt, 1973; 1984; 2009). In particular, Italy's gross external debt position would not grow to an unjustified extent. Financial resources would exist then to finance the investments that are required to foster the economic growth of the European country.

4.2 International transactions and international central banking: the case of Italy

The great watershed between modern national banking systems and the old ones is represented by the foundation of central banks in relatively recent times. The Federal Reserve System, for instance, was created in 1913 after a few unsuccessful attempts in the nineteenth century. However, no central bank has ever lived up to its name until it was able, not long ago, to settle and clear payments between commercial banks by issuing the national monetary currency. It is in fact thanks to the central bank that the national currency is issued and replaces commercial bank money. It is therefore thanks to the central bank that commercial bank money is made homogeneous within the national monetary system. In its function as payment intermediary, central banking allows for the neutrality of money, which becomes a mere means of circulation. National products circulate through the economic system, conveyed by central bank money, a purely numerical tool. No monetary disturbance at the national level can ever be attributed to a failure in the interbank payments system enacted by the central bank.

At the international level, things work differently. No international central bank has ever existed or ever enacted a settlement and clearing system that covered the international monetary space. No monetary transaction has ever been processed by any international monetary intermediation. Indeed, international payments have always been made directly by one national banking system to another, and vice versa. No international currency has ever been issued and, since 1944, the use of national currencies has always been outflanked by the supremacy of the US dollar.

From April 10 to May 19, 1922, the League of Nations convened in Genoa, Italy, at its second international monetary conference. Member countries agreed upon the restoration of the gold-exchange standard system, which was enacted by the League's Financial Committee. As argued by Rueff:

> Under this system, the continental central banks retained all the dollars and sterling they received in order to reinvest them in their place of origin. For instance, every dollar paid into one of these banks was returned on the day it was received to the American economy, since it was immediately invested in the United States money market. Thus the key-currency countries, the United States and Britain, enjoyed the peculiar privilege of being able to buy abroad without having to curb in any way their internal demand. Consequently, their accounts could show a deficit indefinitely, since on the home scene everything went on as if the deficit did not exist … At the same time, the duplication of purchasing power resulting from the expansion of demand in the creditor country, without a corresponding contraction in the debtor country, kept the countries with convertible currencies in a state of chronic inflation … The system, therefore, was doomed, and it eventually collapsed in 1931, during the Depression.
>
> (1964: xi–xii)

Despite the stand taken by a number of politicians and economists in favor of the system – such was the case of Roosevelt's United States in 1934 – the gold-exchange standard was abandoned during World War II and replaced by the dollar-exchange standard.

The creation of the dollar-exchange standard by the nations gathered at the Bretton Woods Conferences in July 1944 was conceived as an attempt to replace the old international monetary system, which had collapsed with the failure of the gold-exchange standard, in order to avoid and put a quick end to the Great Depression of the 1930s. The high hopes of the American delegation lay in the use of a secure currency, the US dollar, as the international means of payments, the value of which was pegged to an ounce of gold. The post-war international monetary system created at the Bretton Woods Conferences in 1944, however, was far from being different, in terms of its economic effects, from the gold-exchange standard. As Rueff observes:

> In 1945 the same monetary system that had driven the world to despair and disaster, and had almost destroyed the civilization it was supposed to stand for, was revived on a much wider scope. But while in 1922 the system had been set up deliberately, this time it was reintroduced by tacit, yet unanimous agreement, without any definite decision or even an informal discussion.
>
> (1964: xii)

The dollar-exchange standard, as argued by Rueff (1964), was far from being the solution to the monetary disorders of the past. Indeed, the system soon proved to be inadequate to deal with the shortage of dollars that soon took place on the global scale. The United States was a world exports leader, with a positive balance of trade. This fact implied that importing countries were paying the US more than what the US was paying for products from the rest of the world. Given the specific nature of the international monetary system set up at Bretton Woods, net importing countries had to finance their imports from the US in US dollars, which proved increasingly difficult until the United States was a net exporter. The aids programs after World War II, such as the Marshall Plan, did not succeed in providing enough US$ credit abroad to solve the dollar shortage outside the United States. Also, the situation became even worse because of the larger and larger gap between the increasing amount of dollars throughout the world and the supply of gold. Because of such a gap, the convertibility of the US dollar into gold became hard to be respected.

The Nixon shock of August 1971 put an end to the dollar-exchange standard system and paved the way to the current free-floating era. By 1971, the United States had become a net commercial importer from the rest of the world and a step further was made by the Jamaica Accords to establish a new world monetary order that was entirely based on national currencies and no longer on the mixed system of the past in which gold had played a major role. International debates about the architecture of the international monetary system had taken place long before (see, for instance, Rueff, 1971; Schumacher, 1943; Stamp, 1963; Triffin, 1961). The British proposal at Bretton Woods, for instance, focused on the creation of an International Clearing Union (ICU) and the use of the Bancor as a new supranational currency to be used to carry out international monetary transactions. Yet, the British plan never came to fruition. Not even the creation of the Special Drawing Right (SDRs) at the IMF, reminiscent of Harry D. White's 1944 call for the creation of drawing rights, has ever come close to Keynes's 1944 plan for an international currency.

After the creation of the current free-floating monetary system, a number of authors, including Steil (2007), have defended the need for the creation of an international monetary unit. As argued by Schmitt (1973; 1984; 2009) and Cencini (2015; 2017), an international currency is required as a component of an international system of payments settlement and clearing (ISPSC) that would avoid the formation of monetary disorders in both net importing- and net exporting countries. As argued by the two economists, the monetary disturbances typical of the gold-exchange and the dollar-exchange standard systems are still present nowadays. In fact, not even the current free-floating era, which was established after the Nixon shock of August 1971 and the Jamaica Accords of January 1976, has been able to remove the inflationary phenomenon which takes place in net creditor countries and a few other monetary disorders of no less importance in net debtor countries.

The Schmitt plan introduces elements of novelty compared to the past. As first argued by Schmitt (1973; 1984), through an international system of clearing and settlement, any country would be simultaneously a net exporter and a net importer. Indeed, any net trade deficit would be matched by an equal amount of financial exports to the rest of the world. Likewise, any net commercial export would be matched by a net purchase of financial securities. International central banking would ensure the identity between commercial and financial imports and exports at the global level, thus eliminating the global imbalance that afflicts the world current account and the world financial and capital account.

Table 7.8 sketches the basic features of the ISPSC proposed by French and Swiss economists Schmitt and Cencini. For the sake of explanation, suppose the parity between the euro, the dollar, and the international currency, IC (€1 = $1 = IC1). Entry 1 shows the availability of bank deposits in the hands of income-holders in the rest of the world. Entries 2 and 3 represent the payment order issued by Italy's commercial importers through Italy's commercial banks and the Bank of Italy. The payment order is taken by the International Central Bank, which authorizes the payment of RW's commercial exporters through the intermediation of RW's central bank (entries 4–6). The payment is authorized by the International Central Bank provided RW's income-holders (individuals, firms, and the state) import financial securities (obligations and company shares, for example) from Italy's financial exporters. The payment is carried out through the intermediation of RW's central bank, the International Central Bank, and the Bank of Italy (entries 7–12).

5 Conclusion

The authorities that have governed Italy over the past 25 years sought to implement a series of reforms to improve the welfare of the Italian population. Indeed, especially in the aftermath of the crisis, a number of labor and pension reforms, for instance, were carried out with the aim of reducing unemployment and producing income inequality and lowering the country's internal and external indebtedness. Yet, none of the public authorities that followed throughout the years – not even when they chose austerity as way out of the crisis – was able to reduce Italy's sovereign debt significantly. In the attempt to reduce the indebtedness of the Italian banking system toward the rest of the world, austerity and left-wing measures proved no better than the right-wing policies of the early 2000s.

Since the creation of the eurozone, the data show that Italy's gross external debt is partly justified by current account debt and total reserves changes. The institutional eye, however, has not yet realized that Italy's gross external debt has changed beyond any justifiable extent. The reason for such over-indebtedness turns out to be the result of the current international payments practice, which leads to the creation of Eurocurrencies in net exporting countries. In particular, the very existence of Eurocurrencies gives rise to inflation in exporting countries and constitutes a means to carry out currency wars, to the detriment of net importing countries. Also, net importing countries experience another monetary disturbance. In fact, even though domestic importers – households, firms, and the state – always spend their incomes to purchase foreign goods and services,

Table 7.8 International settlement and clearing

	Assets		*Liabilities*	
	(2) Commercial importers	€x	Bank of Italy	€x
Commercial imports and financial exports	(12) Bank of Italy	€x	Financial exporters	€x
		Bank of Italy		Assets
	(3) Commercial banks	€x	Italy's commercial banks	
	(11) ICB (financial transactions)	ICx	Commercial banks	€x
		International central bank		
International central banking	(4) Bank of Italy (commercial transactions)	ICx	RW's Central Bank (commercial transactions)	ICx
	(10) RW's central bank (financial transactions)	ICx	Bank of Italy (financial transactions)	ICx
		RW's central bank		
Commercial exports and financial imports	(5) ICB (commercial transactions)	ICx	Commercial banks	\$x
	(9) Commercial banks	\$x	ICB (financial transactions)	ICx
		RW's commercial banks		
	(1) Firms (RW)	\$x	IHs (RW)	\$x
	(6) RW's central bank	\$x	Firms (RW's commercial exporters)	\$x
	(7) IHs (RW's financial importers)	\$x	RW's central bank	\$x
	(8) Firms	\$ (X – x)	IHs	\$ (X – y)

Source: Adapted from Cencini (2015).

the domestic monetary system of net commercial importers always turns out to be indebted. This has been the case of Italy, for instance, the statistics of which show that, through the past 20 years, indeed, the Italian gross external debt position has deteriorated beyond any reasonable prediction.

This shows that, in spite of the fact that the Italian growth model can be labeled debt-led, the indebtedness of Italy's residents has increased much more than in proportiona to their gain in real terms. This chapter has shown a contradiction between the slow economic growth of Italy and its increasingly higher sovereign debt. The mismatch between the excessive debt of the country and its small growth is due to the monetary disorders caused by the system of international monetary transactions.

As argued by Schmitt (1973; 1984), the search for the monetary reasons for the unjustified variation in the gross external debt position of Italy leads to a straightforward conclusion. Indeed, net importing countries incur an unjustified sovereign debt because of the absence of an international system of payments settlement and clearing (ISPSC). Accordingly, an ISPSC should be adopted by national public authorities, including the Bank of Italy, through the intermediation of an international central bank, such as the European Central Bank. Through the establishment of a multilateral system of settling and clearing at the international level, Italy's economic growth would benefit as a result of orderly monetary transactions, since the gross external debt would come to a substantial halt. Through international central banking, indeed, Italy's annual deficits would reduce, compared to the past. Thus, more financial resources could be invested in productive activities, instead of being deployed to finance unjustified indebtedness.

Italy is a "weaker 'Southern Model' with more uncertainty and poor economic performance" (Rangone & Solari, 2012: 1203). Italy and other Southern European countries including Greece, Portugal, and Spain

> were left highly vulnerable to the Eurozone sovereign debt crisis. Efforts by their governments to counter the negative effects of the financial crisis through countercyclical policies in 2008 and 2009 were cut short by the slow rate of accommodation from the European Central Bank and by the rising risk premium on their public debt.
>
> (Perez & Rhodes, 2014: 212)

The economic situation of Italy has even worsened following the strict state rules against COVID-19. As of June 8, 2020, the Italian GDP was expected to decrease by 8.3 percent over the same year (National Statistical Institute, 2020), with negative repercussions on the sovereign debt. A new institutional phase, through the cooperation between the Italian government, the Bank of Italy, and the European Central Bank, should be aimed at analyzing the debt issue, to try and reduce the unjustified burden of country's indebtedness toward foreign nations. The new institutional phase, if it succeeds in reducing the debt level, would reduce financial uncertainty and could trigger economic growth, investing financial resources that, at present, are devoted to financing the unjustified rise in the Italian sovereign debt.

Since 1945, we have again been setting up the mechanism that, unquestionably, triggered the disaster of 1929–1933. We are now watching the consequences, as they follow in their inevitable course. It is up to us to decide whether we are going to let our civilization drift further toward the inevitable catastrophe. For those with foresight, our most pressing duty at this juncture is to impress on Western thinking that monetary matters are serious, that they require deliberate consideration and should be dealt with systematically. Although we are already on the brink of disaster, salvation is still possible if we take decisive action. And the recovery must be inspired by deep conviction, based on a systematic analysis of past experience, and incontrovertible conclusions (Rueff, 1964: xiii).

Acknowledgments

The author is thankful to Alvaro Cencini for his useful comments on a reading of this chapter. The author would also like to express his gratitude to the editors of this book for their comments on a final draft. Responsibility for errors of opinion or fact remains with the author.

Notes

1 COFER and IFS collect allocated and unallocated total reserves, respectively.
2 Even more interestingly, they have shown that all indebted countries face an unjustified change in their gross external debt positions. See, for instance, Schmitt (1973; 1984; 2009) and Cencini (2015; 2017). In this regard, see also Cencini and Rossi (2015) and Carrera (2020) for further statistical evidence and explanations in the case of Spain.

References

Baccaro, L., & Pontusson, J. (2016). Rethinking comparative political economy: The growth model perspective. *Politics and Society.* 44 (2), 175–207.

Barbieri, P., & Scherer, S. (2009). Labour market flexibilization and its consequences in Italy. *European Sociological Review*, 25 (6), 677–692.

Berton, F., Richiardi, M., & Sacchi, S. (2012). *The political economy of work, security and flexibility: Italy in comparative perspective.* Bristol: Policy Press.

Carrera, A. (2020). Spanish trade deficit and reasons for international central banking. In S. Budría (Ed.), *La internacionalización de la empresa española.* Thomson Reuters. Forthcoming.

Cencini, A. (2015). *Elementi di macroeconomia monetaria*. Padova: CEDAM.

Cencini, A. (2017). The sovereign debt crisis: The case of Spain. *Cuadernos de Economia – Spanish Journal of Economics and Finance*, 40 (112), 1–13.

Cencini, A., & Rossi, S. (2015). *Economic and financial crises: a new macroeconomic analysis.* London: Palgrave Macmillan.

Della Sala, V (2004). The Italian model of capitalism: On the road between globalization and Europeanization? *Journal of European Public Policy*, 11 (6), 1041–1057.

Esping-Andersen, G., & Regini, M. (2000). Why deregulate labour markets? *British Journal of Sociology*, 53 (4), 693–696.

Eurostat (2019). Available at: https://ec.europa.eu/eurostat/statistics-explained/index.php?title=Income_poverty_statistics/it.

Government of Italy (2020). Available at: www.governo.it/it/i-governi-dal-1943-ad-oggi/191.

Heimberger, P. & Krowall, N. (2020). Seven 'surprising' facts about the Italian economy. www.socialeurope.eu/seven-surprising-facts-about-the-italian-economy [accessed August 20, 2020].

IMF (1987). *Report on the world current account discrepancy.* Washington, DC: International Monetary Fund.

IMF (1992). *Report on the measurement of international capital flows.* Washington, DC: International Monetary Fund.

IMF (2011). *IMF survey: Assessing the need for foreign currency reserves.* Washington, DC: International Monetary Fund.

IMF (2020). Data: United States. Available at: http://data.imf.org/ (accessed February 2, 2020).

Krugman, P., & Obstfeld, M. (2003). *International economics.* Reading, MA: Addison-Wesley.

Mishkin, F. S. (2019). *Economics of money, banking and financial markets.* Boston: Pearson.

Molina, O., & Rhodes, M. (2007). The political economy of adjustment in mixed market economies: A study of Spain and Italy. In B. Hancké (Ed.) *Beyond varieties of capitalism: Conflict, contradictions and complementarities in the European economy* (pp. 223–252). Oxford: Oxford University Press.

National Statistical Institute (2020). Statistics. Available at: www.istat.it.

Perez, S. A., & Rhodes, M. (2014). The evolution and crises of the social models in Italy and Spain. In J. E. Dølvik & A. Martin (Eds.), *European social models from crisis to crisis: Employment and inequality in the era of monetary integration* (pp. 177–213). Oxford: Oxford University Press.

Picot, G. (2012). *Politics of segmentation: Party competition and social protection in Europe.* London: Routledge.

Picot, G., & Menendez, I. (2017). Political parties and non-standard employment: An analysis of France, Germany, Italy and Spain. *Socio-Economic Review*, 17 (4), 899–919.

Picot, G., & Tassinari, A. (2015). Politics in a transformed labor market: Renzi's labor market reform. *Italian Politics*, 30, 121–140.

Rangone, M., & Solari, S. (2012). From the Southern-European model to nowhere: The evolution of Italian capitalism, 1976–2011. *Journal of European Public Policy*, 19 (8), 1188–1206.

Reinhart, C., & Rogoff, K. (2009). *This time is different: Eight centuries of financial folly.* Princeton, NJ: Princeton University Press.

Rueff, J. (1964). *The age of inflation.* Chicago: Henry Regnery.

Rueff, J. (1971). *The monetary sin of the West.* New York: Macmillan.

Schmitt, B. (1973). *New proposals for world monetary reform.* Albeuve: Castella.

Schmitt, B. (1984). *Les pays au régime du FMI.* Albeuve: Castella.

Schmitt, B. (2009). The theorem of interest. SSRN. Available at: https://papers.ssrn.com/sol3/papers.cfm?abstract_id=1413169 (accessed February 1, 2020).

Schumacher, E. F. (1943). Multilateral clearing. *Economica*, 10 (38), 150–165.

Stamp, M. (1963). The Stamp Plan – 1962 version. In H. G. Grubel (Ed.), *World monetary reform: Plans and issues* (pp. 80–89). Stanford, CA: Stanford University Press.

Steil, B. (2007). The end of national currency. *Foreign Affairs*, 86 (3), 83–96.

Steil, B. (2018). *The Marshall Plan: Dawn of the Cold War.* New York: Simon & Schuster.

Triffin, R. (1961). *Gold and the dollar crisis.* New Haven, CT: Yale University Press.

Triffin, R. (1963). Excerpts from *Gold and the dollar crisis.* In H. G. Grubel (Ed.), *World monetary reform: Plans and issues* (pp. 15–54). Stanford, CA: Stanford University Press.

Trigilia, C., & Burroni, L. (2009). Italy: rise, decline and restructuring of a regionalized capitalism. *Economy and Society,* 38 (4), 630–653.

Vesan, P., & Ronchi, S. (2019). The puzzle of expansionary welfare reforms under harsh austerity: Explaining the Italian case. *South European Society and Politics,* 371–395.

Williams, P. L. (2015). *Operation Gladio.* New York: Prometheus Books.

World Bank (2020a). Data: United States. Available at: https://data.worldbank.org (accessed February 5, 2020).

World Bank (2020b). Data: Italy. Available at: https://data.worldbank.org/country/italy.

World Bank (2020c). Data. Available at: https://data.worldbank.org/ (accessed February 5, 2020).

8 In the eye of the storm

The “success” of the Spanish growth model

Luis Cárdenas, Paloma Villanueva, Ignacio Álvarez and Jorge Uxó

COMPLUTENSE UNIVERSITY OF MADRID
COMPLUTENSE INSTITUTE FOR INTERNATIONAL STUDIES
AUTONOMUS UNIVERSITY OF MADRID
UNIVERSITY OF CASTILLA-LA MANCHA

1 Introduction

This chapter deals with the Spanish growth model from a socio-structural perspective, i.e., combining macroeconomic and institutional factors. We analyze the evolution of this model over the last three decades, from 1995 to 2018, reviewing its main determinants and characteristics, and examining how institutional changes have altered the model.

Spain constitutes a good case study for various reasons. In the first place, it is one of the paradigmatic cases of the so-called Mediterranean mixed economies (Amable, 2003; Molina & Rhodes, 2007), since its situation in terms of economic growth is one of the more successful in this group of economies. In the second place, its labor market is considered to be one of the most segmented with one of the highest non-standard job rates among European countries, which explains the high level of income inequality (Eurofound, 2019; Hipp, Bernhardt & Allmendinger, 2015). Additionally, it allows us to analyze the complex effects of institutional change, as structural reforms in Spain had a significant impact on the country's labor market.

Specifically, the strong yet volatile aggregate demand growth from 1995 to 2018 can be explained by the development of the following six institutional spheres:

1 The mode of production is characterized by an intense process of deindustrialization and tertiarization.
2 Financial market liberalization resulted in a highly concentrated bank sector, which is a common feature of financialization.
3 The internationalization of the economy is mirrored both in an increase in exports and in an increase in financial flows.
4 Economic policies have generally focused on expenditure restraint (reaching its peak during the “austerity era”).
5 Decentralization of collective bargaining and wage moderation are trends that have been accentuated during this period.
6 Liberalization of the labor market institutions has become widespread.

Changes in these institutional spheres have different effects on aggregate demand components, and hence on the post-Fordist growth models (debt-led or export-led). As reflected in Table 8.1, most of these changes had a negative effect on wages per worker and the wage share (as usually found during the post-Fordist era), and this negative effect on the wage share has been translated into a restriction on the growth of aggregate demand. Wage-led economies subject to continuous wage constraints tend to grow below their potential capacity (Onaran & Obst, 2016).

Nevertheless, in the case of Spain, this negative effect on the growth of aggregate demand has been partially compensated for by strong credit inflows and the stagnation of productivity during the 1990s and 2000s. Strong credit inflows allowed for the rapid growth of the Spanish economy until 2008. Furthermore, until that year, the economy generated a high level of employment, which resulted in significant increases in consumption and investment, despite the external and financial imbalances. This employment growth took place in an economy increasingly skewed toward low productivity (and labor-intensive) sectors.

During the post-2010 debt crisis, international authorities (the so-called "Troika") insisted on the need to implement strict internal devaluation processes through labor market reforms and fiscal austerity packages (Afonso, 2019; Baccaro & Howell, 2011; Perez & Matsaganis, 2018). Following the financial market discipline, these institutions imposed this political agenda in Europe's periphery, particularly the Mediterranean countries.

Finally, given the high increase in private leverage and the external deficit, along with the augmentation of investment and consumption, the Spanish growth model during the 1995–2008 period can be categorized as a "debt-financed, consumption-led demand model." The definition of the growth model after the crisis is not as straightforward, as we will see.

Some scholars and institutions hold the liberalization agenda (Baccaro & Howell, 2011) responsible for an export-led recovery in Spain (Perez & Matsaganis, 2019), thus supporting the notion of a successful case study (MEYSS, 2013). Other authors argue that this agenda failed in its purpose (Álvarez, Uxó & Febrero, 2019). According to the former, through the flexibilization of prices and wages, supply-side structural reforms made possible the necessary

Table 8.1 Effects of institutional change on aggregate demand, Spain, 1995–2018

Institutional sphere	*Transformation*	*Macroeconomic variable*	*Effect*
Production regime	Deindustrialization	Productivity	Negative
Financial	Financialization	Aggregate demand	Mixed
International	Globalization	Net exports	Mixed
Wage-labor nexus	Wage moderation	Wage per worker	Negative
Labor market	Liberalization	Wage per worker	Negative
Welfare state	Commodification	Public expenditure	Negative

adjustments to re-establish economic growth. As the mainstream narrative argues, the improvement in price and export competitiveness, fostered by the reduction of unit labor costs, triggered job growth.

In Section 2, we study the economic fundamentals of post-Fordist growth in Spain. Section 3 deals with the main institutional changes of the liberalization trajectory. Section 4 analyzes the effects of reforms on the Spanish growth model. The final section features the conclusion.

2 The post-Fordist growth model in Spain

Starting in the 1980s, western economies vastly modified their economic structures so that their institutional frameworks and economic processes adopted the main features of the post-Fordist era: internationalization, financialization, deindustrialization, and tertiarization. These global tendencies affected western economies' growth models differently.

In this sense, the difference between demand regimes (wage-led as opposed to profit-led) and post-Fordist growth models is very relevant. Most western economies, with a wage-led demand regime, underwent a decrease in the wage share which ultimately had a negative marginal effect. Nonetheless, these economies based their growth models on exogenous and contingent factors, such as financial stimuli, which counterbalanced the wage devaluation process yet resulted in a rather unstable dynamic.

Spain has experienced strong expansionary periods as well as severe economic recessions. Further on in this chapter, we detail the Spanish growth model, focusing on the main post-Fordist features: deindustrialization, financialization, and internationalization.

2.1 A debt-financed consumption-led demand model?

Over the last 25 years, the Spanish business cycle has undergone an expansionary phase, followed by a deep recession and finally a recovery period. The first expansionary phase (1995–2008) was intense in both duration and growth, overtaking most European economies and reaching average year-over-year (YoY) growth rates of 3.4 percent (see Table 8.2). In fact, the 2001–2002 crisis hardly affected the Spanish economy. However, the GDP fall registered during the 2009–2013 recession amounted to -1.8 percent every year, making Spain one of the hardest hit economies in Europe. The recent recovery period has recorded a slower GDP growth (2.7 percent) although it remains higher than that of most European economies.

With regard to employment evolution, job creation was very intense. According to the Economically Active Population Survey, the number of people employed increased by almost 8 million from 1995 to 2007. As a consequence of the new institutional framework (see Section 3), temporary work, part-time work, and internships explained this increase to a great extent (Garcia-Serrano & Malo, 2013; Toharia & Malo, 2000.

Table 8.2 Evolution of demand, employment and wages

Phase	*Years*	*Y*	*E*	*Y/E*	*W*	*W/E*	*W/Y*	*I/Y*	*U*
Expansion	1995–2008	3.4	3.5	-0.1	2.9	-0.6	63.4	28.2	14.0
Recession	2009–2013	-1.8	-3.6	1.8	-2.9	0.7	61.2	24.5	20.2
Expansion	2014–2018	2.7	2.4	0.3	2.1	-0.3	59.4	22.3	19.7

Source: Quarterly National Accounts (QNA), Eurostat. https://ec.europa.eu/eurostat/web/national-accounts

Notes: Average rates of log-differences (%): Y = GDP, E = Employment, Y/E = Labor productivity, W = Wage bill, W/E = unit wage. Annual averages. Percentage points: W/Y = Wage share, I/Y = Investment share, U = Unemployment rate.

Since the 1990s, employment had been very elastic depending on changes in demand. Indeed, employment grew at a yearly rate of 3.5 percent during the 1995–2008 period, while labor productivity stagnated (-0.1 percent). By contrast, employment decreases at a greater rate than the GDP during recessions, while productivity rises (1.8 percent). This reflects the countercyclical behavior of productivity.

The sharp tertiarization and the loss of a productive industrial base, which resulted in a highly labor-intensive economy (Cuadrado & Maroto, 2016), explain this particular job creation pattern. During the most expansionary period (1995–2008), job creation was concentrated in construction, real estate services, company services and retail; that is, low-productivity sectors with low technological progress penetration. Despite this being a common feature among western economies, Spain's capital/labor ratio is relatively low and increases at a slower pace (Buendía, 2020). As a result of this sectoral concentration, capital formation during this period was relatively inefficient, hampering potential wage growth. What is more, productivity even outgrew wages during the first expansionary period (see Table 8.2).

Regardless of the high employment growth and the stagnation of productivity, the unemployment rate remained at high levels (14 percent on average) compared to other European economies, yet it fell from 20 percent (3.9 million people unemployed) in 1994 to a low of 8 percent (2 million) in 2007. This lower unemployment reduction despite impressive job creation can be explained by the evolution of labor supply, which was driven by: (1) an increase in the domestic active population; (2) a constant rise in the participation rate (growing from below 50 percent to over 61 percent) due to the mass incorporation of women in the labor market; and (3) an increase in incoming migrant workers from the 1990s onwards.

Along with low productivity growth, unit real wage growth per worker dropped to -0.6 percent on average, not to mention growing wage inequality among employees. (Bernardi & Garrido, 2008; Martínez-Pastor & Bernardi, 2010). Such behavior can be associated with the concatenation of a series of institutional factors. In mixed Mediterranean economies, the labor relations framework is characterized by the prevalence of tripartite agreements over others such as firm-level agreements. While there is no "bargaining pattern," horizontal and vertical coordination in sectoral agreements tend to ameliorate the agreed-upon conditions depending on the region and the sector (Nonell et al., 2006). Nevertheless, there is no direct link between sectors, and company-level agreements set even lower wage increases than those at a sectoral level.

In these models, the tripartite negotiation agreed on nominal wage moderation. This was theoretically justified by the European convergence context, as inflationary pressures were to be avoided in case of intense job creation. Nonetheless, this translated into the stagnation of real wage growth as a consequence of the spread of non-standard contracts (temporary, part-time, and others) with fewer labor rights and lower wages. These decentralization and deregulation dynamics resulted in a persistent fall in the labor share from the 1980s onwards.

In a wage-led economy like Spain (Álvarez et al., 2019, Cárdenas & Fernández, 2020; Naastepad & Storm, 2006; Onaran & Obst, 2016; Villanueva et al., 2020) with a given income and employment level, real wage stagnation should moderate consumption as well as investment (because of the accelerator effect). Yet, consumption behaved similar to GDP (3.3 percent and 3.4 percent, respectively). This can be examined using a combination of two effects.

First, investment in labor-intensive sectors fostered job creation, resulting in an increase in the wage bill greater than that of unit wages (2.9 percent vs -0.6 percent). As Storm and Naastepad (2017) put it, this powerful employment creation is driven by an employment/productivity trade-off. It follows that the reforms during the post-Fordist era slowed down productivity growth, thus rendering employment more elastic to changes in aggregate demand.

Hence, the labor-intensive-based tertiarization of the economy allowed for a wage moderation strategy to go along with a high employment generation that boosts the wage bill, via the volume effect. Despite their lower wages, the newly employed furthered both private consumption and residential investment, given their greater propensity to consume, the creation of households (Arrazola et al., 2015; Neto, 2005), easy access to credit in the real estate bubble context, and the financialization process, let alone other investment related to construction (retail, transport, public services, etc.).

Second, gross fixed capital formation (GFCF) underwent an increase that was much more vigorous than the remaining aggregate demand components. During the period 1995–2008, GFCF registered a YoY growth of 5 percent, followed by a contraction of -8.8 percent (YoY) during the 2009–2013 recession. When considered in net terms (without depreciation), accumulation growth was even greater.

Regarding the technical composition of investment, equipment saw a greater increase (machinery, transport materials, software and intangible assets), but construction and building prevailed (60–70 percent of total investment). This points to a notable relevance in the growth model (Cosculluela & de Frutos, 2013).

The investment boost, particularly that made in equipment, was mainly financed using loans from abroad (Buendía, 2020). This financing source explains why internal demand was also supported by the evolution of private consumption. For the investment rate (GFCF/GDP) to grow with a stable consumption rate (C/GDP), the external sector has to increase its deficit, thus widening the existing disequilibrium. In other words, collecting foreign savings.

While exports grew at 6 percent YoY (1995–2008), imports grew at a higher pace (7.6 percent YoY). The gap became even wider from 2000 on. So, despite the contribution of imports and exports to trade openness, the external sector had a negative contribution to GDP growth during this period (Figure 8.1). This constitutes a key feature of the first expansionary period. The intense trade and financial openness were responsible for this external imbalance and for the ground-breaking spread of banking credit which is found to be at the root of the real estate bubble and the global financial crisis (Sanabria & Medialdea, 2016). This leveraging process ultimately leads to an investment squeeze.

In the scheme of things, the growing external deficit in goods and services (internationalization) was financed by external capital flows and a strong leveraging process of firms and households (financialization). Foreign savings have therefore played a significant role in compensating for the previously mentioned internal driven restrictions derived from the deindustrialization process. While the high employment volatility associated with the countercyclical behavior of productivity can be interpreted as a consequence of tertiarization, the stagnation of wages can be attributed to labor market flexibilization reforms and the decentralization of collective bargaining. This combination of factors corresponds to a debt-led growth model.

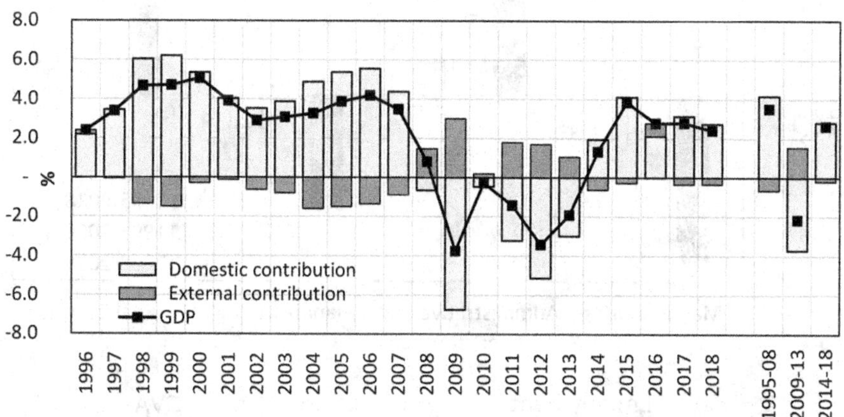

Figure 8.1 Contributions to GDP growth
Source: National Accounts, Eurostat. https://ec.europa.eu/eurostat/web/national-accounts

2.2 The production regime: deindustrialization, tertiarization and privatization

First, since the early 1980s, there has been a deindustrialization process, as the share of GDP and employment corresponding to manufacturing has been significantly reduced (see Figure 8.2), showing a weak specialization and a loss of competitiveness for more complex products with respect to the rest of the world (Alonso, 1999). Although a lower contribution to value added and to employment is a feature common to western economies (see Chapters 4, 7 and 10 on France, Italy, and the United Kingdom, in this book, for example), Spain has seen sharp declines (in share of gross value added (GVA), up to 13 percent in current terms, and 15 percent in constant terms; and even below 15 percent in terms of employment). With regard to capital stock (data from BBVA-IVIE), that which corresponds to industry has lost more than 5pp, falling to less than 23 percent of GDP. On the other hand, there has been a strong increase in capital in the construction, financial and real estate sectors, as well as other private services and public administration.

As Figure 8.2 shows, the weight of manufacturing in employment has fallen by 7.15pp and its weight of GVA by 5.15pp during the period 1995–2018, with most of the decrease concentrated in the years 1995–2008. However, the biggest increases in the structure of employment 5pp are administrative and support services, while real estate has taken over in terms of GVA.

Among the causes that explain this phenomenon are the strong destruction of productive capacities in traditional branches (such as steel and shipbuilding) in the 1980s (Caloghirou, Voulgaris & Zambarloukos, 2000), which were not replaced by new alternative capacities, and the subsequent absence of industrial

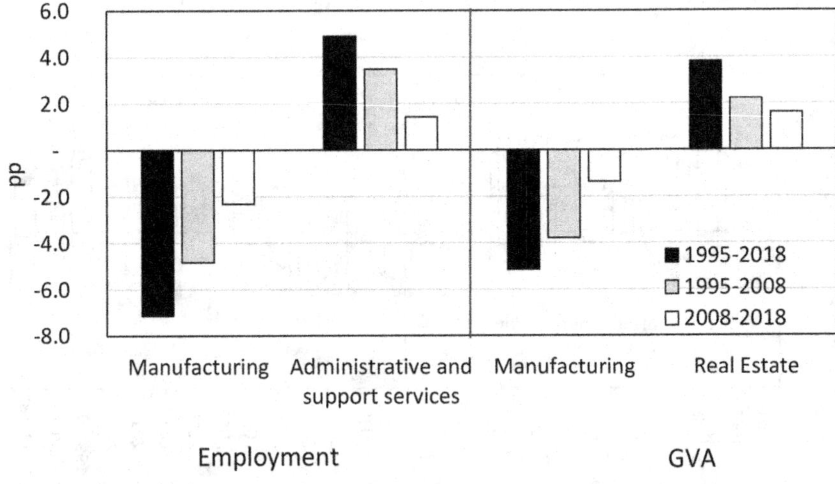

Figure 8.2 Shift-share in employment and real GVA in select branches
Source: National Accounts, Eurostat. https://ec.europa.eu/eurostat/web/national-accounts

policy and strategic decisions by the public authorities aimed at strengthening industrial activity. Likewise, the lack of investment in the sector beginning in the late 1990s, in parallel with the development of the real estate financial bubble, has led to a persistent technological weakness, mirrored in the insufficient dedication of resources to R&D (Castellacci & Álvarez, 2006). The situation has been aggravated by the growing acquisition of Spanish companies by foreign investors, whose transnational strategies in Spain have focused on lines of specialization with lower technological intensity in the international context.

At the same time, there has been a move toward tertiarization, which until 2007 was heavily skewed toward construction and finance (including real estate) and later toward hotel and restaurant services. Thus, the finance-real estate sector increased its relative share to represent, in constant terms, more than 14 percent of GVA in 2007, while the construction sector increased its share to almost 12 percent. Real estate activities alone gained more than 4pp in the weight of GVA between 1995 and 2018 (see Figure 8.2).

Second, with regard to the business structure and functioning of the main markets for goods and services, the formation of a group of large Spanish companies was carried out in relation to the privatization of state-owned companies (Comín, 2008; Vergés, 2000); especially from 1996, when the massive sale of majority share packages took place, resulting in a sharp reduction in the remaining state-owned service companies. Simultaneously, mergers and takeovers also took place among private firms (Buendía, 2020), e.g. large companies in the construction and infrastructure sectors (ACS, FCC, Ferrovial, OHL, Acciona and Sacyr), electric utilities companies (Iberdrola and Fenosa-Gas Natural), and the banking sector (Santander, BBVA, Sabadell) in the context of financial liberalization.

As a result, a considerable share of large, mainly Spanish-owned, companies are companies from a previous process of concentration and privatization of those that were once state-owned (Binda, 2013). This has generated a growing asymmetry between, on the one hand, the small nucleus of large companies with oligopolistic positions in their respective markets, which are capable of increasingly diversifying their product lines; and, on the other hand, a huge number of small establishments, many of which are still run by families. According to the INE's Central Business Directory, at one end of the spectrum only 0.05 percent of companies have more than 500 employees, while at the other end, more than 90 percent have fewer than 10 employees. This produces a business atomization that severely constrains productive capacity, the incorporation of technology and the improvement of labor efficiency, particularly within this small business network.

The strong increase in foreign direct investment in the Spanish economy has led to a majority or exclusive control of certain industrial branches (automotive, chemical, electronics, part of the food industry) and to a significant presence in services such as telecommunications, insurance, large shopping centers, auditing, consulting, and the media, among others. The most frequent entry procedure has been through the purchase of existing companies, while the creation of new companies has occurred solely in certain activities. As a consequence, a significant number of the large existing companies in the Spanish economy are foreign multinationals. According to the INE (Statistics on the Subsidiaries of Foreign Companies in Spain), in 2017, multinational companies accounted for 30 percent of total turnover, rising to 41 percent in the case of industry, and within this sector, 52 percent for chemicals and 58 percent for electrical, electronic and optical material and equipment, reaching a maximum of 81.5 percent for transport material.

This particular business structure composition, with a few large companies and multinationals that account for a large proportion of employment (33 percent of private sector affiliates work for companies with more than 500 workers) and a very high number of small and very small companies, has articulated a social bloc around these large companies and their interests (Molina & Rhodes, 2007; Royo, 2007; Rubio-Mondéjar & Garrués-Irurzun, 2016) that in practice has allowed their political demands to be implemented. One example of this is the demand for the prioritization of company-level agreements, formalized in the early 2000s (Martin & Alós, 2003), and effective in 2012 (as detailed in Section 3).

2.3 Financialization and banking concentration

Beginning in the 1980s, financial liberalization consisted of eliminating regulated ratios and interest rates that limited the management of the assets and liabilities of banks and savings banks, along with the liberalization of internal and external capital movements, including the presence of foreign financial institutions. Parallel to this, the geographical expansion of savings banks was introduced and the concentration of banks was promoted (Pagoulatos, 2003; Perez, 1997). Until 1993, banks avoided external competition thanks to the conditions negotiated by the Spanish government when it joined the EEC. Reforms leading to greater activity in financial markets were also passed, with the increasing participation of foreign capital and the creation of new financial institutions related to capital markets. Thus, companies increased their capacity for external financing, both through bank credit and through increased access to capital markets, increasing the significance of direct investment and other inflows of foreign capital stimulated by the entry into the EEC.

Likewise, monetary and financial conditions were determined by the process that began with the Maastricht Treaty, which consolidated the creation of the single currency and the European Central Bank (ECB), and were strengthened through the functioning of the euro monetary area. The ECB's monetary policy and the functioning of the European money markets led to a fall in real interest rates in all European economies, which was more pronounced in the case of Spain where the difference between the official interest rate and inflation in the consumer price index became negative between 2002 and 2006. The combination of falling rates, a common currency and easy access to external financing (Fuentes, 2009) fostered the expansion of credit within the economy.

This context of monetary laxity acted in conjunction with the financial and real estate boom that began in the second half of the 1990s and became a speculative bubble from the beginning of the following decade. Much of the credit was channeled into the purchase of homes and other properties. Mortgage-backed loans grew to represent 58 percent of the total in 2007, while commercial credit fell to 5 percent.

Three figures help us illustrate the bubble. The first is the exponential growth of residential investment (133 percent between 1995 and 2007, in constant terms) and of free housing prices (201 percent in the same period). The second is the parallel increase in credit expansion with respect to GDP, from 72 percent to 212 percent. This is one of the highest percentages internationally, well above that recorded by most Western countries. The third figure is the increase in the capitalization value of listed companies, which rose from 33 percent to 125 percent of GDP (source: Bank of Spain, www.bde.es/webbde/en/estadis/infoest/bolest3.html).

As leaders of this monetary expansion, banks and savings banks (the latter with an unprecedented expansion) increasingly focused on granting loans related to construction and development credit (companies) and the purchase of property (households). In turn, the need for greater liquidity to further expand this credit policy led to a sharp increase in their foreign debt position, borrowing from European banks and issuing easily negotiable debt securities abroad, which increased the gap between their deposits and loans. Thus, the symptoms of financial fragility (Ruiz, Stupariu & Vilariño, 2015) became increasingly pronounced, since a large part of their assets consisted of long-term mortgage loans (whose recovery depended on the repayment terms of the borrowers), while their liabilities were dominated by short- and medium-term payment demands, which depended largely on international factors.

The dominant position of the large banks is reflected in the distribution of corporate profits. During this period, the profits of the financial and insurance sectors increased their share from 3.7 percent to 7.1 percent of national income. This fact constitutes one of the features of the "financialization" of the economy, along with other features such as: (1) the importance of the financial operations of non-financial companies and households, both in the formation of their income and assets and in their liabilities; (2) the very strong expansion and interconnection of the markets for financial securities, derivative instruments and financed assets (especially real estate); (3) the primacy of financial criteria in the decisions of the state, non-financial companies, and households; and (4) the pendulum influence of the dynamics of the financial markets on the general progress of the economy.

The process of liberalization was accompanied by a greater concentration around a small core of large banks, as a result of five key developments: (1) the bankruptcy at the beginning of the 1980s of medium-sized banks (Urquijo, Catalana, Rumasa) which were acquired by large banks; (2) the crisis in 1993 of a large bank, Banesto, which was ultimately purchased by another one, Santander; (3) the chain of mergers encouraged by financial liberalization; (4) the privatization of public financial institutions, previously grouped around Argentaria in the 1990s; and (5) the crisis beginning in 2008 of many banks and savings banks involved in the previous real estate boom (Dymski, 2013).

The most notable outcomes of this process have been the following (Tortella & Garcia-Ruiz, 2013): (1) the significant reduction in the number of banking institutions; (2) the growing control by five institutions (Santander, BBVA, Caixabank, Bankia and Sabadell) where most of the capital, assets, and banking operations are concentrated; (3) the increase in participation, between 1997 and 2013, by the top five in total assets from 31.4 percent to 54.4 percent (source: Consolidated Banking Data. European Central Bank, https://sdw.ecb.europa.eu/browse.do?node=9689367); (4) the minimal influence of foreign banks; and (5) the disappearance of a public bank with strategic financial objectives.

2.4 Trade openness: export growth and current account deficit

Since the 1980s, the Spanish economy has been definitively inserted into a European and global context that was simultaneously undergoing various major changes, including the intensity of internationalization processes and the growing dominance of finance. However, this insertion took place from a subordinate position, determined by the notable differences in technological capabilities, levels of capitalization, and the type of productive specialization with respect to the main European economies.

Trade in goods grew rapidly, generating a rapid opening to foreign markets, especially those of the EU, where most of Spain's exports and imports are concentrated. This trade reflects, and at the same time reproduces, the conditions of the productive structure, both its specialization and its deficiencies. Intra-industrial trade predominates, although the proportion of agricultural goods and processed foods in exports has continued to be relevant, whereas raw energy materials and other primary goods in imports remained important (Alonso, 1999).

The weight of the export of capital goods is largely due to the important presence of transnational companies (especially automotive) that take advantage of the cost benefits of manufacturing in Spain to sell in Europe and other regions. The other part corresponds to goods of medium and low technological intensity produced by medium-sized Spanish companies. Prior to the decline suffered during the last crisis, export expansion had maintained its share of total world exports (Xifré, 2017).

The contribution of tourism was highly relevant in the period 1995–2008. Despite the negative goods and income balances, the current account balance did not exceed -2/-3 percent of GDP. However, from 2004 onwards, the external deficit was above 6 percent and continued to widen to almost 10 percent in 2007–2008. This deficit highlighted the need for a large volume of external capital, revealing the strong domestic imbalance between investment and domestic savings (Uxó, Paúl & Febrero, 2011). As shown on the demand side, investment growth raised its share of GDP to 30 percent, while gross domestic savings remained at around 20 percent, thus rendering the inflow of foreign savings necessary.

The financing was dependent on direct, portfolio and loan investments from abroad. Direct investment flows grew rapidly (Bajo-Rubio & López-Pueyo, 2002). Most of the inflows were investments from European companies and an increasing proportion was destined to purchase existing Spanish companies, especially in services (70 percent in 2000–2007) and in the industrial branches of chemicals, transport equipment, metallurgy, and food.

In turn, foreign direct investment (FDI) outflows intensified from 1997 on, when the rapid transnationalization began of a group of large Spanish companies in banking, telecommunications, electricity, oil extraction, and construction. This gave rise to the unusual situation experienced in 1999–2001, when there was a net outflow of direct investment. Afterwards, the outflow figures moderated and the net entry balance returned, except in 2006–2007 when a very strong outflow took place, due both to Spanish investments abroad and to the withdrawal of foreign investments that were relocated to other countries. Finally, during the crisis, financial flows moderated in both directions (source: UNCTAD, https://unctad.org/topic/investment/investment-statistics-and-trends).

Therefore, according to the aforementioned figures, the bulk of external financing did not come from FDI but from financial investments made through the purchase of securities and loans. The inflow of portfolio investment (corporate shares and bonds, public debt) has been significant since the 1990s, particularly through stock market purchases and the underwriting of public debt securities. However, the largest increases were recorded, starting in 2004, as the financial and real estate bubble developed. The same thing happened with foreign loans, which increased rapidly during the bubble years and were mostly directed to banks, savings banks (Ruiz, Stupariu & Vilariño, 2015) and certain large companies.

3 Institutional change and structural reforms

The three processes analyzed above (de-industrialization, financialization and internationalization) occurred simultaneously with an economic policy, which shows the consolidation of several features established at end of the 1970s and further reinforced with EU membership, in what is known as the "neo-liberal trajectory" (Baccaro & Howell, 2011): the priority given to market liberalization and privatization, the containment of public expenditure to readjust the budget balance and the active role assumed by the state in making the labor market more flexible, and the fragmentation or decentralization of collective bargaining. This already has had an impact on the growth model (Rey-Araújo, 2020), but especially after the economic crisis when the period of austerity began, there was a further deepening of this trajectory.

3.1 Monetary and fiscal policies in the European Union context

Economic policy has been constrained by the commitments made upon joining the EU (monetary stability, market liberalization, and external openness), in particular by the liberalizing aims demanded after the adoption of the Single European Act and after the Maastricht Treaty. These objectives are in line with previously approved plans such as the Moncloa Pacts (1977) and the Medium-Term Economic Program (1983–1986), which already contained stabilizing guidelines and liberalizing objectives as adjustment programs following the crisis of the mid-1970s (Fina, Meixide & Toharia, 1989; Toharia, 1988). They include the same type of diagnosis of the hierarchy and interdependencies of existing problems and a method for choosing the best strategy to solve them. In contrast to the political limitations of the UCD, the Spanish Socialist Workers' Party (PSOE) had the political power to implement the chosen measures (Martinez-Lucio & Blyton, 1995).

This integration process strengthened the state's action in these areas. Thus, the labor legislation reforms were justified with the aim of rendering the labor market and labor relations more flexible in order to adapt them to the low-inflation European environment. Subsequently, in addition to generating state revenues, the privatization of public enterprises was justified by the requirements of the Single European Act, which was designed to create the European single market and to promote competition in the markets for goods and services (Vergés, 2000). Similarly, the liberalization of the financial sector was understood as a way to promote competition between entities and to improve the allocation of savings (Etxezarreta, 1991).

The entry into the euro eliminated or restricted as much as possible the three usual types of economic policy instruments: monetary, exchange rate, and budgetary policy. As is widely known, monetary policy was left in the hands of the European Central Bank (ECB), whose sole objective was to control price stability, namely, to keep inflation at around 2 percent. The exchange rate policy disappeared within the monetary area and was subordinated to the objective of promoting international capital mobility through a free floating exchange rate, without precise objectives and without an entity responsible for its evolution.

Budgetary policy remained formally within the sovereign powers of each government, but was in fact subject to the containment of the budget deficit below 3 percent of GDP and of public debt to 60 percent. In a European and international context of tax cuts that limited state revenues, a government that did not grant these reductions would be penalized by capital movements. Thus, the deficit limit and revenue restraint became severe restrictions on increasing state spending. Thus, since the signing of the Maastricht Treaty, the entire budgetary policy of each government has also been conditioned by the European context (Gruppe & Lange, 2014; Pavolini et al., 2016).

As a result of this restriction, public expenditure and the fiscal deficit which had reached their maximum in 1995, with percentages of 44.5 percent and 7.2

percent of GDP respectively, fell progressively until, in 2007, the expenditure was 38 percent and the deficit was corrected to present a public surplus since 2005. Consequently, the public debt, which had risen somewhat rapidly to 63 percent of GDP in 1995, subsequently fell to 36 percent in 2007.

The relative fall in expenditure was mainly motivated by lower interest payments and lower transfers resulting from the reduction in unemployment. An example of the latter is the 1992 reforms (Law 22/1992), which tightened up the requirement for access to the contributory benefit by increasing the required prior contribution period from 6 to 12 months and reducing the amount of the benefit (from 80 percent of the regulatory base to 70 percent) and with a maximum duration of 24 months. In addition, starting in 1993 (Law 22/1993), the contribution to be paid by the worker was no longer financed by Social Security but by the beneficiary (with the consequent reduction in the amount). For its part, the increase in income was due to the rapid growth of the economy and not to an increase in tax rates.

However, beginning in 2008, there was a radical change in the budgetary situation (Kickert & Ysa, 2014), first, with the implementation of counter-cyclical spending that rapidly increased the public deficit; and, second, through the application of harsh austerity policies with the aim of drastically reducing spending and the state deficit (Afonso, 2019; Calvo, 2014).

As a result of these restrictions, public expenditure and the fiscal deficit which had reached maximum levels in 1995, with ratios of 44.5 percent and 7.2 percent of GDP respectively, fell progressively until 2007, with an expenditure ratio of 38 percent and deficit correction as of 2005. Consequently, the public debt, which had risen somewhat rapidly to 63 percent of GDP in 1995, fell to 36 percent in 2007.

Finally, starting in the summer of 2008, the change in the financial scenario in Europe and worldwide led to increasingly difficult access to external financing by banks and savings banks that had been heavily indebted in previous years (Ruiz, Stupariu & Vilariño, 2015). Financial fragility gave way to the bankruptcy of many lenders as the economy entered an economic recession that (1) contracted real estate sales and paralyzed new activities linked to the real estate sector; (2) increased the difficulties of indebted companies and households to pay banks and savings banks; and (3) increased the difficulties of the latter in meeting their payments to external creditors.

Then, between 2008 and 2010, the increase in public deficit due to lower tax revenues and the higher (counter-cyclical) expenditures caused by the economic crisis implied that greater financial resources had to be sought abroad, leading to the public debt crisis in Europe (Gruppe & Lange, 2014). The ban in the euro zone on the ECB acting as a lender of last resort to meet these financing needs placed the state and the banks in an increasingly difficult position to obtain financing. This had three interlinked consequences.

The first was the state's growing need to issue debt in markets where demand was falling, meaning that it had to pay higher rates for public debt and face greater difficulties in reaching the volumes requested (Massó, 2016).

This situation, together with the existing instability and uncertainty, encouraged speculative behavior and led to a sovereign debt crisis.

The second consequence was that, in order to rescue a significant part of the bankrupt financial system (assuming the cost of its recapitalization), the state needed external financing provided by European institutions. In order to face the financial and sovereign debt crisis in the eurozone, different official bodies had to be created *ex profeso* to cover the financing. Thus, in 2012, the temporary structures of the European Financial Stability Fund (EFSF) and the European Financial Stability Facility (EFSF) gave way to the European Stability Mechanism (ESM).

The third was the imposition by these European institutions of a very tough "austerity and reform" program (Pavolini et al., 2016). This resulted in a generalized cut in public spending and a significant reduction in the welfare state (Del Pino, 2013; Navarro, 2015).

This was the counterpart of receiving the funding required to restructure the financial system (up to 100 billion euros), through the signing of a Memorandum of Understanding in July 2012. The agreement explicitly placed conditions on funding for the implementation of severe budgetary adjustment measures (Excessive Deficit Protocol) and various reforms (Macroeconomic Imbalance Procedure) required by the EU (Álvarez, Luengo & Uxó, 2013; Blyth, 2013). Sections 3.2 and 3.3 address the institutional changes in collective bargaining mechanisms and labor market institutions that are motivated by these reforms (Cioffi & Dubin, 2016; Meardi, 2018).

3.2 The wage-labor nexus and the industrial relations system in transformation

The Spanish industrial relations system has traditionally been characterized since the 1980s by several key aspects:

1 The predominance of sectoral collective bargaining where the interests of large companies dominate, with much power in the CEOE (Spanish Confederation of Employers' Organizations) as the main employers' organization, and two majority unions (the General Workers' Union, UGT, and the Workers' Commission, CCOO).
2 Significant coverage of collective bargaining based on the "erga omnes principle," which establishes that conditions in a sectoral agreement are automatically extended to all workers in the sector or branch of activity, regardless of whether they belong to the signing union.
3 Guaranteed coverage on the basis of limitations as to the termination of the collective agreement (until 2012, agreement between the parties was necessary) and the principle of ultra-activity of collective agreements prevails, which establishes that its content will continue to apply after the end of its validity until such time as the negotiators reach a new agreement.

4 There is a low rate of union membership as a result of the essentially electoral nature of the formation of Works Councils and bargaining units do not require prior membership to exercise union rights.
5 There are no formal mechanisms for the horizontal coordination of wage demands between activity sectors, but a general framework is established through social dialogue to serve as a reference for all negotiated agreements.

Nonell et al. (2006) analyze vertical and horizontal macro-coordination (including formal and informal practices) and show that, before the economic crisis, governance in the industrial relations system was based on specific legal and cultural elements. However, wage negotiation mechanisms have been conditioned by an income policy consisting of competitive social concertation or competitive corporatism (Ferreiro & Gómez, 2008; Royo, 2007; Sanchez-Mosquera, 2017), according to which wage moderation was a necessary condition for achieving macroeconomic stability.

As mentioned above, the context of the process of integration into the EU, the formation of the Economic and Monetary Union and, afterwards, the signing of the Stability and Growth Pact, which sought to create the conditions for wage moderation with the aim of converging inflation rates in the Member States, are all contributing factors. Of particular note is the fact that inflation in Spain tended to be several points higher than in other European economies, which affected the price competitiveness of companies in the context of rapid trade opening. At this point, it is possible to distinguish three major stages in the evolution of the labor relations framework (Molina, 2014).

The first of these corresponds to the 1980s and lasts until the mid-1990s, when successive PSOE governments actively participated in tripartite wage negotiations with employers and trade unions (Martinez-Alier & Roca, 1987). These governments insisted on the central objectives established since the Moncloa Pacts: priority for monetary stability (control of inflation) and growth in business profits. These are considered the sine qua non conditions for increasing investment and employment, with wages, unemployment and social policy as subsidiary variables of the benefits and advantages granted to companies (Etxezarreta, 1991; Felipe, 2002).

These priorities and objectives required compliance with the same political and social agreements as those found in the Moncloa Pacts: trade union support for the measures agreed to along these lines. At the state level, after the NEA signed in 1981–1982, the first González government promoted the Interconfederal Agreement for 1983 and the Economic and Social Agreement for 1985–1986. In the meantime, the lack of agreement in 1984 was resolved by a government decree, agreed upon by the CEOE with the Minister of Economy. Although these agreements were initially achieved through the support of the UGT, the political differences between this union and the PSOE government had a negative effect on their relationship (Astudillo, 2001). The turning point was marked by the mobilizing capacity shown in the general strike of December 14, 1988 (14-D), once unity of action was achieved among the majority unions.

This translated into both an increase in demand for a "social turn" in economic policy (with some agreements between the socialist government and the trade unions being reached), and a significant increase in wages (from 1988 to 1995, the hourly wage rose by 15 percent, an increase that was greater than the growth in hourly productivity). Taking advantage of the economic expansion and under social pressure, socialist governments also increased social spending through investment in education, expanded social security health coverage, extended the pension system, and improved other benefits.

The second stage (González & Luque, 2014) corresponds to the weakening of the tripartite social agreement system, with the changes introduced, starting in the mid-1990s, being dominated by interconfederal agreements. After the recession of 1993, the capacity of trade unions to influence economic policy weakened considerably. This resulted in a labor reform that gave greater flexibility to dismissals, and a change in the Workers' Statute that allowed the non-application of higher-level agreements on wages, with the requirement of prior agreement between the parties.

In the People's Party governments, first the Inter-Confederal Agreement for Employment Stability was signed in 1997 and then the Inter-Confederal Agreement for Collective Bargaining (ANC). The ANC, which began in 2002 and was subsequently extended or renewed until 2008, established the rule of moderate wage growth as a central criterion for determining wages. It included as reference variables: expected inflation, expected productivity growth and a wage review clause that included the difference between the variation of the consumer price index (CPI) and expected inflation, in order to avoid inflationary spirals. In practice, the increase in the wage range made it impossible for higher-level agreements to be generally applied to all workers and, as a result, real wages were reduced for 10 years (between 1999 and 2007, they contracted by 5 percent).

The labor share suffered a severe setback as the yearly unit wage grew more slowly than the already sluggish productivity growth (see Figure 8.3); this gap is mirrored by the fact that cumulative productivity growth is more than double that of the unit wage.

Profits grew at yearly average rates of almost 5 percent during the two expansionary phases. Over the period 1994–2008, profit growth doubled that of wages. This outcome was implicit in the logic of the economic programs applied by all the governments during this period, following the path set by the Moncloa Pacts (1977): guaranteeing the growth of business profits. To the extent that the increase in labor productivity was weakened, this objective implied that, inexorably, the increase in labor efficiency was mostly absorbed by business profits.

The third stage covers the period starting in 2010, when a new round of interconfederal agreements (Luque & Gonzalez, 2015) began. Known as the Agreement on Employment and Collective Bargaining (AENC), it consisted of three-year coverage and a tighter nominal wage growth moderation strategy, conditioned by the evolution of the economy and/or the sectoral and

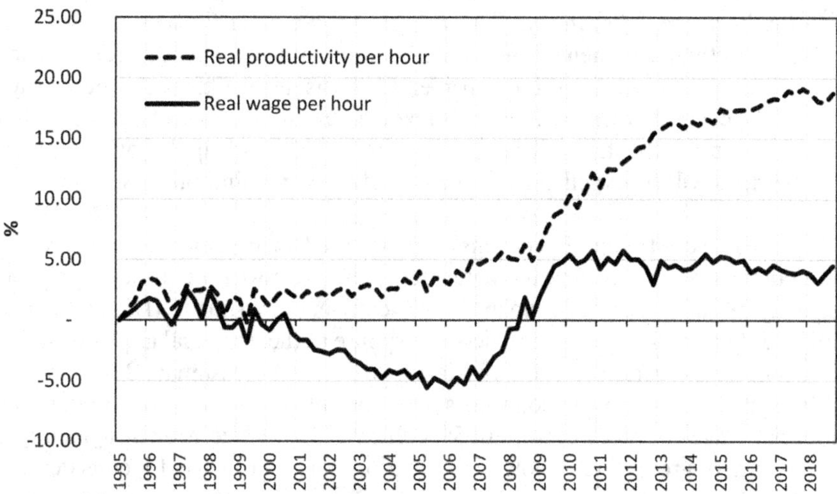

Figure 8.3 Wage-productivity gap (1995–2018)
Source: National Accounts, Eurostat. https://ec.europa.eu/eurostat/web/national-accounts

business situation. This is a policy of wage devaluation, which was accompanied by other fiscal austerity policies implemented by the PSOE and PP governments (Martins, 2017).

Without a doubt, this stage has been characterized by the significant decentralization of collective bargaining (Rocha, 2018) to adapt it to the conditions of individual companies. The labor reforms of 2010 and above all 2012, transformed the orientation of bargaining and collective agreements to be exclusively functional to business performance (Malo, 2015; Muñoz de Bustillo & Pinto, 2018). They were introduced with the following four fundamental measures:

- *Facilities for temporary derogation from collective agreements*: Although the possibility of a derogation had already been contemplated in the 2010 Reform, with the 2012 Reform, the derogation can be made unilaterally by the employer in case of economic, technical, organizational, or production problems. The employer may thus avoid the provisions of the agreement on pay, working hours, or organization of working time, among others.
- *Priority in the application of the company agreement*: The sectoral agreement no longer acts as a base from which economic agents negotiate working conditions, but rather as a mere reference that lacks mandatory enforcement.
- *Possibility of renegotiating the agreement before the end of its term*: This renegotiation can be promoted by any of the parties and aims at the rapid adjustment of the agreed-upon wages to business productivity.

- *Limits to the "ultra-activity" of the agreements*: After the loss of validity of a collective agreement, it will only be automatically extended for a period of one year (and not on an open-ended basis, as was the case previously), in the event that the social agents reach a new agreement before then. After this period, the higher-level agreement, if any, will apply, otherwise the workers will be expelled from the collective bargaining process.

There is no doubt that the reforms have increased the capacity of companies for discretionary action outside the agreements and have weakened the negotiating capacity of unions, thus enabling a wage-driven adjustment (López-Andreu, 2019), despite the increase in conflicts in response to the unilateral implementation of labor reforms (Campos-Lima & Martin-Artiles, 2011; Fishman, 2012).

In recent years, social consensus has continued to focus on moderating nominal wages (Cruces et al., 2015; Köhler, 2018). Wage growth agreements have limited growth to below the inflation rate and have to consider the ECB's inflation target or real productivity growth as a general rule (Fernández, Ibáñez & Martinez, 2016). This is reflected in the successive agreements for Employment and Collective Bargaining (IAENC, IIAENC, IIIAENC), in which maximum increases of between 0.5 percent and 1.5 percent were agreed upon, following the revision on inflation.

This is in line with the theses, held by Uxó et al. (2016) and Muñoz de Bustillo and Esteve (2017), which emphasize that the reforms were not intended to alleviate the structural weaknesses of the labor market, but rather were instruments which, through the weakening of the negotiating position of workers, sought wage devaluation as the main strategy for exiting the crisis and increasing business profits.

Figure 8.4 shows how this subset of reforms was very effective in reducing wages, with significant drops in real wages. In turn, this slowdown in the agreed-upon wage was accompanied by changes in the evolution of the wage drift (the difference between the rates of variation of the effective average wage and the agreed-upon average wage), revealing the consequences of the possibilities of unbundling and temporary non-application of agreements. Figure 8.4 also shows that the relationship between the growth of the effective wage and the agreed-upon wage becomes negative as of the 2009–2013 stage, when it had traditionally been positive (0.25 percent). In other words, collective bargaining underwent an important qualitative change; the wages agreed on in the agreements no longer serve as the basis from which the effective wage increase is negotiated, but rather act as a mere reference around which the negotiators make decisions.

In conclusion, throughout the period 1995–2018, successive changes led to the weakening of the mechanisms for negotiating agreements within the multi-level system that characterizes the Spanish model. The signing of centralized and interconfederal agreements between trade unions and employers organizations did not prevent a growing number of companies applying discretionary criteria on wages and working conditions, using the laxity of legal regulations (del Rio & Fenger, 2019).

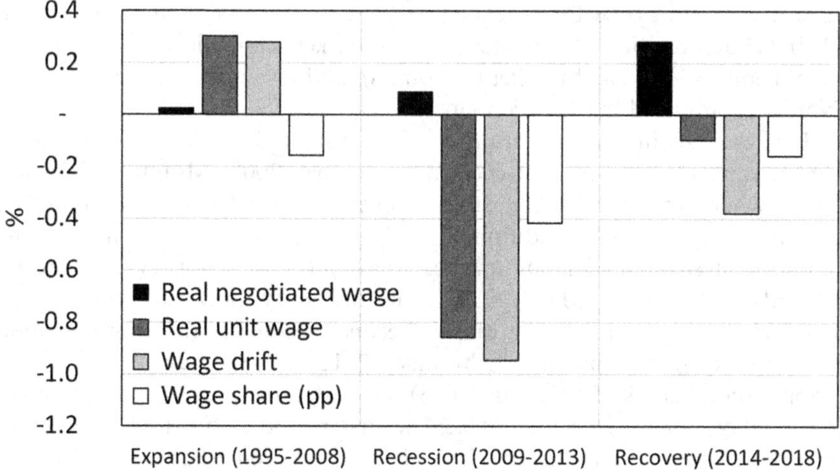

Figure 8.4 Wage growth, 1995–2018
Source: Business and Economic Series Database (BDSICE). Ministry of Economic Affairs and Digital Transformation. http://serviciosede.mineco.gob.es/Indeco/BDSICE/HomeBDSICE.aspx

Thus, the number of employees increased whose companies were not covered by the agreements or were only applying certain clauses, thus changing the content of the agreements at the summit in subsequent rounds of sectoral, provincial, and company negotiation. The tertiarization, financialization and internationalization of production resulted in a loss of importance in sectors that offered jobs with a greater tradition of advocacy and trade unionism, transforming the culture of collective bargaining. These features make it more difficult to unite interests and organizational possibilities among employees in a context of labor polarization (Molina & López-Roldán, 2015).

In addition, the trade unions became progressively weaker in terms of their demands. The process that started in the 1980s can be summed up in the change of position from conflict to cooperation and consensus (González & Luque, 2014; Hamann, 1997; Hamann, Johnston & Kelly, 2012; Koch, 2005; Martinez-Alier & Roca, 1987). Their negotiating position has focused on trying to defend wages and employment. Yet, despite the attempts to modify labor policies (Pulignano, Ortíz & De Franceschi, 2016) to avoid contractual duality (particularly striking is the case of the 1988 general strike), it has not de facto managed to limit the split between covered and uncovered workers, resulting from the process of labor market flexibilization.

3.3 From labor market flexibilization at the margin to deregulation at the core

From a comparative political economy framework, the liberalization policies in the labor market institutions (Etchemendy, 2011) have been summarized in three ideal-typical trajectories related to three varieties of capitalism (Thelen, 2014): (1) deregulation (Anglophone liberal market economies); (2) dualization (Continental coordinated market economies); and (3) embedded flexibilization (Nordic coordinated market economies).

However, Spain has generally been considered a typical case of a Mediterranean mixed-market economy (Amable, 2003; Molina & Rhodes, 2007), where the role of the state is even more relevant than in other countries (Royo, 2009). Additionally, it has been considered as having one of the most segmented labor markets (Doeringer & Piore, 1971; Gordon, Edwards & Reich, 1981) even though inequality between insiders and outsiders is lower than in other dualized economies due to the poor condition of the former (Häusermann & Schwander, 2012).

Some scholars, like Sola et al. (2013), have identified two particular stages of the labor policy since the 1980s. The first period (1984–1994) was characterized by flexibility at the margin (Cebrián et al., 2003; Ferreiro & Serrano, 2001; Toharia & Malo, 2000), i.e. the creation of specific temporary contracts, mainly fixed term for employment promotion and agency contracts. These legal changes substantially modified the Workers Charter ("Estatuto de los Trabajadores").

Indeed, until 1984, non-standard contracts could only be used under very specific circumstances, for instance, for seasonal or transitory tasks and in the case of employers' needs (Garcia-Serrano & Malo, 2013). The main objective of these changes was to reduce the extraordinarily high unemployment rate and to improve the employability of some groups, like young people, via the introduction of flexibility in labor market entry.

One should remember that since the 1980 Workers Charter there have been more than 50 labor reforms, most of them aimed at creating new types of contracts that offered some kind of incentive for companies to use them (generally looser conditions, less protection or fewer bonuses to Social Security contributions). The most important issues from the period 1984–1997 are described below:

- The reform of the Workers Charter (1984) deregulated the use of fixed-term contracts. For instance, the "temporary contract for production needs" has been widely used since then and the reform expanded the "temporary contract for the promotion of employment," extending it to any unemployed worker, and abolishing the hiring ceilings established according to the workforce in the firm. In addition, the reform introduced a list of 16 types of unprotected contract (Albarracín, 2000) and the "causality principle" was relaxed, which created a loophole. As a consequence, there was a very sharp increase in the temporary employment rate.
- The youth employment plan (1988) sought to introduce a far looser use of internship and apprenticeship contracts, reducing the rights and protection of young workers. However, as a result of the 1988 general strike, it was not implemented (Recio & Roca, 1998).

- In 1992, the decree of urgent measures for employment promotion and unemployment protection was passed by the government. It focused on the reduction of unemployment benefits, limiting access by increasing the minimum required contribution period (12 months), the amount (from 80 percent to 70 percent and 60 percent of wages) and duration (maximum 24 months) to contributory unemployment benefits.
- The labor reform of 1994 brought the legalization and authorization of temporary work agencies. Additionally, the reform included proposals from the youth employment plan (1988). Thus, the minimum age for the apprenticeship contract was raised to 25, theoretical training time was reduced (from 25 to 15 per cent of the working day) and the duration was extended from 6 months to 3 years (apprenticeship) and 2 years (internship). Wages could be reduced under the Interprofessional Minimum Wage. Finally, restrictions for part-time contracts were also abolished and the organizational and production causes for fair dismissal were added.

However, during the second period (1997–2012), the institutional reforms focused on a reduction of the dismissal costs for permanent contracts and on enhancing the capacity of the firms to remove employees or significantly modify the working conditions, i.e. flexibility in the labor market exit. The aim of these reforms was to reduce non-standard employment, specifically the temporary employment rate, as it was one of the highest in the world (Polavieja, 2003).

The labor reform of 1997 directly affected permanent contracts, introducing a new type of permanent contract "for the promotion of open-ended hiring" aimed at young workers (people aged 18–29) and for temporary contracts being converted to permanent. This contract had a compensation for unfair dismissal of 33 days per year worked (previously 45 days), with a maximum of 24 monthly payments.

A new reform in 2002 introduced the "express dismissal," in which the employer recognizes the unfairness of the dismissal and deposits within 48 hours in the social court the amount of the corresponding compensation for unfair dismissal. Until 2009, this channel accounted for 30 percent of access to unemployment benefits, while 60 percent was due to the expiration of temporary contracts (the remaining 10 percent was due to other channels of minor relevance). Additionally, this reform imposed a mandatory commitment to this activity, and compliance with the obligations established, as a requirement for entitlement to unemployment benefits.

After the economic crisis in 2008, the diagnosis of the domestic and international authorities was that the Spanish labor market institutions were overwhelmingly inadequate and, as a result, real wages did not fall sufficiently, or quickly enough, to prevent an increase in the unemployment rate. This fact implies that if there had been greater wage flexibility, the severe economic shock would not have caused the unemployment rate to soar.

This narrative shows that, as a consequence of the institutional rigidities of the labor market, during the recession the adjustment mechanism was external, i.e. individual or collective dismissal. In addition, the adjustment was uneven due to the lack of wage flexibility, meaning that dismissals and wage cuts were concentrated in the secondary segment of the labor market. Consequently, those relatively unprotected workers who have temporary and other nonstandard contracts (mainly younger workers and women), were more greatly affected by the wage adjustment.

The policy implication is that a higher level of flexibility should imply a reduction in labor market dualism and a decrease in the unemployment rate (Horwitz & Myant, 2015). Following this prescription, during the period from 2009 to 2013, there were several reforms of flexibilization in the labor market and the industrial relations system (Banyuls et al., 2009). The two most significant were those of 2010 and 2012, as they introduced very profound changes in labor regulations which theoretically aimed at reversing the structural weaknesses of the Spanish labor market, reducing wage-setting rigidity and labor dualism, and resolving the situation of high unemployment. Despite the fact that the 2010 reform was approved by a social-democratic government (the Spanish Socialist Party) and the 2012 reform by a right-wing government (the Popular Party), both reforms were unilaterally imposed by the government via a decree law, thus breaking the social dialogue (Molina & Miguélez, 2013).

The content of the Spanish labor market reforms under austerity is well known (Garcia-Serrano & Malo, 2013; Muñoz de Bustillo & Esteve, 2017; Sola et al., 2013). In a nutshell, the 2010 reform facilitated the procedures and lowered the costs of dismissal (Cruces et al., 2015). The 2012 reform went much further, significantly reducing job protection legislation (dismissal costs and procedures), which was in line with the previous policy objectives of employer associations like the CEOE (Martin & Alós, 2003). Other issues from those labor reforms (Eichhorst, Marx & Wehner, 2017), such as unemployment benefit generosity and coverage, and active labor market policies, played a minor role, which was in line with other South European societies.

Thus, the recent trend of institutional change is identified as a deregulation process within the various iterations of the liberalization approach (Lallement, 2011; Picot & Tassinari, 2017; Prosser, 2016). These reforms played a key role in facilitating unilateral decisions by employers as well as in the collective bargaining of such issues as dismissal, work organization, and working conditions (Köhler & Calleja, 2017). As a result, the discretionary power of employers to increase external, internal and wage flexibility grew considerably (Lasierra, 2007; López-Andreu, 2017).

A review of the main changes hints that the reform occurred at the core of employment protection legislation (EPL) (Cardenas & Villanueva, 2020). First, the compensation for unfair dismissal was reduced to 33 days of gross salary per year worked, with a maximum of 24 monthly payments (previously it was 45 days with a maximum of 42 monthly payments). Meanwhile, the temporary contract compensation was increased from 8 days to 12 days of gross salary per worked year. This was important because "institutions are what actors make of them" (Hauptmeier, 2012).

The fact that the compensation for unfair dismissal is assessed (quantified) beforehand and that the employer can negotiate it in out-of-court procedures (such as conciliation, mediation and arbitration) imply that employers could take this punishment as a sort of a cost for exercising their right to dismiss freely or without cause. In other words, by reducing the compensation for unfair dismissal, the discretionary power of employers was considerably increased. In addition, the previous authorization for collective dismissals was removed and it is no longer necessary to reach an agreement with the employees' representatives.

According to the over-protection narrative (Fernández & Martinez, 2013), the aforementioned changes should modify companies' preferences for permanent contracts, as these become more flexible. As a result, in order to reduce the existing dualism, the differences in employment protection between permanent and temporary contracts have been narrowed, mainly, through the reduction of protections against dismissal of permanent contract holders.

Therefore, the 2012 reform was the first in the last 30 years to reduce the compensation for unfair dismissal. Especially after 1980, when the Workers Charter reduced dismissal compensation from two months (60 days) per year worked, with a maximum of five years (60 monthly payments), to 45 days per year worked (42 monthly payments).

Second, measures were included to encourage open-ended contracts and to reduce entry barriers. Severance pay for temporary contracts is increased from 8 to 12 days per year worked and a worker can only link together temporary contracts for 24 months (before it was 30 months) at the same company or group of companies.

Third, the 2012 reform created a new sort of contract, the "supporting permanent contract for entrepreneurs," which is for companies with fewer than 50 workers (a large percentage of the firms in Spain). Its particularity was that the trial period was set at one year (with no dismissal penalties) instead of six months, and tax incentives and social security bonuses were offered in cases in which the employee was hired as taken out of unemployment.

Fourth, the assumptions for fair dismissals have become increasingly loose over the years. Initially, they could be justified solely for technical reasons and the consent of the labor authority was required. However, the 2010 and 2012 reforms represent a substantial change in the breadth of economic circumstances. After 2012, employers could dismiss fairly in cases where current or expected losses were predicted, or a decrease in the level of sales or income was expected over three consecutive quarters. Additionally, the administrative procedures for carrying out the layoffs (Rigby & Garcia-Calavia, 2013) were reduced, as employers became exempt from justifying the company's financial situation. Moreover, dismissals are left as the only means of adjustment, and administrative authorization for collective dismissals is no longer necessary.

Fifth, in order to promote internal flexibility, the labor reforms allowed companies to substantially modify working conditions unilaterally (wages, working hours, working time, geographical mobility, etc). Specifically, the flexibility of part-time work has increased significantly. Furthermore, employers may implement suspensions of contracts and temporary reductions of working hours without administrative authorization and with public financial support, when there are economic, organizational, or technical reasons to do so.

Hence, the 2010 and 2012 labor market reforms have been particularly successful in achieving EPL reduction, given that they have substantially transformed the legal framework in an attempt to reduce and speed up the compensation for the termination of permanent contracts. The same dynamic is mirrored in the increase in the share of dismissed core workers in 2017 (see Figure 8.5). In 2017, 14 percent of workers with permanent contracts were fired within the first three months and up to 34 percent were fired within their first year. In 2013, the shares of dismissed core workers amounted to 9 percent and 24 percent, respectively. However, Herrero, Cárdenas, and López (2020) hold that there is no evidence of a significant improvement in the unemployment rate due to the latest labor market reforms.

Consequently, a context has been created that is characterized by the destruction of stable jobs, an increase in worker turnover and instability (Fernández-Macías, 2003; Martinez-Pastor, & Bernardi, 2011), and an increase in atypical jobs; not to mention, the loss of purchasing power of wages, an increase in the range and dispersion of wages (Cervini-Plá & Ramos, 2011), and the reduction of labor rights (Fernández et al., 2016), especially in service activities (Bernardi & Garrido, 2008).

4 A new growth model?

Has the Spanish economy experienced a significant change in model as a result of the institutional reforms promoted by the Troika? In this section, we

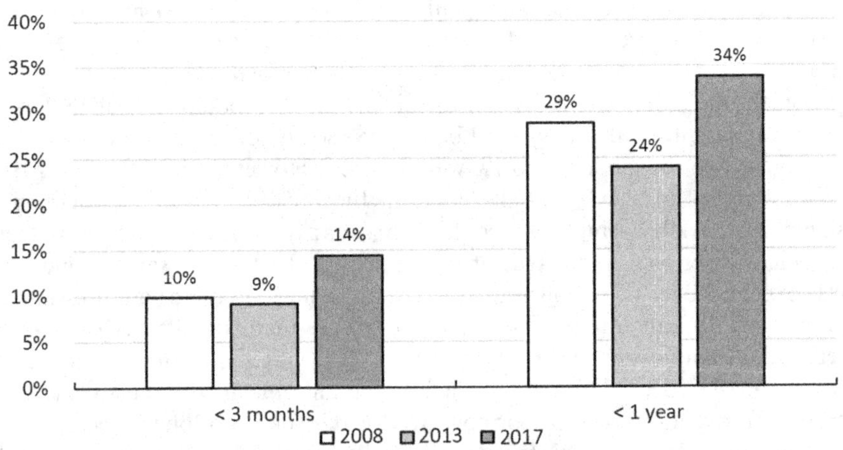

Figure 8.5 Share of dismissed core workers (2008, 2013, and 2017)
Source: Cárdenas & Villanueva (2020).

present some stylized facts related to the evolution of economic growth in the period of recovery (2014–2018). Our results do not support the hypothesis that labor market reforms and wage devaluation have changed the growth model in favor of an export-led model. Private consumption remains the main driver of investment and economic growth, based on the same mechanisms that drove economic growth in the previous expansionary phase. The external sector certainly plays a relevant role in the recovery but, as we will see, this positive balance of the foreign sector is not due so much to an improvement in external competitiveness, but to the lower need to capture savings, as a result of the lower volume of investment over GDP (GFCF/GDP).

4.1 The collapse of aggregate demand growth and net export growth

As discussed above, Spain registered a strong debt-led growth of private investment and consumption in 1995–2008, and a real estate bubble took shape. In the short term, investment is the most volatile component of aggregate demand, and consequently its fluctuations drive changes in production and employment. Meanwhile, consumption has a greater share in aggregate demand and determines the trend evolution of output. Once the global financial crisis explodes, the macroeconomic imbalances accumulated by the Spanish economy become evident (Royo, 2009) and reinforce a sharp decline in private domestic demand. (Febrero & Bermejo, 2013): firms and households are heavily indebted and experience a balance-sheet recession; the credit crunch due to the difficult situation faced by financial institutions prevents the refinancing of past debts; and the bursting of the construction bubble (Garcia, 2010) drives unemployment up (Uxó, Febrero & Bermejo, 2013) and reduces labor incomes.

Household consumption comprises two opposing trends. On the one hand, as economic theory predicts, the decrease in household gross disposable income during the recession translated into a significant induced drop in final consumption expenditure as well, having a procyclical impact. On the other hand, the downward stickiness of some kind of quasi-fixed expenditures led to important reductions in the household savings rate from 2010 onwards, helping to stabilize aggregate demand to some (partial) extent.

The authorities first reacted to the economic crisis by implementing a fiscal stimulus package, including both reductions in taxes and increases in public expenditure. Public demand had a positive contribution to GDP growth of 1.3pp in 2009 (see Figure 8.6), although GDP decreased by 3.6 percent that year. However, between 2011 and 2013 fiscal policy becomes strongly restrictive and procyclical. The change to a restrictive fiscal policy triggered by the sovereign debt crisis had strong negative effects on domestic demand between 2011 and 2013, causing a second recession with severe effects on employment. During those years, the contribution of public consumption and investment in GDP was overwhelmingly negative (-1.3 percent on annual average). In 2013, public investment was 51 percent lower than in 2008 in real terms. The reduction in public demand is amplified by the fiscal multiplier, which had an impact on all economic activity.

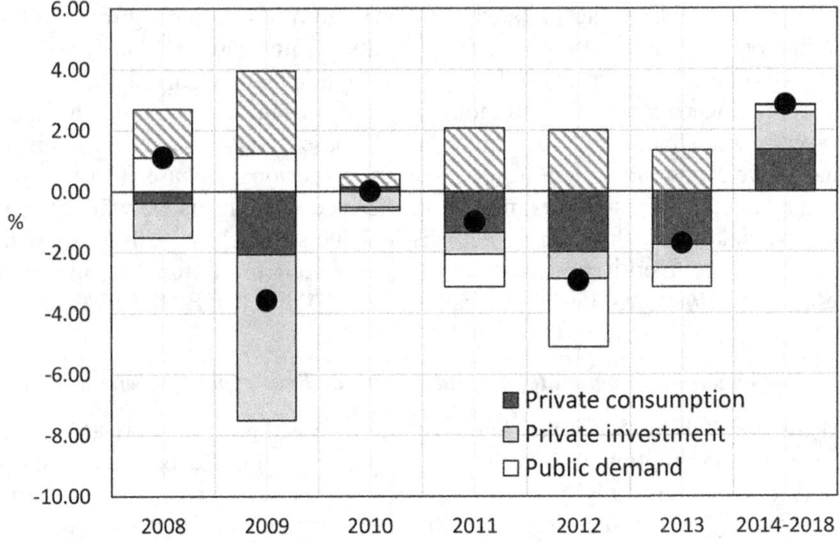

Figure 8.6 Main components of aggregate demand contributions to GDP growth, 2008–2018

Source: National Accounts, Eurostat. https://ec.europa.eu/eurostat/web/national-accounts

One of the most remarkable changes to occur during the double-dip recession is the adjustment of the Spanish external sector, and the positive contribution of net exports to GDP growth. Specifically, the current account balance had gone through a readjustment of 11.6 pp of GDP since the beginning of the crisis, turning a deficit of a -9.6 percent of GDP in 2007 into a current account surplus of 2 percent of GDP in 2018. Most of the adjustment in this period was precisely driven by the collapse of imports, which decreased at an annual average of -4 percent as a consequence of shrinking domestic demand (Villanueva et al., 2020).

Regarding exports, the collapse in international trade provoked a reduction in Spanish exports of goods and services as well (-11 percent in real terms). After recovery from their fall in 2009, exports grow again quickly from 2010 onwards, with a performance similar to that registered during the expansive period before the crisis. The positive performance of export demand is one of the prominent facts that must be taken into account to explain the evolution of GDP in Spain during these years. As was the case with the downward stickiness of quasi-fixed expenditures, after 2010, exports also acted as an element that helped stabilize the aggregate demand of the Spanish economy in the midst of the collapse. In this way, in a context of generalized contraction in the other sources of final demand, export behavior prevented a deeper recession and contributed to the stabilization of economic activity, enabling the return to GDP growth.

Nevertheless, it is important to note that this positive performance of Spanish exports is not a novelty of the post-crisis period. On the contrary, Spanish exports have maintained steady growth since 2000: as Table 8.3 shows, the average annual growth of the export of goods and services in the periods 1995–2008 and 2014–2018 has been similar. These growth rates are not very different from those registered by the eurozone as a whole during these years. Exports are a key factor when explaining the transition from recession to recovery. Nevertheless, the behavior described above casts serious doubt on the idea that cost-competitiveness gains via price factors derived from the internal devaluation policy (Bilbao-Ubillos & Fernández-Sainz, 2019; Xifré, 2017) have triggered an export boom that explains GDP recovery after 2014. The importance of exports is made evident by the fact that they act as a stable source of demand in the absence of other sources.

The export share of GDP increased sharply during the double-dip recession (from 25 percent in 2008 to 32 percent in 2013), and it continued to rise during the recovery period (up to 34 percent in 2017). Notwithstanding, this change is mainly due to the collapse and subsequent stagnation of GDP, whose level in 2017 was approximately the same as in 2007, and not to a supposed export boom.

In the recovery phase (2014–2018), however, we observe an important novelty not observed in other recoveries in the Spanish economy: the current account surplus was maintained and external demand does not have a negative contribution to GDP, as was the case in other expansionary periods.

The reason the external balance deteriorated in other periods of expansion, such as that of 1995–2007, was not due to poor export performance (see Table 8.3), but rather to the high income elasticity of imports. The high income elasticity of Spanish imports caused imports to grow at a very high annual average rate during the 1995–2007 expansion, much higher than that of exports (7.2 percent versus 5.7 percent in real terms). However, during the 2014–2018 expansion, this difference was reduced remarkably (annual average rate of 4.9 percent for imports, versus 4.4 percent for exports, as shown in Table 8.3). As long as exports followed a similar trend in both periods, the difference between the pre-crisis and post-crisis periods relies mainly on the growth rates of imports (Myro, 2018).

The compatibility of an expansionary period with external surpluses during the 2014–2018 period also responded to some temporary factors, like the fall in oil prices or the exceptionally positive trend in tourism due to political problems in other Mediterranean countries, and the decrease in interest rates, which meant a sensible improvement in the income balance. Furthermore, the ratio between imported intermediate products and the total consumption of intermediate products did not decrease (Cárdenas et al., 2020).

4.2 The reproduction of the growth model

The institutional changes of the 2012–2014 period do not seem to have transformed – at least not in a significant way – the Spanish growth model: no "export boom" took place during the 2014–2018 period, nor was there a

Table 8.3 Main components of aggregate demand (1995–2018)

	Year-over-year real growth rate (%)			*Contributions to real GDP growth (%)*			*Share of nominal GDP (%)*		
	1995–2008	*2009–2013*	*2014–2018*	*1995–2008*	*2009–2013*	*2014-2018*	*1995-2008*	*2009–2013*	*2014–2018*
Gross domestic product	3.4	-1.8	2.7	3.4	-1.8	2.7	100.0	100.0	100.0
Domestic demand	3.9	-3.5	2.8	4.1	-3.9	2.8	102.8	99.1	96.7
Final consumption expenditure	3.5	-1.8	2.1	2.8	-1.5	1.6	76.0	78.8	77.6
Household and NPISH	3.3	-2.4	2.4	2.0	-1.5	1.4	58.8	58.4	58.5
Government	4.3	-0.1	1.0	0.8	-0.1	0.2	17.2	20.4	19.1
Gross capital formation	5.1	-8.9	5.8	1.4	-2.5	1.2	26.8	20.4	19.1
Gross fixed capital formation (GFCF)	5.1	-8.3	4.5	1.4	-2.3	1.0	26.3	20.2	18.4
Construction	4.4	-11.7	3.7	1.0	-2.4	0.5	17.1	11.7	8.9
Machinery and equipment	6.0	-5.4	6.1	0.3	-0.4	0.3	7.1	5.3	5.9
External demand	-1.5	6.3	-0.5	-0.6	1.6	-0.2	-2.8	0.9	3.3
Exports of goods and services	5.7	2.3	4.4	1.0	0.4	1.1	25.9	28.6	34.3
Exports of goods	5.9	3.3	3.8	0.7	0.4	0.7	17.8	19.8	23.7
Exports of services	5.3	0.4	5.7	0.3	0.0	0.4	8.1	8.8	10.5
Exports of tourist services	3.3	0.1	6.4	0.1	-0.0	0.2	3.8	3.6	4.4

Imports of goods and services	7.2	-3.7	4.9	1.6	-1.2	1.3	28.7	27.7	31.0
Imports of goods	7.4	-3.3	4.4	1.4	-0.9	0.9	23.7	23.1	25.6
Imports of services	6.4	-5.5	7.4	0.3	-0.3	0.3	5.0	4.6	5.3
Imports of tourist services	8.7	-3.8	10.8	0.1	-0.0	0.1	0.8	0.9	1.2

Source: National Accounts, Eurostat. https://ec.europa.eu/eurostat/web/national-accounts

birth of any new export-led model as a consequence of the wage devaluation policy. Furthermore, and in accordance with our previous studies (Álvarez et al., 2019; Cárdenas et al., 2020; Villanueva et al. 2020), this wage devaluation strategy did not change the character of the Spanish economy from a wage-led economy to a profit-led economy. Lower wages are not the key to explaining the strong recovery in private investment during the recent expansion phase.

The recovery of the Spanish economy follows a classic pattern during these years, which is explained mainly by the recovery of investment due to the effect of the autonomous components of aggregate demand in the trough of the business cycle, together with the impact of some additional temporary effects (evolution of interest rates, oil prices, and fiscal policy). Let's begin by reviewing these conjunctural factors.

In the first place, during the period 2014–2018, the ECB continued to lower official interest rates, maintaining a negative marginal deposit facility rate from 2014 and a main refinancing rate equal to 0 percent from March 2016. Additionally, the central bank implemented other unconventional monetary policy measures such as the asset purchase programs of public and private bonds (Arribas & Cárdenas, 2018). As a result, real interest rates in Spain remained even lower during the recovery period than they had done during the first years of the recession. This fall in interest rates involved a reduction in the financial burden of households and non-financial corporations, increasing household disposable income and profit margins, and therefore reinforcing consumption and investment. This reduction in interest rates also expanded the fiscal space, because the public balance improves as a result of an increase in public revenue coming from higher growth, and a decrease in interest payments.

Additionally, Brent crude oil prices fell from an average of $110 per barrel in the period 2011–2013, to an average of $50 in 2015–2018. Traditionally, the Spanish economy has shown a great dependency on imported oil, with current account and domestic prices being very sensitive to changes in international oil prices. Starting in 2014, the reduction experienced by oil prices permitted an important relief for domestic energy consumption, increasing disposable income and reducing costs for firms. For instance, energy imports would have been 20 billion euros higher in 2017, or the equivalent of 1.7 percent of GDP, given the oil prices of 2014 ($97.22/barrel) rather than the prices of 2017 ($51.57/barrel).

A third crucial factor that explains the rapid economic growth achieved starting in 2015 is the change in fiscal policy, which became clearly expansive that year. Table 8.3 shows that the contribution of public demand – public consumption and public investment – to GDP growth was negative (-0.1 percent) until 2013, while it was slightly positive in the period 2014–2018. The end of fiscal cutbacks helped the private sector to restart economic growth, activating the fiscal multiplier (Uxó et al., 2018 present arguments supporting that the fiscal multiplier was well above 1 percentage point in Spain during this period.). Thus, the recovery after 2014 cannot be explained without considering the softening of fiscal austerity policy.

The fourth factor is endogenous and responds to the dynamics of the business cycle. The variable that leads the cycle change is investment in equipment, as it begins to grow three quarters before the trough. Once investment in equipment changes its trend and starts growing, other components of investment follow, and finally household consumption and GDP begin to grow at the end of 2013. This change in the business cycle is fundamentally due to the effect of the autonomous components of aggregate demand: the downward stickiness of quasi-fixed expenditures of private consumption, as well as exports, are elements that end up stabilizing the business cycle by acting as brakes on the fall in demand, thus avoiding a more serious collapse and determining the change in trend.

The increase in the profit share (the ratio of gross corporate profits to added value) due to wage devaluation was not a main driver of investment recovery because the profit share growth (Salas, 2014) was not accompanied by a parallel increase in the investment share. The reinvestment rate of non-financial corporations (the gross capital formation to gross profits ratio) had been stagnating since 2010 and their current value is still far from the pre-crisis levels.

However, the rise in employment that takes place, once companies start to recover their investment, certainly plays a major role in the economic recovery. As discussed above, this is because in Spain employment is very highly sensitive to the business cycle (due to an industrial structure that is highly specialized in labor-intensive sectors); its creation induces a very rapid growth of consumption, which in turn can be noted in the capacity utilization rate of companies.

Then, once recovery starts, the strong dynamism of household consumption (due to the high sensitivity of employment in the business cycle) reinforces investment and GDP growth. This is due to particularly intense job creation, but also to new reductions in the savings rate. In spite of wage devaluation, the disposable income of households began to rise in 2014, thanks to extensive employment creation. This extensive job creation also allows for a recovery of the GFCF in construction (although starting from very low levels in 2013).

As we can see in Figure 8.7, the growth in household disposable income led to an even greater increase in private consumption (while household disposable income was 50 billion euros higher in 2017 than in 2013, consumption had increased by 73 billion euros), partially financed by a reduction in the household savings rate (from 9.6 percent to 5.7 percent). Therefore, private consumption became one of the main drivers of the recovery.

In addition to the pent-up demand effect, rapid employment creation – even though it was concentrated in low-paying jobs – seems to be the key factor behind this performance of household consumption. Specifically, Martinez and Urtasun (2017) highlight two reasons. First, moving from job destruction to job creation boosts household confidence, reduces the need for precautionary savings and explains the upturn in spending on durable goods. Second, the marginal propensity to consume among individuals who find a

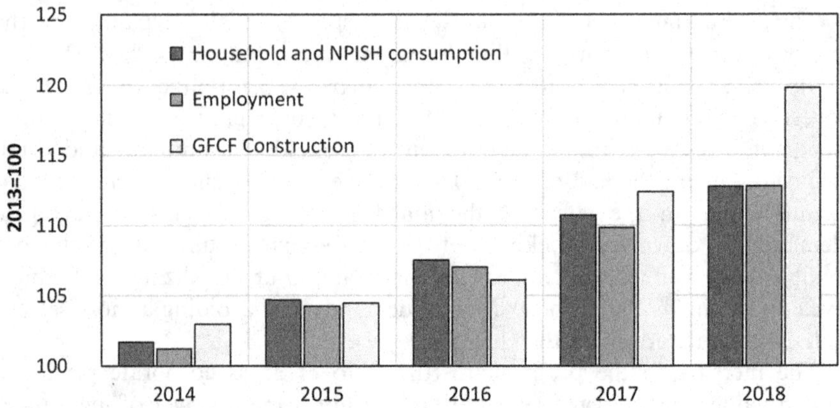

Figure 8.7 Employment, household consumption, and investment in construction during the recovery

Note: 2013 = 100. NPISH = non-profit institutions serving households.

Source: National Accounts, Eurostat. https://ec.europa.eu/eurostat/web/national-accounts

job is higher than it is among the unemployed population, and also higher than those who are currently employed. Therefore, increases in income coming from job creation tend to translate into spending to a high proportion.

All in all, the main driver of the growth model after 2014 is again the increase of private investment, which triggers the multiplier effect on aggregate demand and, along with it, new job creation and household consumption. Due to the high elasticity of employment (measured as the total number of people employed at national level) to GDP, the growth of private investment is robust and induces the very rapid growth of consumption, reinforcing the role of domestic demand in the recovery.

Nevertheless, this new job creation has little to do with the labor reforms adopted during the period 2010–2012. As we can see in Figure 8.8, the relationship between job creation and economic growth, although higher than the eurozone average, remained stable before and after these reforms. Labor reforms in Spain did not modify the elasticity of employment to GDP in the periods of economic expansion (1995–2009 vs. 2014–2018).

The results that the institutional changes of 2010–2012 had on employment are not encouraging. On the one hand, wage devaluation did not translate into greater job creation –labor reforms did not change the relationship between employment and economic growth – since the demand for employment is a derived demand that responds fundamentally to the evolution of aggregate demand. On the other hand, non-standard employment increased dramatically, which covers forms of temporary contracts (including fixed-term, agency, seasonal or discontinuous contracts), part-time contracts (in any of their formulations) and other forms of non-standard contracts (such as training and work experience contracts).

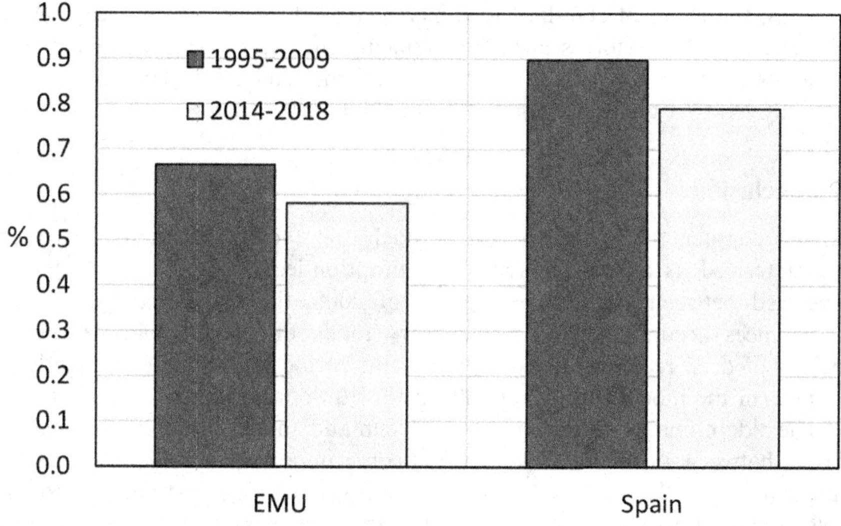

Figure 8.8 Employment-to-GDP elasticity, 1995–2018
Source: National Accounts, Eurostat. https://ec.europa.eu/eurostat/web/national-accounts

During the recession period, 50 percent of the total employment reduction was in standard employment (see Figure 8.9). However, when the economy grows again and job creation takes off, it does so essentially in nonstandard contracts, which outgrow standard ones. This means that the employment created during the economic recovery was focused on precarious employment (70 percent of all new jobs).

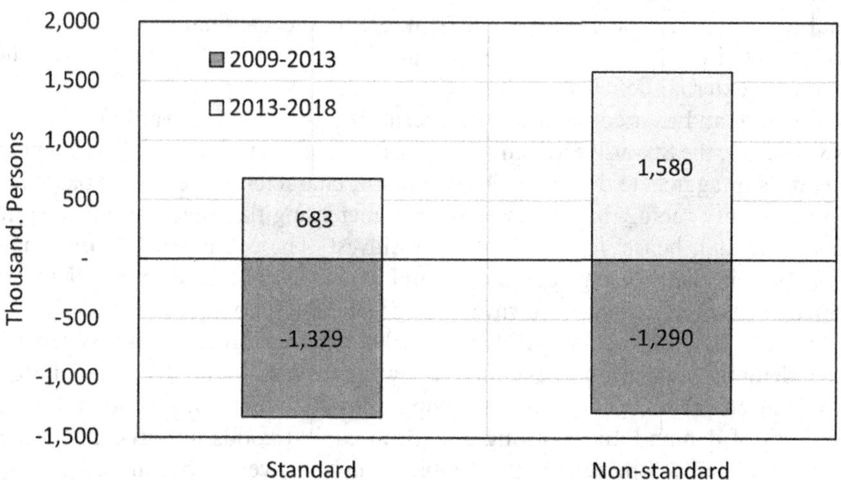

Figure 8.9 Jobs increases during and after the economic crisis, 2009–2018
Source: Statistics from the General Social Security Scheme (GSSS).

Thus, the share of standard jobs has decreased in the last ten years. As a conclusion, labor reforms aimed at reducing the "rigid" aspects of employment protection legislation and decentralizing collective bargaining have actually led to a greater segmentation of the labor market.

5 Conclusion

In this chapter, the Spanish growth model after the Fordist period has been characterized as a "debt-financed consumption-led demand" model, which operated between 1995 and 2008. As of 2008, the major macroeconomic imbalances accumulated by the country made the model collapse, and a period of deep recession began. During this period, an attempt was made to transform the model through significant institutional changes.

The "debt-financed consumption-led demand model" that takes place in Spain between 1995 and 2008 presents some important specificities. First of all, starting in the 1980s, there was significant wage stagnation, due to the reforms that liberalized the labor market and weakened collective bargaining. The strong creation of atypical employment, especially temporary work, broadened the segment of workers who have more unstable working lives, and who therefore receive lower annual wages.

A stagnation in real wages such as that observed in Spain beginning in the 1980s should have led to a restriction in economic growth, since in wage-led economies the marginal effect of a fall in the wage share has contractionary effects. However, two phenomena offset this contractionary effect on aggregate demand.

In the first place, the significant external indebtedness during the 1990s and 2000s – linked to the internationalization of the Spanish economy – promoted the leverage of households and corporations in the context of the real estate bubble, as well as the expansion of bank credit and the financialization of the economy. Furthermore, this foreign indebtedness was able to finance the growing external deficit that was generated during this period.

Second, and as a consequence of a tertiarization process toward labor-intensive sectors, the Spanish economy developed a strong elasticity of employment to changes in aggregate demand. This structural characteristic led to employment growing very rapidly in expansion phases, increasing the average propensity to consume and, hence, for corporations to invest. The counterpart of this characteristic is that, during recessions, employment is destroyed very quickly in Spain, thus reinforcing the downward trend of contractionary periods.

In this way, during the 1990s and 2000s external saving compensated for the demand restrictions generated by wage restraint and by the deindustrialization process. This external saving allowed – through new loans – new sources of demand and a strong growth in capital goods imports, expanding sectors linked to the real estate bubble, which are very labor-intensive. This expansion of labor-intensive sectors would determine the strong growth of employment and consumption during this period.

With the international financial crisis of 2008, external debt quickly ceased, and the model collapsed due to its own imbalances. The housing bubble burst and job destruction was transmitted to investment and private consumption. In this way, financial variables and the sectoral composition of the Spanish economy intensified both the expansionary and recessive cycle of the country. In addition, after the sovereign debt crisis of 2010–2011, public demand was also drastically reduced through austerity policies, which aggravated the duration of the recession (Carballo-Cruz, 2011; Salmon, 2017).

The period of crisis, between 2010 and 2013, is used by Spanish and European authorities to implement significant institutional reforms, particularly in the labor market. The aim of these reforms was to promote a profound change in the economic model, which, however, does not seem to have occurred.

Due to a combination of external and internal factors (Cárdenas et al., 2020), the economy recovered from 2014 to 2018. During this expansion phase, for the first time in a long time, economic growth coexisted with an external surplus. However, this new reality does not seem to be due to a structural change in the model. The external sector deficit was corrected by the positive performance of exports derived from the growth in the world economy, by the drop in international oil prices and, above all, by a sharp drop in domestic demand. The positive contribution of the external sector during the 2014–2018 recovery is due to the fall in imports, and not so much to the recovery of exports. It is the low level of these imports – resulting from a decline in the investment share of GDP with the implementation of fiscal austerity and wage devaluation policies – which largely explains the current account balance during this period. Thus, a change in the growth model toward an export-led model is not verified. Furthermore, the recovery that began in 2014 does not appear to be accompanied by significant changes in the sectoral composition of the economy and the creation of atypical employment becomes even more widespread in this period.

There is a clear line of continuity between the recovery of 2014–2018 and the period prior to the economic crisis: employment maintained a strong elasticity to changes in GDP and continued to be the key determinant of the evolution of the total wage mass (while unit labor costs remained stagnant). Thus, there is a high correlation between the increase in employment and the increase in household consumption and residential investment, despite the fact that this increase in employment occurs mainly in atypical low-paid figures.

Labor market reforms and wage devaluation – policies embedded in a clear neoliberal trajectory – are not the causes of the economic recovery that began in 2014. Exports are not driven by a reduction in wages, but rather by the external demand of the main trading partners. And the rapid job creation is not the result of wage devaluation, but the effect of the recovery of demand and the consequence of a high structural elasticity of employment to GPD derived from the sectoral composition of the economy. In addition, the end of fiscal austerity helped the private sector to reactivate economic growth, triggering the fiscal multiplier. Finally, strong tail winds (low interest rates and low oil prices) supported GDP growth significantly during the 2014–2018 period.

The Spanish economy is an economy that for decades, until the 2008 crisis, followed a debt-led growth model, which was strongly supported by the expansion of private consumption and residential investment, thanks to strong job creation. The crisis and recent institutional reforms tried to create a new export-led model, which, however, has not been borne out. The recovery of the 2014–2018 period therefore raises doubts about the future continuity of the current growth model: the economy did not move toward an export-led model, but the high leverage of households and corporations does not make the debt-led model followed during the previous decades easily repeatable.

Thus, it could be expected that, if the distributional change continues to be adverse for labor and the wage share continues to decline in the years to come, two future possibilities lie ahead. The first possibility is that as the investment share of GDP increases, the external surplus will deteriorate, again turning into an external deficit. The other possibility is that this deterioration in the external surplus will not occur in the coming years, as long as the investment-to-GDP ratio remains structurally low.

References

Afonso, A. (2019). State-led wage devaluation in Southern Europe in the wake of the Eurozone crisis. *European Journal of Political Research*, 58 (3), 938–959.

Albarracín, J. (2000). Neoliberal employment policies. *International Journal of Political Economy*, 30 (2), 56–81.

Alonso, J. A. (1999). Growth and the external constraint lessons from the Spanish case. *Applied Economics*, 31 (2), 245–253.

Álvarez, I., Luengo, F., & Uxó, J. (2013). *Fracturas y crisis en Europa*. Madrid: Clave Intelectual.

Álvarez, I., Uxó, J., & Febrero, E. (2019). Internal devaluation in a wage-led economy: The case of Spain. *Cambridge Journal of Economics*, 43 (2), 335–360.

Amable, B. (2003). *The diversity of modern capitalism*. Oxford: Oxford University Press.

Arrazola, M., de Hevia, J., Romero-Jordán, D., & Sanz-Sanz, J. F. (2015). Long-run supply and demand elasticities in the Spanish housing market. *Journal of Real Estate Research*, 37 (3), 371–404.

Arribas, J., & Cárdenas, L. (2018). Monetary policy as compensatory power? An institutionalist approach to the Eurozone crisis. *Journal of Economic Issues*, 52 (4), 987–1009.

Astudillo, J. (2001). Without unions, but socialist: The Spanish Socialist Party and its divorce from its union confederation (1982–96). *Politics & Society*, 29 (2), 273–296.

Baccaro, L., & Howell, C. (2011). A common neoliberal trajectory: The transformation of industrial relations in advanced capitalism. *Politics & Society*, 39, 521–563.

Bajo-Rubio, O., & López-Pueyo, C. (2002). Foreign direct investment in a process of economic integration: The case of Spanish manufacturing, 1986–1992. *Journal of Economic Integration*, 17 (1), 85–103.

Banyuls, J., Miguélez, F., Recio, A., Cano, E., & Lorente, R. (2009). The transformation of the employment system in Spain: Towards a Mediterranean neoliberalism? In G. Bosch, S. Lehndorff, & S. Rubery (Eds.), *European employment models in flux:*

A comparison of institutional change in nine European countries (pp. 247–270). Basingstoke: Palgrave Macmillan,

Bernardi, F., & Garrido, L. (2008). Is there a new service proletariat post-industrial employment growth and social inequality in Spain? *European Sociological Review*, 24 (3), 299–313.

Bilbao-Ubillos, J., & Fernández-Sainz, A. (2019). A critical approach to wage devaluation: The case of Spanish economic recovery. *The Social Science Journal*, 56 (1), 88–93.

Binda, V. (2013). *The dynamics of big business: Structure, strategy, and impact in Italy and Spain*. London: Routledge.

Blyth, M. (2013). *Austerity: The history of a dangerous idea*. Oxford: Oxford University Press.

Buendía, L. (2020). A perfect storm in a sunny economy: A political economy approach to the crisis in Spain. *Socio-Economic Review*, 18 (2), 419–438.

Caloghirou, Y., Voulgaris, Y., & Zambarloukos, S. (2000). The political economy of industrial restructuring: Comparing Greece and Spain. *South European Society and Politics*, 5 (1), 73–96.

Calvo, N. (2014). Crisis management, re-centralization and the politics of austerity in Spain. *International Journal of Iberian Studies*, 27 (1), 3–20.

Campos-Lima, M. D. P., & Martin-Artiles, A. (2011). Crisis and trade union challenges in Portugal and Spain between general strikes and social pacts. *Transfer*, 17 (3), 387–402.

Carballo-Cruz, F. (2011). Causes and consequences of the Spanish economic crisis: Why the recovery is taking so long. *Panoeconomicus*, 58 (3), 309–328.

Cárdenas, L., & Fernández, R. (2020). Revisiting Francoist developmentalism: The influence of wages in the Spanish growth model. *Structural Change and Economic Dynamics*, 52, 260–268.

Cárdenas, L., & Villanueva, P. (2020). Flexibilization at the core to reduce labor market dualism? Evidence from the Spanish case. *British Journal of Industrial Relations*. doi:10.1111/bjir.12541

Cárdenas, L., Villanueva, P., Álvarez, I., & Uxó, J. (2020). Peripheral Europe beyond the Troika: Assessing the 'success' of structural reforms in driving the Spanish recovery. *Review of Keynesian Economics*, forthcoming.

Castellacci, F., & Álvarez, I. (2006). Innovation, diffusion and cumulative causation changes in the Spanish growth regime, 1960–2001. *International Review of Applied Economics*, 20 (02), 223–241.

Cebrián, I., Moreno, G., Samek, M., Semenza, R., & Toharia, L. (2003). Atypical work in Italy and Spain: The quest for flexibility at the margin in two supposedly rigid labor markets. In S. Houseman & M. Osawa (Eds.), *Nonstandard work arrangements in Japan, Europe and the United States* (pp. 89–129). Kalamazoo, MI: W.E. Upjohn Institute for Employment Research.

Cervini-Plá, M., & Ramos, X. (2011). Long-term earnings inequality, earnings instability and temporary employment in Spain 1993–2000. *British Journal of Industrial Relations*, 50 (4), 714–736.

Cioffi, J. W., & Dubin, K. A. (2016). Commandeering crisis: Partisan labor repression in Spain under the guise of economic reform. *Politics & Society*, 44 (3), 423–453.

Comín, F. (2008). Public enterprises in Spain: Historical cycles and privatizations. *Análise Social*, XLIII (4), 693–720.

Cosculluela, C., & de Frutos, R. F. (2013). Housing investment in Spain, has it been the main engine of growth? *Applied Economics*, 45 (14), 1835–1843.

Cruces, J., Álvarez, I., Trillo, F., & Leonardi, S. (2015). Impact of the euro crisis on wages and collective bargaining in southern Europe: A comparison of Italy, Portugal and Spain. In G. Van Gyes, & T. Schulten (Eds.), *Wage bargaining under the new European economic governance: Alternative strategies for inclusive growth* (pp. 93–137). Brussels: European Trade Union Institute (ETUI).

Cuadrado, J. R., & Maroto, A. (2016). Unbalanced regional resilience to the economic crisis in Spain: A tale of specialisation and productivity. *Cambridge Journal of Regions, Economy and Society*, 9(1), 153–178.

Del Pino, E. (2013). The Spanish welfare state from Zapatero to Rajoy: Recalibration to retrenchment. In B. Field, & A. Botti (Eds.), *Politics and society in contemporary Spain* (pp. 197–216). New York: Palgrave Macmillan.

Del Rio, P., & Fenger, M. (2019). Spanish trade unions against labour market reforms: Strategic choices and outcomes. *Transfer: European Review of Labour and Research*, 25 (4), 421–435.

Doeringer, P. B., & Piore, M. J. (1971). *Internal labor markets and manpower analysis.* Lexington, MA: DC Heath.

Dymski, G. A. (2013). Can relationship banking survive the Spanish economic crisis? *Ekonomiaz*, 84, 182–203.

Eichhorst, W., Marx, P., & Wehner, C. (2017) Labor market reforms in Europe: Towards more flexicure labor markets? *Journal for Labor Market Research*, 51 (3), 1–17.

Etchemendy, S. (2011). *Models of economic liberalization: Business, workers, and compensation in Latin America, Spain, and Portugal.* Cambridge: Cambridge University Press.

Etxezarreta, M. (1991). *La reestructuración del capitalismo en España, 1970–1990.* Madrid: Icaria Editorial.

Eurofound (2019). *Labor market segmentation: Piloting new empirical and policy analyses.* Luxembourg: Publications Office of the European Union.

Febrero, E., & Bermejo, F. (2013). Spain during the Great Recession: Teetering on the brink of collapse. In Ó. Dejuán, E. Febrero, & J. Uxò (Eds.), *Post-Keynesian views of the economic crisis and its remedies* (pp. 266–293). London: Routledge.

Felipe, J. (2002). Unemployment and profitability: The case of Spain. In P. Davidson (Ed.), *A post Keynesian perspective on 21st century economic problems* (pp. 216–243). Cheltenham: Edward Elgar.

Fernández, C. J., Ibañez, R., & Martinez, M. (2016). Austerity and collective bargaining in Spain: The political and dysfunctional nature of neoliberal deregulation. *European Journal of Industrial Relations*, 22 (3), 267–280.

Fernández, C. J., & Martinez, M. (2013). Narratives, myths and prejudice in understanding employment systems: The case of rigidities, dismissals and flexibility in Spain. *Economic and Industrial Democracy*, 34 (2), 313–336.

Fernández-Macías, E. (2003). Job instability and political attitudes towards work: Some lessons from the Spanish case. *European Journal of Industrial Relations*, 9 (2), 205–222.

Ferreiro, J., & Gómez, C. (2008). Is wages policy on the agenda of trade unions again? Voluntary wage moderation in Spain. *Economic and Industrial Democracy*, 29 (1), 64–95.

Ferreiro, J., & Serrano, F. (2001). The Spanish labor market reforms and consequences. *International Review of Applied Economics*, 15 (1), 31–53.

Fina, L., Meixide, A., & Toharia, L. (1989). Reregulating the labor market amid an economic and political crisis. In S. Rosenberg (Ed.), *The state and the labor market* (pp. 107–125). Boston: Springer.

Fishman, R. M. (2012). The politics of industrial relations: Labor unions in Spain. *South European Society and Politics*, 17 (4), 599–601.

Fuentes, I. (2009). Changes in the loan-deposit gap and in its funding in the current decade. *Economic Bulletin* (January).

Garcia, M. (2010). The breakdown of the Spanish urban growth model: Social and territorial effects of the global crisis. *International Journal of Urban and Regional Research*, 34 (4), 967–980.

Garcia-Serrano, C., & Malo, M. A. (2013). Beyond the contract type segmentation in Spain: Country case study on labor market segmentation. Employment Working Paper No. 143. ILO.

González, S., & Luque, D. (2014). Goodbye to competitive corporatism in Spain: Social pacting and conflict in the economic crisis. *REIS*, 148, 79–102.

Gordon, D. M., Edwards, R., & Reich, M. (1981) *Segmented work, divided workers: The historical transformation of labor in the United States.* Cambridge: Cambridge University Press.

Government of Spain (1977). Los pactos de la Moncloa. Texto completo del acuerdo económico y del acuerdo político. Madrid, 8–27 Octubre 1977. Madrid: Servicio Central de Publicaciones / Secretaría General Técnica.

Gruppe, M., & Lange, C. (2014). Spain and the European sovereign debt crisis. *European Journal of Political Economy*, 34, S3–S8.

Hamann, K. (1997). The pacted transition to democracy and labor politics in Spain. *South European Society and Politics*, 2 (2), 110–138.

Hamann, K., Johnston, A., & Kelly, J. (2012). Unions against governments: Explaining general strikes in Western Europe, 1980–2006. *Comparative Political Studies*, 46 (9), 1030–1057.

Hauptmeier, M. (2012). Institutions are what actors make of them: The changing construction of firm-level employment relations in Spain. *British Journal of Industrial Relations*, 50 (4), 737–759.

Häusermann, S., & Schwander, H. (2012) Varieties of dualization? Labor market segmentation and insider-outsider divides across regimes. In P. Emmenegger, S. Häusermann, B. Palier, & M. Seeleib-Kaiser (Eds.), *The age of dualization: The changing face of inequality in deindustrializing societies* (pp. 27–51). Oxford: Oxford University Press,

Herrero, D., Cárdenas, L., & López, J. (2020). Does flexibilization lead to lower unemployment? An empirical analysis of the Spanish labor market. *International Labor Review.* https://doi.org/10.1111/ilrs.12146.

Hipp, L., Bernhardt, J., & Allmendinger, J. (2015). Institutions and the prevalence of nonstandard employment. *Socio-Economic Review*, 13 (2), 351–377.

Horwitz, L., & Myant, M. (2015). Spain's labor market reforms: The road to employment – or to unemployment? Working Paper, March, ETUI.

Kickert, W., & Ysa, T. (2014). New development: How the Spanish government responded to the global economic, banking and fiscal crisis. *Public Money & Management*, 34 (6), 453–457.

Koch, M. (2005). Wage determination, socio-economic regulation and the state. *European Journal of Industrial Relations*, 11 (3), 327–346.

Köhler, H. D. (2018). Industrial relations in Spain – strong conflicts, weak actors and fragmented institutions. *Employee Relations*, 40 (4), 725–743.

Köhler, H. D., & Calleja, J. P. (2017). Spain: A peripheral economy and a vulnerable trade union movement. In S. Lehndorff, H. Dribbusch, & T. Schulten (Eds.), *Rough waters: European trade unions in a time of crises* (pp. 61–81). Brussels: European Trade Union Institute (ETUI).

Lallement, M. (2011). Europe and the economic crisis: Forms of labour market adjustment and varieties of capitalism. *Work, Employment and Society*, 25 (4), 627–641.

Lasierra, J. M. (2007). Labor flexibility and job market segmentation in Spain: A perspective from the labor demand side. *The International Journal of Human Resource Management*, 18 (10), 1858–1880.

López-Andreu, M. (2017). All precarious? Institutional change and turning points in labor market trajectories in Spain. *Employee Relations*, 39 (3), 408–422.

López-Andreu, M. (2019). Employment institutions under liberalization pressures: Analysing the effects of regulatory change on collective bargaining in Spain. *British Journal of Industrial Relations*, 57 (2), 328–349.

Luque, D., & Gonzalez, S. (2015). Austerity and welfare reform in South-Western Europe: A farewell to corporatism in Italy, Spain and Portugal? *European Journal of Social Security*, 17 (2), 271–291.

Malo, M. A. (2015). The impact of Spanish 2012 labor reform on collective bargaining. *Spanish Economic and Financial Outlook*, 4 (3), 17–28.

Martin, A., & Alós, R. (2003). Between decentralization and centralization of collective bargaining: The Spanish case. *Industrielle Beziehungen*, 10 (1), 64–96.

Martínez, M., & Urtasun, A. (2017). The recovery of private consumption in Spain by product type and household. *Economic Bulletin, Bank of Spain*, 2, 2–17.

Martinez-Alier, J., & Roca, J. (1987). Spain after Franco: From corporatist ideology to corporatist reality. *International Journal of Political Economy*, 17 (4), 56–87.

Martinez-Lucio, M., & Blyton, P. (1995). Constructing the post-Fordist state: The politics of labor market flexibility in Spain. *West European Politics*, 18 (2), 340–336.

Martinez-Pastor, J. I., & Bernardi, F. (2011). The flexibilization of the Spanish labor market: Meaning and consequences for inequality from a life-course perspective. In H. Blossfeld, S. Buchholz, D. Hofäcker, & K. Kolb (Eds.). *Globalized labor markets and social inequality in Europe* (pp. 79–107). London: Palgrave Macmillan,

Martins, M. (2017). Crisis and work: An analysis of emergency labour market policies in Portugal, Spain and Greece. *Revista Española de Investigaciones Sociológicas (REIS)*, 158, 3–21.

Massó, M. (2016). The effects of government debt market financialization: The case of Spain. *Competition & Change*, 20 (3), 166–186.

Meardi, G. (2018). Economic integration and state responses change in European industrial relations since Maastricht. *British Journal of Industrial Relations*, 56 (3), 631–655.

MEYSS (2013). *Report evaluating the impact of the labor reform*. Madrid: Ministry of Employment and Social Security.

Molina, O. (2014). Beyond de-centralization: The erosion of collective bargaining in Spain during the Great Recession. *Stato e mercato*, 34 (3), 397–422.

Molina, O., & López-Roldán, P. (2015). Occupational growth and non-standard employment in the Spanish service sector: From upgrading to polarization. In W. Eichhorst, & P. Marx (Eds.), *Non-standard employment in post-industrial labor markets: An occupational perspective* (pp. 110–149). Cheltenham: Edward Elgar.

Molina, O., & Miguélez, F. (2013). From negotiation to imposition: Social dialogue in austerity times in Spain. ILO Working Papers No. 51, September.

Molina, O., & Rhodes, M. (2007). The political economy of adjustment in mixed market economies: A study of Spain and Italy. In B. Hancké, M. Rhodes, & M. Thatcher

(Eds.), *Beyond varieties of capitalism: Conflict, contradictions, and complementarities in the European economy* (pp. 223–252). Oxford: Oxford University Press.

Muñoz de Bustillo, R., & Esteve, F. (2017). The neverending story: Labor market deregulation and the performance of the Spanish labor market. In A. Piasna & M. Myant (Eds.), *Myths of employment deregulation: How it neither creates jobs nor reduces labor market segmentation* (pp. 61–80). Brussels: European Trade Union Institute (ETUI).

Muñoz de Bustillo, R., & Pinto, F. (2018). Against the wind: Industrial relations in Spain during the Great Recession and its aftermath. *Economia & lavoro*, 52 (1), 87–104.

Myro, R. (2018). The sustainability of Spain's trade surplus. *Spanish Economic and Financial Outlook*, 7 (6), 31–43.

Naastepad, C. W. M., & Storm, S. (2006). OECD demand regimes (1960–2000). *Journal of Post Keynesian Economics*, 29 (2), 211–246.

Navarro, V. (2015). Report from Spain: The political contexts of the dismantling of the Spanish welfare state. *International Journal of Health Services*, 45 (3), 405–414.

Neto, M. S. (2005). Analysis of the determinants of new housing investment in Spain. *Housing, Theory and Society*, 22 (1), 18–31.

Nonell, R., Alós-Moner, R., Martín-Artiles, A., & Molins, J. (2006). The governability of collective bargaining. The case of Spain. *Transfer: European Review of Labor and Research*, 12 (3), 349–367.

Onaran, Ö., & Obst, T. (2016). Wage-led growth in the EU15 member-states: The effects of income distribution on growth, investment, trade balance and inflation. *Cambridge Journal of Economics*, 40 (6), 1517–1551.

Pagoulatos, G. (2003). Financial interventionism and liberalization in Southern Europe: State, bankers, and the politics of disinflation. *Journal of Public Policy*, 23 (02), 171–199.

Pavolini, E., León, M., Guillén, A. M., & Ascoli, U. (2016). From austerity to permanent strain? The European Union and welfare state reform in Italy and Spain. In C. De La Porte, & E. Heins (Eds.), *The sovereign debt crisis, the EU and welfare state reform* (pp. 131–157). London: Palgrave Macmillan,

Perez, S. A. (1997). *Banking on privilege: The politics of Spanish financial reform*. Ithaca, NY: Cornell University Press.

Perez, S. A., & Matsaganis, M. (2018). The political economy of austerity in Southern Europe. *New Political Economy*, 23 (2), 192–207.

Perez, S. A., & Matsaganis, M. (2019). Export or perish: Can internal devaluation create enough good jobs in Southern Europe? *South European Society and Politics*, 24 (2), 259–285.

Picot, G., & Tassinari, A. (2017). All of one kind? Labor market reforms under austerity in Italy and Spain. *Socio-Economic Review*, 15 (2), 461–482.

Polavieja, J. G. (2003) Temporary contracts and labor market segmentation in Spain: An employment-rent approach. *European Sociological Review*, 19 (5), 501–517.

Prosser, T. (2016) Dualization or liberalization: Investigating precarious work in eight European countries. *Work, Employment and Society*, 30 (6), 949–965.

Pulignano, V., Ortíz, L., & De Franceschi, F. (2016). Union responses to precarious workers Italy and Spain compared. *European Journal of Industrial Relations*, 22 (1), 39–55.

Recio, A., & Roca, J. (1998). The Spanish socialists in power: Thirteen years of economic policy. *Oxford Review of Economic Policy*, 14 (1), 139–158.

Rey-Araújo, P. M. (2020). The contradictory evolution of "Mediterranean" neoliberalism in Spain, 1995–2008. *Review of Radical Political Economics*. https://doi.org/10.1177/0486613419882122.

Rigby, M., & Garcia-Calavia, M. Á. (2013). The development of extra-judicial systems of collective conflict resolution in Southern Europe: Understanding the Spanish system. *European Journal of Industrial Relations*, 20 (2), 149–156.

Rocha, F. (2018). Strengthening the decentralization of collective bargaining in Spain. In S. Leonardi & R. Pedersini (Eds.), *Multi-employer bargaining under pressure: Decentralization trends in five European countries*. Brussels: European Trade Union Institute (ETUI).

Royo, S. (2007). Varieties of capitalism in Spain: Business and the politics of coordination. *European Journal of Industrial Relations*, 13 (1), 47–65.

Royo, S. (2009). After the fiesta: The Spanish economy meets the global financial crisis. *South European Society and Politics*, 14 (1), 19–34.

Rubio-Mondéjar, J. A., & Garrués-Irurzun, J. (2016). Economic and social power in Spain: Corporate networks of banks, utilities and other large companies (1917–2009). *Business History*, 58 (6), 858–879.

Ruiz, J. R., Stupariu, P., & Vilariño, Á. (2015). The crisis of Spanish savings banks. *Cambridge Journal of Economics*, 40 (6), 1455–1477.

Salas, V. (2014). Corporate profits and the recovery of the Spanish economy. *Spanish Economic and Financial Outlook*, 3 (5), 53–61.

Salmon, K. (2017). A decade of lost growth: Economic policy in Spain through the Great Recession. *South European Society and Politics*, 22 (2), 239–260.

Sanabria, A., & Medialdea, B. (2016). Lending calling: Recession by over-indebtedness: description and specific features of the Spanish case. *Panoeconomicus*, 63 (2), 195–210.

Sanchez-Mosquera, M. (2017). Trade unionism and social pacts in Spain in comparative perspective. *European Journal of Industrial Relations*, 24 (1), 23–38.

Sola, J., Alonso, L. E., Fernández, C. J., & Ibáñez, R. (2013). The expansion of temporary employment in Spain (1984–2010): Neither socially fair nor economically productive. In M. Koch & M. Fritz (Eds.), *Non-standard employment in Europe: Paradigms, prevalence and policy responses*. London: Palgrave Macmillan.

Storm, S., & Naastepad, C. W. M. (2017). Bhaduri–Marglin meet Kaldor–Marx: Wages, productivity and investment. *Review of Keynesian Economics*, 5 (1), 4–24.

Thelen, K. (2014). *Varieties of liberalization and the new politics of social solidarity*. Cambridge: Cambridge University Press.

Toharia, L. (1988). Partial Fordism: Spain between political transition and economic crisis. In R. Boyer (Ed.), *The search for labor market flexibility: The European economies in transition* (pp. 119–139). Oxford: Clarendon Press.

Toharia, L., & Malo, M. A. (2000). The Spanish experiment: Pros and cons of flexibility at the margin. In G. Esping-Andersen & M. Regini (Eds.), *Why deregulate markets?* (pp. 307–335). New York: Oxford University Press.

Tortella, G., & Garcia-Ruiz, J. L. (2013). *Spanish money and banking: A history*. Basingstoke: Palgrave Macmillan.

Uxó, J., Álvarez, I., & Febrero, E. (2018). Fiscal space on the eurozone periphery and the use of the (partially) balanced-budget multiplier: The case of Spain. *Journal of Post Keynesian Economics*, 41 (1), 99–125.

Uxó, J., Febrero, E., & Bermejo, F. (2016). Crisis, unemployment and internal devaluation in Spain. In M. Myant, S. Theodoropoulou, & A. Piasna (Eds.), *Unemployment, internal devaluation and labor market reforms in Europe.* Brussels: European Trade Union Institute (ETUI).

Uxó, J., Paúl, J., & Febrero, E. (2011). Current account imbalances in the Monetary Union and the Great Recession: Causes and policies. *Panoeconomicus*, 58 (5), 571–592.

Vergés, J. (2000). Privatisations in Spain: Process, policies and goals. *European Journal of Law and Economics*, 9 (23), 255–280.

Villanueva, P., Cárdenas, L., Uxó, J., & Álvarez, I. (2020). The role of internal devaluation in correcting external deficits: The case of Spain. *Structural Change and Economic Dynamics*, 54, 282–296. https://doi.org/10.1016/j.strueco.2020.03.008.

Xifré, R. (2017). Non-price competitiveness factors and the export performance: The case of Spain in the Euro area. *Spanish Economic and Financial Outlook*, 6 (3), 55–66.

9 This time was different

The crisis that went past Sweden

Luis Buendía and Pedro M. Rey-Araújo

UNIVERSITY OF LEÓN AND UNIVERSITY OF SANTIAGO DE COMPOSTELA

1 Introduction

After decades of neoliberal hegemony around the world, Sweden is still often held up as embodying an alternative model to the "free-market," deregulated version of capitalism that has become dominant in the Anglo-Saxon countries since the late 1970s and early 1980s, an arguably fairer, more inclusive, and more egalitarian version of capitalism commonly associated with the Nordic countries. Strong social-democratic parties, centralized collective bargaining institutions, low levels of wage dispersion, highly "de-commodifying" and universalist welfare states, high levels of trade union density, or public policies promoting both gender equality in the workplace and a higher degree of co-responsibility at home, are often cited as constitutive features of such "Nordic" type of capitalism.

Nevertheless, after decades of neoliberal restructuring around the world, to what extent does this picture still constitute an accurate description of the current state of affairs in Sweden's political economy? Certainly, many of the constitutive features of the traditional "Swedish model" remain in place which, in turn, keep on setting the Swedish political economy apart from most of its European neighboring countries. Dimensions such as the quality and scope of its welfare state mechanisms; its continued efforts to promote gender equality in the workplace and beyond; the distributive outcomes it keeps to deliver and, especially, its capacity to reconcile the former with sustained economic prowess and international competitiveness, remain unparalleled in the European arena. Nevertheless, while its singularity in that respect has not yet faded away, the Swedish political economy has certainly not remained immune to existing pressures for institutional change along neoliberal lines.

Following a painful and turbulent process of restructuring during the 1980s, a new accumulation pattern was finally consolidated from the early 1990s onwards. Indeed, it is the way the economic crisis of the 1990s was confronted and eventually resolved, rather than the Great Recession, that which holds the ultimate key to apprehend the current configuration of the "Swedish model." As documented throughout this book, in most European countries the onset of the Great Recession has acted as a catalyst for an accelerated process of liberalization and commodification of socio-economic relations. The Swedish case clearly constitutes an exception in this regard. Not only has the Great Recession merely had a short, albeit intense, impact on the Swedish economy but also the institutional transformations it sparked have been significantly limited in scope. Hence, the actual configuration of the Swedish political economy in the aftermath of the Great Recession has shown a great degree of continuity with respect to the preceding period, in terms of both the main features of its institutional environment and its productive specialization.

As indicated in Chapter 1, the Swedish growth-model has so far represented a sort of "via media" between export-led and consumption-led growth models, respectively, insofar as Sweden has managed to reconcile, both before and after the Great Recession, positive current account balances with rising households' consumption levels. Contrary to the situation experienced by other countries, such as Germany, whose export prowess was ultimately achieved at the expense of repressing labor remuneration and, hence, domestic demand, Sweden has consistently managed to avoid such a trade-off between net exports and private consumption. A productive specialization prominently anchored around high-tech manufacturing and high-end services featuring low price elasticity explains, on the one hand, why rising net exports did not require the sustained repression of domestic demand and, on the other, why the Great Recession had such a limited impact upon the Swedish economy.

With respect to the traditional Swedish model, two core differences are to be pointed out. On the one hand, the main source of expanding aggregate demand has no longer been the public sector, as had been the case until the late 1970s, but, rather, private activity. On the other hand, maintaining sound public finances and low levels of inflation has been consolidated as the main policy priorities since the early 1990s, thus abandoning the Swedish government's prior commitment to full employment. In the last instance, such a reconfiguration of public policy priorities reveals a changing balance of forces between capital and labor within the Swedish political economy while, simultaneously, also contributing decisively to consolidate it. This is arguably the core element of the new Swedish model.

The same applies to the various transformations undergone by the Swedish system of industrial relations. First, the new system of coordinated, multi-sectorial collective bargaining has also entailed rising decentralization and individualization of labor relations, insofar as greater scope is left for further negotiation at the firm level, where individual skills and performance, instead of job characteristics, are accorded a greater role in determining wages. Second, previous restrictions on temporary contracts have been partially removed, thus increasing the duality of the labor market. While the proportion of temporary contracts remains comparatively limited, it has nonetheless become a particularly pervasive phenomenon among certain strata such as, prominently, younger workers. Third, animated by the increasing tertiarization of the Swedish economy, the internal cohesion of the trade union movement has been severely curtailed, as white-collar unions, who have ambiguous interests when it comes to reducing earnings inequality, have increased their presence at the expense of the main blue-collar union (LO). These various transformations have increased the internal heterogeneity of the working class, thus negatively affecting its power resources vis-à-vis capital.

These transformations in the productive and industrial relations spheres, respectively, have been accompanied by transformations along similar lines regarding the Swedish political economy's arguably most idiosyncratic institution, namely, the welfare state, which has become less universalistic in scope, and less decommodifying in nature. In this regard, the role of private providers has been increased in certain key areas, such as health or education; contributory private pension schemes have gained prominence with respect to the public system; and the replacement rates and duration of certain benefits, such as those linked to unemployment or sickness, have been reduced. All in all, therefore, the Swedish welfare state has not only left greater scope for private providers but also has proven less effective in insulating individuals from market pressures, being in turn less capable of correcting market-generated social inequalities.

The rest of this chapter will be organized as follows. Section 2 will briefly review the characteristics of the traditional "Swedish model," which remains the inescapable reference point from which to judge the transformations taking place during last decades. Then, the main characteristics of the new growth model, the system of collective bargaining, and the welfare state, respectively, will be explored in detail. While attention will be paid to the consequences of the Great Recession in terms of the institutional restructuring it promoted, as well as the changes experienced by the accumulation pattern, we conclude that the true turning point was the crisis the Swedish economy went through during the early 1990s. The ensuing "Swedish model," while it has not succumbed to existing pressures for institutional transformation along neoliberal lines, has certainly lost much of its previous capacity to decommodify social life, on the one hand, and to correct social inequalities, on the other.

2 The "Swedish model"

The "Swedish model" refers to the interaction among the welfare state, the political aspects, and the economic aspects that help explain the evolution of the former in the case of Sweden. To that extent, we will start by describing Sweden's macroeconomic evolution in Section 3, then we will analyze the framework of labor relations, which we consider an important part of the welfare state understood in its broadest sense and, finally, we will approach the evolution of the welfare state proper, that is, the so-called social wage, which includes income benefits as well as services, as well as the tax system, since it is a powerful redistribution tool, both directly through taxes, and indirectly by financing the social wage. Nonetheless, before exploring in detail the recent period, we first review the origins and history of the "Swedish model," analysis of which is necessary to properly apprehend the nature and stakes of the various transformations introduced during the 1990s.

The "Swedish model" was not a theoretically devised plan resulting in an institutional framework with long-lasting consequences for the welfare of the Swedish people. Rather, it was an institutional setting that resulted from the joint evolution of several other institutional domains, which were born and developed in a context of relatively peaceful relationships among social agents. Following Korpi (1983), we understand the origin of the "Swedish model" to be found in the class compromise that crystalized in the 1938 Saltsjöbaden Agreement, which put an end to three decades of industrial conflict between the main employers association (SAF) and the main trade union (LO). Since the beginning of the century, the SAF and the LO had been involved in several labor conflicts, to an extent that Korpi (1983: 46) stated that the number of days affected by conflicts was the highest of all OECD countries by then. When the Social Democratic Party won the elections in 1932, the SAF adopted an even more radical stance against it and decided to channel funds to the opposing parties, the Liberal Party and the conservative party (Moderates) (Ryner, 2002: 72; Swenson, 2002: 134, 245).

Once the employers accepted the new position of force attained by the labor movement,[1] they accepted the social democratic government's proposal to initiate talks with the labor union, leading to the Saltsjöbaden Agreement, which involved the acknowledgment by the SAF of the unions' right to organize and strike in exchange for, on the one hand, the introduction of certain fiscal advantages and, on the other, the concession by both the unions and the Social Democratic Party that firms' management was the exclusive prerogative of the employers. This agreement came thus to confirm the reformist turn inside the Social Democratic Party, a road they had started to adopt in the 1920s and that involved the acceptance that socialism could be reached through welfare reforms (Meidner 1993: 212). After the end of World War II, and following the trend that other Nordic countries had adopted, the Social Democratic Party and the LO passed a program (the Post-war Program) which included, among other measures, the nationalization of economic sectors. However, the employers and the right-wing parties opposed it. In line with the main conclusions of the Saltsjöbaden Agreement, the Social Democrats finally decided to retreat from any kind of planning (Pontusson, 1992).

Insofar as the government could not implement the policies it considered necessary as long as these would challenge the pre-eminence of the market economy, the only alternative was to have recourse to the use of incentives. The internal logic of the Rehn-Meidner plan has to be understood along these lines. Put forward by two LO economists, Gösta Rehn and Rudolf Meidner, it aimed at promoting economic stabilization through market mechanisms. The idea was to implement restrictive policies to avoid profits from being high enough for wage drift to create inflationary pressures. Active labor market policies and fiscal incentives would work together to achieve full employment in such a restrictive macroeconomic scenario. Finally, the model included the so-called "solidaristic wage policy," according to which only differences regarding the working environment or the nature of the job would justify wage differentials (Erixon, 2008; Pontusson, 1992). Such a model would thus give rise to a continuous process of "creative destruction," since those firms that could not afford to pay higher relative wages to low-skilled workers would have to close, thus resulting into productivity gains for the whole system. However, unemployment pockets would also ensue, which is why, in addition, Sweden became a pioneer regarding the use of active labor market policies to address unemployment problems. In the context of a labor shortage, this idea would be attractive to employers as well (Bonoli, 2014). Finally, the public sector became an employer of last resort, especially during the 1970s crisis, when active labor market policies and public employment creation were crucial to compensate for the effects of the crisis.

The last component on which we want to focus is the expansion of the welfare state. It is important to note that, before World War II, the welfare state in Sweden already included a universal pension system, a compulsory work accident insurance, and a voluntary unemployment program managed by subsidized associations. They were mainly the result of changes and policies implemented under social democratic rule during the 1930s since, before that decade, there was scarcely any national system of social protection, except for the old-age pensions (Valocchi, 1992: 192). Hence, by the end of the 1930s, there was a proper welfare state in Sweden, yet one of limited scope, as most of the social expenditure was spent on combating poverty (Olsson, 1986: 5–6). Despite the existence of programs with broader scope, they had severe limitations. Old-age pensions covered 90 percent of the population, but their replacement rates were certainly low, being between 14 and 27 percent of the previous income; unemployment benefits covered 7 percent of the population and sickness benefits, covered 46 percent of the population. The only income benefit with higher coverage as well as higher replacement rates was the work accident insurance, with around 60 percent on both (Korpi & Palme, 2007).

At the same time the Social Democrats retreated from a politically ambitious program of economic planning and, following the above-mentioned idea that the road to socialism was through enlarging social protection, the government gradually built the most generous welfare state to be found in any capitalist democracy. This was also part of a conscious effort to combine social protection and productivity, that is, a social investment approach in which the country became a leader under the heading of a "productive social policy" (Lindh, 2014: 273–274). The increase of cash benefits accelerated between the 1940s and the 1970s, including the relaxation of qualifying conditions (e.g. a lower retirement age; fewer waiting days for cash benefits) and an increase in both their duration and benefit amounts. Besides that, the government also introduced new benefits (child allowances, housing allowances, a new unemployment subsidy for people who do not qualify for the insurance, etc.) (Berggren, 2005; Olsson, 1986; Sjögren Lindquist & Wadensjö, 2006). Furthermore, the role of the public sector as a provider was increased, as chiefly reflected in the healthcare system, which was fully nationalized (again, through an incentives policy: doctors simply could not afford to compete with the public sector at the official fees once national regulation was implemented, so they moved to the public sector) (Immergut, 1992). The public sector started to provide also new social services with broad coverage, including childcare and elder care (Morel, 2007). As a result, the number of public employees more than tripled (Edvinsson,, 2005).

In sum, by the 1970s, the core elements of the "Swedish model" were an encompassing welfare state, a peaceful framework of labor relations, and the Rehn–Meidner model. The labor movement had become so strong that its demands also became more ambitious, to the point that the Social Democratic government addressed existing inequality problems by taking decisive steps toward co-determination and the so-called "wage-earners funds," a proposal made by Rudolf Meidner involving a gradual socialization of ownership (see Meidner et al., 1978). However, the employers' reaction led the Social Democratic Party to postpone any official decision concerning the funds.

1976 was the year when the Social Democratic Party lost the elections for the first time in decades, and when the world crisis finally hit Sweden's economy. With a right-wing government (which stopped the trend to co-determination), the employers' federation toughened its position and favored a free-enterprise position, financing think-tanks and right-wing parties and even calling for a lock-out in 1980 (Ryner, 2002: 144). That was the beginning of the end of centralized bargaining: in 1983, the engineering employers association abandoned the bargaining system after convincing the corresponding union to follow suit. That trend continued until 1991 when, with a new right-wing coalition in the government, the employers withdrew their representatives from the tripartite bodies.

The cohesion of the labor movement had started to deteriorate when the services sector expanded and unions started to disagree over wage differentials (Meidner, 1993), which explains why in 1983 the main engineering union accepted the employers' proposal to abandon centralized bargaining. This proved a fatal blow to the solidaristic wage policy. Additionally, when the Social Democrats returned to the government in 1982, they introduced a watered-down wage-earners' fund proposal (Whyman, 2003) as part of a whole package of measures which revealed an important modification in the positions they had hitherto advocated. Another part of the latter was a clear support for furthering deregulation with the intention of stimulating economic growth. This was achieved at the cost of creating two asset bubbles in the housing and property markets by the end of the decade (Ryner, 2002).

Despite those important changes in the economic sphere, the welfare state remained chiefly unchanged, with the commitment to full employment intact and even showing improvements in social services and cash benefits. By the end of the 1980s, the Swedish model still showed its main distinctive signs compared to other European welfare states.

3 The macroeconomic evolution since the 1990s

The Swedish economy entered a deep recession in 1991 when the afore-mentioned asset bubbles burst. Once financial intermediaries defaulted on their loans, the Swedish banking system was brought to the brink of collapse, forcing the state either to nationalize the financial institutions in need, or to provide them with special credit lines (Ryner, 2013). Facing speculative attacks against the SEK (the *krona*), the government initially opted for defending the currency by rising domestic interest rates, a decision which, in conjunction with negative wealth effects derived from falling housing prices, could not but further depress aggregate demand. In response, flexible exchange rates were finally implemented in November 1992, while the Central Bank officially adopted an explicit inflation target of 2 percent in January 1993.

Eventually, an export-led recovery was initiated in 1994 (Steinmo, 2013), thereby initiating a new period of intense and uninterrupted economic growth lasting until the onset of the Great Recession (real gross domestic product (GDP) growth averaging 3.33 percent annual growth until 2007). Animated by such vigorous economic expansion, government's budgetary deficits were soon overcome by 1998 (Figure 9.1). Sound public finances over time, in turn,

Figure 9.1 Net lending in the public sector (% GDP)
Source: Own elaboration with data from Statistics Sweden (SCB) (from 1990 to 1992) and AMECO (from 1993 to 2013). ec.europa.eu/.../ameco-database_en

helped to gradually bring down public debt levels (reaching 37% of GDP in 2008). Moreover, current account surpluses became the norm, surpassing 8% in 2007, while inflation levels were consistently kept in check.

While some voices have argued that the new situation represented nothing but a revitalization of the "Swedish model" in a globalized world (e.g. Anxo & Niklasson, 2009), several authors have interpreted these various changes as signaling the onset of a markedly new growth model (e.g. Buendía & Palazuelos, 2014; Erixon, 2011; Schnyder, 2012), chiefly characterized by the dominance of private over public activity as the main growth engine; the establishment of price stability over the attainment of full employment as the main policy priority; an increasing financialization of Sweden's productive structure and society (Belfrage, 2008), and a broad commitment to budgetary stability (Bergman, 2011).

Between 1994 and 2007, two features of the new model prominently stand out from the demand side. On the one hand, in stark contrast to previous periods, private consumption (+2.8 percent yearly, on average) has shown more intense growth than public consumption (+0.7 percent) (Buendía & Palazuelos. 2014). On the other hand, the main drivers of growth have been private investment (+4.95 percent) and, especially, foreign demand (+7.2 percent). This pattern of growth has been labeled an "export-led mercantilist regime" (Stenfors, 2014). However, while the role played by exports growth is undeniable in light of the data presented above, it misses the fact that consumption has also experienced a sustained, albeit more moderate, pattern of expansion (Figure 9.2). As noted by Baccaro and Pontusson (2016), rising levels of private consumption set Sweden apart from other countries, such as Germany, where good export performance was achieved at the expense of repressing labor remuneration and, in consequence, domestic consumption. Rising consumption levels found further support in the evolution of private debt, which registered quite high levels both before and after the Great Recession, according to data from the International Monetary Fund (IMF). Since the mid-1990s to 2007, it went from 180 to 205 percent of the GDP, but then it reached even higher levels, going from 229 to 253 percent of GDP between 2008 and 2018.

The key to such balanced pattern of growth has nonetheless a supply-side explanation, namely, Sweden's successful upgrading of its export profile by shifting into ICT-related manufacturing and services while still retaining a strong presence in traditional manufacturing products (e.g. automobiles) and raw materials, such as wood (Thelen, 2019). Because of the lower price sensitivity of high-tech manufacturing and high-end services, Sweden managed to sustain rising exports without repressing domestic labor remuneration, in turn favoring a gradual expansion of households' consumption levels alongside expanding foreign demand (Baccaro & Pontusson, 2016: 92). The sectors of activity that have registered higher levels of expansion between 1994 and 2007 are, on the one hand, manufacturing (+6 percent yearly) and the ICT sector (+8.4 percent), the latter virtually doubling its weight within GDP during

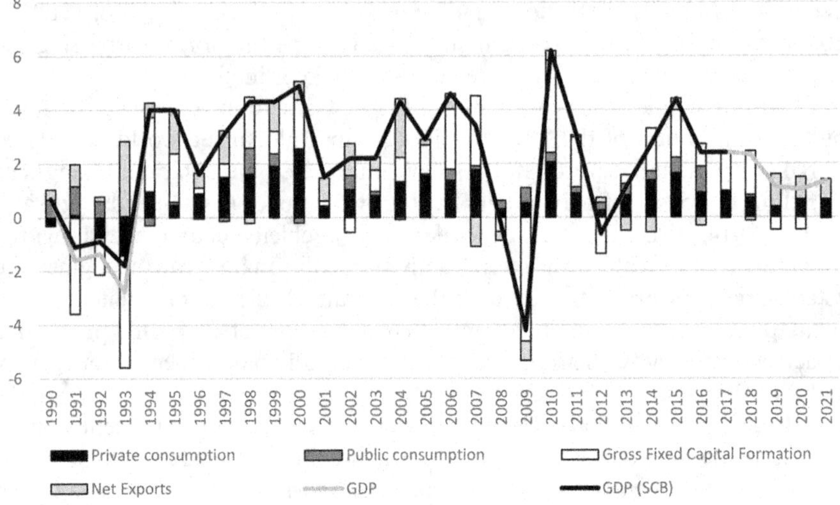

Figure 9.2 Contributions to GDP growth
Source: AMECO. ec.europa.eu/…/ameco-database_en

those years. This shift into the ICT sector was in turn favored by a notable expansion of tertiary education during the 1980s and 1990s (Pontusson, 2011), a conscious governmental effort to increase average computer literacy levels among the population (Thelen, 2019), and by the extensive use of Active Labor Market Policies in the immediate aftermath of the early 1990s crisis (Anxo & Niklasson, 2009). Moreover, such an expansion of the ICT sector also had indirect spillover effects to other sectors of the economy, insofar as it supported sustained labor productivity increases in the economy as a whole (Erixon, 2011).

The onset of the Great Recession in 2008 had a brief, albeit very intense, effect upon the Swedish economy. While the Swedish banking system was virtually unaffected by the US subprime mortgage crisis, it was nonetheless heavily exposed to the Baltic countries, where the effects of the global crisis were compounded by the collapse of their domestic real estate markets (Erixon, 2011). However, the rapid recovery undergone by the Baltic economies, together with the absence of serious credit losses derived from domestic companies' bankruptcies, avoided any serious harm to the Swedish financial system. Nonetheless, the real economy, being very dependent on the export sectors, was intensely affected by weakening international demand. The recession was initiated in the second half of 2008, registering negative real GDP growth in 2009. Despite the slight increase experienced by aggregate consumption in 2009 (+1.5 percent), plummeting levels of private investment (-18 percent) and exports (-14 percent) dragged down real GDP growth (-4.2 percent). Despite its intensity, the recession was finally overcome in 2010, when real GDP bounced back (+6.2 percent), driven by recovering private investment activity (+16.1 percent) and export demand (+10.8 percent).

Such a rapid export-led recovery from the economic downturn, as had been the case in the previous recovery after the 1990s recession, was in turn favored by a weakened currency between 2009 and 2010 and the composition of Swedish exports (raw materials and investment goods), which benefitted from the recovery of international demand from 2010 onwards (Stenfors, 2014). Moreover, contrary to the situation in the previous crisis in the 1990s (Bergman, 2011), Swedish public finances were in significantly good shape at the beginning of the crisis (public debt levels dropping below 40 percent of GDP in 2008). Sound public finances in turn enabled the adoption of several counter-cyclical measured, besides the effect derived from built-in automatic stabilizers, such as increased government grants to municipalities, new programs of investments in infrastructures, a reduction of income tax levels for certain vulnerable groups and social security contributions, together with a significant expansion of active market labor policies (ALMPs) (Anxo, 2012).

The broad contours of the Swedish growth model have barely been affected by the impact of the Great Recession. Between 2010 and 2018, while real GDP grew at a slightly lower rate on average (+2.2 percent yearly), it nonetheless managed to reconcile aggregate consumption growth (+1.8 percent) with exports expansion (+3.4 percent), while maintaining the vigor previously shown by private investment (+4.1 percent). From the supply side, the continuing prowess of ICT services (+4.9 percent), financial services (+4 percent) and professional and administrative services (+4 percent) has been in stark contrast to the relative stagnation experienced by manufacturing (+0.68 percent). In sum, the Great Recession did not cause any sort of drastic transformation in Sweden's political economy.

However, while the main determinants of economic growth in the post-2010 Swedish model do show a great deal of continuity with respect to those operating during the previous period, there are nonetheless significant differences between the two periods. First, growth rates have been considerably lower, mostly because of receding international demand for Swedish exports. Second, manufacturing production has stagnated in real terms since 2010 whereas, in the previous period, only the ICT services' sector had registered higher average rates of yearly growth. Third, the state's economic activity has been more proactive when compared to the previous period. Ample fiscal surpluses were no longer the norm (at least until 2017), while the average rate of public consumption' yearly growth has virtually doubled (although still at a considerably lower level than private consumption's growth). Lastly, while current account surpluses were consistently reproduced over time, they did nonetheless show a markedly downward trend (from +8.15 percent in 2007 to +1.9 percent in 2018).

While Sweden's productive structure has shown a marked continuity since the early 1990s, as noted, another key feature of the Swedish model emerging in the early 1990s has been, as several commentators have pointed out, an ongoing process of "financialization" (e.g. Belfrage, 2008; Belfrage &

Kallifatides, 2018; Christophers, 2013; Ryner, 2013), the source of which is to be found in the restructuring process of the 1980s and early 1990s, when key policy transformations included a radical liberalization of financial markets and monetary flows, a norm-based monetary policy or the implementation of floating exchange rates, resulting in the consolidation of Stockholm as a regional financial center (Belfrage & Kallifatides, 2018). These changes fostered the transformation of the traditional bank-based system into a more market-oriented one, as reflected in the increase experienced throughout the period in the equity-to-loans ratio of Sweden's non-financial corporations, as well as in the continuous increase in stock market capitalization in relation to GDP. Those changes, in turn, have facilitated the increase of private debt levels to reach an all-time high, exactly at the same pace that the public sector reduced its own. Nonetheless, while non-financial corporations have become considerably more market-oriented, the Swedish corporate governance structure has succumbed neither to managerial short-termism nor to the absolute prioritization of maximizing shareholder value (Stenfors, 2014). The reason why is to be found in the preservation of high levels of ownership concentration, as the preservation of controlling mechanisms, such as differential "voting rights," has effectively decoupled share ownership from actual control, in turn sustaining "non-market coordination" in key sectors of the economy. However, while the financialization of the Swedish productive structure remains an incomplete process to date, it has been the most intense in two areas traditionally safeguarded from the operation of market logics, namely, the pension and housing systems (Belfrage & Kallifatides, 2018; Christophers, 2013). These areas will be scrutinized in detail below.

4 The labor market and industrial relations

The economic crisis between 1991–1994 had its most dramatic effects in terms of employment. Committed to restoring the confidence of the international markets, the government refused to undertake currency devaluations, as had been the norm during the 1980s. Instead, a restrictive monetary policy was implemented, in the guise of rising interest rates, accompanied by drastic cuts in public spending. Abandoning its traditional commitment to securing full employment in favor of price stability, such a stance signaled a radical break with the traditional policy priorities of the "Swedish model." In barely three years, more than 500,000 jobs were lost, among which close to 150,000 corresponded to the public sector. Regarding private employment, more than two-thirds of total employment destruction corresponded to manufacturing and construction sectors. In consequence, the unemployment rate rose from 3.8 percent in 1991 to over 10 percent in 1994, despite a 4 percent reduction in activity rates, an unheard-of level in Sweden's recent history (Figure 9.3).

While the economic crisis finally ended in 1994, uninterrupted economic growth for more than a decade had meagre effects in terms of employment creation. Indeed, it was not until 2007, at the very end of the expansion phase,

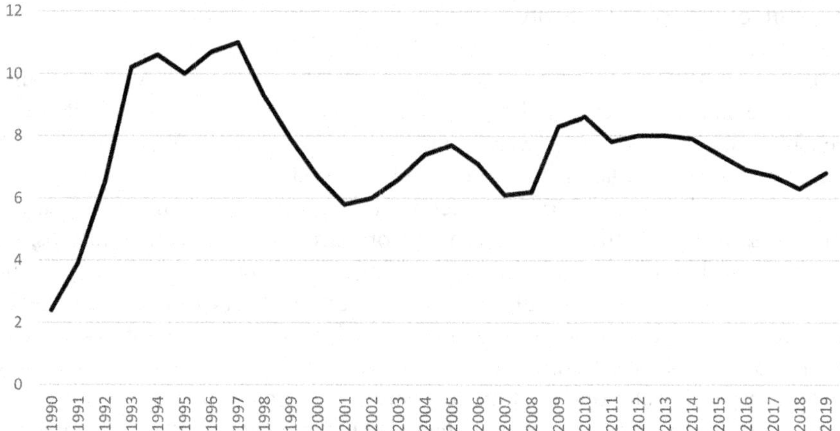

Figure 9.3 Unemployment rate, 1990–2019
Source: AMECO. ec.europa.eu/…/ameco-database_en

when employment levels, in absolute terms, finally surpassed those previously attained in 1991. Contrary to previous phases of sustained economic growth, employment creation between 1994–2008 did correspond exclusively to the private sector, insofar as the public sector destroyed another 30,000 jobs in the course of the expansion. The sectorial composition also differed sharply from previous periods, as the number of manufacturing jobs stagnated, whereas the service sector accounted for half a million new jobs. In sum, employment creation until 2008 was entirely circumscribed to private services.

Regarding the configuration of industrial relations, the main institutional transformation concerned the re-centralization of collective bargaining at the sectorial level. Centralized bargaining, one of the core pillars of the "Swedish model," had unraveled during the turbulent 1980s, featuring high levels of labor unrest and wage-led inflation. The new industrial relations regime was initiated in 1997, when an "Industrial Agreement" (*Industriavtal*) was signed between the main trade unions and the employers confederations in the tradable goods sectors, with the explicit goal of fostering wage increases compatible with economic growth and full employment. A system of coordinated, multi-sectorial bargaining was implemented for most of the private sector which, nonetheless, left ample scope for actual wage determination at the enterprise level. These industrial agreements set a sector-specific norm regarding the size of potential wage increases compatible with price stability, which firm-level agreements were to respect, together with clear procedures concerning the regulation of firm-level negotiations and the resolution of potential industrial disputes by independent mediators. Moreover, this system reinforced the pace-setting role of the export sector regarding wage increases in other sectors (Anxo & Niklasson, 2009). To that extent, a National Mediation Office was set up in 2000 which authorized mediators without the consent of the parties involved, and was explicitly designed to bring wage developments in line with those agreed upon in the sectors exposed to international trade (Ibsen, 2016). This re-centralization of collective bargaining now coexisted, however, with a much higher individualization of wage schemes, insofar as wages were now to be set not only according to job characteristics, but also in relation to individual skills and performance.

Anxo and Niklasson (2009) contend that, despite higher individualization of wages, very high trade union density compared to European standards, on the one hand, and very high rates of coverage of collective agreements, on the other, deliver an institutional framework promoting "negotiated flexibility" between capital and labor representatives, in turn strengthening the institutional pillars of the traditional "Swedish model." However, the relatively balanced power relations existing between capital and labor that stood at the very core of the "Swedish model" have been partially undone, as argued by Baccaro and Howell (2011). While the re-centralization of collective bargaining might give the impression of a revival of the "historical compromise" between capital and labor, the true innovation of the period resides, in the last instance, in the individualization of bargaining and the concomitant increasing differentiation of wages, so that, despite relative institutional continuity at a formal level, a marked liberalization of labor outcomes has actually taken place. Indeed, trade union density levels might not be as good an indicator of the institutional power of the working class as they used to be in the past. While union density declined only slightly until 2006 (Kjellberg, 2011), the internal composition of the trade union movement has nonetheless been significantly altered. Whereas blue-collar unions (LO) have been weakened by occupational changes, the opposite holds in relation to white-collar ones (SACO and TCO), which have a less clear interest when it comes to reducing earnings inequalities. As a result, the internal homogeneity of the working class has been greatly reduced and, therefore, its institutional capabilities have been downgraded accordingly (Bengtsson & Ryner, 2018).

Regarding employment protection, several institutional transformations have significantly increased the duality of the Swedish labor market (Thelen, 2014). Whereas the regulation of open-ended contracts has not been modified since the early 1990s, several legislative measures have been adopted which significantly deregulated the use of fixed-term contracts. The 1997 reform legalized the use of temporary contracts without objective productive reasons, whereas, previously, employers could have recourse to fixed-term contracts only under specific circumstances (e.g. when replacing an absent employee). Nonetheless, certain qualifications were introduced, such as a limitation on employers of having a maximum of five workers under those contracts (Holmlund & Storrie, 2002). Another reform was implemented in 2007 which, on the one hand, lifted the previous limitation regarding the maximum number of employees an employer might have under a temporary contract, while, on the other hand, extended the time an individual worker could be temporarily employed in the same job, from 14 to 24 months within a 5-year period (Svalund & Berglund, 2018). In 2007, 13 percent of employees aged 25–54 had a fixed-term contract, although that figure rose to 57 percent for employees aged 15–24 (the incidence for female workers has been higher, previous figures had been 15.3 percent and 65 percent, respectively).

The Great Recession, as already noted, had but a slight impact upon the Swedish economy. In terms of wage employment losses, the rate of unemployment increased slightly from 6.1 percent to 8.6 percent between 2008 and 2010, accounting for a loss of almost 70,000 jobs, evenly split between the private and public sectors, respectively. However, within private employment, the service sector actually generated 30,000 new jobs whereas close to 75,000 were lost in the manufacturing sector. This pattern of employment creation in the private sector was maintained in the upcoming years, insofar as another 25,000 jobs were lost in manufacturing between 2010 and 2017, thus standing in stark contrast to the behavior of the service sector, where more than 300,000 new jobs were generated during the same period. Regarding public employment, the previous tendency of declining employment levels was brought to a halt, as more than 130,000 new jobs were created between 2010 and 2017. Nonetheless, despite employment levels recovering after 2010, the rate of unemployment remained fairly constant at around 8 percent during the upcoming years, not dropping below 7 percent until 2016. The explanation lies in the fact that rising employment trends coexisted with a concomitant rise in labor participation after 2010. Moreover, while no significant increase in the proportion of fixed-term contracts occurred after 2010, around 50 percent of workers aged 15–24 had a temporary contract in 2018. Indeed, young workers have been much harder hit by the crisis as compared to other age groups. The unemployment rate of workers aged 15–25 rose to 24.8 percent in 2010, and by 2018 it was still 16,8 percent (6.4 percent and 5.2 percent, respectively, for those aged 25–54). The main reasons explaining the comparatively worse situation experienced by younger workers include the higher prevalence of fixed-term contracts among those strata, on the one hand, and the implementation of the seniority principle ("last in, first out") regarding collective dismissals, on the other (Anxo, 2015).

Regarding collective bargaining, no significant changes were experienced after the crisis. The years following the onset of the Great Recession have been characterized by very low levels of labor conflict, while collective agreements kept ensuring widespread wage moderation in successive negotiation rounds (Anxo, 2017). The two-tier collective bargaining set up during the 1990s remained firmly in place after the crisis. However, the internal composition of the trade union movement has been further affected. A crucial event in this respect was the 2006–2007 reform of the unemployment insurance system. In Sweden, the unemployment insurance funds are subsidized by the state and administered by the trade unions themselves (the so-called "Ghent system"), while individual membership is voluntary. After the reform, the state's subsidies to the unemployment insurance funds were severely curtailed, thus significantly increasing the average monthly membership fees. Moreover, the obligation of the different insurance schemes to contribute to an "equalization fund" has been removed, in turn heavily increasing the dispersion of fees in different sectors, membership fees have been higher in those sectors displaying higher levels of unemployment. As a result, half a million workers abandoned the unemployment insurance system in 2008–2009 (Anxo, 2015). Moreover, these sectors, precisely, were the most adversely hit by the crisis, and where the presence of the blue-collar union LO is comparatively much higher, such as manufacturing or low-paid services. As a result, trade union membership has steadily declined ever since, despite being still at very high levels compared to European standards (trade union density has declined by 6 percent between 2007 and 2018), as many young workers have left, or not joined, unions (Svallfors, 2016). Moreover, declining membership has disproportionately affected the blue-collar union LO, whereas white-collar unions have actually seen their membership increase during these years. Given that the latter have a more blurred interest in wage equalization, the internal cohesion of the working class is bound to be further disrupted, and the redistributive character of the Swedish model to be affected accordingly (Gordon, 2019).

In sum, Sweden's labor market has performed comparatively well since the onset of the Great Recession, and several lines of continuity can be identified with respect to previous times, such as the norm-setting role played by the export sector, a centralized collective bargaining system, low levels of labor conflict and comparatively high rates of trade union density. However, the relative balance of power between capital and labor, arguably the defining trait of the labor relations system characteristic of the "Swedish model," has been significantly altered to the benefit of the former. Occupational changes away from manufacturing and the increasing dispersion of wages have reduced the hegemonic position of the blue-collar unions within Sweden's trade union structure. As a result, the solidaristic nature of the Swedish labor market has been severely affected and, therefore, the institutional power of the working class might be expected to decrease accordingly.

5 The evolution of the welfare state

Regarding the development of the Swedish welfare state, it was the crisis in the 1990s, rather than the Great Recession, which had a more significant impact upon it, a trend we have seen before. This is because, on the one hand, the former hit the Swedish economy harder than the latter did but also, on the other hand, because during that crucial crisis there was a right-wing coalition in government which considered it the appropriate moment to introduce several ideologically motivated reforms. If the 1980s were the years when the Social Democratic Party adopted, under the "Third Way" banner, a more pro-market stance concerning several institutional domains, the 1990s were the years when those changes reached the welfare state. In the words of Wahl (2011: 57), Sweden "was among the countries in Europe that liberalized, privatized, contracted out and market-oriented most, during this period – apart from the United Kingdom." This section explores these transformations.

In 1997, the Swedish Prime Minister Göran Persson published a book in Swedish entitled "Those who are in debt are not free" (Erixon, 2011: 320–321), in which he defended the necessity of budget consolidation measures. This idea, shared by other Swedish right-wing parties, was the basis for the austerity program adopted to confront the crisis: in 1995, as a reaction to the increasing public debt, a ceiling on public expenditures was introduced. The intensity of the fiscal austerity measures introduced had no parallel among OECD countries between the early 1970s and the 2008–2011 period (Erixon, 2011: 272): the replacement rates and length of sickness and unemployment benefits were cut (Berggren, 2005; Sjögren Lindquist & Wadensjö, 2006), the indexation of cash benefits came to an end, and the basic pension was reduced twice, in 1993 and in 1996 (Hemerijck, 2013; Kosonen, 2011: 225–226). During those years, the coverage of housing subsidies declined, thus eroding the universality of the system and leading to the increasing role of private housing at the expense of public housing, the stock of which has been severely privatized since then (Hort, 2014: 55–56).

It is important to note that, while some of these cutbacks regarding replacement rates were reversed once the economy started to recover, they never attained their previous levels. As well as that, the Social Services Act of 1998 made social assistance less generous, thus curtailing the system's effectiveness regarding poverty reduction (Kuivalainen & Nelson, 2012). Regarding unemployment benefits, work requirements were further toughened up in the following years, including the obligation to accept a job anywhere in the country after 100 days of being unemployed, even at a wage 10 percent below the unemployment benefit, while, in addition, the right to have the unemployment benefit renewed by joining a labor market program was abolished in 2001 (Bonoli, 2014: 197–198). These transformations signaled a change from welfare to workfare or, to put it in Hemerijck's (2013 165) words, it meant going along "the activation line."

In the case of old age pensions, changes were no less significant. The 1994 pension reform linked pensions to economic, demographic, and financial variables, as it included a small compulsory capitalization component (Belfrage & Ryner, 2009; Carroll & Palme, 2006). As a result, the defined benefit system turned into a defined contribution one, where each person has now to choose which pension fund he or she wants to invest in (Wahl, 2011: 111). Retirement age was also increased from 65 to 67 that year. As a consequence of the 1990s reform, Sweden is now one of the countries with a higher level of coverage of privately funded pensions (nearly 100 percent of the employed population is covered by a mandatory private pension system, while 27.6 percent is also covered by voluntary pension schemes) (Hort, Kings & Kravchenko, 2016: 684).

All these changes led to a continuous decrease in the decommodifying nature of the welfare state, as revealed by the evolution of Scruggs et al.'s (2017) generosity index (see Figure 9.4). As shown below, the decommodification levels increased in a clear trend until the end of the 1980s, the point when a downward trend was consolidated. By 2010, the last available year, the generosity of the Swedish welfare state was even below its level in the 1970s (although still remaining higher than in most other countries).

Regarding public service's provision, the Moderate Party initiated during its government term the so-called "Choice Revolution." Regarding education, a system of vouchers was introduced so that families could choose which provider they preferred, whereas regarding healthcare, public financing was also granted to the choice of a doctor, irrespective of whether it was from the public or the private sector. When the SAP returned to the government, while the latter was canceled, the former was not (Blomqvist, 2004), thus consolidating an increase in the private provision of social services through greater user financing and municipal decentralization (Hemerijck, 2013: 168). As a consequence, tax-financed private employment rose from 10,000–20,000 in 1990 to more than 120,000 in 2012 (Hort, 2014: 34), while private schools increased their share in the upper secondary level from 10.9 to 48.2 percent between 1995 and 2010 (Erixon, 2011: 275). Regarding childcare and elder care, they followed different paths: while childcare improved throughout the

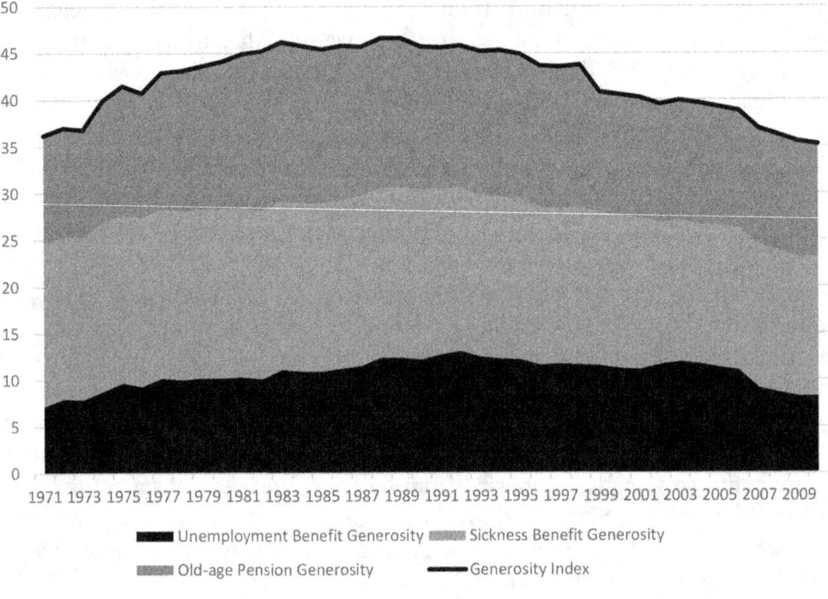

Figure 9.4 The generosity index and its components, 1970–2010
Note: See Scruggs et al. (2017) and its codebook for a definition of each component.
Source: Adapted from Scruggs et al. (2017).

whole period to reach quasi-universal coverage, elder care became more selective and partially privatized, albeit of a higher quality nonetheless (Blomqvist, 2004; Morel, 2007: 183–238, 341–342).

In general, privatizing trends spread throughout all the welfare state, thus challenging the universalization of the whole system. As a result, there has been an increase in class-related segmentation, insofar as middle-class, highly educated parents choose private providers to a much greater extent than other segments of the population do (Kersbergen & Kraft, 2017). In the beginning, those services were mainly provided by non-profit actors, but that quickly changed. Service delivery in those areas is now under the control of large shareholding or private equity companies, which have become powerful actors in the decision-making process regarding how the welfare state is to be organized (Svallfors, 2015).

Another trend that should be highlighted when studying the evolution of the welfare state is that of its increasing financialization, a process singularly acute in the domains of pensions and housing, respectively. The pension reform in the mid-1990s made every Swedish citizen a potential investor as the funded component was managed following portfolio investment strategies (Belfrage & Kallifatides, 2018). As such, a mass investment culture was introduced in the midst of the population's everyday life, with the declared aim of fostering private savings and to reduce the reliance on old-age savings in the public sector.

The other welfare state realm that has clearly been affected by financialization is that of housing. As happened elsewhere, the commodification of the right to dwelling has led to an increase in profits for speculators (which has led to the afore-mentioned real estate bubbles) while, at the same time, the social need for housing had been quite neglected. The Swedish housing market has thus been converted into a hybrid with notable malfunctions (Christophers, 2013). As the public sector has chosen to retreat from intervening in this sector, the right to housing has been seriously challenged by housing prices increasing much faster than wages, thus fostering households' increasing resort to credit which, again, increased the role of the financial sector in the whole system.

Regarding taxes, the Social Democrats were the intellectual authors of the 1991 reform, later known as the "Tax Reform of the Century" (which predicted a revenue reduction worth 6 percent of the GDP, according to pre-reform estimates), which included important rate cuts and a broadening of the tax base. However, conservatives, liberals and the Center Party added new tax cuts for their particular constituencies, which led to an under-financed reform and to an increasing deficit (Steinmo, 2010: 65). The 1991 tax reform introduced a ceiling of 50 percent on the earnings of the top bracket and the tax base was enlarged by imposing VAT taxes on services that had previously been tax-free. For most people, direct taxes became similar to flat rates. In 1994, the Social Democrats introduced a new austerity tax raising the top marginal tax rates for the highest incomes (Hort, 2014: 61–62).

Besides a higher emphasis on labor market activation, the privatization of public services, and cutbacks in cash benefits, another trend worth mentioning concerns the enhancement of social investment. Sweden enjoyed a comparatively advantaged starting point with regards to most other countries in this regard, as manifested, for instance, for instance, in the fact that its parental leave benefits were among the most generous. Nevertheless, in the mid-1990s, the Prime Minister Goran Persson introduced a new approach by declaring it would become the key to combat unemployment. That was the beginning of the "lifelong learning focus" (Jenson, 2014). Along with the pension reform, this was a way to address social security issues. As a part of this program, since 1995 all municipalities had to offer full-time childcare to all children aged between 1 and 12 years old if their parents were working or studying and, from 2001 onwards, also for children whose parents were on parental leave (for 15 weekly hours, at least) (Meagher & Szebehely, 2012). These measures were improved again in the 2000s when a top rate on childcare fees was introduced (Hemerijck, 2013). The downside of this process was that, in the move to a new curriculum, the new focus on skills replaced the old emphasis on the values of equality and democracy.

The result is that, apart from the parental leave benefit of 480 days (with 60 non-transferable days), there is a one-month leave for fathers when the child is born. Both are compensated to 80 percent of the previous earnings. There is also temporary leave when the child is sick (at 80 percent of the previous income) for up to 120 days per year per child until he or she is 8 years old. Additionally, there is a flat-rate child allowance (up to the age of 16 years), complementary study allowances for those between 16 and 19, and a housing allowance for low-income earners with children and income support for single parents (Hort, 2014: 46–47). In sum, Sweden remains a comparatively good country to have children.

In terms of inequality, Sweden became the OECD country where it increased the most, partly as a result of the various changes we have commented upon in previous sections, partly as a consequence of those changes we have just mentioned (OECD, 2015). According to data from Statistics Sweden (*Statistiska centralbyrån*, SCB), the Gini coefficient increased by 35 per cent between 1991 and 2007, whereas the share of income obtained by the richest 1 per cent rose from 4.6 to 8.4 per cent (Figure 9.5). The sources of income that increased the most during those years, in relative terms, were capital gains and capital income, respectively. This development owes a great deal to the 1991 tax reform, which introduced a dual-income tax, thus giving strong incentives to high-income earners to shift their bases from labor to capital incomes (Fritzell et al., 2012: 172; Palme, 2019: 236). Besides that, changes in social assistance caused poverty to notably increase during those years, certainly not as much as it did in other European countries, although to a much greater extent that in other Nordic countries (Kuivalainen & Nelson, 2012: 82). By measuring the difference between primary income and disposable income with data from the SCB, we can see that, while the public sector reduced inequalities by 50 per cent in 1991, it did so only by 39 per cent in 2007.

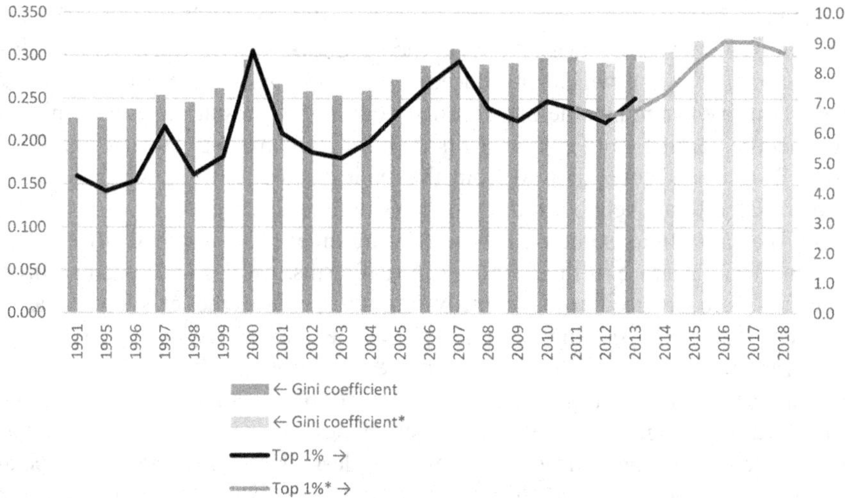

Figure 9.5 Gini coefficient and top 1% income shares, 1991–2018
Note: * denotes a change in the methodology used by SCB.
Source: Adapted from data from Statistics Sweden (SCB).

Two main reasons explain why the Great Recession did not cause crucial transformations in the Swedish welfare state (Palme, 2019: 240). On the one hand, the crisis did not hit Sweden too hard while, on the other, a certain consensus between the parties along the ideological spectrum made it harder to introduce important changes there than in other countries (Bergh, 2011; Erixon, 2011: 276). Paradigmatically, when the crisis started, the conservative Minister of Finance, Anders Borg, pushed for more public investment (Steinmo, 2010: 86). In 2011, despite implementing a fiscal consolidation package, social expenditures increased and, although the reduction of sickness and unemployment insurance was under study, the commitment to the social investment approach remained under the "Boost for Pre-Schools" initiative (2009–2012) (Hemerijck, 2013).

This notwithstanding, some important changes took place around 2008 that need to be considered. The above-mentioned cross-party consensus concerned the concept of the welfare state in general, but not the form that such a welfare state was to adopt. Crucially, as already commented upon in Section 4, the reform of the union membership system meant a direct attack on unions. During their term of office, in addition, the center-right coalition also cut the benefit level of unemployment benefit, while reducing its length and increasing its contributions (Hort, 2014: 47–48). Unions were considered an impediment to the activation policy the coalition wanted to implement in order to increase labor supply and reduce unemployment levels, namely, the *arbetslinjen* (the work-line) policy, which included the tightening up of sickness insurance, household service deductions, a lower amount of unemployment insurance benefits and new active labor market programs (Palviainen, 2019). Nonetheless, the most innovative measure was the adoption of in-work tax credits (*jobbskatteavdraget*), which introduced tax exemptions for income from work (in a country where income benefits are taxable). As a result, taxes were higher for income coming from cash benefits than for job earnings (Hort et al., 2016: 677). Tax expenditures derived from this policy amounted to over three times those related to active labor market policies (Palme, 2019: 240).

At the same time, some cash benefits were indexed to nominal prices, thus leading to a decrease in their amount in real terms, while some social security benefits were reduced, thus contributing to increase the existing distance between the employed and the unemployed, as well as increasing inequality and reducing their effectiveness in decreasing poverty levels. While these measures were aimed at increasing the labor supply, in a recessionary context, they had hardly any effect in that respect. Hence, their main consequence has been a redistribution of resources from people with low incomes from social security, to people with higher incomes accruing from wages (indeed, the higher the income, the greater the tax cut) (Palme, 2019).

The center-right government introduced a new childcare allowance which would allow parents to choose between taking the children to public childcare, on the one hand, or taking care of them at home and being paid the allowance, on the other. Once more, the argument of the freedom of choice came first, despite some voices denouncing it as a "gender trap." However, contrary to the government's expectations, only 1.9 percent of all children aged 1–3 years were cared for at home with support from the care allowances (mainly by women), while the rest of the population kept on relying on childcare (Hort et al., 2016; Meagher & Szebehely, 2012). Along the same lines, a tax deduction for the use of domestic services was introduced (Hort et al., 2016: 680).

Regarding services, perhaps the most relevant concerns the privatization of major hospitals, although that was, once again, previous to the onset of the Great Recession (Hort, 2014: 52). In the case of the pension system, the crisis had important effects inasmuch as pensions had to be lowered to preserve their long-run financial stability, given the financial buffer was affected by the recession. Indeed, since 2010 was an electoral year, the cutback was finally spread through several years ahead in order to avoid voters' punishment (Lindh, 2014: 279).

Finally, regarding taxes, important changes, both just before the Great Recession and immediately afterwards, included the abolishment of the inheritance tax, the wealth tax, and the taxes on residential property. Added to previous trends, they point to a future of increasing inequalities. Indeed, the tax and regulation reforms implemented since the 1980s have facilitated capital gains, while the 2006 reform allowed owners of small companies to shift a larger share of dividends from labor income to capital income (Svallfors, 2015).

After the crisis, inequality kept on growing. In 2017, the Gini coefficient reached an all-time high with 0.322 (slightly decreasing the next year, see Figure 9.5). Also, in 2017, the redistributive capacity of the public sector (measured, again, as the difference between the Gini coefficient before and after government intervention) was 37.35 per cent, the lowest figure in the series (that starts in 1991). The explanation for these trends of increasing inequality lies in several factors. Palviainen (2019) estimates that the effect of some policies such as the *jobbskatteavdraget*, albeit responsible for greater poverty and inequality, is limited compared to changes in the market income distribution and changes in the demographic structure caused by greater immigration flows. Other authors consider that a lower universality in the Swedish welfare state is related to these results also. Concretely, Kersbergen and Kraft (2017: 222) show that rising selectivity and targeting of social policies (due to tighter eligibility criteria and ongoing privatization trends) have caused greater inequality and poverty. Palme (2019: 235), in turn, also blames tax policy changes prior to the crisis for increasing relative poverty rates. In sum, while there have not been significant retrenchment policies as a result of the Great Recession, policy changes introduced before the crisis have worsened the universalism deficit, which we have already commented upon (Palme, 2019: 244). In the future, more inequality is to be expected and although it has not had an impact on the composition of the internal demand (heavily dependent upon consumption, as has been said), it might contribute, along with the proliferation of different debt instruments, to the increase of a private debt that is already very high.

6 Conclusion

Does the new "Swedish model," the one emerging from the economic crisis of the early 1990s, ultimately represent an adaptation of the traditional "Swedish model" to the new competitive pressures articulating the new international environment or, rather, does it constitute a clear deviation from the former and, hence, a markedly different stage in the recent history of Swedish capitalism? Certainly, Sweden keeps on displaying very high levels of trade union density as well as comparatively low levels of income inequality compared to European standards, its welfare state keeps displaying an above-average capacity to decommodify key areas of social life, while the export-oriented sectors keep on playing a pacesetting role, through a recentralized collective bargaining system, regarding the wage determination in those sectors less exposed to international competition. Nonetheless, in stark contrast to the previous period, the trade union movement is, at the moment, much more internally differentiated, revealing in turn a more ambiguous stance regarding the containment and reduction of wage dispersion; inequality does remain low although it has been increasing throughout the whole period, especially with regards to non-wage income; and the recentralization of collective bargaining during the 1990s has nonetheless permitted higher individualization regarding wage determination, leading in turn to higher wage dispersion. At the core of all these changes, in the last instance, lies a shifting balance of forces between labor and capital.

While the singularity of the "Swedish model" remains firmly in place when compared to coexisting growth models within the European arena, it has nonetheless not remained impervious to existing pressures derived from the worldwide demise of Fordism. Through an uneven though profound process of institutional transformation during the late 1970s and 1980s, several areas previously protected from market pressures underwent a sustained process of liberalization and increasing commodification; several previously public enterprises were sold to private hands; while financial capital saw many of the restrictions that had operated upon it in the past eventually removed. In consequence, the relative balance of forces between capital and labor, arguably the key element accounting for the internal coherence of the "Swedish model," has been significantly skewed to the benefit of the former. As a result, competitive pressures have been accentuated, financialization has gained prominence, and social inequalities have been on the rise.

In sum, a new growth model was consolidated following the dramatic economic crisis between 1991–1993 chiefly characterized, first, by the dominance of private over public activity as the main driver of economic growth, second, by the adoption of price stability over the attainment of full employment as the main policy priority and, third, by a new pattern of productive specialization prominently anchored around high-tech manufacturing and high-end services. The latter, in turn, explains why the Great Recession had such a minor impact upon the Swedish economy. Indeed, it is the economic crisis of the 1990s and the way it was confronted and eventually resolved, rather than the Great Recession, which holds the ultimate key to apprehend the current state of affairs of the "Swedish model."

Acknowledgments

Names are given in alphabetical order. Both authors contributed equally to the research.

Note

1 Steinmo (2010) attributes the key to the success of the Social Democrats to the change to a proportional representation electoral system. so that, by the 1930s, when the non-socialist parties also came to accept that, the "Social Democrats would be the dominant party in politics for quite some time."

References

Anxo, D. (2012). From one crisis to another: The Swedish model in turbulent times revisited. In S. Lehndorff (Ed.), *A triumph of failed ideas: European Models of capitalism in crisis* (pp. 27–40). Brussels: ETUI.

Anxo, D. (2015). The Swedish social model: Resilience and success in turbulent times. In D. Vaughan-Whitehead (Ed.), *The European social model in crisis* (pp. 507–552). Cheltenham: Edward Elgar Publishing.

Anxo, D. (2017). Industrial relations and the crisis: The Swedish experience. ILO Working Paper.

Anxo, D., & Niklasson, F. (2009). The Swedish model: Revival after the turbulent 1990s? In G. Bosch, S. Lehndorff, & J. Rubery (Eds.), *European employment models in flux: A comparison of institutional change in nine European countries* (pp. 81–105). Basingstoke: Palgrave Macmillan.

Baccaro, L., & Howell, C. (2011). A common neoliberal trajectory: The transformation of industrial relations in advanced capitalism. *Politics & Society*, 39 (4), 521–563.

Baccaro, L., & Pontusson, J. (2016). Rethinking comparative political economy: The growth model perspective. *Politics & Society*, 44(2), 175–207.

Belfrage, C. (2008). Towards 'universal financialisation' in Sweden? *Contemporary Politics*, 14 (3), 277–296.

Belfrage, C., & Kallifatides, M. (2018). Financialisation and the new Swedish model. *Cambridge Journal of Economics*, 42 (4), 875–900.

Belfrage, C., & Ryner, M. (2009). Renegotiating the Swedish social democratic settlement: From pension fund socialism to neoliberalization. *Politics & Society*, 37 (2), 257–287.

Bengtsson, E., & Ryner, M. (2018). Why no wage solidarity writ large? Swedish trade unionism under conditions of European crisis. In S. Lehndorff, H. Dribbusch, & T. Schulten (Eds.), *Rough waters: European trade unions in a time of crises* (pp. 285–3029). Brussels: ETUI.

Berggren, S. (2005). Kunskapsöversikt över förmåner riktade till barn och barnfamiljer. Working Papers in Social Insurance. Available at: www.forsakringskassan.se/irj/go/km/docs/fk_publishing/Dokument/Rapporter/Working_papers/wp0501_kunskapsoversikt_over_formaner_riktade_till_barn_och_barnfamiljer.pdf.

Bergh, A. (2011). The rise, fall and revival of the Swedish welfare state: What are the policy lessons from Sweden? IFN Working Paper No. 873.

Bergman, M. (2011). Best in class: Public finances in Sweden during the financial crisis. *Panoeconomicus*, 58 (4), 431–453.

Blomqvist, P. (2004). The choice revolution: Privatization of Swedish welfare services in the 1990s. *Social Policy & Administration*, 38 (2), 139–155. https://doi.org/doi:10.1111/j.1467-9515.2004.00382.x.

Bonoli, G. (2014). Active labor market policy and social investment: A changing relationship. In N. Morel, B. Palier, & J. Palme (Eds.), *Towards a social investment welfare state? Ideas, policies and challenges* (pp. 181–204). Bristol: Policy Press.

Buendía, L., & Palazuelos, E. (2014). Economic growth and welfare state: A case study of Sweden. *Cambridge Journal of Economics*, 38 (4), 761–777.

Carroll, E., & Palme, J. (2006). *Inclusion of the European Nordic model in the debate concerning social protection reform: The long-term development of Nordic welfare systems (1890–2005) and their transferability to Latin America in the twenty-first century*. Financiamento del Desarrollo Series. New York: United Nations.

Christophers, B. (2013). A monstrous hybrid: The political economy of housing in early twenty-first century Sweden. *New Political Economy*, 18 (6), 885–911.

Edvinsson, R. (2005). *Growth, accumulation, crisis: With new macroeconomic data for Sweden 1800–2000*. Stockholm: Almqvist & Wiksell International.

Erixon, L. (2008). The Swedish Third Way: An assessment of the performance and validity of the Rehn–Meidner model. *Cambridge Journal of Economics*, 32 (3), 367–393.

Erixon, L. (2011). Under the influence of traumatic events, new ideas, economic experts and the ICT revolution: The economic policy and macroeconomic performance of Sweden in the 1990s and 2000s. In L. Mjøset (Ed.), *The Nordic varieties of capitalism* (pp. 265–330). Bingley: Emerald Group Publishing.

Fritzell, J., Bäckman, O., & Ritakallio, V.-M. (2012). Income inequality and poverty: Do the Nordic countries still constitute a family of their own? In J. Kvist, J. Fritzell, B. Hvinden, & O. Kangas (Eds.), *Changing social equality: The Nordic welfare model in the 21st century* (pp. 165–186). Bristol: Policy Press.

Gordon, J. C. (2019). The perils of vanguardism: Explaining radical cuts to unemployment insurance in Sweden. *Socio-Economic Review*, 17 (4), 947–968.

Hemerijck, A. (2013). *Changing welfare states*. Oxford: Oxford University Press.

Holmlund, B., & Storrie, D. (2002). Temporary work in turbulent times: The Swedish experience. *The Economic Journal*, 112 (480), 245–269.

Hort, S. E. O. (2014). *Social policy, welfare state, and civil society in Sweden*. Vol. II. 3rd enlarged edn. Stockholm: Arkiv förlag.

Hort, S. E. O., Kings, L., & Kravchenko, Z. (2016). Still awaiting the storm? The Swedish welfare state after the latest crisis. In K. Schubert, P. de Villota, & J. Kuhlmann (Eds.), *Challenges to European welfare systems* (pp. 671–691). Cham: Springer International Publishing. https://doi.org/10.1007/978-3-319-07680-5_29.

Ibsen, C. L. (2016). The role of mediation institutions in Sweden and Denmark after centralized bargaining. *British Journal of Industrial Relations*, 54 (2), 285–310.

Immergut, E. M. (1992). *Health politics: Interests and institutions in Western Europe*. Cambridge: Cambridge University Press.

Jenson, J. (2014). Redesigning citizenship regimes after neoliberalism: Moving towards social investment. In N. Morel, B. Palier, & J. Palme (Eds.), *Towards a social investment welfare state? Ideas, policies and challenges* (pp. 61–87). Bristol: Policy Press.

Kersbergen, K. V., & Kraft, J. (2017). De-universalization and selective social investment in Scandinavia? In A. Hemerijck (Ed.), *The uses of social investment* (pp. 216–226). Oxford: Oxford University Press. https://doi.org/10.1093/oso/9780198790488.003.0019.

Kjellberg, A. (2011). The decline in Swedish union density since 2007. *Nordic Journal of Working Life Studies*, 1 (1), 67–93.

Korpi, W. (1983). *The democratic class struggle*. London: Routledge & Kegan Paul.

Korpi, W., & Palme, J. (2007). The Social Citizenship Indicator Program (SCIP). Stockholm: Swedish Institute for Social Research, Stockholm University. Available at: https://dspace.it.su.se/dspace/handle/10102/7.

Kosonen, P. (2011). Experiences from two financial crises in the Nordic welfare states: 1990–93 and 2008–10 compared. In K. Farnsworth & Z. Irving (Eds.), *Social policy in challenging times: Economic crisis and welfare systems* (pp. 219–230). Bristol: Policy Press.

Kuivalainen, S., & Nelson, K. (2012). Eroding minimum income protection in the Nordic countries. In J. Kvist, J. Fritzell, B. Hvinden, & O. Kangas (Eds.), *Changing social equality: The Nordic welfare model in the 21st century* (pp. 69–88). Bristol: Policy Press.

Lindh, T. (2014). Social investment in the ageing populations of Europe. In N. Morel, B. Palier, & J. Palme (Eds.), *Towards a social investment welfare state? Ideas, policies and challenges* (pp. 261–284). Bristol: Policy Press.

Meagher, G., & Szebehely, M. (2012). Equality in the social service state: Nordic childcare models in comparative perspective. In J. Kvist, J. Fritzell, B. Hvinden, & O. Kangas (Eds.), *Changing social equality: The Nordic welfare model in the 21st century* (pp. 89–118). Bristol: Policy Press.

Meidner, R. (1993). Why did the Swedish model fail? *Socialist Register*, 29, 211–228.

Meidner, R., Hedborg, A., & Fond, G. (1978). *Employee investment funds: An approach to collective capital formation*. London: George Allen & Unwin.

Morel, N. (2007). L'Etat face au social: La (re)definition des frontières de l'Etat-providence en Suède. Une analyse des politiques de prise en charge des personnes âgées dépendantes et des jeunes enfants de 1930 à 2005. Thesis, Université Paris I, Panthéon-Sorbonne. Paris.

OECD (2015). OECD income inequality data update: Sweden. Available at: www.oecd.org/sweden/OECD-Income-Inequality-Sweden.pdf.

Olsson, S. E. (1986). Sweden. In P. Flora (Ed.), *Growth to limits: The Western European welfare states since World War II*. Vol. 1, *Sweden, Norway, Finland, Denmark* (pp. 1–116). Berlin: Walter de Gruyter.

Palme, J. (2019). Sweden: In times of two crises. In S. Ólafsson, M. Daly, O. Kangas, & J. Palme (Eds.), *Welfare and the Great Recession: A comparative study* (pp. 228–245). Oxford: Oxford University Press. https://doi.org/10.1093/oso/9780198830962.003.0013.

Palviainen, H. (2019). Changing Nordic model? A policy analysis. EUROMOD Working Paper Series.

Pontusson, J. (1992). *The limits of social democracy: Investment politics in Sweden*. Ithaca, NY: Cornell University Press.

Pontusson, J. (2011). Once again a model: Nordic social democracy in a globalized world. In J. Cronin, G. Ross, & J. Shoch (Eds.), *What's left of the Left: Democrats and social democrats in challenging times* (pp. 89–115). Durham, NC: Duke University Press.

Ryner, M. (2002). *Capitalist restructuring, globalization and the Third Way: Lessons from the Swedish model*. London: Routledge.

Ryner, M. (2013). Swedish trade union consent to finance-led capitalism: A question of time. *Public Administration*, 91 (4), 823–839.

Schnyder, G. (2012). Like a phoenix from the ashes? Reassessing the transformation of the Swedish political economy since the 1970s. *Journal of European Public Policy*, 19 (8), 1126–1145.

Scruggs, L., Jahn, D., & Kuitto, K. (2017). Comparative welfare entitlements dataset 2. Version 2017–09. Available at: www.sp.uconn.edu/~scruggs/wp.htm.

Sjögren Lindquist, G., & Wadensjö, E. (2006). National social insurance – not the whole picture: Supplementary compensation in case of loss of income. Available at: www.regeringen.se/content/1/c6/07/28/34/696f8794.pdf.

Steinmo, S. (2010). *The evolution of modern states: Sweden, Japan, and the United States*. Cambridge: Cambridge University Press.

Steinmo, S. (2013). Governing as an engineering problem: The political economy of Swedish success. In W. Streeck & A. Schäfer (Eds.), *Politics in the age of austerity* (pp. 84–107). Cambridge: Polity.

Stenfors, A. (2014). Financialisation and the financial and economic crises. The case of Sweden. *Financialisation, Economy, Society and Sustainable Development (FESSUD)*, 27.

Svallfors, S. (2015). Politics as organized combat: New players and new rules of the game in Sweden. MPIfG Discussion Paper. Available at: https://ideas.repec.org/p/zbw/mpifgd/152.html.

Svallfors, S. (2016). Politics as organised combat. New players and new rules of the game in Sweden. *New Political Economy*, 21(6), 505–519.

Svalund, J., & Berglund, T. (2018). Fixed-term employment in Norway and Sweden: A pathway to labor market marginalization? *European Journal of Industrial Relations*, 24 (3), 261–277.

Swenson, P. (2002). *Capitalists against markets: The making of labor markets and welfare states in the United States and Sweden*. Oxford: Oxford University Press. http://dx.doi.org/10.1093/0195142977.001.0001.

Thelen, K. (2014). *Varieties of liberalization and the new politics of social solidarity*. Cambridge: Cambridge University Press.

Thelen, K. (2019). Transitions to the knowledge economy in Germany, Sweden, and the Netherlands. *Comparative Politics*, 51 (2), 295–315.

Valocchi, S. (1992). The origins of the Swedish welfare-state: A class analysis of the state and welfare politics. *Social Problems*, 39 (2), 189–200.

Wahl, A. (2011). *The rise and fall of the welfare state*. New York: Pluto Press.

Whyman, P. (2003). *Sweden and the "Third Way": A macroeconomic evaluation*. Farnham: Ashgate.

10 Financial services industry power and labor market polarization in the UK debt-led growth model

Julián López and Adrián Rial

COMPLUTENSE UNIVERSITY OF MADRID AND COMPLUTENSE INSTITUTE FOR INTERNATIONAL STUDIES

1 Introduction

Although some authors hold that the UK was once a corporatist, manufacturing-based national economy, it is now unanimously considered to be a clear example of an Anglo-Saxon liberal market economy (Bickerton, 2018; Edgerton, 2018). That is, a system of market relations between workers and firms, where government regulations and trade unions play only a minor role. As is probably well known, the current model emerged after the crisis of the late 1970s and the subsequent transformations of the economy in the 1980s and 1990s. Following Baccaro and Pontusson (2016) and Lavery (2017; 2019a; 2019b,; 2018), we maintain that this new British growth model can be defined by two axes:

1 The financial axis, that consists of a highly influential financial sector in terms of income generation, employment creation, and external balance.
2 The employment axis, that involves the growing incidence of low-skilled, non-standard jobs in the low-wage sector of the economy.

Describing it in more detail, the model rests on two complementary dynamics. First, the liberalized financial sector and its ancillary industries attract capital inflows from abroad, export financial and professional services, and extend credit to households and firms increasingly dependent on financial markets. Second, low unionization rates, soft employment protection regulations, and immigration from lower-income countries contain labor costs in low-skill services.

However, these sources of continuous growth are also the main instability forces of the regime and are directly related to the 2008 financial crisis and the current Brexit political crisis. On the one hand, credit-fueled consumption generates a rise in households' and firms' indebtedness and, consequently, raises financial fragility across the private sector. As the 2008 financial crisis showed, households' and firms' financial weakness contributed to a rise in defaults and caused liquidity and solvency problems in the private sector as a whole. On the other hand, there are growing income disparities. People and places linked to the financial and professional services sector have higher annual incomes (derived either from capital gains or from labor), better job opportunities, and better career prospects than those linked to low-skill services or declining manufacturing employment. Thus, Brexit can be seen as the largely unpredicted result of the UK inequality problem, because, as some researchers have proven, the social and economic conditions of the most depressed areas were a significant, and perhaps the most important, factor in the EU referendum voting outcome (Becker, Fetzer & Novy, 2017; Fetzer, 2019).

As a consequence, the model produces two main results in terms of economic performance. The first is what we call the "economic puzzle of the UK economy." Despite showing relatively low gross domestic product (GDP) growth rates figures, the UK has the lowest unemployment and highest activity rates in decades. However, at the same time, the high employment growth is not producing higher inflation rates, even though the labor compensation share remains stable and is even increasing.

The second result is the "employment–productivity trap" and refers to the following. On the one hand, during 2010–2015, employment grew faster in industries that were classified as low productivity growth industries (LPGI) in the previous period. On the other hand, much of the slowdown in UK productivity growth is explained by the slowdown of previously high productivity growth industries (HPGI). So the economy is trapped in a productivity–employment problem: Employment creation is concentrated in LPGI, but previous industrial sources of productivity enhancement seem to be exhausted, and turning back to them is not an option.

The chapter proceeds as follows (see Table 10.1). Section 2 describes the economic structural foundations of the UK growth model since the 1980s, regarding output, employment, demand, and income distribution, focusing on those aspects relevant to our goals. Sections 3 and 4 contain a brief analysis of the main institutional characteristics and economic implications of both

Table 10.1 Outline of the chapter

Weakness	*Household indebtedness*		*Wage disparities*	*Slowdown of previous sources of labor productivity growth*	
	The economic puzzle			The employment-productivity trap	
Economic performance	Low inflation rates	Low unemployment rates	Stable labor compensation share	Higher employment growth in LPGI	Slowdown productivity growth in HPGI
	Complementary dynamics				
Political economy axis	Financial axis			Employment axis	

the financial and labor axes. Section 4 interrogates the impact of the financial and political crisis on both. The final section presents a conclusion.

2 Economic performance of the UK growth model

2.1 The UK employment–productivity trap

After the years of the economic crisis of the 1980s and early 1990s, the last two decades have been characterized by stable, decreasing but persistent output growth rates, low unemployment rates, and extremely low productivity rates. Indeed, following the shock of the financial crisis, the economy not only recovered but reinforced the trends of the previous decade dramatically, particularly regarding employment and productivity growth. Thus, in the last quarter of 2019, the unemployment rate was 3.9 percent (the lowest levels since the early 1970s), and productivity growth was virtually 0, according to the last data (Table 10.2).

The employment productivity performance seems to be related to various factors. The first is the relatively low levels of investment. As a proportion of GDP, it only represents 16.7 percent, lower than their corresponding ratios in comparable countries like Japan, Canada, France, or Germany (Pessoa & Van Reenen, 2014). The second is the endogenous link between labor productivity and wages. Although this relationship is far from being clear, some analysts highlight that higher pay may force firms to enhance productivity by investing in new equipment and human capital formation. Because of this reason, they demand a rise in salaries to improve productivity (IPPR, 2018). The third, and perhaps the most important one, is the employment structure of the British economy. Britain has been the country with a higher decline in manufacturing employment, and it is one of the economies more dependent on service activities, which are typically less productive industries (Berry, 2015).

To show whether changes in employment structure have impacted labor productivity growth, we conduct the following exploratory analysis (Figure 10.1). After setting aside all the non-market British industries, we divide the rest of them into four groups (H = high, MH = medium-high, ML = medium-low, and L = low) according to their productivity growth during the periods 1995–2007 and 2010–2015. Then, we calculate employment growth in these groups for the same time interval.

Table 10.2 Evolution of demand, employment and wages

Phase	*Years*	*Y*	*E*	*Y/E*	*W*	*W/E*	*W/Y*	*I/Y*	*U*
Expansion	1995–2007	2.9	0.8	2.1	3.1	2.3	48.3	18.2	5.8
Recession	2008–2009	-2.3	-1.2	-1.1	-2.0	-0.8	50.5	16.2	6.6
Expansion	2010–2017	2.0	1.4	0.6	1.4	0.0	49.2	16.7	6.5

Source. EU KLEMS.https://euklems.eu/

Note: E = employment ; W = wages.

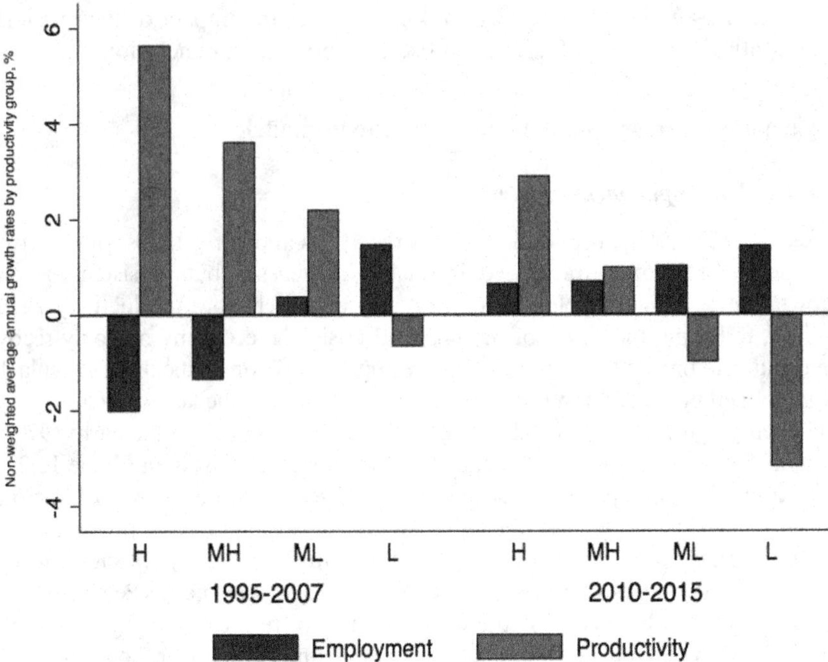

Figure 10.1 Employment growth between 1995 and 2015 by productivity group
Source: Adapted from EUKLEMS data. https://euklems.eu/

Our results, shown in Figures 10.2 and 10.3, point to some relevant questions:

1 Within market activities, employment increases faster in medium-low and low productivity growth industries. Indeed, during the first period, the non-weighted average of employment growth rates is only positive in low productivity growth industries. Regarding the second period, employment grows in the four industry groups but at the expense of lower productivity growth rates. As shown in Figure 10.3, between industries with higher employment growth rates in 2010–2015, most have lower productivity growth rates than those in 1995–2007.
2 This performance is congruent with the employment-productivity trade-off hypothesis, which suggests that job creation in advanced economies is in conflict with productivity enhancement. However, it is important to note that Figure 10.2 displays non-weighted averages by productivity group while Figure 10.3 shows differences in annual growth rates by industry; thus, we are not considering employment and productivity level differences between industries. In other words, Figures 10.2 and 10.3 provide only a tentative approach to the relationship between productivity and employment within industries, but their implications for the economy as a whole should not be understated.

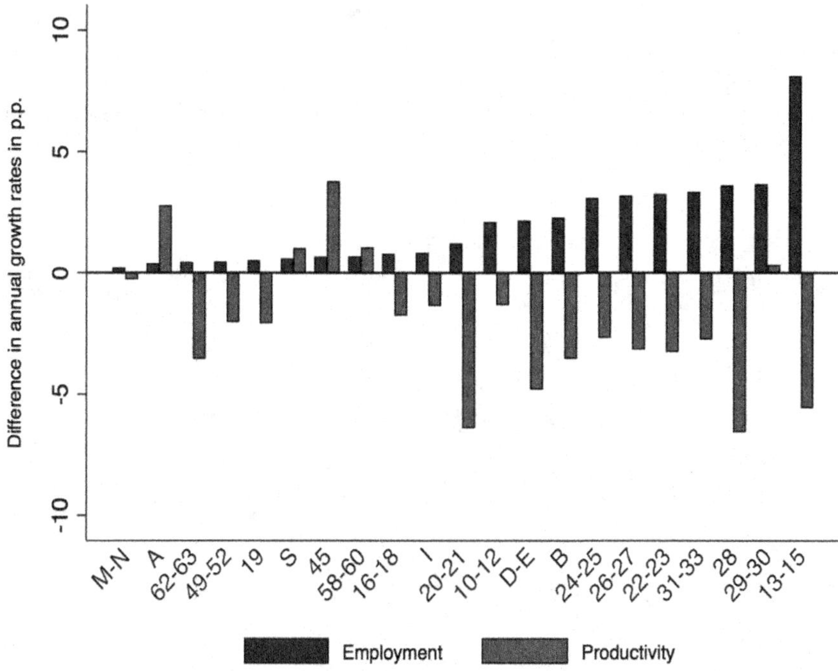

Figure 10.2 Change in employment and productivity growth rates
Source: Adapted from EU KLEMS data. https://euklems.eu/

3 After classifying them by productivity growth in the period 1995–2007, we plotted their productivity values (in logs) against time and rescaled the axis to better show the industry performance over the whole period (1995–2015). Although a decrease or slowdown in productivity can be attributed to almost every industry from 2010–2015, the contrast with respect to the previous period is greater for high and medium-high productivity growth industries. This points to the question of whether or not the slowdown in productivity of the productive industries from the previous period may explain, at least partially, the slowdown of the economy as a whole in 2010–2015.

A more accurate insight can be obtained by calculating the contributions to the aggregate productivity growth of each industry group using the decomposition formula proposed by Nordhaus (2001; 2002). Following this method, the productivity growth of an economy can be calculated as a sum of industry contributions. Besides, these contributions are broken down into three terms. The first is the pure productivity effect (PPE) and measures the contribution to productivity growth that would occur with no changes in the nominal output shares. The second is the Baumol effect (BE), which consists of the interaction between productivity growth and the change in nominal output

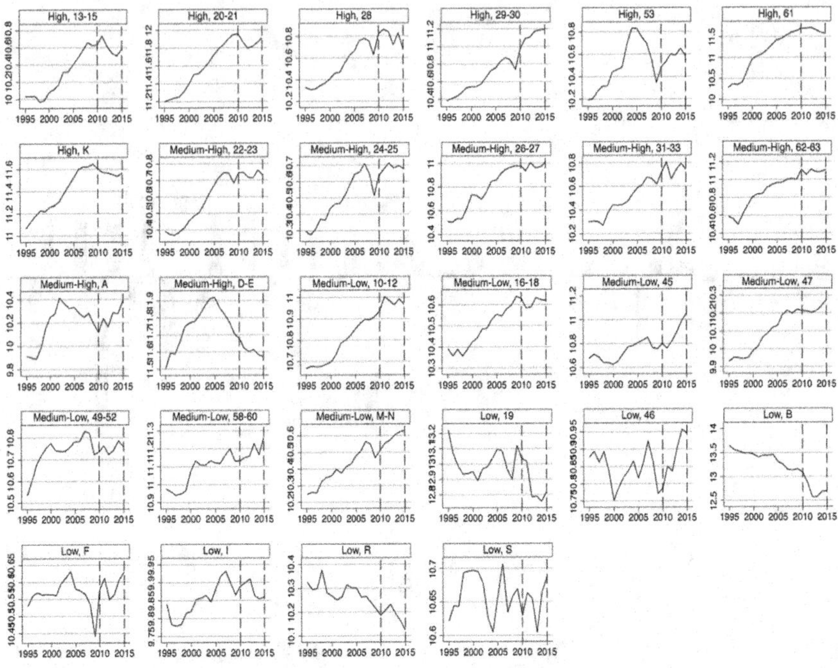

Figure 10.3 Labor productivity in logs by industry
Note: Industry codes given in ISIC Rev.4 – Nace Rev.2, see Appendix/http://www.euklems.net/TCB/2018/ALL_output_Readme_17ii.txt
Source: Adapted from EU KLEMS data. https://euklems.eu/

share with respect to the base year. The third term, the Denison effect (DEN), implies that a productivity enhancement can be obtained if workers are displaced to more productive industries, so when employment grows in more productive industries, those industries are contributing positively to aggregate productivity growth.

Once we obtain each industry contribution, we calculate partial aggregates of every type of contribution (PPE, BE and DEN) by productivity growth group, and then the average for the periods 1996–2007 and 2010–2015 is taken. Figure 10.4 displays the difference between the 2010–2015 and 1996–2007 contributions over productivity growth groups. The results show how the slowdown in productivity growth in industries with a previously non-stationary high productivity performance explains the slowdown in the productivity growth of the UK economy. Only low-productivity-growth industries are positively contributing to the difference in aggregate labor productivity growth with respect to the previous period, probably because demand constraints influence their stationary pattern.

All in all, the data point to two main considerations. First, employment in market activities is growing much faster in industries that, according to the

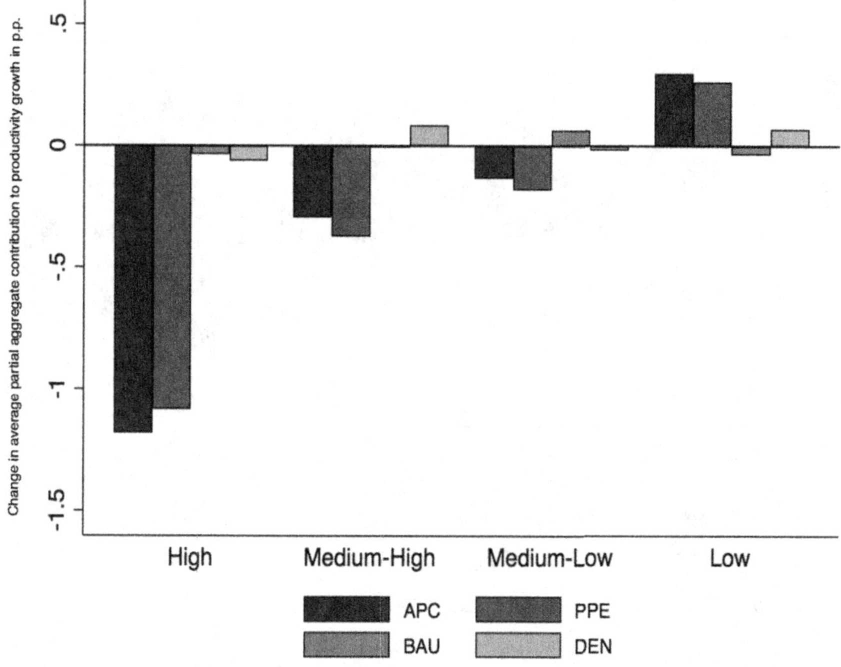

Figure 10.4 Changes in contribution to aggregate labor productivity
Source: Adapted from EU KLEMS. https://euklems.eu/

UK 1994–2007 standards, would be classified as low-productivity-growth industries. Second, at the same time, the more labor-intensive growth pattern observed in the 2010–2015 period cannot be attributed to changes in employment structure but instead to the exhaustion of previous industrial sources of labor productivity growth. Combined, the two facts point to what we call the employment-productivity trap.

2.2 The trade deficit, the deindustrialization process and the UK debt-led growth model

When analyzing the role played by demand, one of the main features that characterizes the British growth model is that the UK needs to sustain a substantial trade deficit in order to achieve a substantial GDP growth rate (Figure 10.5). Even more so, this trade deficit tends to become even larger when there is an economic expansion, yielding a negative contribution to aggregate demand growth (Figure 10.6). As during economic expansions, final consumption expenditure increases its share, while gross capital formation grows at about the same pace as the economy, this deterioration of the trade balance seems to go hand-in-hand with the relative expansion of final consumption rather than with the relative expansion of investment. The

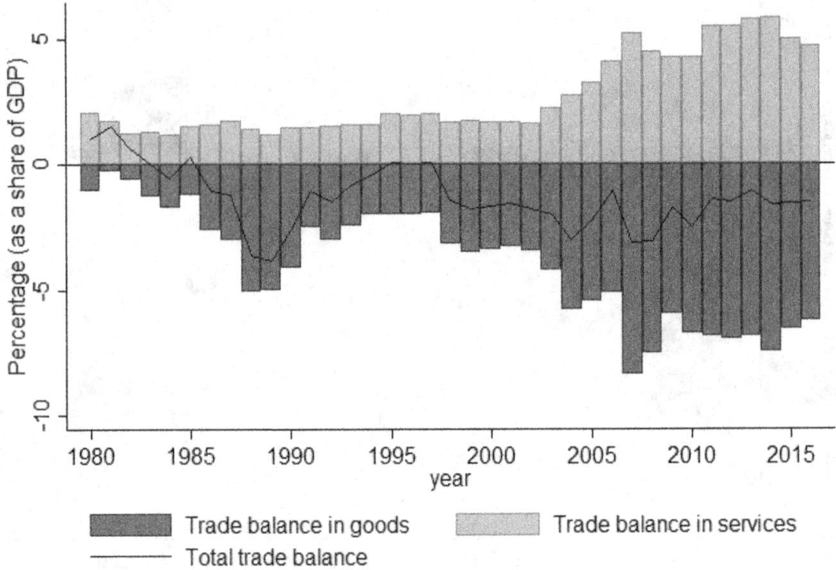

Figure 10.5 Decomposition of the trade balance

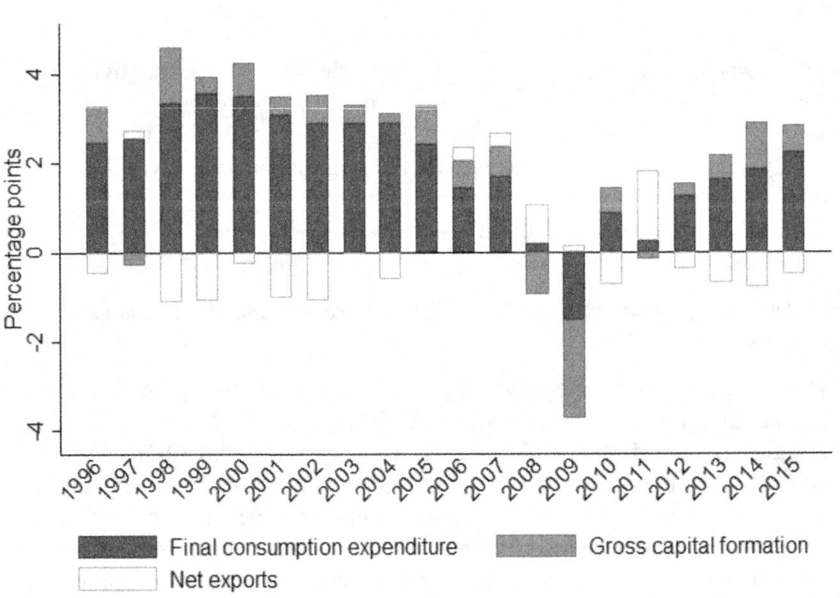

Figure 10.6 Demand contributions to GDP growth

substantial and rising trade deficit (during expansions) of the British economy is linked to the nature of its deindustrialization process.

Even though the literature on structural change has claimed that internal factors such as non-homothetic preferences, that is, heterogeneous income elasticities of demand across sectors- (Clark, 1957; Comin et al., 2015; Foellmi & Zweimüller, 2008; Kongsamut et al., 2001; Pasinetti, 1981), or cross-sector differences in technological conditions (Acemoglu & Guerrieri, 2006; Alvarez-Cuadrado et al., 2017; 2018; Baumol, 1967; Ngai & Pissarides, 2007) play a larger role than ancillary mechanisms such as the changing input-output structure (Berlingieri, 2014; Pasinetti, 1981; 1993; Sposi, 2016) or international trade growth by industry in explaining why economies deindustrialized (Kollmeyer, 2009; Rowthorn & Wells, 1987; Van Neuss, 2018), there is evidence that differences in the degree of deindustrialization across developed or mature economies can be explained to a large extent by the evolution of the trade balance in the manufacturing sector (Rowthorn & Coutts, 2004; Rowthorn & Ramaswamy, 1999).

Given the steady loss of competitiveness suffered by the British manufacturing sector, the UK economy has exhibited a gradual increase in the trade deficit in goods since the early 1980s (Figure 10.6), which has exacerbated its deindustrialization process. This stronger decline in the manufacturing employment shares has key implications for the configuration of the British growth model. First, the UK economy enjoys to a lesser extent the special properties of manufacturing as an engine of growth (Szirmai, 2012): stronger productivity and wage growth, higher returns to scale (Kaldor, 1966; 1968; 1975; McCombie et al., 2002), unconditional convergence in productivity (Rodrik, 2013), stronger linkages with other industries of the economy, higher tradability (which eases the balance of payments constraint) and a stronger development of the capabilities needed to produce more complex products (Hidalgo et al., 2007; Hidalgo & Hausman, 2009). Second, as a result of this weakness in the manufacturing sector, the British economy needs to find alternative sources to fuel growth. As Gräbner et al. (2020) have recently argued, indeed, the degree of competitiveness of the manufacturing sector deeply conditions the growth models that countries follow within the European Union. In order to follow an export-led growth model, the country's manufacturing firms must possess a required level of capabilities to be competitive. If its manufacturing firms do not have these capabilities, then the country needs to rely on the expansion of internal demand to foster growth, which normally gives rise to a trade deficit. In the European economies that have managed to implement a successful growth model based on internal demand (e.g., Spain, Portugal, the UK), debt arose as a key driver of growth, providing a strong stimulus for household expenditure. As a result, these economies followed a debt-led growth model, in which a liberalized financial sector channeled foreign capital inflows and funded a credit extension to fuel growth.

In Section 3, when analyzing the role played by finance, insurance and real estate (FIRE) and business services in the British economy, we provide a more detailed characterization of how these industries shape the UK's debt-led growth model.

2.3 The British economic puzzle

As in many other advanced economies, annual inflation growth rates and annual unemployment rates have persistently declined in the UK since the employment and inflationary crisis of the 1970s and the 1980s. This performance contradicts the inflation-unemployment trade-off assumption, standard in most macroeconomic models. As can be seen in Figure 10.7, while unemployment rates are the lowest they have been in decades, inflation remains stable in the range of 1–3 percent. This is particularly true for our study period, which begins in 1995.

The assumed relationship is perhaps too simplistic. Even leaving aside other influences on price-fixing apart from wages (such as price-demand elasticity), aggregate unemployment reduction does not automatically lead to higher prices, which depend on various factors and, crucially, on workers' bargaining power. This is a non-measurable variable that, in turn, is a function of several measurable ones, such as average labor productivity, national and international trade pressures, technological change, and institutional determinants.

From an income distribution perspective, the labor share of GDP at current market prices may be an accurate indicator of employees' bargaining power.

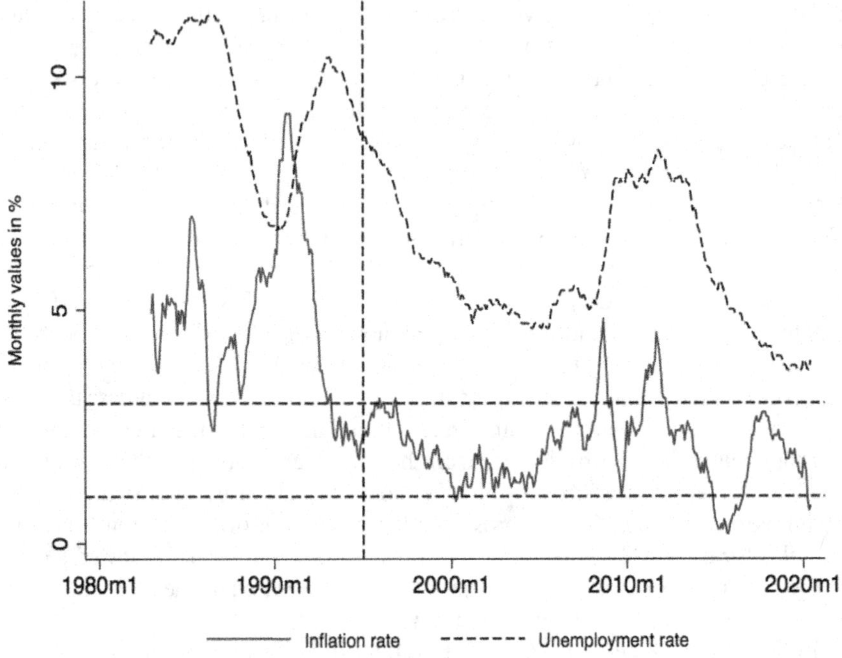

Figure 10.7 Inflation and unemployment rates
Source: OECD short-term labor market statistics and system of national accounts. stats.oecd.org/Index.aspx?DataSetCode=STLABOUR

However, considering this variable performance puts us in a more puzzling situation. As Figure 10.8 shows, between 1995 and 2019, the adjusted and non-adjusted labor share not only remained stable but increased, and their relationship with inflation rates, if any, is negative. The answer, like the devil, is in the details. As Lavery (2019a) has recently noticed, employee compensation is an aggregate of incomes from different workers across heterogeneous industries with very different pay scales. Following the same example mentioned by him, this measure includes the salaries of workers in low-skill sectors and payments received by top executives and managers. In other words, a relatively stable labor share can be hiding great bargaining power differences and, therefore, huge wage disparities between workers across industries and occupations.

In a similar way, Bell and Van Reenen (2010; 2013; 2014) point to the impact of financial sector expansion on extreme wage inequality in the UK. According to their estimations, around 75 percent of the overall increase in the top earners' share of the wage bill can be attributed to the top financial sector employees. Namely, they highlight the importance of bankers' bonuses in the pay raises of top income earners. Although this form of payment has a marginal significance among the rest of percentiles because it is only a minor component of annual earnings, bonuses constitute an important part of annual salary payments for top percentile workers.

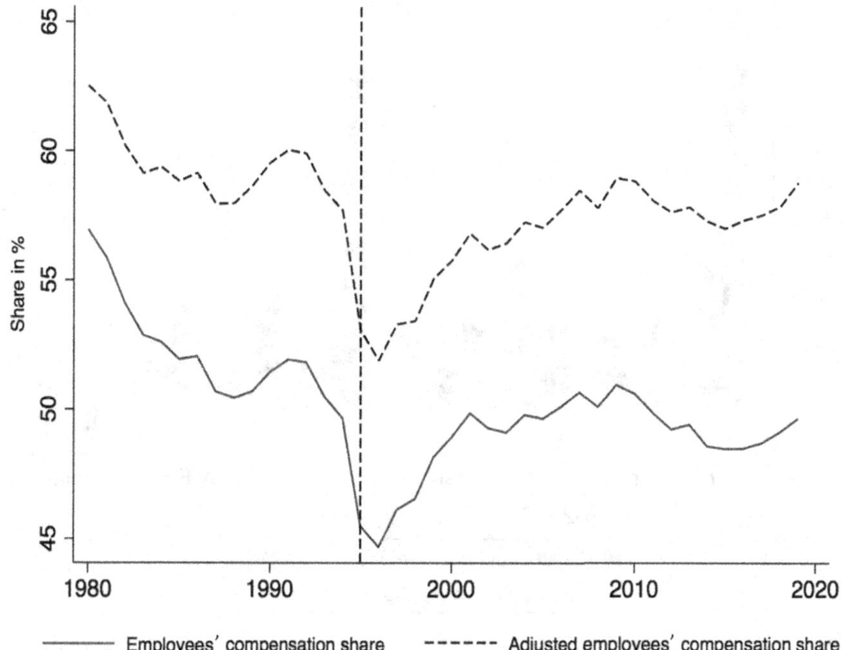

Figure 10.8 Labor share of GDP
Source: OECD system of national accounts. www.oecd.org/sdd/na

3 The financial axis

3.1 The increasing importance of FIRE and business services

In recent decades, the British economy has specialized in business services and finance. Both business services and FIRE have taken over the leading role in fostering economic growth that manufacturing once filled. As Figure 10.9 shows, this pattern of specialization also stands out when compared to the ones exhibited by the three largest EU economies. In the first period (1996–2007), real output in business services and FIRE grew at an outstanding rate in the UK, considerably faster than in the other three economies. In the second period (2010–2015), the British business services industry continued to remarkably outperform those of Germany, France and Italy, while FIRE suffered a strong output slowdown due to the consequences of the financial crisis. Beyond output growth, FIRE's nominal value added share (Table 10.3), which has been significantly higher than those of the other economies, also underscores the importance of FIRE. In contrast to business services and FIRE (the latter in the first period), British manufacturing exhibited mostly stagnant growth, unable to keep pace with the German manufacturing sector or even the French one (in the 1996–2007 period).

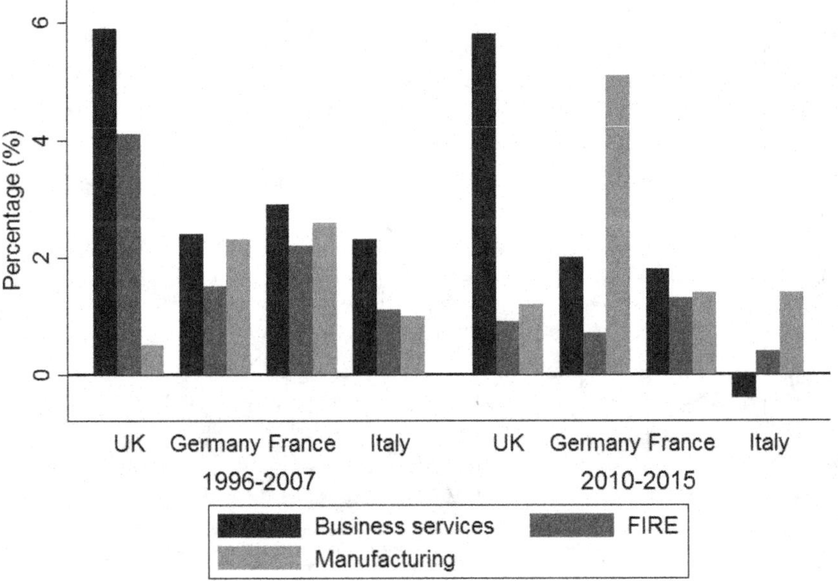

Figure 10.9 Real output growth for selected industries in the four largest European economies

Table 10.3 Nominal value added and employment shares for selected industries in the four largest European economies (%)

	Nominal value added shares			*Employment shares*		
	1995	*2007*	*2015*	*1995*	*2007*	*2015*
The UK						
Business services	8.0	11.0	12.2	11.3	15.1	16.7
FIRE	20.8	21.5	20.9	5.0	5.4	5.2
Manufacturing	17.3	10.0	10.1	17.0	10.7	9.1
Germany						
Business services	9.6	11.0	11.0	7.1	11.9	13.0
FIRE	15.7	16.1	15.1	4.4	4.3	3.9
Manufacturing	22.8	23.4	23.0	21.3	18.8	18.6
France						
Business services	10.7	13.0	13.1	10.2	13.6	14.6
FIRE	14.6	16.8	17.2	4.4	4.3	4.3
Manufacturing	16.6	13.0	11.7	15.0	11.6	9.9
Italy						
Business services	8.2	9.1	9.5	6.4	10.2	11.8
FIRE	14.4	17.7	19.7	3.6	3.6	3.6
Manufacturing	20.9	17.8	16.0	21.3	18.6	15.8

Source: Adapted from EU KLEMS. https://euklems.eu/

Looking at productivity growth across these industries (Figure 10.10), we can see that the productivity performance of British business services contrasts sharply with that of the other three economies. While in Germany, France and Italy, business services seem to behave like a (Baumolian) technologically stagnant industry, in the UK, they exhibit robust productivity growth in both periods. Despite the widespread productivity slowdown suffered by the British economy in 2010–2015, business services barely decreased their productivity growth rate with respect to the first period (-0.3 percentage points). Regarding FIRE, productivity growth in the UK also outperforms (although not as much as business services) that of the other three economies in 1996–2007. However, unlike business services, FIRE experienced a sharp productivity slowdown in the UK during 2010–2015. Lastly, the decline of British manufacturing does not seem to be linked during the first period to a weak productivity growth rate. Indeed, productivity in the British manufacturing sector grew at a similar rate to that of Germany or France in 1996–2007. All in all, it seems that the manufacturing sector in the UK underwent a process of economic restructuring, where only the most competitive and productive parts survived, thereby boosting productivity growth in the sector. In spite of the solid productivity growth achieved in 1996–2007, the British

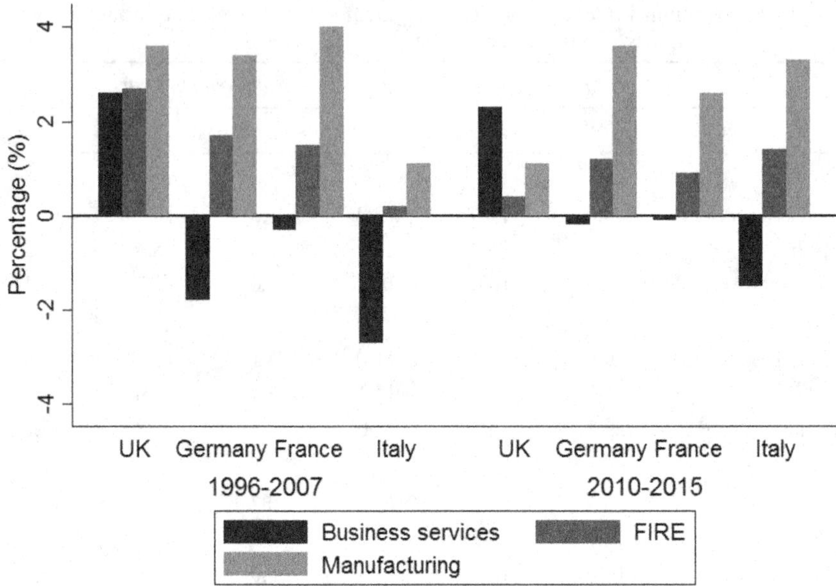

Figure 10.10 Labor productivity growth for selected industries in the four largest European economies

manufacturing sector was also affected by the productivity slowdown that took place in 2010–2015, lagging behind the productivity performance of manufacturing in Germany, France and Italy.

The dynamics of output and productivity across these industries yield a pattern of employment creation that is depicted in Figure 10.11. First, although business services creates employment at a fast rate in each of these four economies, it is remarkable that the UK manages to do so while generating significant productivity gains in this industry. Second, FIRE exhibits a more limited role in creating employment. Nevertheless, the British FIRE industry outperforms, in terms of employment growth, those of Germany, France and Italy. Third, manufacturing employment has generally decreased in all these economies. However, the British manufacturing sector showed the strongest decline during the restructuring process from 1996 to 2007.

As a result of these trends, the employment structure has shifted away from manufacturing toward some services industries, such as business services (Table 10.3). Given the solid productivity performance of business services in the UK, the relative rise of this industry might actually strengthen its role as an engine of growth. On the contrary, in Germany, France and Italy the technologically stagnant nature of business services represent a structural burden for aggregate growth when resources shift to this industry.

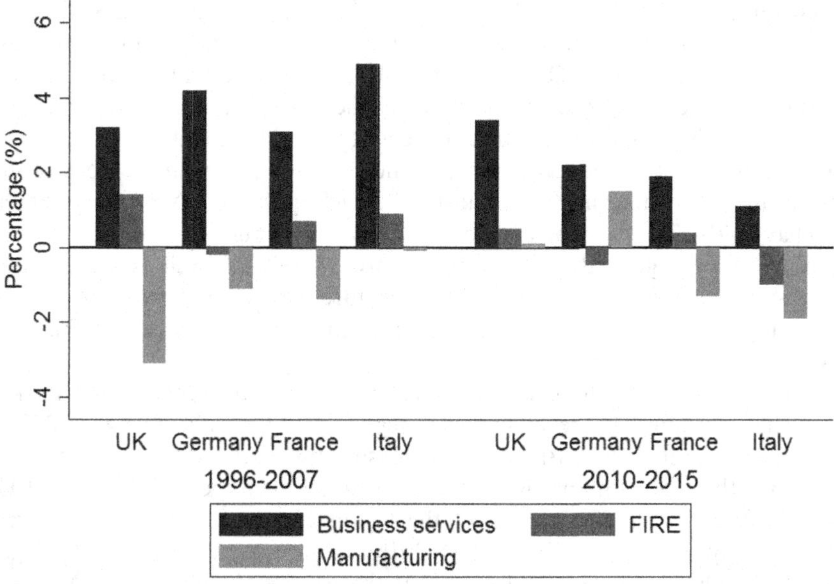

Figure 10.11 Employment growth for selected industries in the four largest European economies

3.2 Explaining the growing importance of FIRE and business services from changes in the British financial regulation context

3.2.1 The four turning points in banking and financial regulation

A set of deep institutional reforms in 1971 began to change the structure and functioning of the UK's banking and financial sector. Before then, the sector was coordinated by the UK Treasury and the Bank of England with a ceiling on interest rates and direct controls on credit. The Competition and Credit Control reform of 1971 relaxed these restrictions as well as those affecting capital provisions. According to Braggion and Ongena (2017), these reforms were in part the result of the growing importance of the City of London as a hub for international capital flows and may explain the transformation from bilateral to multiple banking for corporate financing as well as the formation of a more competitive financial sector.

The second institutional turning point was the "Big Bang" deregulation of the UK financial sector in 1986, which consisted of a set of changes in the structure of the London Stock Exchange (LSE). These included a new electronic trading system, opening membership to previously excluded banks and foreign brokers, end of fixed minimum commission rates for non-members, and removing the division between brokerage and "jobbers" firms, allowing a firm to represent a client and negotiate directly with other brokers. Although the great importance of these reforms is not under discussion, some researchers claim that the "Big Bang" reforms profoundly and abruptly changed the UK financial sector, while others see them as a part of a more gradual transformation initiated in 1975 (Oren & Blyth, 2018; Tanndal & Waldenstrom, 2018). In any case, there seems to be agreement on the example and goal of these legal provisions. With respect to the first element, it should be noted that in 1975, the American Securities and Exchange Commission (SEC) implemented one of the most important reforms in its history, which gave the New York Stock Exchange (NYSE) a significant comparative advantage with respect to the LSE. As for the goal, the "Big Bang" reform of 1986, as well as the previous ones since 1975, aimed to ensure the competitiveness of the LSE (and the UK financial markets as a whole) against other marketplaces to attract financial inflows from abroad.

The next stepping-stone was the creation of the European Single Market and the resulting multilevel financial regulation (James & Quaglia, 2020). This means that, before Brexit, an increasing proportion of legal provisions affecting the UK banking and financial services sector came from the EU, mainly through the direct effect of the European regulations and directives. Accordingly, during the 2000s and 2010s, although the base of the legal system regulating financial activities was the Financial Services and Markets Act 2000 (FSMA, amended in 2013 and 2016) and related national rules, various important legislations affecting crucial aspects of the financial sector were decided outside the UK in EU institutions. This has very important implications in terms of political economy, as we will see in other research (James & Quaglia, 2019b; Moloney, 2017; Quaglia, 2017).

The last turning point was the 2008 global financial crisis (GFC). This great shock revealed some of the fragilities of the financial and non-financial British economy, such as the high leverage ratios of firms, banks, and financial corporations, the extended financial risks linked to highly complex financial products, or the worrying housing bubble and household indebtedness (FSA, 2009a; 2010). Besides, regulatory deficiencies were soon considered one of the GFC's major causes since the competent authorities had failed to avoid the risky financial market practices that led to liquidity and solvency problems (Macneil, 2010).

In this context, the GFC raised a wave of legislations reforming financial regulations at both the UK and EU level. At the national level, the Financial Services Act of 2012 (FSA 2012) and the Bank of England and Financial Services Act of 2016 were part of these post-GFC reformist efforts. They included significant changes with respect to the FSMA of 2000 and changed the system of financial regulation authorities. At the European level, many regulations and directives were adopted, most of them actively contested by UK officials but others receiving support. Facing negotiations at the EU institutions, UK politicians and officials now have heterogeneous views on regulation, both inside and outside of the national territory.

In addition, the Brexit result and subsequent negotiations among British government members put into question the capacity of the financial services industry to protect their preferences. Investment funds and British banks are fully integrated into the EU capital markets and will suffer the consequences of a no-deal Brexit because it will imply severe access restrictions to the Single European Market (Moloney, 2017; James & Quaglia, 2019b; Thompson, 2019).

Consequently, the simplistic relation between financial services industry goals and political preferences should be discussed more thoroughly. Section 3.3 contains an analysis of this question.

3.3 The divergent UK political preferences on financial regulation after the GFC and Brexit

In the European Union, financial norms sources may be classified into four levels, following the Lamfaussy regulatory model. By order of importance, the first would be the legislative rules; the second, the administrative rules; the third, the minor normative and supervisory measures; the fourth, the Commission's monitoring and enforcement. To simplify, we will only consider the first level of legislative rules on financial services. These are adopted by the ECOFIN Council of Member States and the European Parliament as co-legislators, although, in practice, regulations and directives are the outcome of a negotiation between the Parliament, Council, and Commission (Moloney, 2014; 2017). In this sense, UK preferences and influence on EU financial legislation may be traced by analyzing the British participation in these institutions.

Political economy classifies member states of the Council according to their approach to market regulation. Countries like the UK, the Netherlands, or Nordic member states are considered "market-makers" because they usually promote regulations that facilitate the creation and expansion of financial markets. Conversely, others like France, Germany, or Italy are seen as "market-shaping" countries because they are in favor of more constraining rules and suspicious of market-based alternatives to institutional regulations (Howarth & Quaglia, 2017; Quaglia, Howarth & Liebe, 2016). After the GFC, this second group gained in relevance, and more restrictive norms were promoted.

The UK shows opposition to many of these legal initiatives. For example, the EU 2012 Short Selling Regulation was contested by the UK Government, which was worried about market liquidity problems that the regulative framework could cause. In general, between 2009 and 2016, pieces of legislation on alternative funds, including hedge funds, rating agencies, or the Financial Transaction Tax, were resisted by the UK, under Conservative as well as Labour governments (Howarth & Quaglia, 2017; Moloney, 2017; Quaglia, 2017). However, although it is easy to see a connection between the alignment of the UK with weaker financial regulation, on the one hand, and the economic weight of the City and the financial sector, on the other, the picture is more complex in terms of political economy. For example, Britain was in favor of capital requirement rules that were stricter than the ones supported by other European countries and the Commission.

The two cases mentioned at the end of Section 3.3.1 will help us better understand how changes in financial regulation are shaped by the relationship between the financial industry, the regulative authorities, the officials, and the politicians. The first case pointed to the contrast between British political preferences on financial regulation in both the UK and the EU institutions. As we will see in the following sections, the UK regulators and policy-makers show different approaches concerning banking regulation, on the one hand, and capital markets regulation, on the other. To explain this difference, it is important to take into account the political and economic context in which legislation is applied (Buller & Lindstrom, 2013; James & Quaglia, 2019b). The second case was the puzzling situation after the Brexit Referendum results and the difficulties on the part of the City in promoting its preferences during the bargaining between the UK government and the EU institutions (James & Quaglia, 2019b; Thompson, 2019).

3.3.1 Divergent preferences on financial regulation

After the GFC, the majority of the UK public opinion was concerned about instability in the financial services industry, perceiving it as a problem and clamoring for stricter government regulation in the sector (James & Quaglia, 2019a). In this context, the typical regulator's trade-off between financial stability and financial sector competitiveness could be solved in favor of the former, as the voters' pressure on their representatives increased.

Before the GFC, three institutions had regulated the stability of the financial markets in the UK: the Bank of England, the Treasury, and the Financial Services Authority (FSA), the latter of which was a supervisory agency. During that period, the role of FSA was often emphasized and perhaps overstated, partly because it constituted a genuine political issue (against other more complex macro explanations) and partly since the Conservative Opposition could use the performance of the FSA against the government (Hodson & Mabbet, 2009). First, because it was created by a Labour Party government and, second, because their board, while independent, was appointed by the Treasury. Indeed, the FSA admitted regulatory failures in the so-called Turner Review and recommended various measures, such as a rise in capital requirements, counter-cyclical regulations, or greater liquidity legislation and supervision (FSA, 2009b). However, as Macneil (2010) noted, if anything, the recognition of errors was merely implicit, since the FSA only assessed the strictness of the regulatory framework (which, in turn, is based on international rules), not taking into account the agency's potential failures as a banking supervisor.

After the 2010 elections, the new Conservative Government promoted the FSA 2012, a legal reform of the FSMA 2000. This law established the Financial Stability Strategy (FSS) of the Bank of England, the Financial Policy Committee (FPC) as well as two new regulators: the Financial Conduct Authority (FCA) and the Prudential Regulation Authority (PRA). The

FPC is the same body corporate of the FSA but with a new name and different functions. It basically consists of an independent agency for promoting good practices, as well as consumer and competition protection. To accomplish their objectives, the FPC has the functions, among others, of making rules or preparing and issuing codes. As for the PRA, its body corporate is integrated into the Bank of England and is responsible for the UK financial system's stability. To do so, the PRA performs the functions of making rules, preparing and issuing codes, and developing a general regulatory framework. Of all the new measures adopted, the creation of the FPC was particularly important. This new institution has a central role in ensuring financial stability by taking action to remove or reduce systemic risks as those related to high levels of leverage, debt, or credit growth.

According -to James and Quaglia (2019b), these changes strengthened the British authorities' power to impose stricter regulations on banking activities, as recent changes in capital requirements regulation shows. Banks are often suspicious of higher capital requirements because they may negatively affect costs, lending capacity, and profits. However, following the GFC, much more stringent regulation on this matter has been enacted in the UK. As a result, the industry's capacity to impose its preferences decreased, and the state authorities gained the power to promote their own views. For some analysts, this can partly be explained by the previously described institutional changes implied in the FSA 2012. Under the new regulative framework, and in the context of changing ideas on banking regulation, the Bank of England had more power to legislate for the protection of financial stability, mainly through the action of the FPC under the FSS (Bell & Hindmoor, 2017; James & Quaglia, 2019b). Therefore, after implementing new rules and reinforcing the supervision by means of stress-testing procedures, the tier 1 capital ratio for the UK banking sector increased considerably, accomplishing Basel III goals (Bell & Hindmoor, 2017).

The UK carried this ambitious approach to capital requirements rules to the negotiations on the EU Capital Requirement Directive IV (CRD IV). British representatives defended a full implementation of Basel III, which meant the implementation of more stringent rules than those proposed by France and Germany. UK banks showed better leverage and capital ratios at that moment, so the implications of more severe capital rules were probably greater for French and German banking systems (Howarth & Quaglia, 2013; Quaglia, 2019). However, the UK position on negotiations was partly explained by the Bank of England's and the FPC's reinforced roles in the new regulative framework, since this role had given them more capacity to influence national preferences on regulation (James, 2016).

However, the same cannot be applied to capital markets activities. In 2011, under the EU Commission's initiative, the Council and the European Parliament adopted the Directive 2011/61/EU on Alternative Investment Fund Managers (AIFM). This legislation created a legal framework for managers of alternative investment funds, including the so-called hedge funds, and was one of the EU's responses to the political pressures on the financial industry after the GFC. The UK was one of the main opponents of this legal provision, clearly consistent with continental European governments' preferences and, particularly, with France's and Germany's preferences (Awrey, 2011; Buller & Lindstrom, 2013; Quaglia, 2011). In Europe, the hedge funds industry was highly concentrated in the UK and, therefore, was far more powerful in that country than in any in other within the EU, so it is easy to understand why UK officials would perceive the norm as an external imposition that could undermine national comparative advantage in those industries (Awrey, 2011; Buller & Lindstrom, 2013; James & Quaglia, 2019b; Quaglia, 2011; 2019). During the negotiations, concerned about the consequences for the alternative investment funds industry, UK regulators were actively resistant to the adoption of legislation on AIFM at the EU level. When, finally, the draft of the Directive was under discussion, they were at the head of those proposing weaker regulations.

On balance, the financial services industry was not equally affected by recent changes in regulation. While the banking system was perceived as highly problematic, the alternative investment funds industry was seen as a primary source of international competitiveness. Diverse approaches to regulation correspond to UK authorities' different views expressed both at the national and the international levels.

3.3.2 Financial services industry's preferences in the context of Brexit

At first sight, the Brexit referendum results implies a negative shock in the UK financial services industry. After years of negotiations between the UK government and EU institutions, it seems that Brexit probably means severe restrictions in access to the European Single Market for UK-based firms and may imply that some of them will decide to leave the UK, moving their European services to another EU Member State, such as Germany or France (Howarth & Quaglia, 2018; Talani, 2019). Assuming that the UK growth model is led by finance and considering the influence exercised by the financial industry on UK political institutions, it is difficult to understand why the Conservative Government promoted a Brexit referendum that would eventually trigger negative consequences for the City. From this point of view, Johnson's government's negotiating position looks even more striking, as it confirms the fears of a "hard" Brexit with particularly negative consequences for the industry (Armour, 2017).

It is true that the financial services industry is not uniform, but it has heterogeneous preferences and capacities to influence UK political institutions and regulative authorities. As we have described above, following the GFC, the EU adopted various legislation not well received by the alternative investment funds industry (Howarth & Quaglia, 2017; James & Quaglia, 2019a; Thompson, 2019). Indeed, Conservative politicians (including the now Prime Minister Boris Johnson) accused EU institutions of undermining the competitiveness of the

British financial industry (Thompson, 2017; 2019). However, in general terms, the majority of managers, firms, and financial industry associations refused Brexit, defended the Remain option in the EU referendum, and now are clearly against a hard Brexit (Howarth & Quaglia, 2017; James & Quaglia, 2019a; Talani, 2019).

According to James and Quaglia (2019a), three factors can explain the financial industry's unexpected lack of capacity to shape the government's Brexit policy. The first points to the changes in political statecraft. Under Cameron's government, a clear priority in the relations between the UK and the EU was the protection of the British financial services industry's preferences. However, after the referendum, the appointment of Theresa May as Prime Minister, and the subsequent national elections, supporters of hard Brexit got control of the Conservative Party and the government. A new strategy, based on captivating Brexit voters' discontent with the EU, was implemented by the Party (James & Quaglia, 2018; 2019a; Thompson, 2017; 2019). After May's resignation and Boris Johnson's great victory in 2019 (the Conservative Party's best result in decades), the strategy has been reinforced.

The second factor is related to the changes introduced by May's government in the institutional powers to face UK-EU relations. Prime Minister Theresa May created the New Department for Exiting the European Union, which, along with the Prime Minister's Office, have replaced the previous model for EU policy relations. As a result, the negotiations with the EU are now more centralized around the Prime Minister, and the financial services industry's access to those UK officials who are negotiating Brexit is almost closed, as reported by financial industry representatives (James & Quaglia, 2019a).

The third factor is related to the collective organization of the British financial services industry. The main division has been previously described and consists of the opposition between banking and non-banking financial sector. While the former see Brexit as a clear negative shock, an important part of alternative investment funds and assets managers actively support the UK's exit from the EU, since their perception of European institutions as a regulator is mostly influenced by the constraining legal provisions adopted after the GBF, under pressure from France and Germany for more stringent legislation (Howarth & Quaglia, 2017; James & Quaglia, 2019a; Thompson, 2019). To this cleavage, another one within the banking sector is added. In contrast to national and international investment banks, which use the UK as a center for their activities in the European Single Market, retail-focused UK banks have a more distancing position on Brexit, as a great part of their business will probably not be directly affected (James & Quaglia, 2018; 2019a).

To summarize, this section has shown that banking and financial regulation changes certainly underpinned the development of the financial services industry and the City, fostering the UK financial-led growth model. However, leaving aside the more simplistic visions of the relation between the financial industry and political institutions, we have also explained why the GFC and the Brexit Referendum results may imply a significant transformation of these linkages. We do not mean at all that the institutional basis of the model has been dismantled, but we suggest instead that they are part of a complex and dynamic political-economic development.

3.4 The economic impact of the increasing importance of FIRE and business services

As we have stated in this chapter, the UK has specialized in the production of highly competitive financial and business services, which has led to a rising trade surplus in both FIRE and the business services industry. As Figure 10.12 shows, the remarkable magnitude of this surplus also stands out when compared to the trade balances that these industries exhibit in Germany, France, and Italy. However, despite the significant contribution of FIRE and business services to its trade balance, the UK has needed to sustain a large trade deficit in order to achieve a robust GDP growth rate due to the weakness of its manufacturing sector.

The degree of competitiveness of the manufacturing sector deeply conditions the UK growth model, which rely on the expansion of debt to foster household expenditure and aggregate growth, giving rise to a debt-led growth model. As a rising financial hub with a declining degree of capabilities in the manufacturing sector, the UK has actually become one of the most salient cases of debt-led growth.

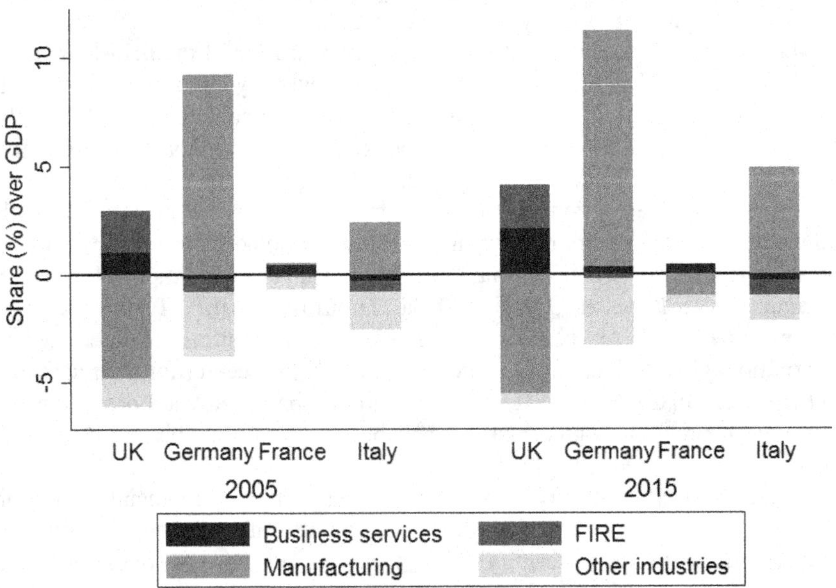

Figure 10.12 Trade balance for selected industries in the four largest European economies

The UK debt-led growth in the period 1995–2007 was characterized by a rapid expansion of credit to the household sector (particularly mortgage debt), which took place in the context of a housing bubble. As Figure 10.13 shows, the household debt to income ratio increased by 65 percentage points from 1995 to 2007. This increase was mostly concentrated between the years 2000 and 2007 (52 percentage points). This credit expansion to the household sector was spurred by several factors, such as (1) the leading international position of the UK financial sector; (2) low interest rates; (3) the availability of foreign capital inflows that financed the UK current account deficit mainly through overseas bank financing; and (4) a wave of financial innovation that, within a liberalized financial sector, developed the securitized credit model in order to increase profitability, while keeping risk at a seemingly low level (FSA, 2009a; 2009b). Besides these factors, as Shiller (2015) argues, in real estate markets there might be a self-reinforcing process between house prices and household debt. House prices grow rapidly when there is a strong increase in demand, so that production cannot keep pace with demand. This increase in prices lead to the expectation of future price increases, which makes households and banks more willing to accept more debt and even higher initial loan-to-value ratios. As a result, demand grows further and house prices keeps increasing, feeding the speculative bubble.

One of the most important implications of this process in terms of the UK growth model was its effect on consumption growth. Besides having eased credit constraints to buy houses, the increase in property prices also led to a

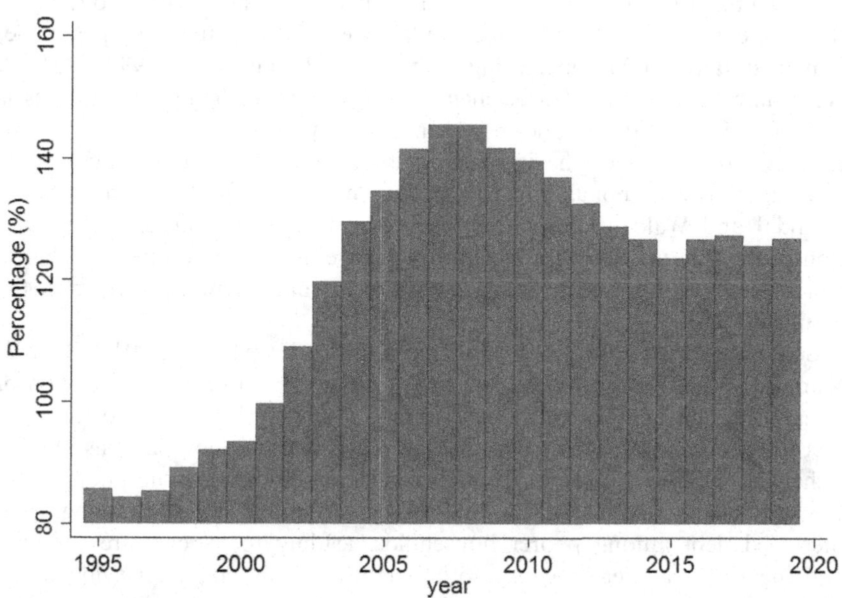

Figure 10.13 Household debt to income ratio

wealth effect that spurred credit availability to finance consumption (Aron et al., 2012; Muellbauer, 2007). Therefore, the UK growth model relied on debt extension for the household sector in 1995–2007.

Even though debt provided a stimulus for growth, it also increased the economy's financial fragility. The outstanding rise in debt in the household and financial sectors, which happened under poor risk assessment, became unsustainable when market confidence weakened and liquidity collapsed. Although debt boosted growth, debt-led growth also set up the conditions that gave rise to the financial crisis. Debt expansion might even have negative consequences for consumption in the medium term, delaying recoveries. There is evidence that highly indebted households in the UK cut consumption expenditure due to tighter credit conditions and increased concern about their ability to repay their debts (Bunn & Rostom, 2014). Besides this negative impact on consumption in the medium term, debt has also vanished as a key driver of consumption growth for the period following the financial crisis. As Figure 10.13 shows, after the speculative bubble burst, the household debt to income ratio decreased until 2015 and has stabilized since that year.

Another implication of the UK debt-led growth model is the rise in inequality. According to Baccaro and Pontusson (2016), the UK has been characterized by the rise in high-end earnings, which has led to higher 90–10 and 90–50 earnings ratios (i.e., the ratio of earnings in the 90th percentile to earnings in the 10th percentile and the 50th percentile, respectively). The former ratio grew by 0.204 units from 1995 to 2011, while the latter increased by 0.11 units from 1994 to 2008. On the other hand, the 50–10 ratio (i.e., the ratio of earnings in the 50th percentile to earnings in the 10th percentile) remained fairly stable, increasing only by 0.02 units from 1994 to 2008. According to Bell and Van Reenen (2010), the rise in high-end earnings is mostly linked to the financial sector. As they show, the financial sector explains 60 percent of the increase in extreme wage inequality due to the substantial rise in bonus pay to workers in this sector. In a similar vein, Tanndal and Waldenström (2018) demonstrate that the financial deregulation in the UK in 1986 then led to an increase in pre-tax top income shares, which seems to have been driven by higher earnings among workers in the financial sector.

Some authors (Behringer & van Treeck, 2019; Frank et al., 2014; Ryoo & Kim, 2014) have claimed that this rise in inequality caused the expansion of household debt and boosted consumption. This may have resulted from the fact that households often try to emulate THE consumption patterns of their richer peers. Since top-income households increased their consumption due to the rise in high-end earning, this rising inequality reduced savings and increased debt among poorer households, leading to expenditure cascades and increasing aggregate consumption. However, the empirical evidence on these mechanisms is far from conclusive (Stockhammer & Wildauer, 2016; Wildauer & Stockhammer, 2018).

3.4 The labor axis

The UK labor market has been characterized by an increasing dualization. Rather than being divided by contract types, this dualization has taken place between workers with different educational levels and incomes (Yoon & Chung, 2016). To a large extent, this process has also been linked to the structural transformation undergone by the UK economy, where employment deindustrialization coincided with this dual pattern of job creation within the service sector. While manufacturing was able to expand employment for low-skill labor and pay above-average wages in the past (with respect to the economy), low-skill labor is now being absorbed into a service sector that is expanding employment at both segments of the labor market, i.e. the low-skill and low-waged segment and the highly skilled and high-waged one.

In order to illustrate this point, we compare the performance in employment (in terms of employees) and wages of three industry groups of the economy: highly skilled services, low-skill services, and manufacturing. Highly skilled services are services that exhibit a share of highly skilled employment above the economy average over the period 2008–2017, while low-skill services show a below-average highly skilled employment share. Skill is measured here by educational attainment, with university graduates being highly skilled and those with intermediate or no formal qualifications being low-skilled (Stehrer et al., 2019). Figure 10.14 shows the results for skill intensity across UK industries. There are seven service industries that, according to our criteria, must be considered highly skilled: information and communication, financial services, business services, public administration, education, health and social work, and arts. Both financial services and business services, which play a leading role in driving the UK's economic growth, exhibit

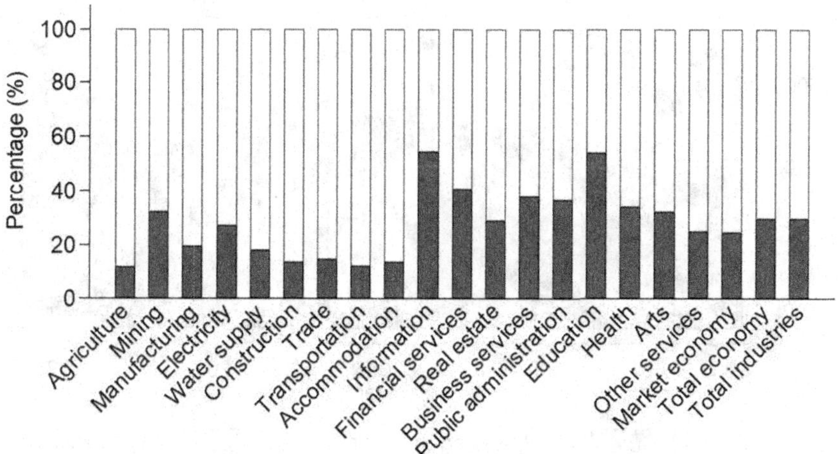

Figure 10.14 Share of employment by educational attainment across industries (averages over the period 2008–2017)

significantly higher shares than the economy (11.2 percentage points more than the economy average for the former, 8.3 points for the latter). On the contrary, trade, transportation, and storage, accommodation and food service activities, real estate and other service activities exhibit a below-average highly skilled employment share and, consequently, are considered low-skill. Interestingly, manufacturing is also a low-skill sector, showing 10 fewer percentage points of highly skilled intensity than the economy.

As Figure 10.15 shows, employment has expanded in both types of service industries, while it has strongly declined in the manufacturing sector. Regarding services, in 1995–2007 employment grew at a significantly faster rate in highly skilled services (2.1 percent) than in low-skill services (1.2 percent), whereas in 2010–2015 the gap between the two narrowed (1.4 percent for the former, 1 percent for the latter). With respect to manufacturing, even though the sector performed significantly poorer in 1995–2007 (-3.1 percent), it also exhibited job destruction in 2010–2015 (-0.6 percent).

Figure 10.16 reports the evolution of the ratio of compensation per employee for selected industries with respect to low-skill services. Both highly skilled services and manufacturing pay a significantly higher compensation per employee than low-skill services. As Figure 10.16 shows, compensation has been (on average over the period) around 30 percent higher in highly skilled services compared to those in low-skill services.

This percentage even increases to 110 percent in certain industries, such as financial services or information and communication. When analysing the

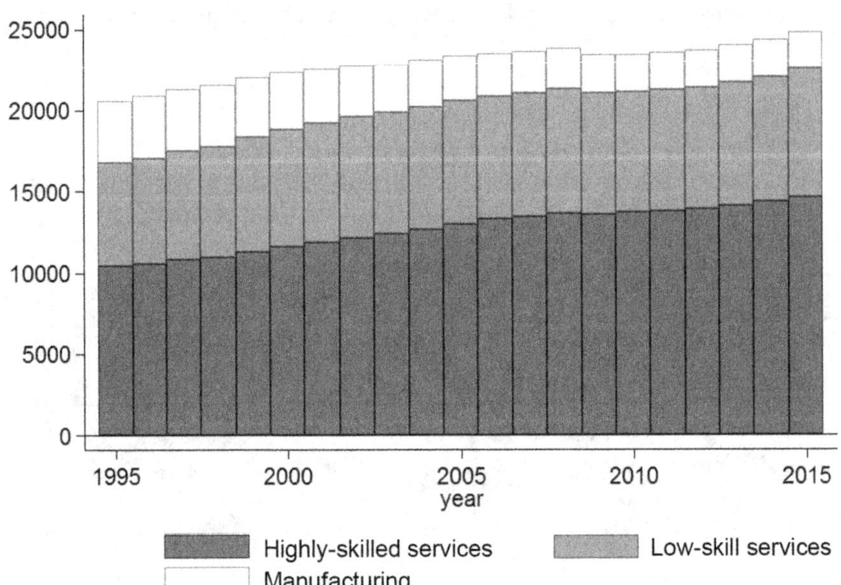

Figure 10.15 Number of employees (thousands) for selected industries

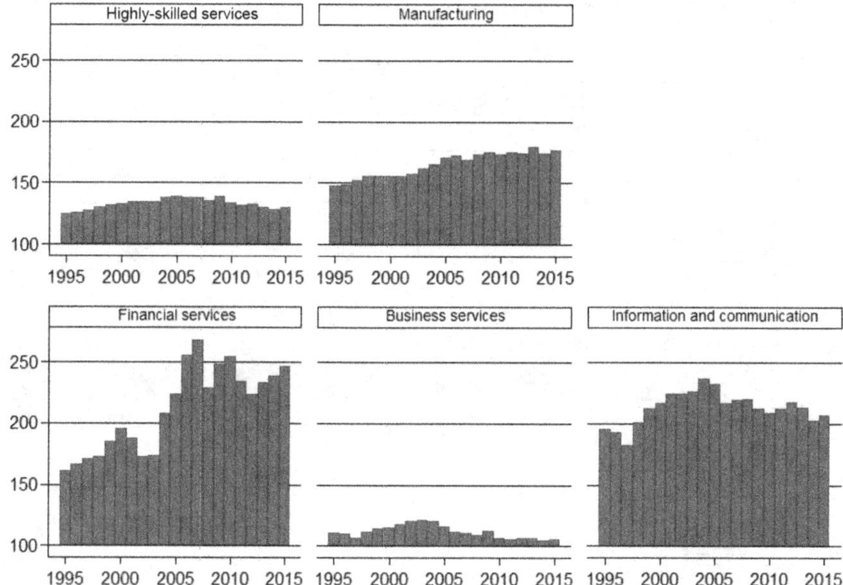

Figure 10.16 Ratio of compensation per employee for selected industries with respect to low-skill services (%)

evolution of the ratio from 1995 to 2015, however, it is important to note that, while the compensation gap for highly skilled services gradually widened before 2007, it began to diminish after the crisis. Regarding manufacturing, this sector exhibits a compensation gap with respect to low-skill services even higher than that of highly skilled services. In manufacturing, compensation has been around 65 percent higher than in low-skill services. Contrary to highly skilled services, the manufacturing sector compensation gap steadily increased both before and after the crisis.

The compensation gap between low-skill services, on one hand, and manufacturing and highly skilled services, on the other, can be attributed, at least to a certain extent, to differences in trade union membership. As depicted in Figure 10.17, trade union membership has consistently been higher in both manufacturing and highly skilled services than in low-skill services. In low-skill services, only 18 percent of employees have been affiliated on average over the period 1995–2019; this percentage rises to 23 percent and 28 percent in manufacturing and highly skilled services, respectively. Although trade union membership has followed a widespread decline over the period across UK industries, manufacturing and highly skilled services have suffered an even stronger decline, thereby eroding the substantial trade union membership gap that they once had with respect to low-skill services.

Overall, the UK labor market has experienced increasing dualization. While the low-skill manufacturing sector, which consistently pays above-

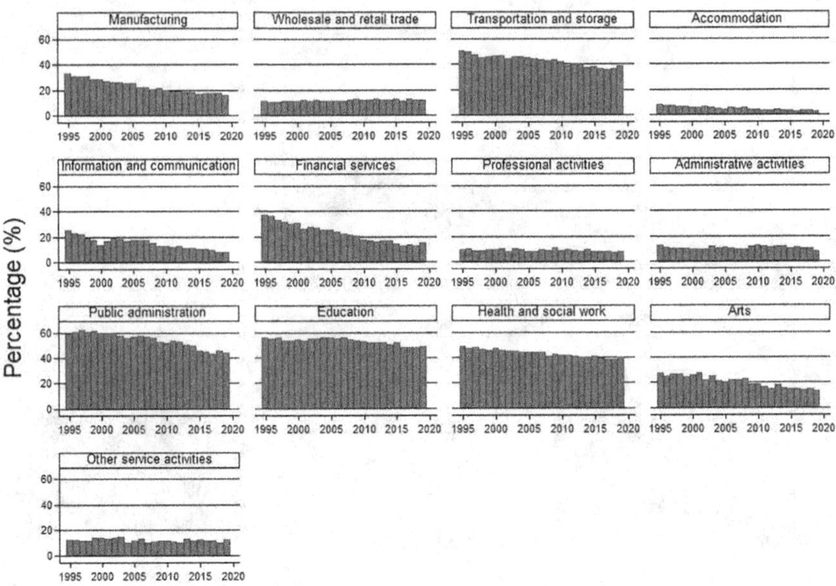

Figure 10.17 Trade union membership as a proportion of employees by industry

average wages, has continued to shed jobs, the service sector is creating employment in both segments of the labor market. However, it seems that the financial crisis has brought important changes to the process of dualization within the service sector. First, employment in highly skilled services has not strongly outgrown that in low-skill services after the crisis. Second, whereas compensation per employee increased faster in highly skilled services from 1996 to 2007, low-skill services moderately reduced the compensation gap from 2008 to 2015. As a result, it seems that the process of dualization might have slowed down after the financial crisis.

4 Conclusion

In this chapter we have shown several stylized facts that define the UK growth model during the years after the Great Recession.

Regarding supply factors, the UK economy exhibits low productivity growth rates because of the slowdown of productivity growth in industries that showed high productivity growth in the previous period and, to a lesser extent, because of employment growth in low productivity growth industries. As a result, aggregate growth mainly relies on employment expansion, leading to the lowest unemployment rates in decades. Nevertheless, this low unemployment rate does not yield higher inflation rates.

With respect to demand, one of the main features that characterizes the British growth model is the UK's need to sustain a substantial trade deficit in order to achieve a substantial GDP growth rate. Moreover, this trade deficit tends to become even larger when there is economic expansion. The substantial and rising trade deficit (during expansions) of the British economy is linked to the steady loss of competitiveness suffered by its manufacturing sector and has exacerbated its deindustrialization process. This process has key implications for the configuration of the British growth model. Since UK manufacturing firms do not have the required level of capabilities to be competitive, then the economy needs to rely on the expansion of debt to provide a strong stimulus for household expenditure. As a result, the UK economy follows a debt-led growth model, in which a liberalized financial sector channels foreign capital inflows, and funds credit extension to fuel growth.

Regarding income distribution, we find two significant facts. First, the labor share remains fairly stable and, second, there is a rise in wage inequality. These stylized facts yield two results in terms of economic performance that we have labeled "The economic puzzle of the UK economy" and "The employment-productivity trap." The first result combines low unemployment rates, high participation rates, low GDP growth rates, and stable inflation rates. The second consists of the reallocation of employment toward LPGI and the slowdown of productivity growth in HPGI. Likewise, both results rest on political economy dynamics that are mutually dependent and refer to the recent evolution of what we have called the financial and the labor axes.

Regarding the financial axis, in Section 3.1 we showed how successive transformations both in the regulatory context and in financial regulation itself contributed to assign a key role to the financial services industry in the UK economy and to reinforce its competitive advantage in the world economy. However, after the Great Recession and Brexit, we have seen that it would be an oversimplification to describe the relationship between the financial services industry and the regulator as a mere subordination. Even though every British government at every level acknowledges the importance of the financial sector and the City in the UK growth model, the British government's preferences are defined by a myriad of factors, such as the state of public opinion or the relative power of certain regulatory authorities.

With respect to the labor axis, in Section 3.2 we argued that the UK labor market has been characterized by an increasing dualization. This process has also, to a large extent, been linked to the structural transformation undergone by the UK economy, where employment deindustrialization coincides with this dual pattern of job creation within the service sector. While in the past, manufacturing was able to expand employment for low-skill labor and pay above-average wages (with respect to the economy), low-skill labor is now being absorbed into a service sector that is expanding employment at both segments of the labor market, i.e., both the low-skill and low-waged segment and the highly skilled and high-waged one. However, it seems that the financial crisis has brought important changes in the process of dualization within the service sector. First, highly skilled services have not strongly outgrown low-skill services in terms of employment after the crisis. Second, whereas compensation per employee increased faster in highly skilled services from 1996 to 2007, low-skill services have moderately reduced the compensation gap from 2008 to 2015. As a result, it seems that the process of dualization might have slowed down after the financial crisis.

References

Acemoglu, D., & Guerrieri, V. (2006). Capital deepening and non-balanced economic growth. *Journal of Political Economy*, 116, 467–498.

Alvarez-Cuadrado, F., Long, N. V., & Poschke, M. (2017). Capital-labor substitution, structural change, and growth. *Theoretical Economics*, 12, 1229–1266.

Alvarez-Cuadrado, F., Long, N.V., & Poschke, M. (2018). Capital-labour substitution, structural change and the labor income share. *Journal of Economic Dynamics & Control*, 87, 206–231.

Armour, J. (2017). Brexit and financial services. *Oxford Review of Economic Policy*, 33 (S1), S54–S69.

Aron, J.*et al.* (2012). Credit, housing collateral, and consumption: evidence from Japan, the UK and the US. *Review of Income and Wealth*, 58 (3), 397–423.

Awrey, D. (2011). The limits of EU hedge fund regulation. *Law and Financial Markets Review*, 5 (2), 119–128.

Baccaro, L., & Pontusson, J. (2016). Rethinking comparative political economy: The growth model perspective. *Politics & Society*, 44 (2), 175–207.

Baumol, W. (1967). Macroeconomics of unbalanced growth: The anatomy of urban crisis. *American Economic Review*, 57 (3), 415–426.

Becker, S., Fetzer, T., & Novy, D. (2017). Who voted for Brexit? A comprehensive district level analysis. *Economic Policy*, 32 (92), 601–650.

Behringer, J., & van Treeck, T. (2019). Income distribution and growth models: A sectoral balances approach. *Politics & Society*, 47 (3), 303–332.

Bell, B., & Van Reenen, J. (2010). Bankers' pay and extreme wage inequality in the UK. Centre for Economic Performance, CEPSP21.

Bell, B., & Van Reenen, J. (2013). Extreme wage inequality: Pay at the very top. *American Economic Review*, 103 (3), 153–157.

Bell, B., & Van Reenen, J. (2014). Bankers and their bonuses. *The Economic Journal*, 124 (574), F1–F21.

Bell, S., & Hindmoor, A. (2017). Structural power and the politics of bank capital regulation in the United Kingdom. *Political Studies*, 65 (1), 103–121.

Berlingieri, G. (2014). Outsourcing and the rise in services. CEP Discussion Paper No. 1199. London: London School of Economics, Centre for Economic Performance.

Berry, C. (2015). The final nail in the coffin: Crisis, manufacturing decline, and why it matters. In J. Green, C. Hay, & P. Taylor-Gooby (Eds.), *The British growth crisis*. London: Palgrave.

Bickerton, C. (2018). *Brexit and the British growth model: Towards a new social settlement*. London: Policy Exchange.

Braggion, F., & Ongena, S. (2017). Banking sector deregulation, bank–firm relationships and corporate leverage. *The Economic Journal*, 129, 765–789.

Buller, J., & Lindstrom, N. (2013). Hedging its bets: The UK and the politics of European financial services regulation. *New Political Economy*, 18 (3), 391–409.

Bunn, P., & Rostom, M. (2014). Household debt and spending. *Bank of England Quarterly Bulletin*, Q3, 304–315.

Ciarli, T., Meliciani, V., & Savona, M. (2012). Knowledge dynamics, structural change and the geography of business services. *Journal of Economic Surveys*, 26 (3), 445–467.

Ciriaci, D., Montresor, S., & Palma, D. (2015). Do KIBS make manufacturing more innovative? An empirical investigation of four European countries. *Technological Forecasting and Social Change*, 95, 135–151.

Clark, C. (1957). *The conditions of economic progress*. London: Macmillan.

Comin, D., Lashkari, D., & Mestieri, M. (2015). Structural change with long-run income and price effects. NBER Working Paper No. 21595.

Dumagan, J. (2013). A generalized exactly additive decomposition of aggregate productivity growth. *Review of Income and Wealth*, 59 (1), 157–168.

Edgerton, D. (2018). *The rise and fall of the British nation: A twentieth century history*. London: Allen Lane.

Fetzer, T. (2019). Did austerity cause Brexit? *American Economic Review*, 109 (11), 3849–3886.

Foellmi, R. & Zweimüller, J. (2008). Structural change, Engel's consumption cycles and Kaldor's facts of economic growth. *Journal of Monetary Economics*, 55, 1317–1328.

Frank, R., Levine, A., & Dijk, O. (2014). Expenditure cascades. *Review of Behavioral Economics*, 1 (1–2), 55–73.

FSA (2009a). *Financial risk outlook*. London: Financial Services Authority.

FSA (2009b). *The Turner Review: A regulatory response to the global banking crisis*. London: Financial Services Authority.

FSA (2010). *Financial risk outlook*. London: Financial Services Authority.

Gräbner, C.*et al.* (2020). Is the Eurozone disintegrating? Macroeconomic divergence, structural polarization, trade and fragility. *Cambridge Journal of Economics*, 44 (3), 647–669.

Guerrieri, P., & Meliciani, V. (2005). Technology and international competitiveness: The interdependence between manufacturing and producer services. *Structural Change and Economic Dynamics*, 16 (4), 489–502.

Hidalgo, C., & Hausmann, R. (2009). The building blocks of economic complexity. *Proceedings of the National Academy of Sciences of the United States of America*, 106 (26), 10570–10575.

Hidalgo, C.*et al.* (2007). The product space conditions the development of nations. *Science*, 317, 482–487.

Hodson, D., & Mabbett, D. (2009). UK economic policy and the global financial crisis: Paradigm lost? *Journal of Common Market Studies*, 47 (5), 1041–1061.

Howarth, D., & Quaglia, L. (2013). Banking on stability: The political economy of new capital requirements in the European Union. *Journal of European Integration*, 35 (3), 333–346.

Howarth, D., & Quaglia, L. (2017). Brexit and the single European financial market. *Journal of Common Market Studies*, 55 (S1), 149–164.

Howarth, D., & Quaglia, L. (2018). Brexit and the battle for financial services. *Journal of European Public Policy*, 25 (8), 1118–1136.

IPPR (2018). *Prosperity and Justice: A plan for the new economy. Final Report of the IPPR Commission on Economic Justice*. Cambridge: Polity Press.

James, S. (2016). The domestic politics of financial regulation: Informal ratification games and the EU capital requirement negotiations. *New Political Economy*, 21 (2), 187–203.

James, S., & Quaglia, L. (2018). The Brexit negotiations and financial services: A two-level game analysis. *The Political Quarterly*, 89 (4), 560–567.

James, S. & Quaglia, L. (2019a). Why does the United Kingdom (UK) have inconsistent preferences on financial regulation? The case of banking and capital markets. *Journal of Public Policy*, 39 (1), 177–200.

James, S., & Quaglia, L. (2019b). Brexit, the City and the contingent power of finance. *New Political Economy*, 24 (2), 258–271.

James, S., & Quaglia, L. (2020). *The UK and multi-level financial regulation: From post-crisis reform to Brexit*. Oxford: Oxford University Press.

Kaldor, N. (1966). *Causes of the slow rate of economic growth of the United Kingdom: An inaugural lecture*. Cambridge: Cambridge University Press.

Kaldor, N. (1968). Productivity and growth in manufacturing industry: A reply. *Economica*, 35 (140), 385–391.

Kaldor, N. (1975). Economic growth and the Verdoorn Law. A comment on Mr Rowthorn's article. *The Economic Journal*, 85 (340), 891–896.

Kollmeyer, C. (2009). Explaining deindustrialization: How affluence, productivity growth, and globalization diminish manufacturing employment. *American Journal of Sociology*, 114, 1644–1674.

Kongsamut, P., Rebelo, S., & Xie, D. (2001). Beyond balanced growth. *Review of Economic Studies*, 68, 869–882.

Kox, H., & Rubalcaba, L. (2007). Analysing the contribution of business services to European economic growth. Bruges European Economic Research Papers No. 9.

Lavery, S. (2017). "Defend and extend": British business strategy, EU employment policy and the emerging politics of Brexit. *The British Journal of Politics and International Relations*, 19 (4), 696–714.

Lavery, S. (2018). The legitimation of post-crisis capitalism in the United Kingdom: Real wage decline, finance-led growth and the state. *New Political Economy*, 23 (1), 27–45.

Lavery, S. (2019a). *British capitalism after the crisis*. New York: Springer International Publishing.

Lavery, S. (2019b). The UK's growth model, business strategy and Brexit. In C. Hay & D. Bailey (Eds.), *Diverging capitalisms* (pp. 149–170). New York: Springer International Publishing.

McCombie, J., Pugno, M., & Soro, B. (2002). *Productivity growth and economic performance: Essays on Verdoorn's Law*. New York: Palgrave Macmillan.

Moloney. N. (2014). *EU securities and financial markets regulation*. Oxford: Oxford University Press.

Moloney, N. (2017). Bending to uniformity: EU financial regulation with and without the UK. *Fordham International Law Journal*, 40(5), 1335–1371.

Muellbauer, J. (2007). *Housing credit and consumer expenditure*. Paper presented at Housing, Housing Finance and Monetary Policy: Proceedings of the Federal Reserve Bank of Kansas City Symposium. Jackson Hole, Wyoming, 30 August–1 September 2007, Federal Reserve Bank of Kansas City, pp. 267–334.

Ngai, L., & Pissarides, C. (2007). Structural change in a multi-sector model of growth. *American Economic Review*, 97, 429–443.

Nordhaus, W. (2001). Alternative methods for measuring productivity growth. National Bureau of Economic Research, Working Paper No. 8095.

Nordhaus, W. (2002). Productivity growth and the new economy. *Brookings Papers in Economic Activity*. Washington, DC: Brookings Institution.

Oren, T., & Blyth, M. (2018). From Big Bang to big crash: The early origins of the UK's finance-led growth model and the persistence of bad policy ideas. *New Political Economy*, 24 (5), 605–622.

Pasinetti, L. (1981). *Structural change and economic growth: A theoretical essay of the dynamics of the wealth of nations.* Cambridge: Cambridge University Press.

Pasinetti, L. (1993). *Structural economic dynamics: A theory of the economic consequences of human learning.* Cambridge: Cambridge University Press.

Pessoa, J., & Van Reenen, J. (2014). The UK productivity and jobs puzzle: Does the answer lie in wage flexibility? *The Economic Journal*, 124, 433–452.

Quaglia, L. (2011). The 'old' and 'new' political economy of hedge funds regulation in the European Union. *West European Politics*, 34 (4), 665–682.

Quaglia, L. (2017). European Union financial regulation, banking union, capital markets union and the UK. *SPERI Paper* 38. Sheffield: Sheffield Political Economy Research Institute.

Quaglia, L. (2019). European Union financial regulation, banking union, capital markets union and the UK. In C. Hay & D. Bailey (Eds.), *Diverging capitalisms: Britain, the City of London and Europe* (pp. 99–124). New York: Springer International Publishing.

Quaglia, L., Howarth, D., & Liebe, M. (2016). The political economy of European capital markets union. *Journal of Common Market Studies*, 54, 185–203.

Reinsdorf, M. (2015). Measuring industry contributions to labour productivity change: A new formula in a chained Fisher index framework. *International Productivity Monitor*, 28, 3–26.

Rodrik, D. (2013). Unconditional convergence in manufacturing. *Quarterly Journal of Economics*, 128 (1), 165–204.

Rowthorn, R., & Coutts, K. (2004). De-industrialisation and the balance of payments in advanced economies. *Cambridge Journal of Economics*, 28 (5), 767–790.

Rowthorn, R., & Ramaswamy, R. (1999). Growth, trade, and deindustrialization. *International Monetary Fund Staff Papers*, 46, 18–41.

Rowthorn, R., & Wells, J. R. (1987). *De-industrialization and foreign trade.* Cambridge: Cambridge University Press.

Ryoo, S., & Kim, Y. (2014). Income distribution, consumer debt and keeping up with the Joneses. *Metroeconomica*, 65 (4), 585–618.

Shiller, R. (2015). *Irrational exuberance.* 3rd edn. Princeton, NJ: Princeton University Press.

Sposi, M. (2016). Evolving comparative advantage: Sectoral linkages, and structural change. Dallas: Federal Reserve Bank of Dallas, Globalization and Monetary Policy Institute.

Stehrer, R.*et al.* (2019). Industry level growth and productivity data with special focus on intangible assets. Statistical Report, 8. Vienna: Vienna Institute for International Economic Studies.

Stockhammer, E., & Wildauer, R. (2016). Debt-driven growth? Wealth, distribution and demand in OECD countries. *Cambridge Journal of Economics*, 40 (6), 1609–1634.

Szirmai, A. (2012). Industrialisation as an engine of growth in developing countries. *Structural Change and Economic Dynamics*, 23, 406–420.

Talani, L. S. (2019). "Pragmatic adaptation" and the future of the City of London: Between globalisation and Brexit. In C. Hay & D. Bailey (Eds.), *Diverging capitalisms: Britain, the City of London and Europe* (pp. 43–71). New York: Springer International Publishing.

Tang, J., & Wang, W. (2004).Sources of aggregate labour productivity growth in Canada and the United States. *Canadian Journal of Economics*, 37 (2), 421–444.

Tanndal, J., & Waldenström, D. (2018). Does financial deregulation boost top incomes? Evidence from the Big Bang. *Economica*, 85, 232–265.

Thompson, H. (2017). Inevitability and contingency: The political economy of Brexit. *The British Journal of Politics and International Relations*, 19 (3), 434–449.

Thompson, H. (2019). The limits of the City's structural power: The City's offshore interests and the Brexit referendum. In C. Hay & D. Bailey (Eds.), *Diverging capitalisms: Britain, the City of London and Europe* (pp. 73–97). New York: Springer International Publishing.

Van Neuss, L. (2018). Globalization and deindustrialization in advanced countries. *Structural Change and Economic Dynamics*, 45, 49–63.

Wildauer, R., & Stockhammer, E. (2018). Expenditure cascades, low interest rates, credit deregulation or property booms? Determinants of household debt in OECD countries. *Review of Behavioral Economics*, 5 (2), 85–121.

Yoon, Y., & Chung, H. (2016). New forms of dualization? Labour market segmentation patterns in the UK from the late 90s until the post-crisis in the late 2000s. *Social Indicators Research*, 128 (2), 609–631.

11 Financial and economic crisis within the EU

Consequences for the Polish banking institutional system

Marcin Roman Czubala Ostapiuk

NATIONAL DISTANCE EDUCATION UNIVERSITY (UNED)

1 Introduction

The systemic transformation in Poland has given rise to a wide number of scenarios, from an economic, political, and social point of view, creating a new panorama within the framework of the post-communist country. This restructuring was accompanied by the emergence of a series of problems to be solved, receiving a response of a structural nature from the political leaders of the moment.

In the literature on the subject, taking into account the development process of the European welfare systems, great attention has been paid to the importance not only of organisms, but also dependent mechanisms (Cerami, 2010: 233). However, this process and its results, as well as the attempts to classify it, have not been free from controversy. It should be remembered, for example, that the functioning of the restored Polish parliamentary democracy and the holding of competitive elections also had an influence, in a certain way and as an additional factor, limiting the institutional modifications of the welfare system after the collapse of the Soviet bloc.

Regarding the initial transitional reforms, in a state where the economy was characterized by hyperinflation, external indebtedness and chronic shortages, there is no doubt that its objective was to establish a market economy, thus allowing the development of new strategies and solutions for a country seeking to rebuild institutional coherence.

Its first phase, referring to the first decade since 1989, marked by the creation of new state agencies and the development of various political processes, was closely linked to major economic changes shaping the course of the country's transformation and its integration with international economies. The reform package orchestrated by the Finance Minister Leszek Balcerowicz included liberalization of the national economy and increased market competition (Kaliński, 2005: 11–12). To do this, the banking sector was reformed, in addition to eliminating preferential credits and subsidies to state-owned companies. Similarly, foreign trade experienced a strong opening-up so that greater access to the national market and tax benefits for foreign capital were witnessed, thus seeking not only to attract, but also to sustain external investment as an important factor in development. In the same way, a fixed exchange rate was introduced, and inflation was reduced through a series of fiscal solutions. Finally, a gradual process of privatization of national companies was launched, not to mention the incentives for the creation of new entities.

In other words, an aggregate of neoliberal economic reforms occurred through which extensive economic deregulation was allowed, introducing a set of changes that, despite some setbacks and the negative short-term effects, allowed the final results to be marked by an early recovery, presenting the correct functioning of the entire state economy.

On the other hand, in the second phase of this transition, characteristic of the subsequent decade, we saw reflected the greater adaptation (limited by the differential results of the first stage) of this new panorama to the welfare system that characterized the developed neoliberal economies of the time. We also witnessed a series of efforts made to reduce the effects of the threat of a second economic downturn. In any case, establishing a market economy, without having ample capital and adequate knowledge, not to mention limited access to the markets of the Western countries, was not an easy task. As a result, among others, Poland experienced a slowdown in economic activity and public debt increased. This scenario was especially visible in the years 2001 and 2002.

Nonetheless, we must not forget that during the second phase, and through the "second-generation economic reforms," the essential focus was placed on foreign investment, and implementing fiscal and labor market deregulation reforms, thus seeking to provide further progress in preferential treatment for potential investors. Without underestimating the other factors that clearly interacted in the economic situation of the country under analysis, we observe that the established actions paid off, especially considering gross domestic product (GDP) growth in the 2004–2008 period and the stock of foreign direct investment (FDI) in the mid-2000s.

Discussing the recent global economic recession of 2008, and in contrast to the other economies of the European Union, the results offered by Poland can be considered to be relatively positive. The Slavic country did not suffer an appreciable crisis, even in the more difficult moments for the European Community project and its members, although it must be remembered that GDP growth experienced two moments of significant deceleration (in 2009, as well as in 2012 and 2013), while the unemployment rate grew (especially in 2012), however, not at levels comparable with its neighboring countries. Furthermore, we must not forget that public spending, after 2008, remained relatively high (in relation to GDP). Undoubtedly, the preparations for Euro 2012 and the receipt of Structural Funds from the European Union budget, the relatively good regulation and the lack of the collapse of the national financial and banking system (along with its expansive activity), the wide domestic market, together with the devaluation of the national currency against the euro and the US dollar (due to Poland's lack of membership in the European monetary zone) helped to keep the economy in good shape compared to the rest of its community partners (Piątkowski, 2013: 11).

What is more, as we have previously underlined, foreign investment played an important role in modernizing and increasing the competitiveness of the Polish economy (Maciejewska, Mrozowski & Piasna, 2016). The approach in question was maintained, even after the end of the systemic transition period, becoming a characteristic of the "dependent market economy" of Poland.

In short, it was an expression of the channeling of the national economy toward exports and the flexibility of the labor market, combined with significant social spending, even if focused on potential foreign investors (Bernaciak, 2017). That is to say, a series of evident neoliberal policy prescriptions were applied, especially since the systemic transition that the country suffered, and that underline a focus on boosting domestic demand, inclusive of the contribution of the foreign sector (which was variable, depending on the period of analysis) to overall economic growth (Marks-Bielska & Nazarczuk, 2012: 27–29).

Finally, the orientation toward economic development, as well as the social determination to be a member of NATO (the North Atlantic Treaty Organization) and the European Union, were the main motivations for both the reforms of public institutions and the changes in neoliberal economic policies implemented since the late 1990s.

Undoubtedly, the accession of Poland as an EU member facilitated the institutional and financial support of the European Community, which was part of the economic success of the Slavic partner. However, its own particular characteristics were not unimportant either. In other words, a stable business environment that allowed entities to implement long-term development strategies. Likewise, the participation of the public sector in the generation of GDP or the state employment rate had shown (since the early 1990s) a downward trend. At the same time, the number of jobs in entities with foreign capital has been growing, demonstrating, once again, how open the country is to foreign investment.

Regarding the models of capitalism established by Amable, it is important to note that Poland, like the other states of Central and Eastern Europe, does not fit uniformly into the proposed classification. Presenting heterogeneous results, we observe how the countries in question bet on different perspectives in the process of systemic transformation, both with reference to the perception of the "market economy" and institutional solutions to be developed. To summarize, Poland is clearly a hybrid example where the capitalism model undergoes variations according to the institutional environment analyzed (Rapacki & Czerniak, 2018).

In any case, the balance between the greater opening-up of the market and the preservation of elements of the welfare state and/or protectionism, foreign direct investment (promoted through tax incentives, among others) and the certain dominance of external ownership in key sectors, such as industry or financial and banking services, skilled but relatively cheap labor (which is also subject to flexible labor market regulation) or the production of complex and durable consumer goods remain some of its main features, suggesting deregulation as the type of liberalization path perhaps most akin to the Polish case.

Therefore, the main aim of this chapter is to carry out an analysis of the institutional changes that have occurred in Poland since 1989, focusing this study on the changes introduced in the banking sector. Moreover, we scrutinize the possible correlation of these institutional facts with the evolution of aggregate demand and the transformations of the growth model.

Finally, taking into account the peculiarities of the country in question, and in comparison with other chapters in this volume, this contribution significantly broadens the time frame in order to complete the vision and analysis developed, also to provide a more comprehensive perspective of the Polish case. This is a crucial exercise in order to better understand the process of formation and development of the chosen sector in Poland and that has witnessed different stages of economic, political and social transformation.

2 The Polish banking sector after the systemic transformation of 1989

The changes in the Polish banking sector, its role and importance in the context of the country as a whole, as a result of the reforms implemented as an effect of the systemic transition, mean that we can treat this area of the economic system as a clear example of the transformation of the economy, in other words, the state and its institutional reconstruction, as well as adaptation to future membership of international organizations, especially the European Union.

2.1 The legislative, organizational and ownership changes

Thanks to the 1982 legislative changes, the banking system underwent some liberalization, with the National Bank of Poland (NBP) becoming a more independent entity, although still with many limitations. Especially, and despite the fact that its presidency has been separated from the Ministry of Finance, the establishment of banking entities in the form of joint-stock companies continued to require prior permission from the government.

Later, the work of a group of experts, which began in 1986 under the direction of the central bank, gave its results through the Banking Law (Ustawa Prawo bankowe, Dz.U., 1989, nr 4 poz. 21) and the Law on the National Bank of Poland (Ustawa Prawo bankowe, Dz.U., 1989, nr 4 poz. 22), both approved by the lower house of the Polish Parliament in 1989. Replacing the initial reforms (implemented in the early 1980s), among others, they drastically liberalized the bases of creation and activity of new entities (including those of a private nature), in conjunction with substantial changes in the institutional organization of the sector (also introducing the concept of legal entity), based on the experience of other highly developed states (Baszyński, 2011: 169–171).

The National Bank of Poland also acquired all the typical functions and objectives for entities of like character: to be a lender of last resort, to define and execute monetary policy, to establish interest rates and reserve requirements, to promote the smooth operation and the stability of the banking system, supervising the solvency and compliance with the specific regulations, also having appropriate procedures, referring to the healing, liquidation and bankruptcy of the entities, among others. Besides, through the amendment to the Constitution of the People's Republic of Poland, its independence was increased, the NBP being permanently separated from the rest of the government administration.

The above-mentioned Balcerowicz reform package allowed greater implementation of a liberal banking model and eliminated the credit plan as a control tool by the central bank (Wilczyński, 1994: 65). Regarding the denationalization of banking, the 1992 reforms extended the operation of the Law on the privatization of state-owned companies (Ustawa o prywatyzacji przedsiębiorstw państwowych, Dz.U, 1990, nr 51 poz. 298) to the sector in question, the acting Minister of Finance being responsible for this process. Additionally, the functioning of the employee councils (a characteristic body of state entities of the communist era) was removed, while the independence of the NBP was further reinforced, also establishing provisions regarding the appointment and dismissal of its president.

The Polish banking system, thanks to the legal modifications implemented, has also undergone a series of substantial changes in its organization. In the first place, based on the 1982 reform and the provisions of the 1988 Council of Ministers, a process has begun to create nine new public entities,[1] supported by the existing central bank branches, and which began to be operational in early 1989 (Baszyński, 2011: 172).

Territorially separated, they fully represented around 50 percent of the sector. Their independence, although supposedly broad, in this initial phase, was marked by the appointment of their directors by the head of government. Through their work, supervised and coordinated by the Council of Banks (existing between 1989 and 1992), headed by the president of the central bank, they assumed much of the deposit and credit responsibilities of the NBP. Over time, these regional banks expanded their territorial scope through branches located outside their main area, however, the opening of new entities significantly reduced not only their participation in the sector as a whole, but also their balance sheet.

In 1991, when the commercialization process was completed, the first step toward its transfer to private hands, the nine organizations had administrative boards and supervisory bodies. In the following year, they signed their twinning agreements with Western European banks. In any case, we must not forget that during the first decade of transformation, state control over modifications of the banking sector was very visible, while any entry and the activity of a foreign entity were based on the structures of the already existing organizations.

Second, and in parallel to the described events, the Bank Gospodarstwa Krajowego (BGK), reactivated after years of inaction, was granted authority to issue Treasury bonds. On the other hand, both within the public and business sectors, we observe the development of the initiative in favor of the establishment of new banking entities, starting, for example, with the Bank of Social and Economic Initiatives,[2] the Bank of Housing Development,[3] and/or Bank for Environmental Protection.[4] Correspondingly, even with the contribution of private capital, Wschodni Bank Cukrownictwa SA were founded in Lublin, Bank Cukrownictwa Cukrobank SA in Wrocław, and Bank Rozwoju Cukrownictwa SA in Poznań, linked to the sugar industry, or Bank Energetyki SA in Radom, related to the energy sector (Bałtowski & Miszewski, 2005: 328). Not to mention Bank Handlowy in Warsaw and Cuprum Bank SA.

In any case, all of them underwent a series of substantial changes, cessation of their activity or absorption by other entities, both banking and private companies. Only two of them (the Bank for Environmental Protection and the Bank for Social and Economic Initiatives), until Poland joined the European Union, preserved their development capacity and organizational continuity, largely thanks to their links with foreign banking entities in the 1990s.

With respect to purely private banks, their extensive foray into the national scene was the result of the liberalization of the banking law together with the lax conditions on the issuance of new licenses. Nonetheless, with low capital and without properly qualified human resources, their expansion capacity turned out to be limited, not putting the dominance of the nine at risk. This was also the case of entities with foreign capital that began operating in Poland (gradually) since 1990.

Third, we must talk about the currency exchange offices that, thanks to the Currency Law (Ustawa Prawo dewizowe, Dz.U., 1989, nr 6 poz. 33) and the ordinance of the presidency of the National Central Bank, were able to start operating in 1989. The initial boom in their foundation has been decreasing in time, basically due to the consequent reforms and restrictions implemented. Another phenomenon was shadow banking. That is, the entities whose aim was to cover some of the basic banking activities, without appropriate permits or the necessary equity for doing so. Put simply, they developed their operations based on the Law on economic activity (Ustawa o działalności gospodarczej, Dz.U., 1988, nr 41 poz. 324).

2.2 The supervisory policies

The first years of systemic transformation were marked by the failure of the Polish central bank to fulfill the functions of control and supervision of the sector, especially with regard to commercial entities.

With the approval of the banking law, at the beginning of 1989, the basic amount needed to open an entity was only 4 million zloty, being slightly increased in subsequent years. Through this stipulation, the legislator sought to encourage private investment, especially of foreign origin, which was reflected in the less orthodox licensing policy and the implementation of a package of tax reductions. Moreover, the origin of the initial capital used was not reviewed, omitting the rigidity of some of the other requirements to be fulfilled, as well as allowing the accumulation of property in the hands of one person. A whole series of rulings were eliminated, to a large extent, by the Banking Law of 1992 (Ustawa o zmianie ustawy Prawo bankowe i niektórych innych ustaw, Dz.U., 1992, nr 20 poz. 78) that forced each entity to have more than one owner, while the initial capital used could not present any kind of commitment.

The setback in the country's economic performance, inclusive of the legislation that was implemented, forced the Polish central bank also to tighten its licensing policy. The basic amount threshold was increased to 70 million zloty, while, since 1993, the EU standard equivalent of ECU 5 million has been implemented. Likewise, with the aim of strengthening the position of Polish banks, equal treatment was applied to all entities, regardless of the origin of their capital, whether domestic or foreign. In this way, the number of licenses issued dropped significantly, limiting the permits of foreign organizations to operate in the Slavic country or to take over any existing national entity. This is an example of the strengthening of an oligopolistic structure in the sector and the important governmental influence in its organization.

It should also be noted that bank supervision was a completely new function within the framework of the National Bank of Poland. A truly non-existent reality in the context of the previous political and economic system, the introduction of which was reflected in the performance of the country's new economic system.

The recommendations, issued to commercial banks (this was the format used, given the inadequacy of the banking law of the time) and later (with its 1992 update) converted into orders, allowed the central entity to further shape the national banking system. Since 1990, commercial banks have been obliged to provide the NBP with information on the level of coverage of assets with equity on a monthly basis. Not to mention, starting in 1991, a new bank account plan was developed for the sector as a whole, unifying in a certain way national accounting with transnational standards and norms.

2.3 *The financial position of the banking entities*

In the first years of their activity, Polish banks obtained very satisfactory financial results, mainly thanks to the difference between the interest rates of the offered loans and the deposits in conditions of high inflation, not to mention the relatively low capital availability, but with a significant return.

As an example of the inequality existing in the economic system of Poland, the profits obtained and their accumulation (in the case of the sector in question, and which also exceeded the profits of the business environment) were clearly wasted. Bad management, the effects of the business cycle, and the transfer of funds to private hands were only some of its causes.

In the second half of 1991, due to the poor conditions of the national economy as a whole, the banking supervision in the making and the lax requirements to be able to operate in the market, the percentage of bad debts held by banks (8 percent of corporate loans) doubled (Wilczyński, 1994: 67–68). Also, at the end of the following year, these commitments already exceeded 30 percent of their total.

The gross profitability and the real income of the banks decreased. While their net income showed an upward trend, one in three loans was bad. Many of the commercial and corporate banks had to deal with a situation of possible bankruptcy. Regarding the large public entities, their condition was not the best either. These not only did not adequately face up to the new reality of a liberated economy, but also had to suffer a series of financial commitments provided to public companies (before the transition) that made their situation more difficult (Baszyński, 2011: 173).

In an environment of liquidations and bank failures, several entities were absorbed by others, that were larger and had more capital. Although, thanks to the Law on financial restructuring of companies and banks (Ustawa o restrukturyzacji finansowej przedsiębiorstw i banków oraz o zmianie niektórych ustaw, Dz.U., 1993, nr 18 poz. 82), the stabilization of the sector in question has been possible. Through long-term bonds, issued by the Treasury to the value of 40 billion zloty, they sought to recapitalize the country's banking system. In this way, the beneficiary entities were able to apply a series of corrective procedures, including obtaining property rights, which ultimately improved their situation.

2.4 Ownership and organizational transformation within the 1993–1997 period: privatization and consolidation of the banking sector

First, the privatization of banks in Poland commenced with the aforementioned program of the Ministry of Finance, which started in 1991 (Baszyński, 2011: 174). Through its approval, the initiative in question passed from the hands of the NBP to an executive body of the state. From the nine systemic public entities, two were chosen, Wielkopolski Bank Kredytowy in Poznań (WBK) and Bank Śląski in Katowice (BŚ), which presented the best economic-financial conditions, without the need for recapitalization.

The Allied Irish Bank turned out to be the definitive strategic investor in case of the former, while the initial public offering (IPO) of the second entity (in 1993) was linked to the acquisition of about 26 percent of its shares by the Dutch entity ING and another 30 percent by small investors (Bałtowski & Miszewski, 2005: 338).

The third of the nine public banks at the time, Bank Przemysłowo-Handlowy of Krakow (BPH), underwent privatization in June 1994. The prevailing recession of the Stock Exchange partially forged the success of this process. Despite this, in 1998, it managed to gain as a strategic investor the German entity Bayerische HypoVereinsbank. In conclusion, in the period 1993–1997, six public banks were privatized through the capital market.

Second, through the consolidation process, the objective was for the banking entities with the best returns, as well as those with partial participation of foreign capital in them, to acquire the weakest entities, incorporating them into their structures. This was an approach that had been promoted since the second half of 1993 and that aimed to avoid possible privatization due to the direct entry of foreign entities, thus maintaining a certain degree of state control over the sector and its development.

Applied to three of the nine public banks – Bank Depozytowo-Kredytowy in Lublin, Pomorski Bank Kredytowy in Szczecin and Powszechny Bank Gospodarczy in Łódź – these entities were merged (in 1996) with Bank Pekao SA. Two years later its shares were admitted to public listing, in addition to being released on the Warsaw Stock Exchange. At the end of 1998, the group also underwent a series of internal reforms, leading to a real merger. Finally, in 1999, most of its share capital was acquired by Unicredito Italiano and Allianz AG (Kaliński, 2005: 21).

Similarly, PKO BP, the largest national bank, underwent a series of profound modifications. The new statute, established in 1992, increased the capital of earnings at the disposal of the entity. Its new Supervisory Board was inaugurated in 1993, giving it a broader range of competencies and methods of operation, comparable to a business entity. All this with the aim of increasing state control over it and promoting the commercial orientation of the organization. As of 2000, the entity in question entered the phase of its commercialization, making its debut on the Warsaw Stock Exchange in 2004.

Third, in accordance with the new policy of the Polish central bank on the issuance of licenses, since 1994, obtaining licenses had been linked to the participation of the entity in question in a restructuring process of a national bank. In this way, the legislator sought to clean up the system of clearly weak or declining entities, which allowed the large international financial institutions to appear on the Polish market.

Starting in 1997, the government's view was modified, abandoning in a certain way the objective of consolidation and protectionism of the national banking sector, included in the political project of its predecessor government. Thanks to a privatization program (through which the sale of majority stakes in Treasury shares to foreign entities was allowed) in 1999, the partial sales of two large public banks – PBH SA and Bank Zachodni SA – were formalized.

However, in 2000–2001, we observed two key mergers for the whole of the Polish system. These transactions included, on the one hand, Bank Zachodni SA and Wielkopolski Bank Kredytowy SA, as well as Bank Przemysłowo-Handlowy SA and Powszechny Bank Kredytowy SA, on the other. In the same way, both new entities were part of the important banking groups of Poland. In short, up to 29 organizations experienced a merger or purchase by other banks, a particularly active process in the 1998–2002 period. In this way, the first years of the millennium were characterized by the establishment of new entities, based on Polish private capital. Unlike the banks founded at the beginning of the systemic transformation process, often immature and poorly managed, these entities seemed to be a stable and lasting element of the national banking sector.

Finally, with regard to cooperative banks, purely state-owned in the communist era, their number dropped after 1989. Due to the consolidation process, their presence in the national economic environment has decreased nearly three times, causing at the same time a reinforcement of the sector. Even so, and despite the variations in the banking sector as a whole and the conversion into one of its elements of a stable nature, it is important to note that the representation of cooperative entities nowadays cannot be compared with the time before the country's systemic transformation (Wilczyński, 1994: 70).

3 The Polish banking sector and the European Union

3.1 Changes in the Banking Law and its adaptation to the EU requirements

The Constitution of Poland (Konstytucja Rzeczypospolitej Polskiej uchwalona przez Zgromadzenie Narodowe w dniu 2 kwietnia, 1997, nr 78 poz. 483), adopted in 1997, reinforced the role of the country's central bank in its entire institutional structure. Moreover, while strengthening its independence, it emphasized its responsibility in the design and execution of the state's monetary policy.

Correspondingly, the new Banking Law (Ustawa Prawo bankowe, Dz.U., 1997, nr 140 poz. 939) and the Law on the National Bank of Poland (Ustawa o Narodowym Banku Polskim, Dz.U., 1997, nr 140 poz. 938), approved in 1997, introduced a series of changes and updates in the organization of the sector, in particular, taking into account the experience of the new stage in the development of the state economy after the communist era. Through its provisions, many of the aspects already included in the analogous legislative acts, approved in 1989, were detailed. The aim was to improve the legal framework, eliminating existing deficiencies and errors. In this way, the aspects relating to the founding of new banking entities, the requirements regarding initial capital or powers available to the Boards of Directors were specified. Along with the aim of greater adaptation to community legislation, it sought to adjust national regulations to the requirements set in the context of the European Union, placing much more emphasis on banking supervision, including the surveillance of entities with foreign capital, as well as the privatization of the national banking system. Finally, part of the powers of the president of the NBP were assumed by new collegiate bodies (headed by him) (Baszyński, 2011: 178–182):

- *The Banking Supervision Commission*: responsible for issuing licenses and supervising commercial banks, introduced a series of rules regarding solvency, liquidity, and concentration indices, among others. This introduced a whole set of novel provisions, in accordance with Community standards, in the context of the Polish banking sector. In the period of its validity (1998–2007), the agency in question issued only nine licenses for the establishment of banking entities, these being, to a large extent, foreign, and thus ensuring the stability of the sector and prudent management of banks in the national environment. Since January 2008, its functions have been assumed by the Polish Financial Supervision Commission (which also incorporated into its framework the activities of the Insurance and Pension Funds Supervision Commission, along with the Securities and Exchange Commission).

- *The Monetary Policy Council*: in charge of monetary policy matters, especially interest rates.
- Another important body was the *Bank Guarantee Fund*. Thanks to its implementation and operation, the partial deposit guarantee (previously only applicable to some of the public banks) was extended to all banking entities, while the legal gap regarding the rehabilitation of banks has been covered. Through the Law on the Bank Guarantee Fund (Ustawa o Bankowym Funduszu Gwarancyjnym,, Dz.U., 1995, nr 4 poz. 18), the legal basis has been established both to facilitate financial assistance to entities threatened with bankruptcy (also allowing the reorganization of said entities) and to establish a payment system for the funds accumulated in the bank (up to a specific amount) in case of lack of their disposal. In addition, the Fund's activity covered all entities present in the national market, subsequently adapting to Community legislation.

Among the other entities to highlight are also (Baszyński, 2011: 182–183):

- *The National Clearing House*, beginning its activity in 1993, implemented an electronic interbank clearing system, ELIXIR. Used by all national entities since 1998, it allowed great advances in the development of the sector, facilitating the flow of information and interbank settlement. Along, in recent years, it has implemented a series of new technological solutions such as the optical reading of bank documents or the public key certificate management system.
- *The Union of Polish Banks*, established in 1991, is an autonomous organization whose main objective is to represent and defend the interests of the whole banking sector before the executive and legislative branches of the state. It seeks to modernize the entire sector through initiatives related to the recruitment of human resources, sharing of good practices among its members, training activities and others, being a permanent element of the national banking scene.
- *The Credit Information Office*, independent from the banking entities, is an entity that acts as an intermediary (based on the current Banking Law), providing (in cooperation with the other agents of the system) information about customers and their financial commitments, as well as on unreliable debtors.

3.2 The economic crisis and its effects on the Polish banking sector

The effects of the Great Recession, which began in the US real estate and mortgage markets, were reflected in the context of the European Union monetary zone due to the mutual transmission channels between national economies. Additionally, its intensity depended on the structural characteristics of the conjunctures of the states, together with the existing connections, their asymmetry, the speed of infection, among others (Chudik & Fratzscher, 2011).

The scenario in question also demonstrated a dysfunction both in the credit sector and in its supervision, i.e., the entry into a phase of economic stagnation and the growth of public debt, as well as the coordinated response by the Member States (with a special emphasis on countries where the currency is the euro). As well, it is necessary to remember that the banks were one of its key elements. Not only causing the spread of the effects of the collapse on a global scale (due to its importance in the development processes of the market economy), both in 2007 and after 2011, but also becoming beneficiaries of intervention and assistance policies, promoting the public debt of many of the Community States.

The economic recession in question also revealed one behavior of the Polish economy different from that of the other countries in the region. Thus, for example, the high activity in the mortgage markets related to the low level of conditionality of the borrowers, a wide use of securitizations and credit derivatives to transfer the related risks or the growth of the unregulated sector were not typical of the Polish market.

Nonetheless, and in relation to the potential channels of contagion to the national financial sector, the analysis carried out by the Polish Financial Supervision Commission (in line with the studies of the European Central Bank) revealed the lack of confidence, the dislocation of the market (understood due to the important and rapid changes in prices and the weakening of exchange rates), as well as indirect effects as the main entry channels of external shocks (Komisja Nadzoru Finansowego, 2009: 8). In the other direction, through the approach used by the central bank, the direct path (formed by the credit, financing, and market channel) was highlighted, on the one hand, and the indirect path, on the other, considering other factors of transmission of recession from abroad to be external (the macroeconomic, capital, the confidence crisis, etc.) (Narodowy Bank Polski, 2008). In short, and based on both approaches, we highlight the degeneration of confidence in financial institutions, a series of macroeconomic effects linked to the weakening of the situation in Poland and in the international context, also the deterioration of the banking sector and changes in the credit and indirect market channel, as the main factors to take into account in the case of Poland.

In any case, the lack of participation of the Polish banking sector in the American subprime mortgage market allowed the transmission market channel of the economic recession to have no effect in their case. In other words, the control of national banking entities by foreign investors could have caused a series of risks (given the deterioration of the economic situation of the mother entities). On the other hand, the financing and capital channels did not prove to be a determining factor and of a direct nature, and did not contribute to the expansion (in Poland) of the crisis phenomena.

However, the aforementioned deterioration in confidence, due to the dependence of national agencies on their strategic investors, was perceived as the first effect of the international financial crisis in the Polish banking context. In summary, and despite a situation of structural excess liquidity in the sector, we witnessed a significant contraction of assets in the interbank market (Stola, 2015: 93).

Likewise, the macroeconomic channel turned out to be another important transmission medium for the Polish economy. Despite the good results of the economic parameters and their causes (described above), the worsening of conditions in the framework of the other member countries of the European Union, the slowdown in their economic situations and the need for public intervention through the rescue of the banks affected all the economic indicators in Poland. In this way, we observe the reduction in its exports, the decrease in the gross domestic product, the increase in the unemployment rate and the weakening of the national currency, among others.

Its impact was even greater, given that it facilitated the transmission of crises through other, indirect, means, further conditioning the banking sector. The tightening of the bank lending policy (mentioned above), as well as the reduction in the supply of credit (due to economic uncertainty and growing capital restrictions) can be considered some of its results (which still continue to affect the other European entities, while in the national case in question they remained until the end of 2012). Nor should we forget the rising cost of loans due to fluctuations between foreign currency and the national currency or the effects on the balance sheets of banking entities, the consequences of the transmission of the crisis to the Polish sphere, this time, through the credit and market indirect channel. In brief, Poland suffered from the relationship between the rapid entry of negative effects of the crisis through direct channels, but limited in time, and the impact of their access through indirect channels, extended over time, and with long-term damaging results.

Conversely, the international economic and financial crisis significantly affected the European banking sector and its configuration. Through a series of structural, profitability and security indicators, we observe how its size in relation to the gross domestic product of the EU Member States has been decreasing. Like its exercise in the credit market, the profitability of the sector's activities as a whole has been declining.

As a result of its negative effects, member countries have been implementing a series of measures with the aim of restoring confidence and security in the banking sector. Among them, the increase in the level of the entities' own capital, the promotion of their resistance to external shocks, as well as the different solutions to reduce the risks of a systemic contraction in the future.

As for the Polish banking sector, in the current economic recession phase, we observe its intense progress (compared to the other EU states), reducing the differences in its development with respect to the sectors of the European Union (especially in the 2008–2013 period). Its high resistance to a difficult environment, caused by the economic and financial crisis, was mainly due to the lack of its impact on the national banking structure and its characteristics described above (especially its limited development, the experience of systemic transformation, and a restrictive regulatory system), as well as the general absence of participation by Polish entities in toxic bank assets. At the same time, we are also witnessing its high efficiency, even in the post-crisis era.

In any case, the indicated development gap is still significant, showing the results of the key indicators and market penetration rates in Poland to be less than other community banking sectors. Besides, any study on such is hampered, given the changes in the environment arising from the crisis (both in fiscal and financial matters), so that it is very difficult to identify a reference state in order to make a comparative analysis that includes the Polish banking sector.

Regarding the financing structure of Polish banks, deposits from non-financial institutions are their most important source. The vast majority of their liabilities correspond to financial and non-financial entities, while the rest is made up of its own resources. Despite this, it must be remembered that the scheme in question varies slightly depending on the distribution of the property and the type of activity carried out by the entity analyzed. Thus, banks that are part of foreign financial groups take advantage of foreign resources to a greater extent than entities with predominantly national capital. Regarding subordinated liabilities and the issuance of own debt securities, their importance within the framework of the sector is limited. However, we observe a financial gap, the result of the difference between the credits granted to non-financial institutions and their deposits, which banks seek to reduce by issuing debt securities or raising funds abroad (assuming the exchange risk).

Next, and taking into account the lack of major changes due to the recession, we can say that the financing structure of the Polish banking sector is relatively stable. The impact of the crisis has not been significant, at least in a direct way. Thanks to a demanding supervision system (compared to other European countries), the banking sector has not claimed any financial help, either from the public sector or its different bodies. Likewise, the capitalization of the entities is sufficient, complying with the requirements established by the Basel III Accord.

Also, the control of the banking sector entities by companies with Polish assets (mostly state agencies) is growing, which shows an increase in the influence on commercial banking assets by national capital. Bank mergers and the use of existing synergies, the improvement in the balance of payments, as well as greater facilities in obtaining financing in periods marked by the economic slowdown are some of the awaited benefits. Moreover, it is expected that the systemic entities (with dominant national capital) will support, always maintaining the said established supervision and control standards, the different activities with the aim of promoting economic growth in Poland.

Regarding possible problems, we must not forget the long-term liquidity requirements (especially taking into account the lack of savings culture in the country under analysis), a scenario that may have a solution, for example, based on the issuance of bank documents with long maturities. The creation of the Polish Development Fund (a strategic state-owned body) is another of the government responses to this phenomenon. Through its instruments, it serves business entities, local governments and individuals, seeking to encourage economic, social and sustainable development, in addition to promoting savings.

Finally, the reform of European economic governance introduced in 2011 involved the establishment of the banking union in the context of the EU. Despite the fact that its regulatory framework is common to all EU Member States, its organizational structure (joint and centralized) places special emphasis on the euro zone. At the same time, the other European Union countries have the possibility of voluntary but not compulsory participation.

Through its main objective, guaranteeing the stability of financial systems and executing the restructuring and orderly liquidation processes of banking entities threatened with insolvency, it seeks to facilitate the supervision and resolution processes (especially in the case of banks whose activities cross the borders of a state), avoiding possible future crises and the expansion of their negative effects. In addition, the activity carried out through its different pillars should improve the economic situation and the labor markets, together with reducing the costs associated with the rescue of banking entities with public funds.

Among the main risks in its execution and effectiveness, we can highlight the possible conflict in the determination of powers and responsibilities between the different bodies that make up the banking union in question, as well as the difficulties in accessing the European Stability Mechanism by the banking entities, among others. In any case, there is no doubt that the banking sectors of the member countries whose currency is the euro will be the best protected against possible financial stability imbalances. Thanks to the European Systemic Risk Board and the Single Supervisory Mechanism, the European Central Bank must also be considered a key part of the new macro- and micro-prudential supervision system.

Regarding the member countries that are not part of the eurozone, but participate in the banking union, despite the improvement in their situation, the activity of the European Central Bank (ECB) and its capacities are significantly reduced due to the limitations of its intervention in these national environments. Even so, the aforementioned cooperation facilitates long-term financing and a decrease in the cost of obtaining funds from national banks, as well as greater access to information. Likewise, we must not forget that the legal framework referring to the second pillar of the banking union, the Single Resolution Mechanism and its application, binds all member countries. Nonetheless, countries that are not part of the banking union cannot access the capital funds of the European Stabilization Mechanism, nor the specific subsidies provided by the ECB. In other words, this is a series of benefits that can be very interesting for Poland, although they entail a set of expenses and a certain loss of independence.

Among other positive elements, we can also highlight the improvement in the perception of the security of the Polish banking sector in the eyes of foreign investors, easier access to long-term financing and a decrease in the cost of obtaining resources from national banks, inclusive of a growth in the issuance of foreign bonds by national banking entities.

In any case, the partial implementation of the banking union, the brief length of the supervision process by the European Central Bank, the limitation of capacities granted to cooperating countries whose currency is not the euro, along with the current conditions of the banking sector continue to make the attractiveness of this project reduced for Poland (Lepczyński, 2014: 97–98). However, we must remember that changes in the European environment may accelerate Poland's decision regarding the establishment of closer ties within the framework of the project in question. In particular, this depends on the progress in its completion, the number of participating states (especially those not yet associated), as well as its correct functioning in the period of a probable economic recession.

4 The Polish welfare and growth model: final appointments

Returning to the general characteristics of the country (developed in Section 1), along with the institutional evolution of the Polish banking system, we observe that Poland's systemic transition was a truly complex process. The different aspects of its development, including the plurality of its internal context, the simultaneous initiation of reforms in all spheres of its nature, as well as the peaceful nature of the shift toward democracy and the market economy, were only some of its characteristics.

Despite the fact that the time frame of this research focuses on a period beginning in 1989, it must be remembered that attempts to open up the socialist economy go back to the time before the fall of the Soviet Union. In any case, the speed and implementation of the progress of the reforms that were part of this transformation have been favored not only by national interest groups, but also by external pressure, world markets and the international community.

Through the initial phase of the establishment of the capitalist system in Poland, at the suggestion of the International Monetary Fund and the World Bank, a set of neoliberal solutions were chosen (Dahl, Piskorska, & Olszewski, 2015: 76–77): a low inflation rate, the moderation of public spending, the reduction of indebtedness, and high growth. This approach was widely applauded by international capital (an important aspect that we will highlight again later). However, its certain lack of adaptation to the Polish context provided an increase in public debt and significant inflation (as indicated above), as well as a fragmentary effect of the reforms implemented.

In the same way, social policy was based on a series of drastic cuts in public spending, the reduction of unemployment benefits, the flexibilization of the labor market, the decentralization of family policy and restrictions in the field of social protection. Also, the modernization of Polish industry linked it to foreign direct investment, promoting a wide range of tax incentives or subsidies so that, following the aforementioned path of neoliberalism, investors and transnational entities gained a strong position. The privatization of the banking sector or the liberalization of the financial market were other examples of measures taken. This was wholly rational, but often too advanced (considering the timing and level of development of the post-communist country's economy). In other words, the reforms approved were according to a Western vision that in many respects omitted the historical and social context of the Polish state in question.

On the other hand, accession to the European Union turned out to be another key event for Poland and its modernization. The legal and institutional adaptation of the national economy to the Community regulatory model, one of the conditions for its incorporation into the European project, triggered a phenomenon of Europeanization of the Polish reality. In particular, this involved a unilateral adjustment to the conditions of the European Community, allowing an adaptation of the segments of the public agenda and their complementarity by the Community institutions.

In reference to the varieties of capitalism and the description of the case of Poland according to the stipulated classification, it is necessary to remember that Poland presents clearly heterogeneous solutions. The appearance of representative singularities for liberal market economies (LMEs) (the type of regulation of the labor market, labor relations, and existing social inequality) shows Poland can be defined by a slightly liberal level of coordination (⊠ukowski, 2014: 78). At the same time, the combination of the market and coordinated regulation, as well as a certain degree of statism, bring it closer to the model of coordinated market economies (CME). Overall, a hybrid situation that (at first) invites us to classify it as a mixed market economy (MME), characterized by a lack of complementarity between the different forms of coordination of its spheres and the tendency to converge toward an LME model.

However, the existence of extensive literature on the subject of the phenomenon of systemic transformation in the countries of Central and Eastern Europe confirms the need for a particular and separate perspective on these events. In this way, it is necessary to highlight the model of the dependent economy (DME), an approach that is more fully applicable to Poland (Muszyński, 2016: 119). Among its main characteristics that coincide with the Polish paradigm we can underline:

- Foreign direct investment as one of the main sources of investment capital; the existing imbalance between the availability of national capital and the inflow of foreign capital, not to mention the concentration of the

crucial part of exports within the strategic sectors of the economy. Also, the influence of international capital and the dependence on its decisions.
- The distribution and unification of the limited coordination model; intermediary institutions (trade unions, associations, and chambers, etc.) without great influence over the decision-making processes.
- Investment in the research, development and innovation sector, included in national and/or regional development strategies, is considered crucial, although its private endowment remains very low.
- Skilled but relatively cheap labor; low-tech companies; the reluctance to pay for the training of employees in work environments.
- The lack of mobility and the dynamism of the labor market, as well as the patterns of a stable and universal corporatist structure; a social policy based on extensive public spending, but not consistent in the long term.
- The presence of the state sector in the economy as a whole; a mercantilist model of representation of interests and a growing state of market institutions.

Considering the Great Recession and its effects on the Polish economy, during the crisis period we observed a dynamic of reduced economic growth, but without significant instability features. Despite this, the decline in exports, the reduction in the rate of foreign direct and domestic investment, the deterioration of the situation in the labor market, the depreciation of the national currency or the increase in inflation, were their main consequences (Muszyński, 2016: 105–106).

It is important to stress that the reaction of the country's situation to world and European events, given its particular characteristics, presented a certain delay, providing real room for maneuver to the executive. Consequently, there were two areas of activity that underwent a series of notable reforms: the environment of the workers, as well as the main area of this study.

In relation to the first area, through the legislative changes introduced, the following changes were promoted:

- liberalization of labor laws: longer settlement periods; the elimination of the limits of use of contracts of determined duration;
- the flexibility of working time: individual working time mechanisms;
- reduction of labor costs: subsidies to employers in financial difficulties with the aim of covering the salaries of employees; financial aid to pay for participation in training courses and postgraduate studies for employees whose working time has been reduced.

These are a set of legislative milestones through which it was sought, mainly, to promote the economic growth of the country. All this in accordance with the adjustment of the existing institutional model and reinforcing the comparative advantages of the national economy (low labor costs and the possibility of free adaptation of work accustomed to changing demand).

In the framework of labor relations, the specific deregulation approach also meant the replacement of collective organization mechanisms in favor of "free-market" agreements, taking one more step toward a path of liberalization that is increasingly deep and characteristic of liberal economies. In other words, a scenario applauded by the representatives of employers and foreign investors.

Regarding the second area, and in addition to the above-mentioned sections, it should simply be recalled that the possible destabilization of the financial system due to the effect of existing global connections, together with the increase in the requirements for granting loans (and therefore the decrease of investments) did not turn out to have a great impact on the economy of Poland as a whole. As already indicated, this was largely due to the limited role of financial institutions and risk operations in the Polish economy, as well as the set of decisions adopted in order to promote domestic, foreign and investment demand (short-term reforms in response to the situation in question).

Further, the structural adaptation of the sector was the result of the profound changes in the European economic governance model as of 2011, although with a moderate impact due to Poland's non-membership of the euro zone. Even so, it must be emphasized that the incorporated adaptations significantly strengthened the existing system.

Consequently, a battery of complex solutions was instigated, determined by the existing comparative advantages and the intention to reinforce them, also the use of the crisis as an excuse to approve legal and institutional modifications in accordance with the political program of the ruling party of the moment. The group of mechanisms that seems to be contradictory, nevertheless, are compatible with each other.

Considering the macroeconomic evolution of the state and its growth model, the Great Recession did not introduce substantial changes. In fact, the most important systemic reforms (an unusual and large-scale advance), introduced after 1989 in response to numerous problems for which there were no previously proven solutions or procedures, took place even before Poland's accession to the European Union, however, belonging to the European club was an additional and indispensable impulse in its deepening.

Rapid economic growth and dynamic development can be considered the main qualities of the country's success. However, the mechanics of the process in question, the methods used for its completion, as well as the adaptation to Western structures significantly limited the possibility of implementing a model of its own and different from the one promoted, in a certain way, externally.

Since the systemic transition, the participation of the state in GDP and the labor market has been decreasing. The attraction of vigorous foreign direct investment, which presents a clearly positive balance (being one of the most articulated among EU members), strong domestic demand, dynamic exports and the profile of a net beneficiary of the community budget are also distinctive, positioning Poland within the domestic demand-led model. The reality is that Poland has not undergone relevant change as a result of the Great Recession, as it was also gradually undergoing change in the period prior to it.

Finally, the balance of the systemic changes introduced, and their effects must be considered as positive. The establishment of an efficient and competitive market economy, the development of an active private sector, the increase in national income, democratic institutions and a rule of law, as well as the growing presence of Poland in the international environment make up some of its major milestones. This was an attempt at transformation and a quest to be able to decide on its own destiny.

5 Conclusion

This chapter offers a series of relevant conclusions:

1 The changes introduced in the banking sector in Poland were one of the most important elements in the systemic transformation of the country. Likewise, its organization, structure, and institutional order are one of the best examples of this modification of the renewed Polish growth model. A set of liberal reforms that sought rapid economic growth, not to mention meeting the conditions of accession to the different international organizations, especially the European Union, were applied.

2 Thanks to the process started at the end of the 1990s, we observed the establishment of private commercial banking entities (increasingly disconnecting the sector in question from state ownership), the increase in the role and the modification in the functions of the central bank, the regeneration of the existing institutional system, introducing new rules of operation and conduct, as well as the establishment of a series of unprecedented institutions, among others, in line with the capitalist market economy systems.

3 In its development process, the Polish banking sector also experienced the entry of foreign investors into the national environment (a characteristic of the area analyzed, although we are currently witnessing its progressive return to Polish influence), the expansion of capital from commercial banks to other specialized segments of the financial market, along with a set of changes in the scope of its ownership and restructuring understood by a process of mutual mergers and acquisitions.

4 Due to the aforementioned changes, the Polish banking system has reached sufficient institutional and functional maturity, allowing its cooperation and integration with the other modern banking systems of the EU Member States. The improvement in the training of banking personnel, the expansion of the product offer and the increase in the quality of the loan portfolio, the promotion of the stability and financial security of the system or the technological advances in the provision of its services offer some examples.

5 With regard to the transmission channels of external shocks, the confidence channel, the macroeconomic channel, as well as the indirect channels (market and credit) should be considered as the main crisis inputs in the case of the Polish financial sector.

6 At the same time, the conservative approach, especially in reference to lending policy and supervision of the commercial bank segment, inclusive of an extensive supervisory system, significantly reduced the negative effects of the eurozone crisis on Poland's economy (avoiding recession, but not a slowdown in the dynamics of economic growth). Its financial structure, clearly stable, also made it easier to avoid the need for any public intervention through bailouts, either by the government or the country's central bank.

7 The Polish banking system, characterized by more restrictive regulations and recommendations, compared to other European countries, can be considered modern, stable and safe (to a large extent, the effect of its development and experience gained as a result of the country's systemic transformation). Further, these conditions have made it possible, in times of recession, to promote its effectiveness and reduce the gap in its development in reference to the other banking sectors of the EU (although this is still significant).

8 Currently, the Polish economy is characterized, among others, by a balance between the greater openness of the market and the pursuit of the preservation of elements of the welfare state, direct foreign investment, with a certain dominance of external property in key sectors such as financial and banking industry or services, skilled but relatively cheap labor, as well as the production of complex and durable consumer goods. This is a set of characteristics that position it within the domestic demand-led growth model.

9 Correspondingly, it follows the path of promoting competitiveness and greater social responsibility. In other words, social policy and inclusive economic growth are the key aspects of this perspective. Through this, an ever-deeper link is sought between both elements in order to strengthen the role of national capital in the country's economic structure, also to develop its export and innovative approach, making it less prone to external shocks. Nor should it be forgotten that this development model also includes strengthening the banking sector as an essential part of the state economy, while many other structural factors still require improvement. Regarding the macroeconomic evolution of Poland and its growth model, despite certain adaptations to the changing international and community context, the Great Recession did not represent a factor of substantial adjustments for Poland.

10 Undoubtedly, one of the next aims of the Polish economy is also the intensification of working to enter, successfully, the euro zone (accession was postponed due to the world financial crisis and historical differences in the development of the Polish economy compared to other Western European conjunctures). In other words, this is a task that will facilitate economic growth and the improvement of the material conditions of society. However, this goal requires a macroeconomic policy defined by sound public finances, adequate coordination of monetary and fiscal

policy, as well as a policy aimed at guaranteeing the effective functioning of market mechanisms.

11 One determining factor that can accelerate the entry of Poland into the eurozone is its participation in the project of its banking union. Through the reform of European economic governance, the European Union has made significant progress in establishing a revised institutional and supervisory system, seeking to improve economic, financial, and budgetary security. Nonetheless, despite this, banking union remains an incomplete set of mechanisms and is still at the implementation phase. Taking into account the current condition of the Polish banking sector, this is still a project of little interest to Poland, as well as raising a number of unknowns regarding its involvement.

12 Due to its development after 1989, in conjunction with its gradual deepening in time, we observe a clear hybridization of its growth model. That is, institutional matrices that show similarities with some different models of Western European capitalism, however, manifest a certain simultaneous deficit of institutional complementarity. The present heterogeneity suggests its framing as a mixed market economy with the tendency to converge to an LME model. In any case, we consider its greater adaptation to the definition of the dependent marking economy, an approach that more fully captures the issue of Poland. This is an example of individual and diverse capitalism, neoliberal in nature, but determined by the search for a compromise between commodification and the protection of the welfare state and protectionism.

13 In summary, this research has shown a set of reforms introduced in Poland and changes whose balance must be valued as positive. An adaptation to Western growth standards, the establishment of a rule of law and the promotion of the international position of the country. A remarkable process of transformation and improvement, also belonging to the EU project provides impetus and promises important additional progress.

Notes

1 Bank Gdański, Pomorski Bank Kredytowy in Szczecin, Powszechny Bank Gospodarczy in Łódź, Powszechny Bank Kredytowy in Warsaw, Bank Przemysłowo-Handlowy in Cracow, Wielkopolski Bank Kredytowy in Poznań, Bank Depozytowo-Kredytowy in Lublin, Bank Śląski in Katowice and Bank Zachodni in Wrocław.

2 Bank Inicjatyw Społeczno-Ekonomicznych.

3 Bank Rozwoju Budownictwa Mieszkaniowego.

4 Bank Ochrony Środowiska.

References

Acemoglu, D., Johnson, S., & Robinson, J. (2005). Institutions as the fundamental cause of long-run growth. In P. Aghion, & S. Durlauf (Eds.), *Handbook of economic growth*, vol. 1A. Amsterdam: Elsevier.

Amable, B. (2003). *The diversity of modern capitalism*. Oxford: Oxford University Press.

Bałtowski, M., & Miszewski, M. (2005). *Transformacja gospodarcza w Polsce*. Wydawca: Wydawnictwo Naukowe PWN.

Baszyński, A. (2011). Sektor bankowy. In W. Jarmołowicz & K. Szarzec (Eds.), *Liberalne przesłanki polskiej transformacji gospodarczej*. Warsaw: Polskie Wydawnictwo Ekonomiczne.

Bernaciak, M. (2017). Coming full circle? Contestation, social dialogue and trade union politics in Poland. In S. Lehndorff, H. Dribbusch, & T. Schulten (Eds.), *European trade unions in a time of crises*. Brussels: ETUI.

Cerami, A. (2010). The politics of social security reforms in the Czech Republic, Hungary, Poland and Slovakia. In B. Palier (Ed.), *A long goodbye to Bismarck?: The politics of welfare reform in continental Europe*. Amsterdam University Press.

Chudik, A., & Fratzscher, M. (2011). Identifying the global transmission of the 2007–2009 financial crisis in a GVAR model. *European Economic Review*, 55 (3), 325–339.

Dahl, M., Piskorska, B., & Olszewski, P. (2015). *Europejskie doświadczenia z demokracją i gospodarką rynkową. Przykład dla Ukrainy*. Warsaw: Elipsa.

Flejterski, S. (2011). Banki jako współsprawcy, współofiary i współbeneficjenci globalnego kryzysu finansowego. In J. L. Bednarczyk & W. Przybylska-Kapuścińska (Eds.), *Od kryzysu do ożywienia. Dylematy współczesnej polityki finansowej*. Warsaw: CeDeWu.

Gorzelak, G. (2010). Kryzys finansowy w krajach Europy Środkowej i Wschodniej. In A. Tucholska (Ed.), *Europejskie wyzwania dla Polski i jej regionów*. Warsaw: Ministerstwo Rozwoju Regionalnego.

Jakóbik, W. (2000). *Zmiany systemowe w Polsce a struktura gospodarki*. Warsaw: WN PWN.

Kalinski, J. (2005). Gospodarka Polski w procesie transformacji ustrojowej (1989–2002). In E. Czarny (Ed.), *Gospodarka polska na przełomie wieków: od A do Z*. Warsaw: Narodowy Bank Polski.

Kołodko, G. W. (1999). *Od szoku do terapii. Ekonomia i polityka transformacji*. Warsaw: Poltex.

Komisja Nadzoru Finansowego (2009). *Polski rynek finansowy w obliczu kryzysu finansowego w latach w latach 2008–2009*. Warsaw.

Konopczak, M., Sieradzki, R., &Wiernicki, M. (2010). Kryzys na światowych rynkach finansowych - wpływ na rynek finansowy w Polsce oraz implikacje dla sektora realnego. *Bank i Kredyt*, 6.

Konstytucja Rzeczypospolitej Polskiej uchwalona przez Zgromadzenie Narodowe w dniu 2 kwietnia (1997). R., przyjęta przez Naród w referendum konstytucyjnym w dniu 25 maja 1997 r., podpisana przez Prezydenta Rzeczypospolitej Polskiej w dniu 16 lipca 1997 r., Dz.U. 1997 nr 78 poz. 483. Warsaw.

Kornai, J. (1995). The principles of privatization in Eastern Europe. In K. Z. Poznanski (Ed.), *The evolutionary transition to capitalism*. Boulder, CO: Westview Press.

Laeven, L. (2011). Banking crises: A review. *The Annual Review of Financial Economics*, 3 (1).

Lepczyński, B. (2014). *Konsekwencje przystąpienia Polski do unii bankowej*. Gdansk: Instytut Badań nad Gospodarką Rynkową.

Lipowski, A. (2000). *Dualizm transformacji. Przypadek Polski 1990–1998*. Warsaw: INE PAN.

Maciejewska, M.; Mrozowicki, A. & Piasna, A. (2016). The silent and crawling crisis: International competition, labour market reforms and precarious jobs in Poland. In M. Myant, S. Theodoropoulou, & A. Piasna (Eds.), *Unemployment, internal devaluation and labour market deregulation in Europe*. Brussels: ETUI.

Marks-Bielska, R., & Nazarczuk, J. M. (2012). Uwarunkowania wzrostu gospodarczego Polski w latach 2001–2010, w kontekście modelu wzrostu Solowa. *Optimum. Studia Ekonomiczne*, 2 (56), 21–33.

Muszyński, K. (2016). Czynniki sterujące antykryzysową polityką prawa pracy w Polsce w latach 2009–2013. *Profilaktyka społeczna i resocjalizacja*, 29, 99–126.

Narodowy Bank Polski (2008). Raport o stabilności systemu finansowego. June.

Nazarczuk, J. (2013). Wpływ światowego kryzysu finansowego na gospodarkę Polski i jej regionów. In R. Kisiel & M. Wojarska (Eds.), *Wybrane aspekty rozwoju regionalnego*. Olsztyn: Fundacja "Wspieranie i Promocja Przedsiębiorczości na Warmii i Mazurach."

Pater, R., & Skica, T. (2011). Skutki kryzysu gospodarczego lat 2007–2009 dla sfery realnej polskiej gospodarki na tle Unii Europejskiej. *Barometr Regionalny*, 1 (23), 29–41.

Piątkowski, M. (2013). Polski Nowy Złoty Wiek od peryferii Europy do jej centrum. World Bank Policy Research Working Paper No. WPS6639.

Rapacki, R. & Czerniak, A. (2018). Emerging models of patchwork capitalism in Central and Eastern Europe: Empirical results of subspace clustering. *International Journal of Management and Economics*, 54 (4), 251–268.

Sawicka, J., & Rykowska J. (2010). Wpływ kryzysu gospodarczego na przyszłość Polski w strefie euro. *Zeszyty Naukowe Polityki Europejskie, Finanse i Marketing*, 4 (53), 341–350.

Schadler, S., Mody, A., Abiad, A., & Leigh, D. (2006). Growth in the Central and Eastern European countries of the European Union. IMF Occasional Paper No. 252.

Stockhammer, E. (2016). Neoliberal growth models, monetary union and the Euro crisis: A post-Keynesian perspective. *New Political Economy*, 21 (4), 365–379.

Stola, E. (2015). Kryzysy finansowe a bezpieczeństwo działalności banków komercyjnych. *Zeszyty Naukowe Szkoły Głównej Gospodarstwa Wiejskiego "Ekonomika i Organizacja Gospodarki Żywnościowej,"* 109, 85–96.

Ustawa o Bankowym Funduszu Gwarancyjnym, Dz.U. (1995). nr 4 poz. 18. Warsaw, December 14, 1994.

Ustawa o działalności gospodarczej, Dz.U. (1988). nr 41 poz. 324. Warsaw, December 23, 1988.

Ustawa o Narodowym Banku Polskim, Dz.U. (1989). nr 4 poz. 22. Warsaw, January 31, 1989.

Ustawa o Narodowym Banku Polskim, Dz.U. (1997). nr 140 poz. 938. Warsaw, August 29, 1997.

Ustawa o prywatyzacji przedsiębiorstw państwowych, Dz.U. (1990). nr 51 poz. 298. Warsaw, July 13, 1990.

Ustawa o restrukturyzacji finansowej przedsiębiorstw i banków oraz o zmianie niektórych ustaw, Dz.U. (1993). nr 18 poz. 82. Warsaw, February 3, 1993.

Ustawa o zmianie ustawy Prawo bankowe i niektórych innych ustaw, Dz.U. (1992). nr 20 poz. 78. Warsaw, February 14, 1992.

Ustawa Prawo bankowe, Dz.U. (1989). nr 4 poz. 21. Warsaw, January 31, 1989.

Ustawa Prawo bankowe, Dz.U. (1997). nr 140 poz. 939. Warsaw, August 29, 1997.

Ustawa Prawo dewizowe, Dz.U. (1989). nr 6 poz. 33. Warsaw, February 15, 1989.

Wilczyński, W. (1994). Transformacja gospodarki polskiej po pięciu latach - 1989–1994. *Ruch Prawniczy, Ekonomiczny i Socjologiczny*, 3, 63–76.

Żukowski, R. (2014). Wyłaniająca się odmiana kapitalizmu w Polsce w ujęciu Varietes of Capitalism – próba wstępnej oceny. In J. Osiński, K. Negacz, & K. Obłąkowska-Kubiak (Eds.), *Polityka publiczna 10 lat Polski w Unii Europejskiej*. Warsaw: Oficyna Wydawnicza Szkoła Główna Handlowa w Warszawie.

12 Conclusion

Luis Cárdenas and Javier Arribas

COMPLUTENSE UNIVERSITY OF MADRID AND COMPLUTENSE INSTITUTE FOR INTERNATIONAL STUDIES

The research questions posed in this book have been developed through each chapter examining a European national economy. The answers obtained in each case have varied, depending, as is to be expected, on the characteristics of the economy being studied. The following sections are the answers to the research questions posed, based on the results obtained.

1 The first research question

The first research question is the placing of each country in its own category among the different types of comparative political economy (CPE). In the development of this book, we have followed the usual CPE classification in which we distinguish between three main groups (liberal market economies, LME, coordinated market economies, CME, and mixed market economies, MME), together with their geographical location (continental, Nordic, Mediterranean, and Eastern Europe). Based on this classification we obtain:

1 LME (liberal market-based economies/Anglo-Saxon countries): characterized by the great importance of price competition and the opening of their goods markets, along with highly sophisticated financial markets and combined with low social protection and high labor flexibility (e.g. the United Kingdom).
2 Continental CME: these coordinated market economies place a moderate importance on price competition and a relatively high importance on quality competition based on non-price coordination, combined with relatively high employment protection, more limited external flexibility, and moderately strong trade unions with the capacity for wage bargaining coordination (e.g. Germany, France).
3 Nordic CME (social-democratic/Nordic capitalism): the Nordic countries tend to have quality-based rather than price-based competition and a high degree of non-market coordination, although with a strong openness to competition and foreign investment. Their labor markets are characterized by moderate employment protection, but with stronger trade unions and coordinated or centralized wage bargaining (e.g. Sweden).

4 Mediterranean MME (South European countries): the European Mediterranean economies are characterized by competition that is essentially based on price with little coordination outside the market and a significant presence of small and medium enterprises along with some large multinationals. The labor market has a high degree of duality between different types of workers and relatively centralized collective bargaining (e.g. Italy, Spainm and Greece).
5 East European MME countries: whose main characteristic is dependence on foreign direct investment, especially from continental West European countries, and offering advantageous conditions to serve as an intermediate link in global value chains (GVCs) through competition based essentially on price and relatively cheap inputs. Labor relations are predominantly at the company level, with little union bargaining power and legal protection, resulting in flexible markets (e.g. Poland).

2 The second research question

In addition, the following questions were raised which were resolved through the research in the chapters of this book. Has the institutional structure that existed prior to the Great Recession been transformed? Or was it previously transformed?

In the French case, after the Great Recession, successive political initiatives have attempted to change the legislative conditions regulating the institutional features characteristic of the French economy. Thus, under the presidency of François Hollande (2012–2017) and, subsequently, Emmanuel Macron (2017–), reforms affecting the functioning of the economy were promoted in this regard. Both leaders saw their popularity severely eroded as a result and had to amend some of their initial plans. Moreover, the starting point of the reformers was similar. In both cases, the loss of competitiveness and the high level of unemployment in the French economy were attributed to the alleged malfunctioning of institutions linked to the functioning of the labor market. In both cases, they were based on the example of Germany.

In the German case, between the late 1990s and early 2000s, major changes were introduced that affected the industrial relations system and contract law (the "Hartz reforms"). These changes had a particular impact on the coverage rate of collective bargaining and on employment protection, decisively changing the institutional basis of the German labor market.

In Italy, there were reforms after the Great Recession. The technocrat, pro-austerity government of the crisis years adopted a Pension Reform and a Jobs Act which were very unpopular. In later years, other center or left-wing governments implemented a number of reforms in an attempt to increase employment levels. In the Renzi era, the major reforms were those affecting the Jobs Act, trying to alleviate the dualism of the Italian labor market and recalibrate Italian labor market policy and its disregard for involving the unions. Between 2012 and 2018, the different Italian governments implemented a series of welfare measures alongside retrenchment and liberalization.

In the Spanish case, the institutional reforms have been far-reaching (with a great impact for those relating to the labor market). The processes of deindustrialization, financialization, and internationalization took place simultaneously with economic policy, which shows the consolidation of several features established since the end of the 1970s and reinforced by joining the EU. Priority was given to the liberalization of markets and privatization, the containment of public expenditure to balance the budget, the active role assumed by the state in making the labor market more flexible and the fragmentation or decentralization of collective bargaining. The economic crisis was followed by a period of austerity that led to a further focus on this path.

In the case of Greece, as previously happened in Spain, substantial changes were taking place in an attempt to adapt the country's economy to European requirements and, therefore, the institutional changes were taking place before the Great Recession. The institutional changes and reforms have been profound and have sometimes involved traumatic processes through which the socio-economic structure of Greece has been severely modified. The liberalization plan for Greece's entry into the euro was similar to that of other Mediterranean economies and was based on mass privatizations at the same time as the economy was opened up to competition with other Eurozone countries. Despite failing to meet the Maastricht criteria, Greece embraced free trade within the eurozone while having an uncompetitive production structure and lost the option of currency devaluation as a means to maintain competitiveness. During the period of our analysis, a profound transformation of the Greek economic structure took place, consisting of: (1) a process of deindustrialization, privatization, and tertiarization; (2) the liberalization of the financial markets, together with important modifications to the financing of economic agents; (3) the privatization of public companies and a clear commitment to contain public spending; (4) the correction of the current account deficit; and (5) increased inequality, loss of workers' rights, and liberalization of the labour market institutions.

When analyzing Sweden, it can be seen that the reforms were approved before the Great Recession, in some respects maintaining the differences between Sweden and the rest of continental Europe. An uneven but profound process of institutional transformation took place during the late 1970s and 1980s, through which several areas previously protected from market pressures underwent a sustained process of liberalization and increasing commodification. For example, several previously public enterprises were sold into private hands, while financial capital saw many of the restrictions that had been placed upon it in the past eventually removed. The process of financial liberalization undertaken during the 1980s led to the emergence of two asset-price bubbles in the housing and property markets, respectively, whose eventual deflation led to a severe crisis between 1991–1993, at which point it started a painful process of economic adjustment. Indeed, it is the economic crisis of the 1990s, and the way it was tackled and eventually resolved, rather than the Great Recession, which ultimately hold the key to understanding the actual configuration of the "Swedish model" nowadays.

In recent decades, the British economy has specialized in business services and finance. Both business services and finance, insurance, and real estate (FIRE) have taken over the leading role in fostering the economic growth that manufacturing once filled. A set of deep institutional reforms in 1971 began to change the structure and functioning of the UK's banking and financial sector. Before then, the sector was coordinated by the UK Treasury and the Bank of England with a ceiling on interest rates and direct controls on lending. The Competition and Credit Control policy of 1971 relaxed these restrictions as well as those affecting capital provisions. The second institutional turning point was the "Big Bang" deregulation of the UK financial sector in 1986, which consisted of a set of changes to the structure of the London Stock Exchange. These included a new electronic trading system, membership being opened up to previously excluded banks and foreign brokers, the end of fixed minimum commission rates for non-members, and the removal of the division between brokerage and "jobber" firms, allowing firms to represent a client and negotiate directly with other brokers. The next stepping-stone was the creation of the European Single Market and the resulting multilevel financial regulation. The last key point was the 2008 Global Financial Crisis. This great shock revealed some of the British economy's financial and non-financial fragilities, such as the high leverage ratios of firms, banks, and financial corporations, the extended financial risks linked to highly complex financial products and the worrying housing bubble and level of household indebtedness. The UK labor market has been characterized by increasing dualization. This process has also been linked to the structural transformation undergone by the UK economy, where the deindustrialization of employment coincided with this dual pattern of job creation within the service sector.

Finally, the Polish case also stems from changes made at the end of the Soviet period (although reforms had been carried out prior to this) and, therefore, the Great Recession is not a milestone for the modification of the country's institutions. The changes introduced in Poland's banking sector were one of the most important elements of the country's systemic transformation. A set of liberal reforms were aimed at rapid economic growth, as well as meeting the conditions for membership of various international bodies, especially the European Union. Thanks to the process initiated at the end of the 1990s, we saw the establishment of private commercial banks, the increase in the role and modification of the functions of the central bank, the regeneration of the existing institutional system, as well as the establishment of a series of new institutions, among others, in line with the capitalist market economy systems, allowing the entry of foreign investors into the national environment.

3 The third research question

If the institutional structure has been transformed, can any of the liberalization paths specified in the literature be identified (deregulation, dualization, or flexisecurity)? Is there a dominant social group or social block associated with it?

The results for the countries analyzed show that in the group made up of Spain, France, the United Kingdom, Greece, and Poland, the phenomenon of "deregulation" has occurred. Among the group of countries analyzed, this is the most common form of liberalization. In contrast, the liberalization processes in countries, such as Italy and Germany, have been characterized as "dualization." Finally, in the case of Sweden, we have the classic paradigm of the economies of the north of Europe and, therefore, according to the analysis carried out it can be classified as "embeddedness flexibilization."

4 The fourth research question

What macroeconomic developments, before and after the Great Recession, can be observed in the economy? Do these developments represent a particular growth model (GM) according to the three categories proposed in the literature (debt-led, export-led, or domestic demand-led)? Has there been any relevant change in the growth model before and after the Great Recession?

As discussed in Chapter 2, three types of GM have been proposed in this book: debt-led, export-led, and domestic demand-led, depending on whether or not the external balance deteriorates as a result of the weight of private consumption and investment, since this simultaneously shows the dynamics and structure of aggregate demand. With regard to consumption and investment in Germany, Spain, France, Greece, Italy, Poland, Sweden, and the United Kingdom during the period 1995–2007 and subsequently during the period 2008–2018, in order to check whether the previous GMs have been maintained or transformed, we look at Figure 12.1 and Figure 12.2.

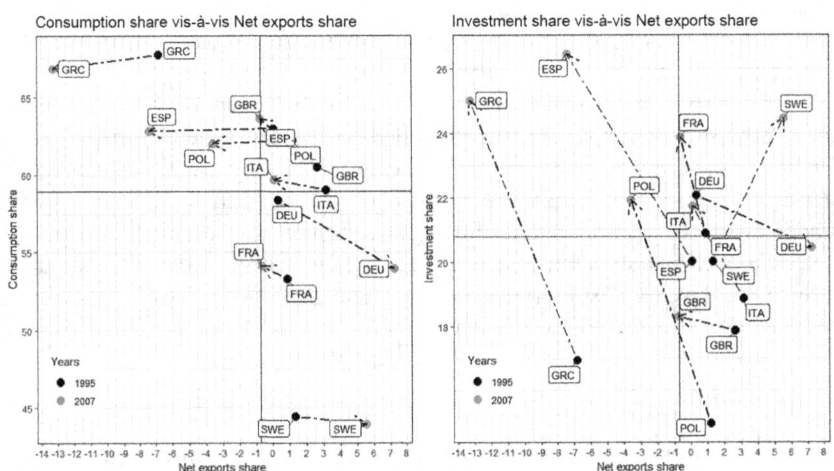

Figure 12.1 Consumption and investment vs. net exports, 1995–2007
Source: Adapted from OECD database.

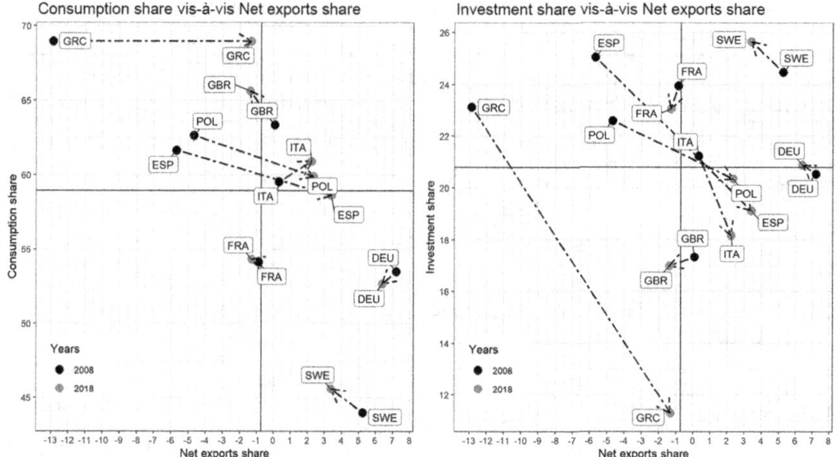

Figure 12.2 Consumption and investment vs. net exports, 2008–2018
Source: Adapted from OECD database.

During the period 1995–2007 (Figure 12.1), investment share (measured as Gross Capital Formation over GDP in real terms) can be seen to be the main element explaining the evolution of net exports. Most economies see their net exports over GDP decrease as investment increases, while consumption shows no great variation and remains stable at over 60 percent (with the exception of the UK where consumption increases by more percentage points than investment itself). Germany has a relationship in the opposite direction, with the weight of investment and consumption decreasing while the trade balance expands. In contrast, Sweden shows a significant increase in both investment and net exports, with a moderate fall in consumption.

After analyzing the first period, in the years from 2008 to 2018 (Figure 12.2), the same behavior patterns can also be seen. First, Spain, Greece, Italy, and Poland significantly reduced their investment share, which led to an improvement in their trade balance. This suggests that the linear and negative relationship between investment effort and net exports has been maintained. Second, the United Kingdom and France see a fall in their investment share while their foreign balance continues to deteriorate, as a result of an increase in the weight of consumption. Third, in the case of Sweden and Germany, there are also some changes. After the crisis they show similar dynamics, increasing their share of investment and consumption while moderately reducing their net exports.

Therefore, the trade-offs analyzed in the first period continue after 2008. The main difference is that mixed market economy (MME) countries have had to correct their net export balance by reducing domestic demand. Therefore, in most of the countries analyzed, there is a trade-off between

Table 12.1 Summary of the results obtained in the analysis of the different countries proposed

Variety of capitalism	*Variety of liberalization*	*Country*	*Pre-crisis growth model*	*Post-crisis growth model*
Continental CME	Dualization	Germany	Export-led	Export-led
Nordic CME	Embedded flexibilization	Sweden	Domestic demand-led	Domestic demand-led
CME Continental	Deregulation	France	Domestic demand-led	Domestic demand-led
LME Anglo-Saxon	Deregulation	the UK	Debt-led	Debt-led
MME Mediterranean	Deregulation	Spain	Debt-led	Domestic demand-led
MME Mediterranean	Dualization	Italy	Domestic demand-led	Domestic demand-led
MME Mediterranean	Deregulation	Greece	Debt-led	Export-led
MME Eastern European	Deregulation	Poland	Domestic demand-led	Export-led

consumption and/or investment with respect to net exports, these trade-offs being what give rise to the two GMs indicated in the literature.

To conclude, and by way of summary, Table 12.1 shows the countries analyzed, which are clear representatives of the GMs identified.

Index

Page numbers in italics refer to figures. Page numbers in bold refer to tables.

Printed in the United States
by Baker & Taylor Publisher Services